CHILTON'S
REPAIR & TUNE-UP GUIDE
FORD
1968 to
1979

**Custom • Custom 500 • Galaxie 500 • XL • LTD • LTD Brougham
LTD Landau • Ranch Wagon • Country Sedan • Country Squire**

D0891035

Managing Editor KERRY A. FREEMAN, S.A.E.
Senior Editor RICHARD J. RIVELE, S.A.E.
Editor ROBERT F. KING JR.

President WILLIAM A. BARBOUR
Executive Vice President RICHARD H. GROVES
Vice President and General Manager JOHN P. KUSHNERICK

CHILTON BOOK COMPANY
Radnor, Pennsylvania
19089

Manufactured in the United States of America

34567890   876543210

Chilton's Repair & Tune-Up Guide: Ford 1968–79
ISBN 0-8019-6842-9 pbk.

Library of Congress Catalog Card No. 78-20254

The Chilton Book Company expresses its appreciation to the Ford
Motor Company, Dearborn, Michigan.

Although the information in this guide is based on industry sources
and is as complete as possible at the time of publication, the possibility exists that the manufacturer made later changes which could not
be included here. While striving for total accuracy, Chilton Book
Company cannot assume responsibility for any errors, changes, or
omissions that may occur in the compilation of this data.

Part numbers listed in this book are not recommendations by Chilton
for any product by brand name. They are references that can be used
with interchange manuals and aftermarket supplier catalogs to locate
each brand supplier's discrete part number.

SAFETY NOTICE
Proper service and repair procedures are vital to the safe, reliable
operation of all motor vehicles, as well as the personal safety of those
performing repairs. This book outlines procedures for servicing and
repairing vehicles using safe, effective methods. The procedures contain many NOTES, CAUTIONS and WARNINGS which should be
followed along with standard safety procedures to eliminate the possibility of personal injury or improper service which could damage the
vehicle or compromise its safety.

It is important to note that repair procedures and techniques, tools
and parts for servicing motor vehicles, as well as the skill and experience of the individual performing the work vary widely. It is not possible to anticipate all of the conceivable ways or conditions under
which vehicles may be serviced, or to provide cautions as to all of the
possible hazards that may result. Standard and accepted safety precautions and equipment should be used when handling toxic or flam-
mable fluids, and safety goggles or other protection should be used
during cutting, grinding, chiseling, prying, or any other process that
can cause material removal or projectiles.

Some procedures require the use of tools specially designed for a
specific purpose. Before substituting another tool or procedure, you
must be completely satisfied that neither your personal safety, nor
the performance of the vehicle will be endangered.

Contents

Quick Reference Specifications

For quick and easy reference, complete this page with the most commonly used specifications for your vehicle. The specifications can be found in Chapters 1 through 3 or on the tune-up decal under the hood of the vehicle.

TUNE-UP

Firing Order _____

Spark Plugs:

    Type _____

    Gap (in.) _____

Point Gap (in.) _____

Dwell Angle (°) _____

Ignition Timing (°) _____

    Vacuum (Connected/Disconnected) _____

Valve Clearance (in.)

    Intake _____   **Exhaust** _____

CAPACITIES

Engine Oil (qts)

    With Filter Change _____

    Without Filter Change _____

Cooling System (qts) _____

Manual Transmission (pts) _____

    Type _____

Automatic Transmission (pts) _____

    Type _____

Differential (pts) _____

    Type _____

COMMONLY FORGOTTEN PART NUMBERS

Use these spaces to record the part numbers of frequently replaced parts.

PCV VALVE   **OIL FILTER**   **AIR FILTER**

Manufacturer _____   **Manufacturer** _____   **Manufacturer** _____

Part No. _____   **Part No.** _____   **Part No.** _____

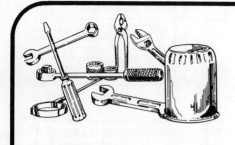

General Information and Maintenance

HOW TO USE THIS BOOK

This book has been written to help the Ford owner perform maintenance, tune-ups and repairs on his automobile. It is intended for both the novice and for those more familiar with auto repairs. Since this book contains information on very simple operations (Chapters 1 and 2) and the more involved ones (Chapters 3–10), the user will not outgrow the book as he masters simple repairs and is ready to progress to more difficult operations.

Several things were assumed of you while the repair procedures were being written. They are mentioned here so that you will be aware of them. It was assumed that you own, or are willing to purchase, a basic set of hand tools and equipment. A skeletal listing of tools and equipment has been drawn up for you.

For many repair operations, the factory has suggested a special tool to perform the repairs. If it was at all possible, a conventional tool was substituted for the special tool in these cases. However, there are some operations which cannot be done without the use of these tools. To perform these jobs correctly, it will be necessary to order the tool through your local Ford dealer's parts department.

Two basic rules of automobile mechanics deserve mentioning here. Whenever the left-side of the car is referred to, it is meant to specify the driver's side. Likewise, the right-side of the car means the passenger's side. Also, most screws, nuts, and bolts are removed by turning counterclockwise and tightened by turning clockwise.

Before performing any repairs, read the entire section of the book that deals with that job. In many places a description of the system is provided. By reading this first, and then reading the entire repair procedure, you will understand the function of the system you will be working on and what will be involved in the repair operation, prior to starting the job. This will enable you to avoid problems and also to help you learn about your car while you are working on it.

While every effort was made to make the book as simple, yet as detailed as possible, there is no substitute for personal experience. You can gain the confidence and feel for mechanical things needed to make auto repairs only by doing them yourself. If you take your time and concentrate on what you are doing, you will be amazed at how fast you can learn.

TOOLS AND EQUIPMENT

Now that you have purchased this book and committed yourself to maintaining your car, a small set of basic tools and equipment will prove handy. The first group of items should be adequate for most maintenance and light repair procedures:

 Sliding T-bar handle or ratchet wrench;
 ⅜ in. drive socket wrench set (with 12 in. breaker bar);
 Universal adapter for socket wrench set;
 Flat blade and phillips head screwdrivers;
 Pliers;
 Adjustable wrench;
 Locking pliers;
 Open-end wrench set;
 Feeler gauge set;
 Oil filter strap wrench;
 Brake adjusting spoon;
 Drift pin;
 Torque wrench;
 and, of course, a hammer.

Along with the above mentioned tools, the following equipment should be on hand:

 Scissors jack or hydraulic jack of sufficient capacity;
 Jackstands of sufficient capacity;
 Wheel blocks;
 Grease gun (hand-operated type);
 Drip pan (low and wide);
 Drop light;
 Tire pressure gauge;
 Penetrating oil (spray lubricant);
 and a can of waterless hand cleaner.

In this age of emission controls and high priced gasoline, it is important to keep your car in proper tune. The following items, though they will represent an investment equal or greater to that of the first group, will tell you everything you might need to know about a car's state of tune:

 12-volt test light;
 Compression gauge;
 Manifold vacuum gauge;
 Power timing light;
 and a dwell-tachometer.

SERIAL NUMBER IDENTIFICATION

Vehicle Identification Number

The official vehicle identification number for title and registration purposes is stamped on a metal tag, which is fastened to the top of

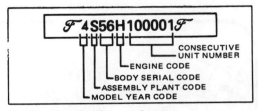

Vehicle identification number tag

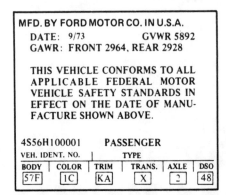

Vehicle certification label—1973–79

the instrument panel. The tag is located on the driver's side, visible through the windshield. The first digit in the vehicle identification number is the model year of the car (0—1970, 4—1974, etc.). The second digit is the assembly plant code for the plant in which the vehicle was built. The third and fourth digits are the body serial code designations (2-dr sdn, 4-dr sdn). The fifth digit is the engine code which identifies the type of engine originally installed in the vehicle (see "Engine Codes" chart). The last six digits are the consecutive unit numbers which start at 100,001 for the first car of a model year built at each assembly plant.

Vehicle Certification Label (1970–79)

The vehicle certification label is attached to the left door lock pillar on 2-door models and on the rear face of the driver's door on 4-door models. The top half of the label contains the name of the vehicle manufacturer, date of manufacture and the manufacturer's certification statement. On 1973 and later models, the top half of the label also contains the gross vehicle weight rating and the front and rear gross vehicle axle ratings. The gross vehicle weight rating is useful in determining the load carrying capacity of your car. Merely subtract the curb weight from the posted gross weight and what is left over is how

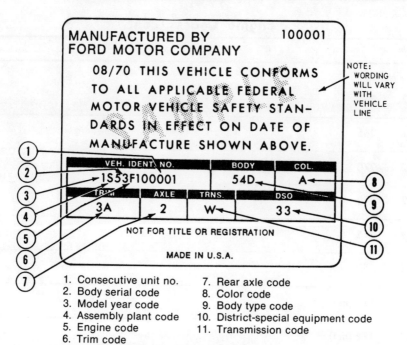

1. Consecutive unit no.
2. Body serial code
3. Model year code
4. Assembly plant code
5. Engine code
6. Trim code
7. Rear axle code
8. Color code
9. Body type code
10. District-special equipment code
11. Transmission code

Vehicle certification label—1970–72

Engine Codes

Disp	Bbl	Hp	'68	'69	'70	'71	'72	'73	'74	'75	'76	'77	'78	'79
6-Cylinder Models														
240	1	103 (net)					V							
240	1	140				V								
240	1	150	V	V	V									
8-Cylinder Models														
302	2	140 (net)					F						F	F
302	2	210	F	F	F	F								
351W	2	153, 162 (net)*					H	H	H				H	H
351C	2	163 (net)					H	H	H					
351M	2	148 (net)								H				
351M	2	152 (net)									H	H	H	H
351	2	240				H								
351	2	250			H									

Engine Codes (cont.)

Disp	Bbl	Hp	'68	'69	'70	'71	'72	'73	'74	'75	'76	'77	'78	'79
8-Cylinder Models														
390	2	255				Y								
390	2	265		Y	Y									
390	2	270	Y		Y									
390	2	280	X											
390	4	315	Z											
400	2	158 (net)									S		S	S
400	2	170 (net)							S					
400	2	172 (net)					S	S						
400	2	180 (net)									S	S		
400	2	260				S								
428	4	340	Q											
428PI	4	360	P	P	P									
429	4	208, 212 (net)*					N	N						
429PI	4	NA					P							
429	4	320		K	K	K								
429	4	360	N	N	N	N								
429PI	4	370				P								
460	4	202 (net)									A	A	A	
460	4	195, 218, 220 (net)*							A	A				
460	4	200, 208, 212 (net)*					A	A						
460PI	4	226 (net)									C	C	C	
460PI	4	267, 274, 275 (net)*						C	C					

PI Police Interceptor
* Net horsepower rating varies with model application

Transmission Codes

Type	'68	'69	'70	'71	'72	'73	'74	'75	'76	'77	'78	'79
3-speed manual	1	1	1	1	—	—	—	—	—	—	—	—
4-speed manual	5	6	—	—	—	—	—	—	—	—	—	—
C4 automatic	W	W	W	W	W	W	W	—	—	—	W	W
FMX automatic	X	X	X	X	X	X	X	X	X	X	X	X
CW automatic	—	—	—	—	—	—	Y	Y	—	—	—	—
C6 automatic	U	U	U	U	U	U	U	U	U	U	U	U
C6 automatic special (towing)	Z	Z	Z	Z	Z	Z	Z	Z	Z	Z	Z	Z

Rear Axle Ratio Codes

Ratio	'68	'69	'70	'71	'72	'73	'74	'75	'76	'77	'78	'79
2.26 : 1	—	—	—	—	—	—	—	—	—	—	—	G
2.47 : 1	—	—	—	—	—	—	—	—	—	—	B	—
2.50 : 1	—	—	—	—	—	—	—	—	—	—	1(J)	—
2.73 : 1	—	—	—	—	—	—	—	—	—	—	—	8(H)
2.75 : 1	1(A)	2(K)	2(K)	2(K)	2(K)	2(K)	2(K)	2(K)	2(K)	2(K)	2(K)	—
2.80 : 1	3(C)	4(M)	4(M)	—	—	—	—	—	—	—	—	—
3.00 : 1	5(E)	6(O)	6(O)	6(O)	6(O)	6(O)	6(O)	6(O)	6(O)	6(O)		
3.07 : 1	—	—	B	B	—	—	5(E)	5(E)	—	—	—	—
3.08 : 1	—	—	—	—	—	—	—	—	—	—	—	Y
3.10 : 1	9	7(P)	—	—	—	—	—	—	—	—	—	—
3.25 : 1	7(G)	9(R)	9(R)	9(R)	9(R)	9(R)	9(R)	9(R)	9(R)	9(R)	—	—
3.50 : 1	8	—	—	—	—	—	—	—	—	—	—	—

NOTE: *Figures in Parentheses indicate locking differential.*

much you can haul around. The bottom half of the vehicle certification label contains the vehicle identification number (as previously described), the body type code, the exterior paint color code, the interior trim color and material code, the rear axle code (see "Rear Axle Codes" chart), the transmission code (see Transmission Codes" chart) and the district and special order codes.

The vehicle certification label is constructed of special material to guard against its alteration. If it is tampered with or removed, it will be destroyed or the word "VOID" will appear.

ROUTINE MAINTENANCE

Maintenance Interval Chart

The numerals in the maintenance chart represent the suggested intervals between service in thousands of miles or number of months, whichever occurs first.

4,000 miles or 4 months	4
6,000 miles or 6 months	6
8,000 miles or 8 months	8
12,000 miles or 12 months	12
18,000 miles or 18 months	18
24,000 miles or 24 months	24
30,000 miles or 30 months	30
36,000 miles or 36 months	36
As Needed	A/N
Does not apply	—

Air Filter Replacement

At the recommended intervals in the maintenance chart, the air filter element must be replaced. If the vehicle is operated under severely dusty conditions, the element should be changed sooner. On all six and 8 cylinder models, the air filter cover is retained with a single wing nut on top of and in the center of the cover. To replace the element, unscrew the wing nut, lift off the cover and discard the old element.

While the air cleaner is removed, check the choke plate and external linkage for freedom of movement. Brush away all dirt and spray the plate corners and linkage with a small amount of penetrating cleaner/lubricant such as CRC®.

Wipe the air filter housing clean with a solvent-moistened rag and install the new element with the word "FRONT" facing the front of the car. Install the cover and wing nut finger-tight.

Fuel Filter Replacement

Every 12,000 miles or 12 months, the fuel filter must be replaced. The filter is located inline at the carburetor inlet. The procedure for replacing the fuel filter is as follows:

1. Remove the air filter.
2. Loosen the retaining clamp(s), securing the fuel inlet hose to the fuel filter. If the hose has crimped retaining clamps, these must be cut off and replaced.
3. Pull the hose off the fuel filter.
4. Unscrew the fuel filter from the carburetor and discard the gasket, if so equipped.
5. Install a new gasket, if so equipped, and screw the filter into the carburetor.
6. Install a new retaining clamp onto the fuel hose. Push the hose onto the fuel filter and tighten the clamp.
7. Start the engine and check for leaks.
8. Install the air filter.

Crankcase Filler Cap Cleaning

At the recommended intervals in the maintenance chart, the oil filler cap must be cleaned. Disconnect the positive crankcase ventilation hose from the cap and lift the cap from the rocker cover. Soak the cap in kerosene or mineral spirits to clean the internal element of sludge and blow-by material. After agitating the cap in the solution, shake the cap dry. Reinstall the cap and connect the hose.

Crankcase Ventilation Filter (in Air Cleaner) Replacement

At the recommended intervals in the maintenance chart, or sooner if the car is operated in dusty areas, at low rpm, for trailer towing, or if the car is used for short runs preventing the engine from reaching operating temperature, the crankcase ventilation filter in the air cleaner must be replaced. Do not attempt to clean this filter.

To replace the filter, simply remove the air filter cover and pull the old crankcase filter out of its housing. Push a new crankcase filter into the housing and install the air filter cover.

Maintenance Interval Chart

Operation	'68	'69	'70	'71	'72	'73	'74	'75	'76	'77–'79	See Chapter
ENGINE											
Air cleaner replacement—6 cyl	12	12	12	12	12	—	—	—	—	—	1
Air cleaner replacement—V8	24	24	24	24	12	12	24	20	20	30	1
Air intake temperature control system check	12	12	12	12	12	12	12	15	15	20	4
Carburetor idle speed and mixture, fast idle, throttle solenoid adj	12	12	12	12	12	12	24	15	15	22.5	2, 4
Cooling system check	12	12	12	12	12	12	12	15	15	12	1, 3
Coolant replacement; system draining and flushing	24	24	24	24	24	24	24	40	40	45	1
Crankcase breather cap cleaning	6	6	6	6	6	12	12	20	20	30	1
Crankcase breather filter replacement (in air cleaner)	—	24	24	6	6	8	24	20	20	30	1
Distributor breaker points inspection	12	12	12	12	12	12	6	—	—	—	2
Distributor breaker points replacement	12	12	12	12	12	24	24	—	—	—	2
Distributor cap and rotor inspection	12	12	12	12	12	24	①	15	15	22.5	2
Drive belts adjustment	12	12	12	12	12	12	12	15	15	22.5	1
Evaporative control system check; inspect carbon canister	—	—	12	12	12	12	24	20	20	30	4

Maintenance Interval Chart (cont.)

Operation	'68	'69	'70	'71	'72	'73	'74	'75	'76	'77–'79	See Chapter
ENGINE											
Exhaust control valve (heat riser) lubrication and inspection	6	6	6	6	6	8	6	15	15	15	1
Exhaust gas recirculation system (EGR) check	—	—	—	—	—	12	12	15	15	15	4
Fuel filter replacement	12	12	12	12	12	12	6	15	10	10	1
Ignition timing adjustment	12	12	12	12	12	12	②	⑥	⑥	⑥	2
Intake manifold bolt torque check (V8 only)	12	12	12	12	12	24	12	15	15	15	3
Oil change	6	6	6	6	6	4	6	5	5	7.5	1
Oil filter replacement	6	6	6	6	6	8	12	10	10	15	1
PCV system valve replacement, system cleaning	12	12	12	12	12	12	24	20	20	22.5	4
Spark plug replacement; plug wire check	12	12	12	12	12	12	③	15	15	22.5	2
Themactor air injection system check	12	12	—	—	—	—	24	15	15	22.5	4
CHASSIS											
Automatic transmission band adjustment	④	⑤	⑤	⑤	⑤	⑤	⑤	⑤	⑤	⑤	6
Automatic transmission fluid level check	6	6	6	6	6	8	12	15	15	15	1

Service										
Brake system inspection, lining replacement	30	30	30	30	24	24	25	30	30	9
Brake master cylinder reservoir fluid level check	6	6	6	6	8	12	15	30	30	1
Clutch pedal free-play adjustment	6	6	6	—	—	—	—	—	—	6
Front suspension ball joints and steering linkage lubrication	36	36	36	36	36	36	30	30	30	1
Front wheel bearings cleaning, adjusting and repacking	30	30	30	30	24	24	25	30	30	9
Manual transmission fluid level check	6	6	6	—	—	—	—	—	—	1
Power steering pump reservoir fluid level check	6	6	6	6	4	6	15	15	15	1
Rear axle fluid level check	6	6	6	6	8	12	15	15	15	1
Steering arm stop lubrication; steering linkage inspection	6	6	12	12	12	12	15	15	15	1

① Conventional ignition—24; electronic ignition—18
② Conventional ignition—12; electronic ignition—18
③ Conventional ignition—12; electronic ignition—18
④ Normal service—36,000 mi. only; severe (fleet) service—6,000/18,000/36,000 mi. intervals
⑤ Normal service—12,000 mi. only; severe (fleet) service—6,000/18,000/30,000 mi. intervals
⑥ Periodic adjustment unnecessary

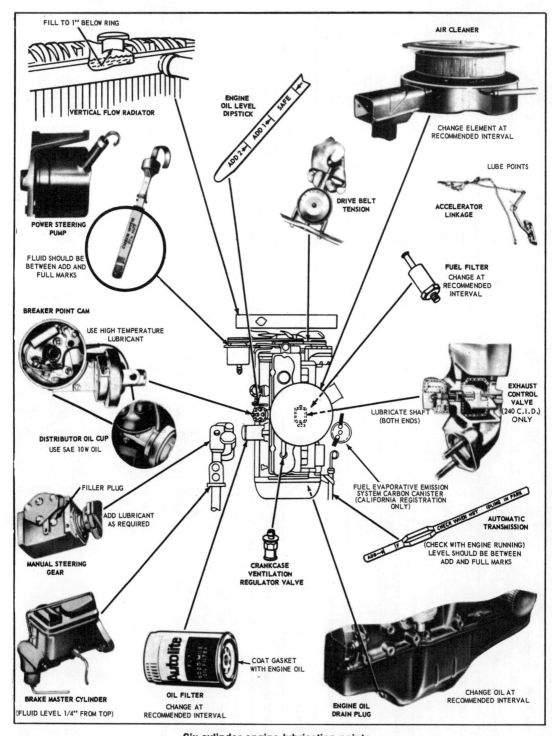

Six-cylinder engine lubrication points

Positive Crankcase Ventilation (PCV) Valve

See "Emission Controls Component Service" in Chapter 4.

Evaporative Control System Canister

See "Emission Control Component Service" in Chapter 4.

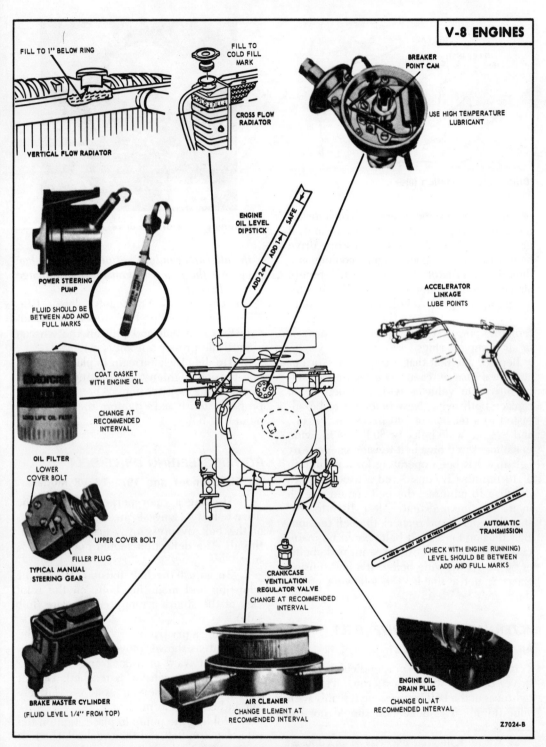

V-8 ENGINES

FILL TO 1" BELOW RING

VERTICAL FLOW RADIATOR

FILL TO COLD FILL MARK

CROSS FLOW RADIATOR

BREAKER POINT CAM

USE HIGH TEMPERATURE LUBRICANT

POWER STEERING PUMP

FLUID SHOULD BE BETWEEN ADD AND FULL MARKS

ENGINE OIL LEVEL DIPSTICK

ADD 2   ADD 1   SAFE

ACCELERATOR LINKAGE LUBE POINTS

COAT GASKET WITH ENGINE OIL

CHANGE AT RECOMMENDED INTERVAL

OIL FILTER

LOWER COVER BOLT

UPPER COVER BOLT

FILLER PLUG

TYPICAL MANUAL STEERING GEAR

CRANKCASE VENTILATION REGULATOR VALVE
CHANGE AT RECOMMENDED INTERVAL

AUTOMATIC TRANSMISSION

(CHECK WITH ENGINE RUNNING) LEVEL SHOULD BE BETWEEN ADD AND FULL MARKS

BRAKE MASTER CYLINDER
(FLUID LEVEL 1/4" FROM TOP)

AIR CLEANER
CHANGE ELEMENT AT RECOMMENDED INTERVAL

ENGINE OIL DRAIN PLUG
CHANGE OIL AT RECOMMENDED INTERVAL

Z7024-B

V8 engine lubrication points

Exhaust Gas Recirculation System Component Cleaning

See "Emission Controls Component Service" in Chapter 4.

Drive Belt Adjustment

Once a year or at 12,000 mile intervals, the tension (and condition) of the alternator, power steering (if so equipped), air condi-

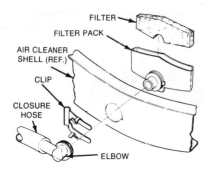

Crankcase ventilation filter

Adjusting alternator (fan drive) belt tension

tioning (if so equipped), and Thermactor air pump drive belts should be checked, and, if necessary, adjusted. Loose accessory drive belts can lead to poor engine cooling and diminish alternator, power steering pump, air conditioning compressor or Thermactor air pump output. A belt that is too tight places a severe strain on the water pump, alternator, power steering pump, compressor or air pump bearings.

Replace any belt that is so glazed, worn or stretched that it cannot be tightened sufficiently. On vehicles with matched belts, replace both belts. New belts are to be adjusted to a tension of 140 lbs (½ in., ⅜ in., and $^{15}/_{32}$ in. wide belts) or 80 lbs (¼ in. wide belts) measured on a belt tension gauge. Any belt that has been operating for a minimum of 10 minutes is considered a used belt. In the first 10 minutes, the belt should stretch to its maximum extent. After 10 minutes, stop the engine and recheck the belt tension. Belt tension for a used belt should be maintained at 110 lbs (all except ¼ in. wide belts) or 60 lbs (¼ in. wide belts). If a belt tension gauge is not available, the following procedures may be used.

ALTERNATOR (FAN DRIVE) BELT

All except 1979 with 351

1. Position a ruler perpendicular to the drive belt at its longest run. Test the tightness of the belt by pressing it firmly with your thumb. The deflection should not exceed ¼ in.

2. If the deflection exceeds ¼ in., loosen the alternator mounting and adjusting arm bolts.

3a. On 1968–72 V8 and 6 cylinder models, use a pry bar or broom handle to move the alternator toward or away from the engine until the proper tension is reached.

CAUTION: *Apply tension to the front of*

the alternator only. Positioning the pry bar against the rear end housing will damage the alternator.

3b. On 1973–78 V8 models, place a 1 in. open-end or adjustable wrench on the adjusting arm bolt and pull on the wrench until the proper tension is achieved.

4. Holding the alternator in place to maintain tension, tighten the adjusting arm bolt. Recheck the belt tension. When the belt is properly tensioned, tighten the alternator mounting bolt.

POWER STEERING DRIVE BELT

All Six-Cylinder and 1971–72 V8 Models

1. Holding a ruler perpendicular to the drive belt at its longest run, test the tightness of the belt by pressing it firmly with your thumb. The deflection should not exceed ¼ in.

2. To adjust the belt tension, loosen the adjusting and mounting bolts on the front face of the steering pump cover plate (hub side).

3. Using a pry bar or broom handle on the pump hub as shown, move the power steering pump toward or away from the engine until the proper tension is reached. Do not pry against the reservoir as it is relatively soft and easily deformed.

4. Holding the pump in place, tighten the adjusting arm bolt and then recheck the belt tension. When the belt is properly tensioned tighten the mounting bolts.

1973–79 V8 Models (except '79 351 V8)

1. Position a ruler perpendicular to the drive belt at its longest run. Test the tightness of the belt by pressing it firmly with

your thumb. The deflection should be about ¼ in.

2. To adjust the belt tension, loosen the three bolts in the three elongated adjusting slots at the power steering pump attaching bracket.

3. Turn the steering pump drive belt adjusting nut as required until the proper deflection is obtained. Turning the adjusting nut clockwise will increase tension and decrease deflection; counterclockwise will decrease tension and increase deflection.

4. Without disturbing the pump, tighten the three attaching bolts.

AIR CONDITIONING COMPRESSOR DRIVE BELT

1. Position a ruler perpendicular to the drive belt at its longest run. Test the tightness of the belt by pressing it firmly with your thumb. The deflection should not exceed ¼ in.

2. If the engine is equipped with an idler pulley, loosen the idler pulley adjusting bolt, insert a pry bar between the pulley and the engine (or in the idler pulley adjusting slot), and adjust the tension accordingly. If the engine is not equipped with an idler pulley, the alternator must be moved to accomplish this adjustment, as outlined under "Alternator (Fan Drive) Belt."

3. When the proper tension is reached, tighten the idler pulley adjusting bolt (if so equipped) or the alternator adjusting and mounting bolts.

THERMACTOR AIR PUMP DRIVE BELT

1. Position a ruler perpendicular to the drive belt at its longest run. Test the

Arrows point out attaching bolts. Turning adjusting nut clockwise increases tension—counterclockwise decreases tension

tightness of the belt by pressing it firmly with your thumb. The deflection should be about ¼ in.

2. To adjust the belt tension, loosen the adjusting arm bolt slightly. If necessary, also loosen the mounting belt slightly.

3. Using a pry bar or broom handle, pry against the pump rear cover to move the pump toward or away from the engine as necessary.

CAUTION: *Do not pry against the pump housing itself, as damage to the housing may result.*

4. Holding the pump in place, tighten the adjusting arm bolt and recheck the tension. When the belt is properly tensioned, tighten the mounting bolt.

1979 351 V8 Engines

1979 Ford LTD's equipped with the 351 V8 feature a single wide ribbed V-belt that drives the water pump, alternator, and power steering pump. To install a new belt, simply retract the belt tensioner with a pry bar and slide the old belt off the pulleys. Slip on a new belt and release the tensioner. The spring powered tensioner eliminates the need for periodic adjustments.

Fluid Level Checks

ENGINE OIL

The oil level in the engine should be checked at fuel stops. The check should be made with the engine warm and switched off for a period of about one minute so that the oil has time to drain down into the crankcase. Pull out the dipstick, wipe it clean and reinsert it. The level of the oil must be kept within the "SAFE" area (on older models between the "ADD" and "F" marks), above the "ADD 1" mark on the dipstick. If the oil level is kept above the "SAFE" area, heavy oil consumption will result. If the level remains below the "ADD 1" mark, severe engine damage may result. The "ADD 1" and "ADD 2" refer to US measure quarts. Remember that in Canada, the Imperial measure quart is used and it is equal to 1.2 US quarts. When topping up, make sure that the oil is the same type and viscosity rating as the oil already in the crankcase.

MANUAL TRANSMISSION FLUID

At the recommended intervals in the maintenance schedule, the fluid level in the manual transmission should be checked. With the car standing perfectly level, apply the parking brake, set the transmission in Neutral, stop the engine and block all four wheels. Wipe all dirt and grease from the filler plug on the side of the transmission. Using a sliding T-bar handle or an adjustable wrench, remove the filler plug. The lubricant should be level with the bottom of the filler hole. If required, add SAE 90 manual transmission fluid to the proper level using a syringe. Install the filler plug.

AUTOMATIC TRANSMISSION FLUID

At the recommended intervals in the maintenance schedule, the automatic transmission fluid level should be checked. The level should also be checked if abnormal shifting behavior is noticed. With the car standing on a level surface, firmly apply the parking brake. Run the engine at idle until normal operating temperature is reached. Then, with the right foot firmly planted on the brake pedal, shift the transmission selector through all the positions, allowing sufficient time in each range to engage the transmission. Shift the selector into Park (P). With the engine still running, pull out the transmission dipstick, located at the right rear of the engine compartment. Wipe it clean and reinsert it, pushing it down until it seats in the tube. Pull it out and check the level. The level should be between the "ADD" and "FULL" marks. Add AFT Type F as required through the dipstick tube.

CAUTION: *Do not overfill the transmission, as foaming and loss of fluid through the vent may cause the transmission to malfunction.*

BRAKE MASTER CYLINDER FLUID

At the recommended intervals in the maintenance schedule, the fluid in the master cylinder should be checked. Before checking the level, carefully wipe off the master cylinder cover to remove any dirt or water that would fall into the fluid reservoir. Then push the retaining clip to one side and remove the cover and seal. The fluid level should be maintained at ¼ in. from the top of the reservoir. Top up as necessary with heavy-duty brake fluid meeting DOT 3 or 4 specifications.

COOLANT

The coolant level in the radiator should be checked on a monthly basis, preferably when the engine is cold. On a cold engine, the coolant level should be maintained at one inch below the filler neck on vertical flow radiators, and 2½ in. below the filler neck at the "COLD Fill" mark on crossflow radiators. On cars equipped with the Coolant Recovery System, the level is maintained at the "COLD LEVEL" mark in the translucent plastic expansion bottle. Top up as necessary with a mixture of 50% water and 50% ethylene glycol antifreeze, to ensure proper rust, freezing and boiling protection. If you have to add coolant more often than once a month or if you have to add more than one quart at a time, check the cooling system for leaks. Also check for water in the crankcase oil, indicating a blown cylinder head gasket.

CAUTION: *Exercise extreme care when removing the cap from a hot radiator. Wait a few minutes until the engine has time to cool somewhat, then wrap a thick towel around the radiator cap and slowly turn it counterclockwise to the first stop. Step back and allow the pressure to release from the cooling system. Then, when the steam has stopped venting, press down on the cap, turn it one more stop counterclockwise and remove the cap.*

REAR AXLE FLUID

At the recommended intervals in the maintenance schedule, the rear axle fluid level should be checked. With the car standing perfectly level, apply the parking brake, set the transmission in Park or 1st gear, stop the engine and block all four wheels. Wipe all dirt and grease from the filler plug area. Using a sliding T-bar handle (⅜ in.) or an adjustable wrench, remove the filler plug. The fluid level must be maintained at ½ in. from the bottom of the filler plug hole.

To check the fluid level in the axle, bend a clean, straight piece of wire to a 90° angle and insert the bent end of the wire into the axle while resting it on the lower edge of the filler hole. Top up as necessary with SAE 90 hypoid gear lube, using a suction gun or kitchen baster. Install the filler plug.

MANUAL STEERING GEAR LUBRICANT

If there is binding in the steering gear or if the wheels do not return to a straight-ahead position after a turn, the lubricant level of the steering gear should be checked. Remove the filler plug using a ¹¹/₁₆ in. open-end wrench and remove the lower cover bolt using a ⁹/₁₆ in. wrench, to expose both holes. Slowly turn the steering wheel to the left until it stops. At this point, lubricant should be rising in the lower cover bolt hole. Then slowly turn the steering wheel to the right until it stops. At this point, lubricant should be rising in the filler plug hole. If the lubricant does not rise when the wheel is turned, add a small amount of SAE 90 steering gear lubricant until it does. Replace the cover bolt and the filler plug when finished.

POWER STEERING RESERVOIR FLUID

At the recommended intervals in the maintenance schedule, the fluid level in the power steering reservoir (if so equipped) should be checked. Run the engine until the fluid reaches operating temperature. Turn the steering wheel from lock-to-lock several times to relieve the system of any trapped air. Turn off the engine. Unscrew the cap and dipstick assembly from the reservoir. The level must be maintained between the "FULL" mark and the end of the dipstick. Top up as necessary with ATF Type F.

BATTERY ELECTROLYTE

The fluid level in the battery cells should be checked on a monthly basis and more frequently in hot, dry weather. To top up the battery, ordinary tap water may be used except in areas known to have a high mineral or alkali content in the water. In these areas, distilled water must be used. The fluid level should be maintained at the "FILL TO RING" mark. If water is added during freezing weather, drive the car for several miles afterward to mix the water and the battery

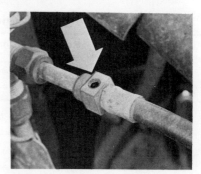

Air conditioning sight glass—typical

electrolyte. If water is needed frequently, check for a cracked battery case or a faulty voltage regulator or alternator.

CAUTION: *Keep lighted cigarettes or any other flame or spark, away from the open battery cells. Highly combustible hydrogen gas is always present in the cells.*

AIR CONDITIONING REFRIGERANT

Once a year, before hot weather sets in, it is advisable the check the refrigerant charge in the air conditioner system. This may be accomplished by looking at the sight glass located in the engine compartment, next to the radiator. First, wipe the sight glass clean with a cloth wrapped around the eraser end of a pencil. Connect a tachometer to the engine with the positive line connected to the distributor side of the ignition coil and the negative line connected to a good ground, such as the steering box. Have a friend operate the air conditioner controls

Capacities

Year	ENGINE No. Cyl Displacement (Cu In.)	Engine Crankcase Add 1 Qt For New Filter	TRANSMISSION Pts To Refill After Draining			Drive Axle (pts)	Gasoline Tank (gals) ■	COOLING SYSTEM (qts)	
			Manual		Automatic			With Heater	With A/C
			3-Speed	4-Speed					
'68	6—240	4	3.5	—	See	5	25	13	13
	8—302	4	3.5	—	chart	5	25	13.7	13.7
	8—390	4	3.5	4.0	below	5	25	20.2	20.2
	8—427	5	—	4.0		5	25	20.6	20.6
	8—428	4	—	4.0		5	25	19.4	19.4

Capacities (cont.)

Year	ENGINE No. Cyl Displacement (Cu In.)	Engine Crankcase Add 1 Qt For New Filter	TRANSMISSION Pts To Refill After Draining			Drive Axle (pts)	Gasoline Tank (gals) ■	COOLING SYSTEM (qts)	
			Manual						
			3-Speed	4-Speed	Automatic			With Heater	With A/C
'69	6—240	4	3.5	—		5	24.5	14.3	14.3
	8—302	4	3.5	—		4.5	24.5	15.4	15.6
	8—390	4	3.5	—		4.5	24.5	20.1	20.5
	8—428P	4	—	—		4.5	24.5	19.7	19.7
	8—429	4	—	4.0		4.5	24.5	20.5	21.5
'70	6—240	4	3.5	—		5	24.5	14.4	14.4
	8—302	4	3.5	—		4.5	24.5	15.4	15.6
	8—351	4	3.5	—		4.5	24.5	16.5	16.9
	8—390	4	3.5	—		4.5	24.5	20.1	20.5
	8—428P	4	—	—		4.5	24.5	19.7	19.7
	8—429	4	—	—	See	4.5	24.5	18.6	19.0
'71	6—240	4	3.5	—	chart	5	22.5	14.1	14.1
	8—302	4	3.5	—	below	4.5	22.5	15.2	15.6
	8—351	4	3.5	—		4.5	22.5	16.3	16.7
	8—390	4	—	—		4.5	22.5	20.3	26.3
	8—400	4	—	—		4.5	22.5	17.6	17.6
	8—429	4	—	—		4.5	22.5	18.8	18.8
'72	6—240	4	—	—		4	22	14.2	14.2
	8—302	4	—	—		4.5	22	15.2	15.2
	8—351	4	—	—		4.5	22	16.3	16.3
	8—400	4	—	—		5	22	17.7	18.3
	8—429	4	—	—		5	22	18.8	19.5

Capacities (cont.)

Year	ENGINE No. Cyl Displacement (Cu In.)	Engine Crankcase Add 1 Qt For New Filter	TRANSMISSION Pts To Refill After Draining			Drive Axle (pts)	Gasoline Tank (gals) ■	COOLING SYSTEM (qts)	
			Manual		Automatic			With Heater	With A/C
			3-Speed	4-Speed					
'73	8—351	4	—	—		4.5	22	16.3	16.3
	8—400	4	—	—		5	22	17.7	18.3
	8—429	4	—	—		5	22	18.8	19.5
'74–'77	8—351	4	—	—		4.5	22③④	16.3	①
	8—400	4	—	—		5	22③④	18.0	18.0
	8—460	4②	—	—		5	22③④	19.4	19.4
'78	8—302	4	—	—		5	24.2	16.9	16.9
	8—351	4	—	—		5	24.2	16.9	16.9
	8—400	4	—	—		5	24.2	16.9	16.9
	8—460	4	—	—		5	24.2	18.6	19.0
'79	8—302	4	—	—		3.5	19.0	13.3	13.4
	8—351	4	—	—		4.0	19.0	13.3	13.4

① 351W—17.1 qts; 351C—16.3 qts; 351M—16.3 qts
② 460 Police Interceptor—7½ qts with filter and oil cooler
③ 1975–77 Sedans—24.2 gals
④ Sedan with auxiliary fuel tank—32.3 gals
   Wagon with auxiliary fuel tank—29.0 gals
■ Station wagons:
   '68–'70—20 gals
   '71—22 gals
   '72–'78—21 gals
P Police
— Not applicable

AUTOMATIC TRANSMISSION REFILL CAPACITIES (Pts)

Year	Code▲	Capacities
'68–'69	U, Z	26
'68–'79	W	20.5
68–'76	X, Y	22
'70–'79	U, Z	25.5

▲ Transmission code can be found on the serial number plate or the vehicle certification label.

while you look at the sight glass. Have your friend set the dash panel control to maximum cooling. Start the engine and idle at 1,500 rpm. While looking at the sight glass, signal your friend to turn the blower switch to the High position. If a few bubbles appear immediately after the blower is turned on and then disappear, the system is sufficiently charged with refrigerant. If, on the other hand, a large amount of bubbles, foam or froth continue after the blower has operated for a few seconds, then the system is in need of additional refrigerant. If no bubbles appear at all, then there is either sufficient refrigerant in the system, or it is bone dry. The way to clear this question up is to have your friend turn the blower switch off and on (engine running at 1,500 rpm) about every 10 seconds or so while you look at the sight glass. This will cycle the magnetic clutch. If the system is properly charged, bubbles will appear in the sight glass a few seconds after the blower is turned off and disappear when the blower is turned on. If no bubbles appear when the blower is in the "OFF" position, then the system should be serviced by an authorized dealer and checked for leaks.

Tires

The tread wear of the tires should be checked about twice a year. Tread wear should be even across the tire. Excessive wear in the center of the tread indicates overinflation. Excessive wear on the outer corners of the tread indicate underinflation. An irregular wear pattern is usually an indication of improper front wheel alignment or incorrect wheel balance. On a vehicle with improper front wheel alignment, the car will tend to pull to one side of a flat road if the steering wheel is released while driving the car. Incorrect wheel balance will usually produce vibrations at high speeds. When the front wheels are out of balance, they will produce vibration in the steering wheel, while rear wheels out of balance will produce vibration in the floor pan of the car.

TIRE PRESSURE

One way to prolong tire life is to maintain proper pressure in the tires. This should be checked at least once a month and should be done with the tires cold (not driven for one hour). If you check the tire pressure when the tires are warm, you will obtain a falsely high reading. Refer to the sticker attached to the rear face of the right-hand door or attached to the inside of the glove compartment door. Snow tires require a 4 psi cold increase in the rear tire pressure above that listed in the chart. For example, an H78 x 15 snow tire will require 30 psi to be properly inflated. Under no circumstances must the maximum inflation pressure, which is stamped on the sidewall of the tire, be exceeded. If you plan to do any trailer towing,

it is recommended that tire pressure (cold) be increased by 6 psi on the rear wheels, again being careful not to exceed the maximum inflation pressure.

TIRE ROTATION

Another way to prolong tire life is to rotate the tires at regular intervals. These intervals depend on the type of tire and on the type of driving you do, but generally they should be about 6,000 miles or twice a year, or sooner if abnormal wear due to front end misalignment is apparent. Follow the accompanying tire rotation diagram for the types of tires your car is equipped with; conventional (bias-ply or bias-belted) or radial-ply. Because of the design of radial-ply tires, it is imperative that they remain on the same side of the car and travel in the same direction. Therefore, in a 4-tire rotational sequence, the front and rear radial tires of the same side are merely swapped. Studded snow tires, radial or conventional, are just as choosy about the direction they travel in. If you equip your car with studded snow tires, mark them "LR" or "RR" prior to removal so that next year they may be installed on the same side of the car. If a studded snow tire that was used on the left rear wheel one year is installed on the right rear wheel the next year, the result will be a dangerous condition where the studs pull out of the tire and are flung to the rear. Remember, never mix radial, belted, and/or conventional type tires on your car. Always make sure that all tires and wheels are of the same size, type and load-carrying capacity.

Coolant Draining and Flushing

At two-year intervals, or if the coolant is rusty or dirty in appearance, the cooling system must be drained and flushed. To drain the system, place a catch pan beneath the petcock (drain cock) at the bottom of the radiator and open the petcock by rotating it counterclockwise. Then, using a ⅜ in. wrench or socket, remove the cylinder block drain plug(s), taking care to catch the old coolant. On six-cylinder models, the drain plug is located at the right rear of the block, in front of the starter. On V8 Models, there are two drain plugs, one on each side of the block.

To remove rust, sludge and other foreign matter from the cooling system, a cooling system cleaner should be used in the engine prior to flushing. Flushing may be accomplished either by inserting a garden hose

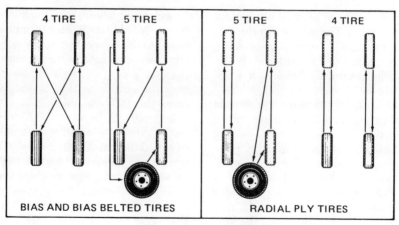

Tire rotation diagrams

into the radiator cap opening, or by using special pressure flushing equipment available at many service stations. In either case, the flushing should be done with the thermostat removed. When using the pressure flushing method, it is advisable to make sure that the cylinder head bolts are tightened to specifications to prevent possible coolant leakage into the cylinders.

The procedure for flushing is as follows: Run the engine at operating temperature for several minutes to circulate the cooling system cleaner. Using a towel, carefully remove the radiator cap, in two stages, allowing the pressure flushing fitting into the radiator. Open the radiator petcock and remove the engine drain plug(s). Run the engine at fast idle until the water is coming out clear. Shut off the engine and then remove the garden hose or the pressure flusher. Close the petcock and install the drain plug(s). Inspect the radiator and heater hoses for cracks, bulges or soft spots and replace as required. Replace the thermostat.

Consult the capacities chart and fill the radiator to within one inch of the filler neck on standard systems or to the top on Coolant Recovery Systems with a mixture of 50% water and 50% ethylene glycol antifreeze. Install the radiator cap, turning it only to the first position (off pressure), thereby allowing the system to bleed of all trapped air bubbles. On cars equipped with a Coolant Recovery System, fill the plastic bottle to the "COLD LEVEL" mark then install the bottle cap. Start the engine and allow it to reach operating temperature. Recheck the coolant level and add as required. Check the system for leakage.

NOTE: *On Coolant Recovery Systems, add coolant only to the plastic bottle.*

Battery Care

Every six months or 6,000 miles, the battery's state of charge should be checked with a hydrometer. A fully-charged battery should have a hydrometer reading of 1.260–1.310 specific gravity at 80° F electrolyte temperature. To correct readings for temperature variations add 0.004 to the hydrometer reading for every 10° F that the electrolyte is above 80° F; subtract 0.004 for every 10° F below 80° F electrolyte temperature. The readings obtained in all six cells should be nearly equal. If any cell is markedly lower, it is defective. If this low reading is not improved by charging, the battery should be replaced, particularly before cold weather sets in. When charging a weak or sulphated (brownish color of electrolyte) battery, the slow charging method must be used. Never allow electrolyte temperature to exceed 120° F during charging.

Inspect the battery terminals for a tight fit on the poles and check for corrosion. Remove any deposits with a wire brush and coat the terminals, after placing them on the poles, with vaseline to prevent further corrosion.

Check the battery case for cracks or leakage.

LUBRICATION

Oil Recommendations

When adding the oil to the crankcase or changing the oil or filter, it is important that oil of an equal quality to original equipment be used in your car. The use of inferior oils may void your warranty. Generally speaking, oil that has been rated "SE, heavy-duty detergent" by the American Petroleum Institute will prove satisfactory.

Oil of the SE variety performs a multitude of functions in addition to its basic job of reducing friction of the engine's moving parts. Through a balanced formula of polymeric dispersants and metallic detergents, the oil prevents high temperature and low temperature deposits and also keeps sludge and dirt particles in suspension. Acids, particularly sulphuric acid, as well as other by-products of combustion of sulphur fuels, are neutralized by the oil. These acids, if permitted to concentrate, may cause corrosion and rapid wear of the internal parts of the engine.

It is important to choose an oil of the proper viscosity for climatic and operational conditions. Viscosity is an index of the oil's thickness at different temperatures. A thicker oil (higher numerical rating) is needed for high temperature operation, whereas thinner oil (lower numerical rating) is required for cold weather operation. Due to the need for an oil that embodies both these characteristics in parts of the country where there is wide temperature variation within a small period of time, multigrade oils have been developed. Basically, a multigrade oil is thinner at low temperatures and thicker at high temperatures. For example, a 20W–40 oil exhibits the characteristics of a 20 weight oil when the car is first started and the oil is cold. Its lighter weight allows it to travel to the lubricating surfaces quicker and offer less resistance to starter motor cranking than, let's say, a straight 30 weight oil. But after the engine reaches operating temperature, the 20W–40 oil begins acting like a straight 40 weight oil, its heavier weight providing greater lubricating protection and less susceptibility to foaming than a straight 30 weight oil. Whatever your driving needs, the oil viscosity-temperature chart should prove useful in selecting the proper grade. The SAE viscosity rating is printed or stamped on the top of every oil container.

Fuel Recommendations

It is important that you use fuel of the proper octane rating in your car. Octane rating is based on the quantity of anti-knock compounds added to the fuel and it determines the speed at which the gas will burn. The lower the octane rating, the faster it burns. The higher the octane, the slower the fuel will burn and a greater percentage of compounds in the fuel prevent spark ping (knock), detonation and preignition (dieseling). Check your owner's manual for the correct fuel for your car.

Changing Engine Oil and Filter

At the recommended intervals in the maintenance schedule, the oil and filter are changed. After the engine has reached operating temperature, shut it off, firmly apply the parking brake, block the wheels, place a drip pan beneath the oil pan and remove the drain plug. Allow the engine to drain thoroughly before replacing the drain plug. Place the drip pan beneath the oil filter. To remove the filter, turn it counterclockwise using a strap wrench. Wipe the contact surface of the new filter clean of all dirt and coat the rubber gasket with clean engine oil. Clean the mating surface of the adapter on the block. To install, hand turn the new filter clockwise until the gasket just contacts the cylinder block. Do not use a strap wrench to install. Then hand-turn the filter ½ additional turn. Unscrew the filler cap on the valve cover and fill the crankcase to the proper level on the dipstick with the recommended grade of oil. Install the cap, start the engine and operate at fast idle. Check the oil filter contact area and the drain plug for leaks.

Oil Viscosity– Temperature Chart

When outside temperature is consistently	Use SAE viscosity number
SINGLE GRADE OILS	
—10° F to 32° F	10W
10° F to 60° F	20W-20
32° F to 90° F	30
Above 60° F	40
MULTIGRADE OILS	
Below 32° F	5W-30 *
—10° F to 90° F	10W-30
Above —10° F	10W-40
Above 10° F	20W-40

* When sustained high-speed operation is anticipated, use the next higher grade.

Certain operating conditions may warrant more frequent oil changes. If the vehicle is used for short trips, where the engine does not have a chance to fully warm-up before it is shut off, water condensation and low temperature deposits may make it necessary to change the oil sooner. If the vehicle is used mostly in stop-and-go traffic, corrosive acids and high temperature deposits may necessitate shorter oil changing intervals. The shorter intervals also apply to industrial or rural areas where high concentrations of dust and other airborne particulate matter contaminate the oil. Finally, if the car is used for towing trailers, a severe load is placed on the engine causing the oil to "thin-out" sooner, making necessary the shorter oil changing intervals.

EXHAUST CONTROL VALVE LUBRICATION

1968–71 240 Six, 1968–69 390, 428 V8

Some models are equipped with exhaust control (heat riser) valves located near the head pipe connection in the exhaust manifold. These valves aid initial warmup in cold weather by restricting exhaust gas flow slightly. The heat generated by this restriction is transferred to the intake manifold where it results in improved fuel vaporization.

The operation of the exhaust control valve should be checked every 6 months or 6,000 miles. Make sure that the thermostatic spring is hooked on the stop pin and that the tension holds the valve shut. Rotate the counterweight by hand and make sure that it moves freely through about 90° of rotation. A valve which is operating properly will open when light finger pressure is applied (cold engine). Lubricate the shaft bushings with a mixture of penetrating oil and graphite. Operate the valve manually a few times to work in the lubricant.

Chassis Greasing

FRONT SUSPENSION BALL JOINTS

Every 3 years or 36,000 miles, the upper and lower ball joints must be lubricated. Fords are not equipped with grease fittings at the ball joints. Instead, they use plugs, one at the top of the upper ball joint and another at the underside of the lower ball joint, which must be removed prior to greasing.

If you are using a jack to raise the front of the car, be sure to install jack stands, block the rear wheels and fully apply the parking brake. If the car has been parked in a temperature below 20° F for any length of time, park it in a heated garage for a half an hour or so until the ball joints loosen up enough to accept the grease. Wipe all accumulated dirt from around the ball joint lubrication plugs. Remove the plugs with a $^3/_{16}$ in. socket wrench. Using a hand-operated, low pressure grease gun fitted with a rubber tip and loaded with a suitable chassis grease, force lubricant into the joint only until the joint boot begins to swell.

NOTE: *Do not force lubricant out of the rubber boat as this destroys the weathertight seal.*

Install the grease plugs.

STEERING LINKAGE

At the recommended intervals in the maintenance schedule, the steering linkage must be lubricated. Grease fittings are not installed from the factory. Instead, plugs are used, which must be removed prior to lubrication. The linkage may be lubricated without raising the car.

If the car has been parked in a temperature below 20° F for any length of time, park it in a heated garage for a half an hour or so until the linkage joints loosen up enough to accept the grease. Wipe all accumulated dirt from around the steering joint plugs at each tie-rod end. Remove the plugs with a $^3/_{16}$ in. socket wrench. Using a hand-operated, low pressure grease gun fitted with a rubber tip and loaded with suitable chassis grease, force lubricant into the holes. When grease begins to escape from the hole, insert the plugs.

STEERING ARM STOPS

At the recommended intervals in the maintenance schedule, the steering arm stops must be cleaned and lubricated. The stops are located on the inside of the steering arm and at the upturned end of the suspension strut where the strut attaches to the lower control arm. Clean all friction points and apply a suitable chassis grease as per the chassis lubrication diagram.

MANUAL TRANSMISSION AND CLUTCH LINKAGE

On models so equipped, apply a small amount of chassis grease to the pivot and friction points of the transmission and clutch linkage as per the chassis lubrication diagram.

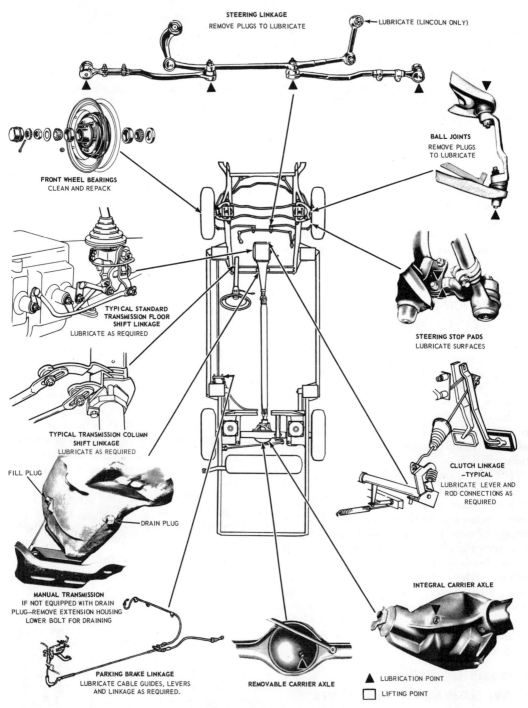

STEERING LINKAGE
REMOVE PLUGS TO LUBRICATE

◄ LUBRICATE (LINCOLN ONLY)

BALL JOINTS
REMOVE PLUGS
TO LUBRICATE

FRONT WHEEL BEARINGS
CLEAN AND REPACK

TYPICAL STANDARD
TRANSMISSION FLOOR
SHIFT LINKAGE
LUBRICATE AS REQUIRED

STEERING STOP PADS
LUBRICATE SURFACES

TYPICAL TRANSMISSION COLUMN
SHIFT LINKAGE
LUBRICATE AS REQUIRED

FILL PLUG

DRAIN PLUG

CLUTCH LINKAGE
–TYPICAL
LUBRICATE LEVER AND
ROD CONNECTIONS AS
REQUIRED

INTEGRAL CARRIER AXLE

MANUAL TRANSMISSION
IF NOT EQUIPPED WITH DRAIN
PLUG–REMOVE EXTENSION HOUSING
LOWER BOLT FOR DRAINING

PARKING BRAKE LINKAGE
LUBRICATE CABLE GUIDES, LEVERS
AND LINKAGE AS REQUIRED.

REMOVABLE CARRIER AXLE

▲ LUBRICATION POINT

☐ LIFTING POINT

Ford chassis lubrication points

AUTOMATIC TRANSMISSION LINKAGE

On models so equipped, apply a small amount of 10W engine oil to the kickdown and shift linkage pivot points.

PARKING BRAKE LINKAGE

At yearly intervals or whenever binding is noticeable in the parking brake linkage, lubricate the cable guides, levers and linkage with a suitable chassis grease.

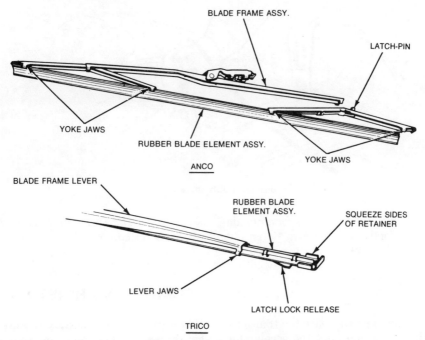

BLADE FRAME ASSY.

LATCH-PIN

YOKE JAWS

RUBBER BLADE ELEMENT ASSY.

YOKE JAWS

ANCO

BLADE FRAME LEVER

RUBBER BLADE
ELEMENT ASSY.

SQUEEZE SIDES
OF RETAINER

LEVER JAWS

LATCH LOCK RELEASE

TRICO

Wiper blade element refill

BODY LUBRICATION

At 12 month intervals, the door, hood and trunk hinges, checks, and latches should be greased with a white grease such as Lubriplate®. Also the lock cylinders should be lubricated with a few drops of graphite lubricant.

DRAIN HOLE CLEANING

The doors and rocker panels of your car are equipped with drain holes to allow water to drain out of the inside of the body panels. If the drain holes become clogged with dirt, leaves, pine needles, etc., the water will remain inside the panels, causing rust. To prevent this, open the drain holes with a screwdriver. If your car is equipped with rubber dust valves instead, simply open the dust valve with your finger.

WIPER BLADE REPLACEMENT

Depending on the type of weather, amount of use or the amount of snow removing chemicals used in your area, the recommended interval for replacement of wiper blades will vary. After making sure that the windshield glass surface is free of all oil, tree sap or other foreign substance that cannot be easily wiped off, check the wiper pattern for streaking. If the blades are cracked or the pattern is streaked or uneven, replace the blades. Replace any blade in question. It will be far cheaper than replacing a scratched windshield later.

PUSHING, TOWING AND JUMP STARTING

When using jumper cables to jump start a car, a few precautions must be taken to avoid both charging system damage and damage to yourself should the battery explode. The old "positive to positive and negative to negative" jumper cable rule of thumb has been scrapped for a new revised procedure. Here it is. First, remove all of the battery cell covers and cover the cell openings with a clean, dry cloth. Then, connect the positive cable of the assist battery to the positive pole of your battery and the negative cable of the assist battery to the engine block of your car. This will prevent the possibility of a spark from the negative assist cable igniting the highly explosive hydrogen and oxygen battery fumes. Once your car is started, allow the engine to return to idle speed before disconnecting the jumper cables, and don't cross the cables. Replace the cell covers and discard the cloth. Now if your car fails to start by jump starting and it is equipped with manual transmission, it may be push started. Cars equipped with automatic transmission cannot be pushstarted. If the bumper of the

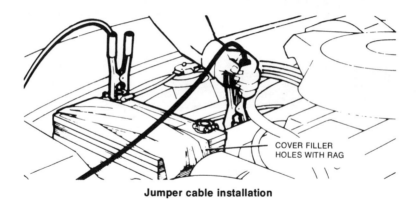

COVER FILLER
HOLES WITH RAG

Jumper cable installation

car pushing you and your car's bumper do not match perfectly, it is wise to tie an old tire either on the back of your car or on the front of the pushing car. This will avoid unnecessary trips to the body shop. To push start the car, switch the ignition to the "ON" position (not the "START" position) and depress the clutch pedal. Place the transmission in Third gear and hold the accelerator pedal about halfway down. When the car speed reaches about 10 mph, gradually release the clutch pedal and the engine should start.

If all else fails and the car must be towed to a garage, there are a few precautions that must be observed. If the transmission and rear axle are in proper working order, the car can be towed with the rear wheels on the ground for distances under 15 miles at speeds no greater than 30 mph. If the transmission or rear is known to be damaged or if the car has to be towed over 15 miles or over 30 mph, the car must be towed with the rear wheels raised and the steering wheel locked so that the front wheels remain in the straight-ahead position.

NOTE: *If the ignition key is not available to unlock the steering and transmission lock system, it will be necessary to dolly the* *car under the rear wheels with the front wheels raised.*

JACKING AND HOISTING

When it becomes necessary to raise the car for service, proper safety precautions must be taken. Fords are equipped with bumper jacks. These jacks are fine for changing a tire, but never crawl under the car when it is supported only by the bumper jack. If the jack should slip or tip over, as jacks sometimes do, you would be pinned under 2 tons of automobile.

When raising the car with the bumper jack to change a tire, follow these precautions: Fully apply the parking brake, block the wheel diagonally opposite the wheel to be raised, stop the engine, place the gear lever in Park (automatic) or 1st or Reverse gear (manual), and make sure that the jack is firmly planted on a level, solid surface. On 1968–70 Fords, the jack should be positioned beneath the bumper inboard of the bumper-to-frame brackets. On 1971 and later models, notches are provided in the bumpers to insert the jack hook.

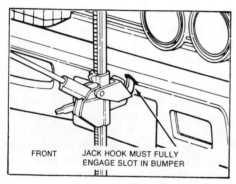

FRONT   JACK HOOK MUST FULLY
ENGAGE SLOT IN BUMPER

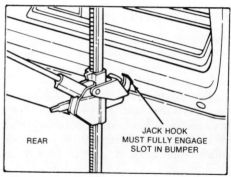

REAR

JACK HOOK
MUST FULLY ENGAGE
SLOT IN BUMPER

Bumper jack installation—1971–77 models

If you are going to work beneath the car, always install jackstands beneath an adjacent frame member. When using a floor jack, the car may be raised at a frame rail, front cross-member, or at either front lower arm strut connection.

The best way to raise a car for service is to use a garage hoist. There are several different types of garage hoists, each having their own special precautions. Types you most often will encounter are the drive-on (ramp type), the frame contact and the twin post or rail type. On all types of hoists, avoid contact with the steering linkage as damage may result. When using a drive-on type, make sure that there is enough clearance between the upright flanges of the hoist rails and the underbody. When using a frame contact hoist, mae sure that all four of the adapter pads are positioned squarely on a frame rail. When using a twin post or rail type, make sure that the front adapters are positioned squarely beneath the lower control arms and the rear adapters positioned carefully beneath the rear axle housing at points no further outboard than one inch from the circumference welds near the differential housing (to prevent shock absorber damage). Always raise the car slowly, observing the security of the hoist adapters as it is raised.

NOTE: *If it is desired to unload the front suspension ball joints for purposes of inspection, position the jack beneath the lower control arm of the subject ball joints.*

2

Tune-Up and Troubleshooting

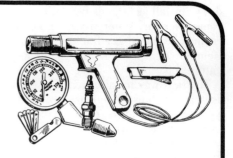

TUNE-UP PROCEDURES

The tune-up is a routine maintenance operation which is essential for the efficient and economical operation, as well as the long life of your car's engine. The interval between tune-ups is a variable factor which depends upon the way you drive your car, the conditions under which you drive it (weather, road type, etc.), and the type of engine installed in your car. It is generally correct to say that no car should be driven more than 12,000 miles between tune-ups, especially in this age of emission controls and fuel shortages. If you plan to drive your car extremely hard or under severe weather conditions, the tune-ups should be performed at closer intervals. High performance engines require more frequent tuning than other engines, regardless of weather or driving conditions.

The replaceable parts involved in a tune-up include the spark plugs, breaker points and condenser (unless equipped with breakerless ignition), distributor cap, rotor, spark plug wires and the ignition coil high-tension (secondary) wire. In addition to these parts and the adjustments involved in properly adapting them to your engine, there are several adjustments of other parts involved in completing the job. These include carburetor idle speed and air/fuel mixture, ignition timing, dwell angle (unless equipped with breakerless ignition), and valve clearance adjustments.

This section gives specific procedures on how to tune-up your Ford and is intended to be as complete and basic as possible. Following this chapter, there is another more generalized section for tune-ups which includes trouble-shooting diagnosis for the more experienced weekend mechanic.

CAUTION: *When working with a running engine, make sure that there is proper ventilation. Also make sure that the transmission is in Neutral (unless otherwise specified) and the parking brake is fully applied. Always keep hands, long hair, clothing, neckties and tools well clear of the hot exhaust manifold(s) and radiator. When the ignition is running, do not grasp the ignition wires, distributor cap, or coil wire, as a shock in excess of 20,000 volts may result. Whenever working around the distributor, even if the engine is not running, make sure that the ignition is switched off.*

Spark Plugs

The job of the spark plug is to ignite the air/fuel mixture in the cylinder as the piston approaches the top of the compression stroke. The ignited mixture then expands

Tune-Up Specifications

When analyzing compression test results, look for uniformity among cylinders rather than specific pressures.

Year	ENGINE No. Cyl Displacement (cu in.)	hp	SPARK PLUGS Type	Gap (in.)	DISTRIBUTOR Point Dwell (deg)	Point Gap (in.)	IGNITION TIMING (deg)▲ Man Trans	Auto Trans	VALVES Intake Opens ■(deg)●	Fuel Pump Pressure (psi)	IDLE SPEED (rpm)▲ Man Trans°	Auto Trans
'68	6—240	150	BF-42	.034	35-40	.027	6B	6B	12	4-6	600	500
	8—302	210	BF-32	.034	24-29	.021	6B	6B	16	4-6	625	550②
	8—390	270	BF-32	.034	24-29③	.021③	6B	6B	13	4½-6½	625	550
	8—390	315	BF-32	.034	24-29③	.021③	6B	6B	16	4½-6½	625	550
	8—428	345	BF-32	.034	24-29③	.021③	6B	6B	16	4½-6½	625	550
	8—428PI	360	BF-32	.034	26-31	.017	—	6B	18	4½-6½	—	600
'69	6—240	150	BF-42	.034	35-40	.027	6B	6B	12	4-6	775/550	550
	8—302	210	BF-42	.034	24-29③	.021③	6B	6B	16	4½-6½	650	550②
	8—390	270	BF-42	.034	24-29③	.021③	6B	6B	13	4½-6½	650	550
	8—428PI	360	BF-32	.034	24-29③	.021③	—	6B	18	4½-6½	—	600
	8—429	320	BF-42	.034	26-31	.017	—	6B	16	4½-6½	—	550
	8—429	360	BF-42	.034	24-29③	.021③	6B	6B	16	4½-6½	650	550

Tune-Up Specifications (cont.)

When analyzing compression test results, look for uniformity among cylinders rather than specific pressures.

ENGINE			SPARK PLUGS		DISTRIBUTOR		IGNITION TIMING (deg)▲		VALVES Intake Opens ■(deg)●	Fuel Pump Pressure (psi)	IDLE SPEED (rpm)▲	
Year	No. Cyl Displacement (cu in.)	hp	Type	Gap (in.)	Point Dwell (deg)	Point Gap (in.)	Man Trans	Auto Trans			Man Trans°	Auto Trans
'70	6—240	150	BF-42	.034	35-40	.027	6B	6B	12	4-6	800/500	500
	8—302	210	BF-42	.034	24-29	.021	6B	6B	16	4-6	575 [800/500]	575 [600/500]
	8—351	250	BF-42	.034	24-29	.021	10B	10B	11	5-7	575 [700/500]	575 [600/500]
	8—390	270	BF-42	.034	24-29③	.021③	6B	6B	13	5-7	570/500	600/500
	8—428PI	360	BF-32	.034	24-29	.021	—	6B	18	4½-6½	—	600/500
	8—429	320	BRF-42	.034	24-29③	.021③	—	6B	16	5-7	—	600/500
	8—429	360	BRF-42	.034	24-29③	.021③	6B	6B	16	5-7	700/500	600/500
'71	6—240	140	BRF-42	.034	33-38	.027	6B	6B	18	4-6	800/500	600/500
	8—302	210	BRF-42	.034	24-29	.021	6B	6B	16	4-6	575 [800/500]	575 [650/500]
	8—351W	240	BRF-42	.034	24-29	.021	6B	6B	11	5-7	575 [775/500]	575 [600/500]
	8—351C	240	ARF-42	.034	24-29	.021	—	6B	12	5-7	—	625/550

8—390	255	BRF-42	.034	24-29	.021	—	6B	13	5-7	—	600/475
8—400	260	ARF-42	.034	26-31	.017	—	10B(6B)	17	5-7	—	625/500
8—429PI	370	ARF-42	.034	27½-29½	.020	—	10B	32	5-7	—	650/500
8—429	320	BRF-42	.034	24-29③	.021③	—	4B	16	5-7	—	600
8—429	360	BRF-42	.034	24-29③	.021③	4B	4B	16	5-7	700	600
'72											
6—240	103	BRF-42	.034	35-39	.027	—	6B	18	4-6	—	500
8—302	140	BRF-42	.034	26-30	.017	—	6B	16	5-7	—	575 [600/500]
8—351W	153	BRF-42	.034	26-30	.017	—	6B	11	5-7	—	575 [600/500]
8—351C	163	ARF-42	.034	26-30	.017	—	6B	12	5-7	—	600/500
8—400	172	ARF-42	.034	26-30	.017	—	6B	17	5-7	—	625/500
8—429	208	BRF-42	.034	26-30	.017	—	10B	8	5-7	—	600/500
8—429PI	NA	ARF-42	.034	26-30	.017	—	10B	32	Electric	—	650/500
'73											
8—351W	153	BRF-42	.034	26-30	.017	—	6B	11	5-7	—	575 [600/500]
8—351C	163	ARF-42	.034	26-30	.017	—	6B	12	5-7	—	600/500
8—400	172	ARF-42	.034	26-30	.017	—	6B	17	5-7	—	625/500

Tune-Up Specifications (cont.)

When analyzing compression test results, look for uniformity among cylinders rather than specific pressures.

| ENGINE | | | SPARK PLUGS | | DISTRIBUTOR | | IGNITION TIMING (deg)▲ | | VALVES | Fuel Pump Pressure (psi) | IDLE SPEED (rpm)▲ | |
Year / No. Cyl Displacement (cu in.)		hp	Type	Gap (in.)	Point Dwell (deg)	Point Gap (in.)	Man Trans	Auto Trans	Intake Opens ■(deg)●		Man Trans°	Auto Trans
'73	8—429	208	BRF-42	.034	26-30	.017	—	10B	8	5-7	—	600/500
	8—429PI	NA	ARF-42	.034	26-30	.017	—	10B	32	Electric	—	650/500
'74	8—351W	162	BRF-42	.034④	26-30	.014-.020	—	6B	15	4-6	—	[600/500]
	8—351C	163	ARF-42	.044	26-30	.014-.020	—	14B	19½	5½-6½	—	[700/500]
	8—400	170	ARF-42	.044⑧	⑥	⑥	—	12B	17	5½-6½	—	[625/500]
	8—460	195	ARF-52	.054⑦	⑥	⑥	—	14B	8	5½-6½	—	[650/500]⑤
	8—460PI	275	ARF-52	.054	⑥	⑥	—	10B	18	Electric	—	[700/500]
'75	8—351M	148	ARF-42	.044	⑥	⑥	—	8B	19½	5½-6½	—	[700/500]
	8—400	158	ARF-42	.044	⑥	⑥	—	6B	17	5½-6½	—	[625/500]
	8—460	218	ARF-52	.044	⑥	⑥	—	14B	8	6.2-7.2	—	[650/500]
	8—460PI	226	ARF-52	.044	⑥	⑥	—	14B	18	Electric	—	[650/500]

'76	8—351M	152	ARF-52	.044	⑥	—	12B⑨	19½	6½–7½	—	[650/500]
	8—400	180	ARF-52	.044	⑥	—	10B	17	6½–7½	—	[650/500]
	8—460	202	ARF-52	.044	⑥	—	8B⑩	8	7.2–8.2	—	[650/500]
	8—460PI	202	ARF-52	.044	⑥	—	8B⑩	8	Electric	—	[650/500]
'77	8—351M	All	ARF-52	.050	⑥	—		19½	6½–7½	—	
	8—400	All	ARF-52	.050	⑥	—		17	6½–7½	—	
	8—460	All	ARF-52-6	.060	⑥	—		8	7–8	—	
'78	8—302	All	ARF-52 (ARF-52-6)	.050 (.060)	Electronic	—	14B	16	5½–6½	—	650
	8—351W	All	ARF-52 (ARF-52-6)	.050 (.060)	Electronic	—	4B	23	4–6	—	650
	8—351M	All	ARF-52 (ARF-52-6)	.050 (.060)	Electronic	—	12B(16B)	19½	6½–7½	—	650
	8—400	All	ARF-52 (ARF-52-6)	.050 (.060)	Electronic	—	13B(16B)	17	6½–7½	—	650
	8—460	All	ARF-52 (ARF-52-6)	.050 (.060)	Electronic	—	10B	8	7¼–8¼	—	580
	8—460	PI	ARF-52-6	.060	Electronic	—	16B	18	7¼–8¼	—	580

Tune-Up Specifications (cont.)

When analyzing compression test results, look for uniformity among cylinders rather than specific pressures.

ENGINE			SPARK PLUGS		DISTRIBUTOR		IGNITION TIMING (deg)△		VALVES Intake Opens ■(deg)●	Fuel Pump Pressure (psi)	IDLE SPEED (rpm)△	
Year	No. Cyl Displacement (cu in.)	hp	Type	Gap (in.)	Point Dwell (deg)	Point Gap (in.)	Man Trans	Auto Trans			Man Trans°	Auto Trans
'79	8—302	All	ARF-52	.050	Electronic		—	14B	16	5½—6½	—	650
	8—351W	All	ARF-52	.050	Electronic		—	4B (EECII)⑪	23	4-6	—	650

▲ See text for procedure
● Figures in parentheses indicate California engine
■ All figures Before Top Dead Center
* Figures in brackets are for solenoid equipped vehicles only. In all cases where two figures are separated by a slash, the first is for idle speed with solenoid energized and the second is for idle speed with solenoid disconnected and automatic transmission in Neutral.

① Adjust mechanical lifters, intake and exhaust, to .025 inch with engine hot
② A/C off
③ For engines equipped with single diaphragm distributors, adjust point dwell to 26-31 degrees and point gap to .017 inch
④ .044 on California models
⑤ 675/500 for California engines
⑥ Solid State (breakerless) ignition
⑦ .044 on California models
⑧ .054 on California models
⑨ 8BTDC @ 650 rpm in California

⑩ 14BTDC @ 650 rpm in California
⑪ California engines have variable EEC II timing; see the text for a description.
B Before Top Dead Center
C Cleveland
NA Not available
PI Police Interceptor
TDC Top Dead Center
W Windsor
— Not applicable
M Modified Cleveland design

and forces the piston down on the power stroke.

The average life of a spark plug is approximately 12,000 miles. This is, however, dependent on the mechanical condition of the engine, the type of fuel that is used, and the type of driving conditions under which the car is used. For some people, spark plugs will last 5,000 miles and for others, 15,000 or 20,000 miles.

Your car came from the factory with resistor spark plugs. Resistor spark plugs help to limit the amount of radio frequency energy that is given off by the automotive ignition system. Radio frequency energy results in the annoying buzzing or clicking you sometimes hear on your radio or the jumping picture you see on your TV when a car pulls into the driveway.

The electrode end of the spark plug (the end that goes into the cylinder) is also a very good indicator of the mechanical condition of your engine. If a spark plug should foul and begin to misfire, you will have to find the condition that caused the plug to foul and correct it. It is also a good idea to occasionally give all the plugs the once-over to get an idea how the inside of your engine is doing. A small amount of deposit on a spark plug, after it has been in use for any period of time, should be considered normal.

NOTE: *1975 and later Fords use special high-temperature spark plug wires on selected cylinders. This is necessary due to the high heat conditions generated by late model emission control equipment, particularly catalytic converters. These high-temperature wires consist of a silicone jacket over silicone insulation. They are easily identified by their white lettering (yellow for standard cables), and the fact that they have "S" for silicone shown next to the vendor identification on the cable. If you find it necessary to replace your spark plug wires, be sure to use the special silicone wires in the specified locations. Standard wires will quickly fail due to the high heat conditions.*

REMOVAL AND INSTALLATION

Every six months or 6,000 miles, the spark plugs should be removed for inspection. At this time they should be cleaned and re-gapped. At 12-month or 12,000-mile intervals, the plugs should be replaced.

Prior to removal, number each spark plug wire with a piece of masking tape bearing the cylinder number. Remove each spark plug wire by grasping its rubber boot on the end and twisting slightly to free the wire from the plug. Using a $^{13}/_{16}$ in. (BF or BRF plugs) or $^5/_8$ in. (ARF plugs) spark plug socket, turn the plugs counterclockwise to remove them. Do not allow any foreign matter to enter the cylinders through the spark plug holes.

Consult the spark plug inspection chart in Step 4.6 of the "Trouble-shooting" section when in doubt about plug condition. If the spark plugs are to be reused, check the porcelain insulator for cracks and the electrodes for excessive wear. Replace the entire set if one plug is damaged. Clean the reusable plugs with a stiff wire brush. Uneven wear of the center or ground electrode may be corrected by leveling off the unevenly worn section with a file.

The gap must be checked with a feeler gauge before installing the plug in the engine. With the ground electrode, a wire gauge of the proper diameter must pass

Cleaning plug with file

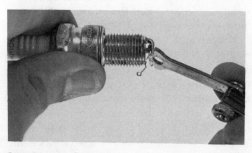

Gapping spark plug

Silicone Cable Usage

Engine	Cylinders Using Silicone Wire
351M	2–3–4–6–7–8
400	2–3–4–6–7–8
460	2–3–4–6

through the opening with a slight drag. If the air gap between the two electrodes is not correct, the ground electrode must be bent to bring it to specifications.

After the plugs are gapped correctly, they may be inserted into their holes and hand-tightened. Be careful not to cross-thread the plugs. Torque the plugs to the proper specification with a $^{13}/_{16}$ or $^5/_8$ in. socket and torque wrench. Install each spark plug wire on its respective plug, making sure that each spark plug end is making good metal-to-metal contact in its wire socket.

Breaker Points and Condenser

NOTE: *All 1975 and later models, 1974 models sold in California, and most 1974 models sold in the 49 states (except some early 351 V8 equipped models) use the new breakerless (solid state) ignition system.*

The points and condenser function as a circuit breaker for the primary circuit of the ignition system. The ignition coil must boost the 12 volts (V) of electrical pressure supplied to it by the battery to about 20,000 V in order to fire the spark plugs. To do this, the coil depends on the points and condenser for assistance.

The coil has a primary and a secondary circuit. When the ignition key is turned to the "on" position, the battery supplies voltage to the primary side of the coil which passes the voltage on to the points. The points are connected to ground to complete the primary circuit. As the cam in the distributor turns, the points open and the primary circuit collapses. The magnetic force in the primary circuit of the coil cuts through the secondary circuit and increases the voltage in the secondary circuit to a level that is sufficient to fire the spark plugs. When the points open, the electrical charge contained in the primary circuit jumps the gap that is created between the two open contacts of the points. If this electrical charge was not transferred elsewhere, the material on the contacts of the points would melt and that all-important gap between the contacts would start to change. If this gap is not maintained, the points will not break the primary circuit. If the primary circuit is not broken, the secondary circuit will not have enough voltage to fire the spark plugs. Enter the condenser.

The function of the condenser is to absorb the excessive voltage from the points when they open and thus prevent the points from becoming pitted or burned.

There are two ways to check breaker point gap: with a feeler gauge or with a dwell meter. Either way you set the points, you are adjusting the amount of time (in degrees of distributor rotation) that the points will remain open. If you adjust the points with a feeler gauge, you are setting the maximum amount the points will open when the rubbing block on the points is on a high point of the distributor cam. When you adjust the points with a dwell meter, you are measuring the number of degrees (of distributor cam rotation) that the points will remain closed before they start to open as a high point of the distributor cam approaches the rubbing block of the points.

There are two rules that should always be followed when adjusting or replacing points. *The points and condenser are a matched set; never replace one without replacing the other. If you change the point gap or dwell of the engine, you also change the ignition timing. Therefore, if you adjust the points, you must also adjust the timing.*

INSPECTION

Disconnect the secondary cable from the coil at the center of the distributor cap. On the distributors using cap clasps to secure the cap, pry the retaining clasps from either side of the cap using a flat blade screwdriver. On distributors using cross-head screws with "L-shaped" levers to secure the cap, press down on the screw head with a flat blade screwdriver and while maintaining pressure, rotate the screw head and retaining lever in either direction to free it from the distributor body. Then, lift off the cap (wires installed) and position it to one side.

Mark the position of the rotor by scribing a mark on the distributor body. Pull the rotor straight up and off. Discard it if it is cracked, burned or excessively worn at the tip. Insert a screwdriver between the stationary and breaker arms of the points and examine the condition of the contacts. Replace the points if the contacts are blackened, pitted, or if the metal transfer exceeds that of the specified point gap (see "Tune-Up Specifications Chart"). Also replace the points if breaker arm has lost its tension (nonadjustable types) or if the rubbing block has become worn or loose. Contact points that have become slightly burned (light gray) may be cleaned with a point file.

In order for the points to function properly, the contact faces must be aligned. The

CONDITION	CAUSED BY
BURNED	INCORRECT VOLTAGE REGULATOR SETTING. RADIO CONDENSER INSTALLED TO THE DISTRIBUTOR SIDE OF THE COIL.
EXCESSIVE METAL TRANSFER OR PITTING	INCORRECT ALIGNMENT. INCORRECT VOLTAGE REGULATOR SETTING. RADIO CONDENSER INSTALLED TO THE DISTRIBUTOR SIDE OF THE COIL. IGNITION CONDENSER OF IMPROPER CAPACITY. EXTENDED OPERATION OF THE ENGINE AT SPEEDS OTHER THAN NORMAL.

Breaker point troubleshooting

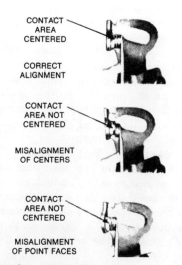

CONTACT AREA CENTERED

CORRECT ALIGNMENT

CONTACT AREA NOT CENTERED

MISALIGNMENT OF CENTERS

CONTACT AREA NOT CENTERED

MISALIGNMENT OF POINT FACES

Breaker point contact alignment

Rotating engine manually

alignment must be checked with the points closed. To close the points, install an open-end wrench on the crankshaft pulley/damper bolt and turn the engine over in its normal direction of rotation until the points can be seen to close.

NOTE: *This may be more easily accomplished with the spark plugs removed.*

If the contact faces are not centered, bend the stationary arm to suit. Never bend the breaker arm. Discard the points if they cannot be centered correctly.

REPLACEMENT

To replace the points and condenser, loosen the nut at the center of the point assembly and slide the distributor primary lead and the condenser lead away from the terminal. Then remove the condenser retaining screw and the point assembly retaining screw(s) and remove the points and condenser. While the points are out, clean the distributor base plate with an alcohol-soaked rag to remove any oil film that might impede completion of the ground circuit. Lubricate the breaker cam lobes with a very light coating of silicone base grease.

Install the new points and condenser and tighten their retaining screws. Connect the electrical leads for both at the primary terminal. Make sure that the contacts are aligned horizontally and vertically as previously described.

The breaker points must be correctly gapped before proceeding any further. Install an open-end wrench on the crankshaft pulley/damper bolt and turn the engine over by hand in the normal direction of rotation

Adjusting point gap

until the rubbing block on the point assembly is resting on the high point of a breaker cam lobe. Loosen the point attaching screws slightly. Insert a feeler gauge of the proper thickness between the point contacts (see "Tune-Up Specifications Chart")

NOTE: *Wipe the feeler gauge clean of any grease or oil which will contaminate the point contacts.*

The gap is correct when the loosely held feeler gauge passes through the contacts with a slight drag. If the gap needs adjusting, insert the tip of a screwdriver in the notch beside the points and twist to open or close the gap as necessary. Then, without disturbing the setting, tighten the breaker point attaching screw(s). Recheck the gap after tightening.

If a dwell meter is available, proceed to "Dwell Angle Setting." If the meter is not available, proceed to replace the rotor on top of the distributor shaft, making sure that the tab inside the rotor aligns with the slot on the distributor shaft. Position the distributor cap on top of the distributor. On distributors using cap clasps to secure the cap, snap the clasps into the slots in the cap. On distributors using cross-head screws with "L-shaped" levers to secure the cap, press down on the screw head and rotate the retaining boss on the distributor body, and then release the screw. Check that the cap is fully seated, and that the spark plug wires fit snugly into the cap. Connect the secondary cable from the coil at the distributor cap. Proceed to "Ignition Timing Adjustment."

Dwell Angle Setting

NOTE: *On cars equipped with breakerless (solid state) ignition, dwell is electronically controlled and cannot be adjusted.*

The dwell angle is the number of degrees of distributor cam rotation through which the breaker points remain fully closed (conducting electricity). Increasing the point gap decreases dwell, while decreasing the point gap increases dwell.

Using a dwell meter of known accuracy, connect the red lead (positive) wire of the meter to the distributor primary wire connection on the positive (+) side of the coil, and the black ground (negative) wire of the meter to a good ground on the engine (e.g. thermostat housing nut).

The dwell angle may be checked either with the distributor cap and rotor installed and the engine running, or with the cap and rotor removed and the engine cranking at starter speed. The meter gives constant reading with the engine running. With the engine cranking, the reading will fluctuate between zero degrees dwell and the maximum figure for that angle. While cranking, the maximum figure is the correct one for that setting. Never attempt to change dwell

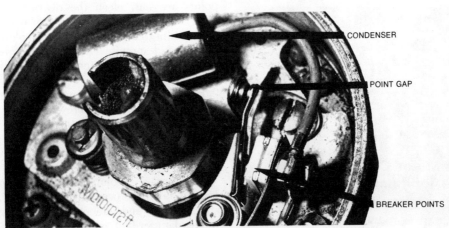

Checking point gap

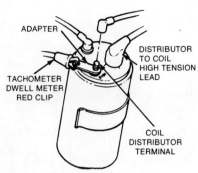

Installing dwell/tachometer adapter on coil (1974 and earlier models)

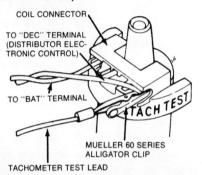

Attaching dwell/tachometer lead to coil connector (1975 and later models)

angle while the ignition is on. Touching the point contacts or primary wire connection with a metal screwdriver may result in a 12 volt shock.

To change the dwell angle, loosen the point retaining screw slightly and make the approximate correction. Tighten the retaining screw and test the dwell with the engine cranking. If the dwell appears to be correct, install the breaker point protective cover, if so equipped, the rotor and distributor cap, and test the dwell with the engine running. Take the engine through its entire rpm range and observe the dwell meter. The dwell should remain within specifications at all times. Great fluctuation of dwell at different engine speeds indicates worn distributor parts.

Following the dwell angle adjustment, the ignition timing must be checked. A 1° increase in dwell results in the ignition timing being retarded 2° and vice versa.

Ford Motor Company Solid-State Ignition

BASIC OPERATING PRINCIPLES

In mid 1974, Ford Motor Company introduced in selected models its new Solid-State Ignition System. In 1975, it became standard equipment in all cars in the Ford lineup. This system was designed primarily to provide a hotter spark necessary to fire the leaner fuel/air mixtures required by today's emission control standards.

The Ford Solid-State Ignition is a pulse-triggered, transistor controlled breakerless ignition system. With the ignition switch "on", the primary circuit is on and the ignition coil is energized. When the armature spokes approach the magnetic pick-up coil assembly, they induce a voltage which tells the amplifier to turn the coil primary current off. A timing circuit in the amplifier module will turn the current on again after the coil field has collapsed. When the current is on, it flows from the battery through the ignition switch, the primary windings of the ignition coil, and through the amplifier module circuits to ground. When the current is off, the magnetic field built up in the ignition coil is allowed to collapse, inducing a high voltage into the secondary windings of the coil. High voltage is produced each time the field is thus built up and collapsed.

Although the systems are basically the same, Ford refers to their solid-state ignition in several different ways. 1974–76 systems are referred to simply as Breakerless systems. In 1977, Ford named their ignition system Dura-Spark I and Dura-Spark II. Dura-Spark II is the version used in all states except California. Dura-Spark I is the system used in California V8's only. Basically, the only difference between the two is that the coil charging currents are higher in the California cars. This is necessary to fire the leaner fuel/air mixtures required by California's stricter emission laws. The difference in coils alters some of the test values.

Ford has used several different types of wiring harness on their solid-state ignition systems, due to internal circuitry changes in the electronic module. Wire continuity and color have not been changed, but the arrangement of the terminals in the connectors is different for each year. Schematics of the different years are included here, but keep in mind that the wiring in all diagrams has been simplified and as a result, the routing of your wiring may not match the wiring in the diagram. However, the wire colors and terminal connections are the same.

Wire color-coding is critical to servicing the Ford Solid-State Ignition. Battery current reaches the electronic module through

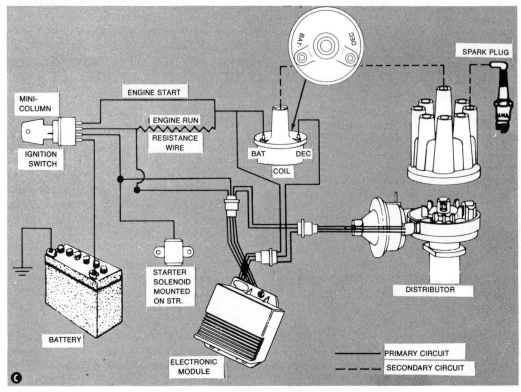

Ford solid state ignition schematic

either the *white* or *red* wire, depending on whether the engine is cranking or running. When the engine is cranking, battery current is flowing through the *white* wire. When the engine is running, battery current flows through the *red* wire. All distributor signals flow through the *orange* and *purple* wires. The *green* wire carries primary current from the coil to the module. The *black* wire is a ground between the distributor and the module. Up until 1975, a *blue* wire provides transient voltage protection. In 1976, the *blue* wire was dropped when a zener diode was added to the module. The *orange* and *purple* wires which run from the stator to the module must *always* be connected to the same color wire at the module. If these connections are crossed, polarity will be reversed and the system will be thrown out of phase. Some replacement wiring harnesses were sold with the wiring crossed, which complicates the problem considerably. As previously noted, the *black* wire is the ground wire. The screw which grounds the black wire also, of course, grounds the entire primary circuit. If this screw is loose, dirty, or corroded, a seemingly incomprehensible ignition problem will develop. Several other cau-

tions should be noted here. Keep in mind that on vehicles equipped with catalytic converters, any test that requires removal of a spark plug wire while the engine is running should be kept to a thirty second maximum. Any longer than this may damage the converter. In the event you are testing spark plug wires, do not pierce them. Test the wires at their terminals only.

TROUBLESHOOTING THE FORD SOLID-STATE IGNITION SYSTEM

NOTE: *Ford has substantially altered their 1978 and later electronic ignition test procedure. Due to the sensitive nature of the system and the complexity of the test procedures, it is recommended that you refer to your dealer if you suspect a problem in your 1978 and later electronic ignition system. The system can, of course, be tested by substituting known good components (module, stator, etc.)*

This system, which at first appears to be extremely complicated, is actually quite simple to diagnose and repair. Diagnosis does, however, require the use of a voltmeter and an ohmmeter. You will also need several jumper wires with both blade ends and alligator clips.

The symptons of a defective component within the solid state system are exactly the same as those you would encounter in a conventional system. Some of these symptoms are:

Hard or no starting

Rough Idle

Poor fuel economy

Engine misses while under load or while accelerating

If you suspect a problem in your ignition system, first perform a spark intensity test to pinpoint the problem. Using insulated pliers, hold the end of one of the spark plug leads about ½ in. away from the engine block or other good ground, and crank the engine. If you have a nice, fat spark, then your problem is not in the ignition system. If you have no spark or a very weak spark, then proceed to the following tests.

Stator Test

To test the stator (also known as the magnetic pickup assembly), you will need an ohmmeter. Run the engine until it reaches operating temperature, then turn the ignition switch to the "off" position. Disconnect the wire harness from the distributor. Connect the ohmmeter between the orange and purple wires. Resistance should be between 400 and 800 ohms. Next, connect the ohmmeter between the black wire and a good ground on the engine. Operate the vacuum advance, either by hand or with an external vacuum source. Resistance should be zero ohms. Finally, connect the ohmmeter between the orange wire and ground. Resistance should be over 70,000 ohms in both cases. If any of your ohmmeter readings differ from the above specifications, then the stator is defective and must be replaced as a unit.

If the stator is good, then either the electronic module or the wiring connections must be checked next. Because of its complicated electronic nature, the module itself cannot be checked, except by substitution. If you have access to a module which you know to be good, then perform a substitution test at this time. If this cures the problem, then the original module is faulty and must be replaced. If it does not cure the problem or if you cannot locate a known-good module, then disconnect the two wiring harnesses from the module, and, using a voltmeter, check the following circuits:

NOTE: *Make no tests at the module side of the connectors.*

1. Starting circuit—Connect the voltmeter leads to ground and to the corresponding female socket of the white male lead from the module (you will need a jumper wire with a blade end). Crank the engine over. The voltage should be between 8 and 12 volts.

2. Running circuit—Turn the ignition switch to the "on" position. Connect the voltmeter leads to ground and the corresponding female socket of the red male lead from the module. Voltage should be battery voltage plus or minus 0.1 volts.

3. Coil circuit—Leave the ignition switch "on". Connect the voltmeter leads to ground and to the corresponding female socket of the green male lead from the module. Voltage should be battery voltage plus or minus 0.1 volts.

If any of the preceding readings are incorrect, inspect and repair any loose, broken, frayed or dirty connections. If this doesn't solve the problem, perform a battery source test.

Battery Source Test

To make this test, *do not* disconnect the coil. Connect the voltmeter leads to the BAT terminal at the coil and a good ground. Connect a jumper wire from the DEC terminal at the coil to a good ground. Make sure all lights and accessories are off. Turn the ignition to

When you're working on the electronic ignition, unplug the module connectors here. Leave the module side alone or you'll short the module out

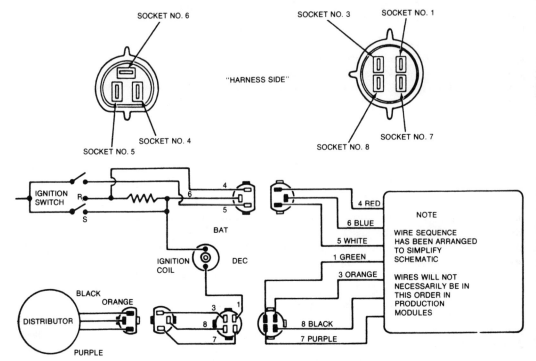

1975 electronic ignition wiring schematic

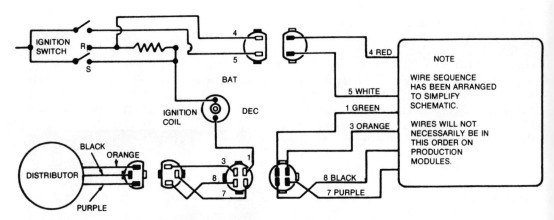

1976 electronic ignition wiring schematic

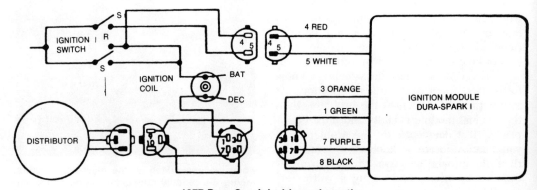

1977 Dura Spark I wiring schematic

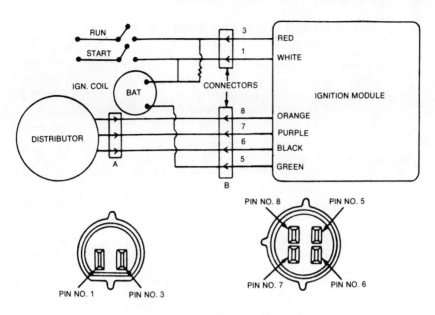

ELECTRONIC MODULE CONNECTORS—HARNESS SIDE

1977 Dura Spark II wiring schematic

the "on" position. Check the voltage. If the voltage is below 4.9 volts (11 volts for Dura-Spark I), then check the primary wiring for broken strands, cracked or frayed wires, or loose or dirty terminals. Repair or replace any defects. If, however, the voltage is above 7.9 volts (14 volts for Dura-Spark I), then you have a problem in the resistance wiring and it must be replaced.

It should be noted here that if you do have a problem in your electronic ignition system, most of the time will be a case of loose, dirty or frayed wires. The electronic module, being completely solid-state, is not ordinarily subject to failure. It is possible for the unit to fail, of course, but as a general rule, the source of an ignition system problem will be somewhere else in the circuit.

1975 Test Sequence

	Test Voltage Between	*Should Be*	*If Not, Conduct*
Key On	Socket #4 and Engine Ground	Battery Voltage ± 0.1 Volt	Module Bias Test
	Socket #1 and Engine Ground	Battery Voltage ± 0.1 Volt	Battery Source Test
Cranking	Socket #5 and Engine Ground	8 to 12 volts	Cranking Test
	Jumper #1 to #8 Read #6	more than 6 volts	Starting Circuit Test
	Pin #7 and Pin #8	½ volt minimum AC or any DC volt wiggle	Distributor Hardware Test

1975 Test Sequence (cont.)

	Test Voltage Between	Should Be	If Not, Conduct
Key Off	Socket #7 and #3	400 to 800 ohms	Magnetic Pick-up
	Socket #8 and Engine Ground	0 ohms	(Stator) Test
	Socket #7 and Engine Ground	more than 70,000 ohms	
	Socket #3 and Engine Ground		
	Socket #4 and Coil Tower	7000 to 13,000 ohms	Coil Test
	Socket #1 and Pin #6	1.0 to 2.0 ohms	
	Socket #1 and Engine Ground	more than 4.0 ohms	Short Test
	Socket #4 and Pin #6	1.0 to 2.0 ohms	Resistance Wire Test

1976 Test Sequence

	Test Voltage Between	Should Be	If Not, Conduct
Key On	Socket #4 and Engine Ground	Battery Voltage ± 0.1 Volt	Battery Source Test
	Socket #1 and Engine Ground	Battery Voltage ± 0.1 Volt	Battery Source Test
Cranking	Socket #5 and Engine Ground	8 to 12 volts	Check Supply Circuit (starting) through Ignition Switch
	Jumper #1 to #8 Read #6	more than 6 volts	Starting Circuit Test
	Pin #3 and Pin #8	½ volt minimum AC or any RC volt wiggle	Distributor Hardware Test

	Test Voltage Between	Should Be	If Not, Conduct
Key Off	Socket #8 and #3	400 to 800 ohms	Magnetic Pick-up
	Socket #7 and Engine Ground	0 ohms	(Stator) Test
	Socket #8 and Engine Ground	more than 70,000 ohms	
	Socket #3 and Engine Ground	more than 70,000 ohms	
	Socket #4 and Coil Tower	7000 to 13,000 ohms	Coil Test
	Socket #1 and Engine Ground	more than 4.0 ohms	Short Test

1977 Test Sequence

	Test Voltage Between	Should Be	If Not, Conduct
Key On	Socket #4 and Engine Ground	Battery Voltage ± 0.1 volts	Module Bias Test

1977 Test Sequence (cont.)

	Test Voltage Between	Should Be	If Not, Conduct
Key On	Socket #1 and Engine Ground	Battery Voltage ± 0.1 volts	Battery Source Test
Cranking	Socket #5 and Engine Ground	8 to 12 volts	Cranking Test
	Jumper #1 to #8—Read Coil "Bat" Term. & Engine Ground	more than 6 volts	Starting Circuit Test
	Sockets #7 and #3	½ volt minimum wiggle	Distributor Hardware Test

	Test Resistance Between	Should Be	If Not, Conduct
Key Off	Sockets #7 and #3 Socket #8 and Engine Ground Socket #7 and Engine Ground Socket #3 and Engine Ground	400 to 800 ohms 0 ohms more than 70,000 ohms more than 70,000 ohms	Magnetic Pick-up (Stator) Test
	Socket #4 and Coil Tower	7000 to 13,000 ohms	Coil Test
	Socket #1 and Coil "Bat" Term.	1.0 to 2.0 ohms Breakerless & Dura-Spark II 0.5 to 1.5 ohms	
	Socket #1 and Engine Ground	more than 4 ohms	Short Test
	Socket #4 and Coil "Bat" Term. (Except Dura-Spark I)	1.0 to 2.0 ohms Breakerless	Resistance Wire Test
		0.7 to 1.7 ohms Dura-Spark II	

Electronic Engine Control II System (EEC II)

Beginning in 1979, Ford's new Electronic Engine Control II System (EEC II) is used on California models with the 351 engine. EEC II is essentially a more sophisticated version of the EEC I system used on the 1978 Versailles.

The EEC II system consists of two separate systems, a monitoring system and an output system, reporting to and controlled by, a microcomputer called an Electronic Control Assembly (ECA). The input or monitoring system consists of a network of sensors which gather data on engine operating conditions and relays this data to the ECA. The ECA then analyzes the data and sends out electrical signals to the various devices in the output system. According to the signals received from the computer, these devices can alter ignition timing, EGR flow, carburetor air/fuel ratio, and thermactor (air pump) flow.

MONITORING SYSTEM

The monitoring or input system consists of six separate sensors which monitor seven different conditions which affect emissions and drivability.

These sensors consist of:

(1) Barometric and Manifold Absolute Pressure Sensor
(2) Engine Coolant Temperature Sensor
(3) Throttle Position Sensor
(4) Crankshaft Position Sensor
(5) Exhaust Gas Oxygen Sensor
(6) EGR Valve Position Sensor

Barometric and Manifold Absolute Pressure Sensor (BMAP)

The barometric and manifold absolute pressure sensor is actually two sensors combined. The BMAP monitors manifold absolute pressure (barometric pressure minus manifold vacuum), and atmospheric pressure. The BMAP is located on the inner fender well.

Engine Coolant Temperature Sensor (ECT)

The ECT is located at the heater outlet fitting at the front of the intake manifold. As its name implies, it monitors the temperature of the engine coolant.

Throttle Position Sensor (TP)

The Throttle Position Sensor supplies the ECA with information about one of the following operating modes:
    Closed throttle
    Part throttle
    Wide open throttle
    Basically, the TP sensor is a potentiometer mounted on the carburetor. The ECA receives and analyzes the data transmitted by the TP, and uses this data to determine spark advance, EGR valve flow, air/fuel ratio, and thermactor air flow.

Crankshaft Position Sensor (CP)

Since with the EEC II system, there is nothing inside the distributor except the rotor,

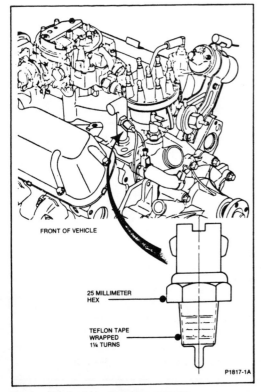

FRONT OF VEHICLE

25 MILLIMETER HEX

TEFLON TAPE WRAPPED 1¼ TURNS

P1817-1A

Engine coolant temperature sensor

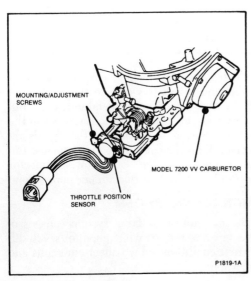

MOUNTING/ADJUSTMENT SCREWS

MODEL 7200 VV CARBURETOR

THROTTLE POSITION SENSOR

P1819-1A

Throttle position sensor

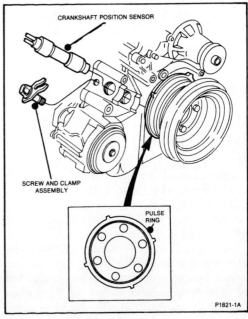

CRANKSHAFT POSITION SENSOR

SCREW AND CLAMP ASSEMBLY

PULSE RING

P1821-1A

Crankshaft position sensor

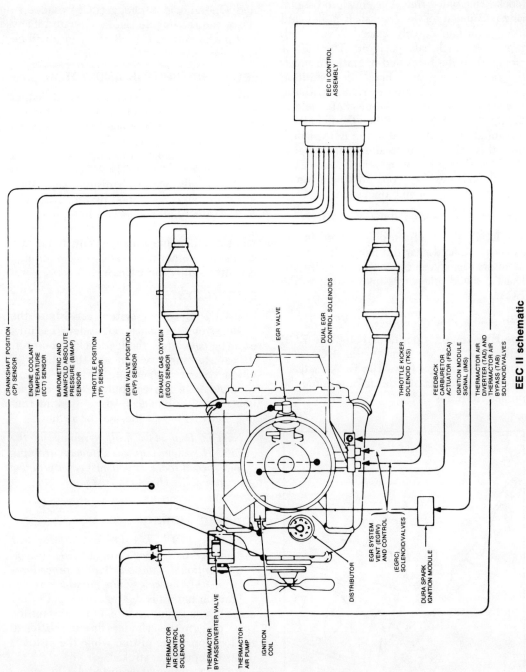

CRANKSHAFT POSITION (CP) SENSOR

ENGINE COOLANT TEMPERATURE (ECT) SENSOR

BAROMETRIC AND MANIFOLD ABSOLUTE PRESSURE (B/MAP) SENSOR

THROTTLE POSITION (TP) SENSOR

EGR VALVE POSITION (EVP) SENSOR

EXHAUST GAS OXYGEN (EGO) SENSOR

EGR VALVE

DUAL EGR CONTROL SOLENOIDS

EEC II CONTROL ASSEMBLY

THROTTLE KICKER SOLENOID (TKS)

FEEDBACK CARBURETOR ACTUATOR (FBCA)

IGNITION MODULE SIGNAL (IMS)

THERMACTOR AIR DIVERTER (TAD) AND THERMACTOR AIR BYPASS (TAB) SOLENOID/VALVES

THERMACTOR AIR CONTROL SOLENOIDS

THERMACTOR BYPASS/DIVERTER VALVE

THERMACTOR AIR PUMP

IGNITION COIL

DISTRIBUTOR

EGR SYSTEM VENT (EGRV) AND CONTROL (EGRC) SOLENOID/VALVES

DURA SPARK IGNITION MODULE

EEC II schematic

some method of establishing reference timing is necessary. Accurate reference timing is therefore achieved by using a pulse ring in the crankshaft pulley in conjunction with a crankshaft position sensor mounted on the block. The pulse ring is a powdered metal ring positioned on the crankshaft pulley and fitted with four equally spaced lobes which represent crankshaft position. The CP is mounted on the block and operates in much the same fashion as a breakerless ignition pickup coil. As the pulse ring rotates with the crankshaft, it interrupts the magnetic field at the tip of the CP sensor. When the field is interrupted, a signal is sent to the ECA, which uses this information to determine engine RPM, and crankshaft position. The ECA then determines the proper timing advance required for best engine operation.

Exhaust Gas Oxygen Sensor (EGO)

The EGO is a small sensor mounted in the exhaust manifold near the flange. The EGO monitors the oxygen concentration of the exhaust gas and relays this information to the ECA.

EGR Valve Position Sensor (EVP)

The EVP sensor is positioned atop the EGR valve, and relays a signal to the ECA concerning exhaust gas flow. The ECA analyzes this and other data in order to determine the proper EGR flow.

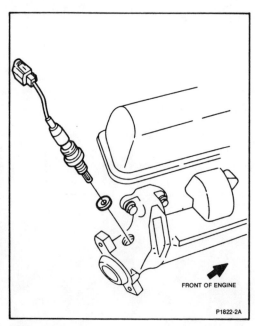

FRONT OF ENGINE

P1822-2A

EGO sensor

ELECTRONIC CONTROL ASSEMBLY

The ECA is essentially a minicomputer consisting of a processor assembly and a calibration assembly. The ECA is protected against total failure by a system known as the Limited Operational Strategy (LOS) mode. In this mode the engine can be operated if any part of the system fails. Performance will be poor, however.

EEC II DISTRIBUTOR AND ROTOR

The distributor used with the EEC II system contains nothing but a unique bi-level rotor. The rotor is fixed in place during assembly and should not be removed except for replacement. Installation requires the use of a special alignment tool. The EEC II distributor has no advance mechanisms, since all ignition timing is controlled by the ECA. The EEC II distributor is locked into place during engine assembly and rotational adjustment is impossible. In any event, timing adjustments are not necessary, since all timing is controlled by the ECA.

OUTPUT SYSTEM

The EEC II output system consists of the EGR system, thermactor air system, the dual catalytic converter, the feedback carburetor, the canister purge system, and the unique ignition system. Depending upon the signals received from the computer, these components can alter fuel/air mixture, ignition timing, EGR flow, and thermactor air flow.

> NOTE: *Diagnosis and/or repair of the EEC II system requires extensive training and special tools. If you suspect a problem in your EEC II system, see your dealer.*

Ignition Timing

> NOTE: *1979 LTD's sold in California are equipped with Ford's new EEC II system. Conventional ignition timing procedures are neither necessary nor possible.*

Ignition timing is the measurement in degrees of crankshaft rotation of the instant the spark plugs in the cylinders fire, in relation to the location of the piston, while the piston is on its compression stroke.

Ignition timing is adjusted by loosening the distributor locking device and turning the distributor in the engine.

Ideally, the air/fuel mixture in the cylinder will be ignited (by the spark plug) and just beginning its rapid expansion as the piston passes top dead center (TDC) of the compression stroke. If this happens, the piston will be beginning the power stroke just as the compressed (by the movement of the piston) and ignited (by the spark plug) air/fuel mixture starts to expand. The expansion of the air/fuel mixture will then force the piston down on the power stroke and turn the crankshaft.

It takes a fraction of a second for the spark from the plug to completely ignite the mixture in the cylinder. Because of this, the spark plug must fire before the piston reaches TDC, if the mixture is to be completely ignited as the piston passes TDC. This measurement is given in degrees (of crankshaft rotation) *before* the piston reaches *top dead center* (BTDC). If the ignition timing setting for your engine is six degrees (6°) BTDC, this means that the spark plug must fire at a time when the piston for that cylinder is 6° before top dead center of its compression stroke. However, this only holds true while your engine is at idle speed.

As you accelerate from idle, the speed of your engine (rpm) increases. The increase in rpm means that the pistons are now traveling up and down much faster. Because of this, the spark plugs will have to fire even sooner if the mixture is to be completely ignited as the piston passes TDC. To accomplish this,

the distributor incorporates means to advance the timing of the spark as engine speed increases.

The distributor in your Ford has two means of advancing the ignition timing. One is called centrifugal advance and is actuated by weights in the distributor. The other is called vacuum advance and is controlled by that large circular housing on the side of the distributor.

In addition, some distributors have a vacuum-retard mechanism which is contained in the same housing on the side of the distributor as the vacuum advance. The function of this mechanism is to retard the timing of the ignition spark under certain engine conditions. This causes more complete burning of the air/fuel mixture in the cylinder and consequently lowers exhaust emissions.

Because these mechanisms change ignition timing, it is necessary to disconnect and plug the one or two vacuum lines from the distributor when setting the basic ignition timing.

If ignition timing is set too far advanced (BTDC), the ignition and expansion of the air/fuel mixture in the cylinder will try to force the piston down the cylinder while it is still traveling upward. This causes engine "ping," a sound which resembles marbles being dropped into an empty tin can. If the ignition timing is too far retarded (after, or

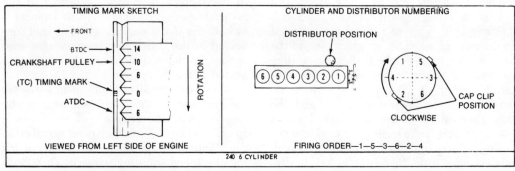

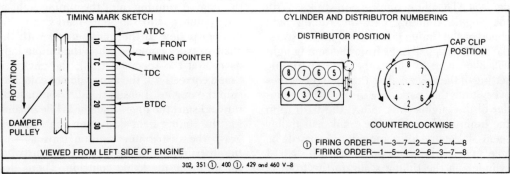

Pointer and timing mark locations—all except EEC II.

Distributor locknut

Timing light aimed at timing marks

ATDC), the piston will have already started down on the power stroke when the air/fuel mixture ignites and expands. This will cause the piston to be forced down only a portion of its travel. This will result in poor engine performance and lack of power.

Ignition timing adjustment is checked with a timing light. This instrument is connected to the number one (No. 1) spark plug of the engine. The timing light flashes every time an electrical current is sent from the distributor, through the No. 1 spark plug wire, to the spark plug. The crankshaft pulley and the front cover of the engine are marked with a timing pointer and a timing scale. When the timing pointer is aligned with the "O" mark on the timing scale, the piston in No. 1 cylinder is at TDC of its compression stroke. With the engine running, and the timing light aimed at the timing pointer and timing scale, the stroboscopic flashes from the timing light will allow you to check the ignition timing setting of the engine. The timing light flashes every time the spark plug in the No. 1 cylinder of the engine fires. Since the flash from the timing light makes the crankshaft pulley seem stationary for a moment, you will be able to read the exact position in the No. 1 cylinder on the timing scale on the front of the engine.

NOTE: *All 1974 and later engines are equipped with conventional and "monolithic" timing features. The monolithic system employs a timing receptacle located at the front of all engines. The receptacle is designed to accept an electronic probe which connects to digital read-out equipment. On cars equipped with electronic ignition, Ford recommends that only timing lights of the inductive pickup type be used as conventional timing lights may give a false reading due to the higher coil charging currents.*

Ford recommends that the ignition timing be checked every 12 months or 2,000 miles. The timing adjustment should always follow a breaker point gap and/or dwell angle adjustment, and be performed with the engine at normal operating temperature.

Locate the crankshaft damper/pulley and timing pointer at the front of the engine, and clean them with a solvent-soaked rag or wire brush so that the marks can be seen. Scribe a mark on the crankshaft damper/pulley and pointer with chalk or luminescent (day glo) paint to highlight the correct timing setting. Disconnect the vacuum hose(s) at the distributor vacuum capsule and plug it (them) with a pencil, golf tee, or some other small tapered object. Connect a stroboscopic timing light to the No. 1 cylinder spark plug (see "Firing Order" illustrations in Chapter 3) and to the battery terminals, according to the manufacturer's instructions. Also connect a tachometer to the engine, with one lead connected to the distributor primary wire connection at the coil and the other lead connected to a good ground.

Make sure that all of the timing light wires and tachometer wires are well clear of the engine. Start the engine and set the idle speed (if necessary) to the speed specified in the "Tune-Up Specifications" chart, using the idle speed adjusting screw(s). Then, with the engine running, aim the timing light at the pointer and at the marks on the damper/pulley. If the marks made with the chalk or paint coincide when the timing light flashes (at the specified rpm), the engine is timed correctly. If the marks do not coincide, stop the engine. Loosen the distributor locknut and start the engine again. While observing the timing light flashes on the markers, grasp the distributor vacuum capsule—not the distributor cap—and rotate the distributor until the marks do coincide. Then, stop the engine and tighten the distributor locknut, taking care not to disturb the setting. As a final check, start the engine once more to make sure that the timing marks still align.

NOTE: *If necessary, readjust the idle speed to that listed in the tune-up specs. Timing is correct only at the specified rpm.*

Once the engine is timed, reconnect the vacuum hose(s) to the distributor. Readjust, if necessary, the curb idle to specifications as outlined under "Idle Speed and Mixture Adjustment." Finally, remove the timing light and tachometer from the engine.

Carburetor

This section contains only carburetor adjustments as they normally apply to engine tune-up. Descriptions of the carburetor and complete adjustment procedures can be found in Chapter 4, under "Fuel System."

When the engine in your car is running, air/fuel mixture from the carburetor is being drawn into the engine by a partial vacuum which is created by the downward movement of the pistons on the intake stroke of the four-stroke cycle of the engine. The amount of air/fuel mixture which enters the engine is controlled by throttle plate(s) in the bottom of the carburetor. When the engine is not running the throttle plate(s) is (are) closed completely blocking off the bottom of the carburetor from the inside of the engine. The throttle plates are connected, through the throttle linkage, to the accelerator in the passenger compartment of the car. After you start the engine and put the transmission in gear, you depress the accelerator to start the car moving. What you actually are doing when you depress the accelerator is opening the throttle plate(s) in the carburetor to admit more of the air/fuel mixture to the engine. The farther you open the throttle plates in the carburetor, the higher the engine speed becomes.

As previously stated, when the engine is not running, the throttle plates in the carburetor are closed. When the engine is idling, it is necessary to open the throttle plate slightly. To prevent having to keep your foot on the accelerator when the engine is idling, an idle speed adjusting screw was added to the carburetor. This screw has the same effect as keeping your foot slightly depressed on the accelerator. The idle speed adjusting screw contacts a lever (the throttle lever) on the outside of the carburetor. When the screw is turning in, it opens the throttle plate on the carburetor, raising the idle speed of the engine. This screw is called the curb idle adjusting screw, and the procedures in this section will tell you how to adjust it.

In addition to the curb idle adjusting screw, most engines have a throttle solenoid positioner. Ford has found it necessary to

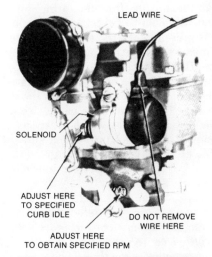

Carter YF with throttle solenoid positioner

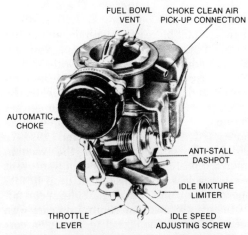

Carburetor adjustment—1969–71 Carter YF

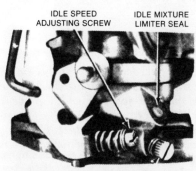

Carburetor adjustments—1968 Carter YF

raise the idle speed on these engines to obtain a smooth engine idle. When the key is turned "off," the current to the spark plugs is cut off and the engine normally stops running. However, if an engine has a high operating temperature and a high idle speed, it is possible for the temperature of the cylinder, instead of the spark plug, to ignite the air/fuel mixture. When this happens, the engine continues to run after the key is turned off. To solve this problem, a throttle solenoid was added to the carburetor. The solenoid is a cylinder with an adjustable plunger and an electrical lead. When the ignition key is turned to "on," the solenoid plunger extends to contact the carburetor throttle lever and raise the idle speed of the engine. When the ignition key is turned "off," the solenoid is de-energized and the solenoid plunger falls back from the throttle lever. This allows the throttle lever to fall back and rest on the curb idle adjusting screw. This closes the throttle plates far enough so that the engine will not run on.

Since it is difficult for the engine to draw the air/fuel mixture from the carburetor with the small amount of throttle plate opening that is present when the engine is idling, an idle mixture passage is provided in the carburetor. This passage delivers air/fuel mixture to the engine from a hole which is located in the bottom of the carburetor below the throttle plates. This idle mixture passage contains an adjusting screw which restricts the amount of air/fuel mixture which enters the engine at idle. The procedures given in this section will tell how to set the idle mixture adjusting screw(s).

NOTE: *With the electric solenoid disengaged, the carburetor idle speed adjusting screw must make contact with the throttle lever to prevent the throttle plates from jamming in the throttle bore when the engine is turned off.*

IDLE SPEED AND MIXTURE ADJUSTMENTS

NOTE: *In order to limit exhaust emissions, plastic caps have been installed on the idle fuel mixture screw(s) which prevent the carburetor from being adjusted to an overly rich idle fuel mixture. Under no circumstances should these limiters be modified or removed. A satisfactory idle should be obtained within the range of the limiter(s).*

Autolite 1101, Carter YF, Motorcraft 2100, Motorcraft 2150, Autolite 4100, Motorcraft 4300, Carter Thermo-Quad, Motorcraft 4350

1. Start the engine and run it at idle until it reaches operating temperature (about 10–20 minutes, depending on outside temperatures). Stop the engine.

2. Check the ignition timing as outlined under "Ignition Timing Adjustment."

3. Remove the air cleaner, taking note of the hose locations, and check that the choke plate is in the open position (plate in vertical position). Check the accompanying illustrations to see where the carburetor adjustment locations are. If you cannot reach them with the air cleaner installed, leave it off temporarily.

4. Attach a tachometer to the engine, with the positive wire connected to the distributor side of the ignition coil, and the negative wire connected to a good ground, such as an engine bolt.

NOTE: *In order to attach an alligator clip to the distributor side (terminal) of the coil (primary connection), it will be necessary to lift off the connector and slide a female loop type connector (commercially available) down over the terminal threads. Then push down the rubber connector over the loop connector and you have made yourself a little adaptor, to which you can connect the alligator clip of your tachometer.*

5. All idle speed adjustments are made with the headlights off (unless otherwise specified on the engine decal), with the air conditioning off (if so equipped), with all vacuumm hoses connected (unless otherwise specified), with the throttle solenoid positioner activated (connected, if so equipped), and with the air cleaner on. The only problem here is that on many cars, the adjustments cannot be reached with the air cleaner installed. On these problem cars, you will have to adjust the idle speed approximately 50–100 rpm higher with the air cleaner removed so that the setting is correct when the air cleaner is installed. Also, if the air cleaner is removed, disconnect and plug the vacuum hoses (all 1973–79 models, and 1971–72 351C and 400 models), for the vacuum operated heated air intake system to prevent a vacuum leak and subsequent drop in idle speed and quality. Finally, all idle speed adjustments are made in Neutral on cars with manual transmission, and in Drive on cars equipped with automatic transmission.

AUTOLITE MODEL 1101 1-V

AUTOLITE MODELS
2100 2-V AND 4100 4-V

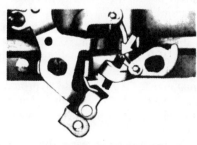

AUTOLITE MODEL 4300 4-V

Idle speed screw locations

NOTE: *Make sure that the parking brake is applied and all four wheels blocked.*

6a. On cars not equipped with a throttle solenoid positioner, the idle speed is adjusted with the curb idle speed adjusting screw. Start the engine. Turn the curb idle speed adjusting screw inward or outward until the correct idle speed (see "Tune-Up Specifications" chart) is reached, remembering to make the 50–100 rpm allowance if the air cleaner is removed.

6b. On cars equipped with a throttle solenoid positioner, the idle speed is adjusted with solenoid adjusting screw (nut), in two stages. Start the engine. The higher speed is adjusted with the solenoid connected. Turn the solenoid adjusting screw (nut) on 1 or 4 barrel carburetors, or the entire bracket on 2 barrel carburetors, inward or outward until the correct higher idle speed (see "Tune-Up Specifications" chart) is reached, remembering to make the 50–100 rpm allowance if the air cleaner is removed. After making this adjustment on cars equipped with 2 barrel carburetors, tighten the solenoid adjusting locknut. The lower idle speed is adjusted with

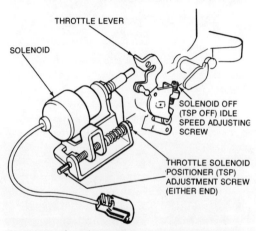

THROTTLE LEVER

SOLENOID

SOLENOID OFF
(TSP OFF) IDLE
SPEED ADJUSTING
SCREW

THROTTLE SOLENOID
POSITIONER (TSP)
ADJUSTMENT SCREW
(EITHER END)

Throttle solenoid positioner adjustment—Motorcraft 2100, 2150, 4300, 4350

IDLE MIXTURE LIMITERS

Idle mixture limiters installed—Motorcraft 4300 shown

the solenoid lead wire disconnected near the harness (not at the carburetor). Place automatic transmission equipped cars in Neutral for this adjustment. Using the curb idle speed adjusting screw on the carburetor, turn the idle speed adjusting screw inward or outward until the correct lower idle speed (see "Tune-Up Specifications" chart) is reached, remembering again to make the 50–100 rpm allowance if the air cleaner is removed. Finally, reconnect the solenoid, slightly depress the throttle lever and allow the solenoid plunger to fully extend.

7. If removed, install the air cleaner and connect the hoses for the heated intake air system. Recheck the idle speed. If it is not correct, Step 6 will have to be repeated and the approximate corrections made.

8. To adjust the idle mixture, turn the idle mixture screw(s) inward to obtain the smoothest idle possible within the range of the limiter(s). After adjusting the mixture, it may be necessary to readjust the idle speed as outlined in Step 6.

9. Turn off the engine and disconeect the tachometer.

NOTE: *If any doubt exists as to the proper idle mixture setting for your car, have the exhaust emission level checked at a diagnostic center or garage with an exhaust (HC/CO) analyzer.*

Motorcraft 2700 Variable Venturi Carburetor

This carburetor was introduced in 1977 for use on California cars equipped with the 302 V8. In 1978, its usage was expanded, and in 1979 it was installed on all LTD's equipped with the 302 V8. This carburetor differs substantially in both theory and operation from the rest of the carburetors discussed here. For a complete description of this carburetor, along with adjustment and overhaul procedures, see Chapter 4.

Catalytic Converter Precautions

Since 1975, Fords have been equipped with catalytic converters to clean up exhaust emissions after they leave the engine. Naturally, lead-free fuel must be used in order to avoid contaminating the converter and rendering it useless. However, there are other precautions which should be taken to prevent a large amount of unburned hydrocarbon from reaching the converter. Should a sufficient amount of HC reach the converter, the unit could overheat, possibly damaging the converter or nearby mechanical components. There is even the possibility that a fire could be started. Therefore, when working on your car, the following conditions should be avoided:

1. The use of fuel system cleaning agents and additives.

2. Operating the car with a closed choke or a submerged carburetor float.

3. Extended periods of engine run-on (dieseling).

4. Turning off the ignition with the car in motion.

5. Ignition or charging system failure.

6. Misfiring of one or more spark plugs.

7. Disconnecting a spark plug wire while testing for a bad wire or plug, or poor compression in one cylinder.

8. Push or tow-starting the car, especially when hot.

9. Pumping the gas pedal when attempting to start a hot engine.

Troubleshooting

The following section is designed to aid in the rapid diagnosis of engine problems. The systematic format is used to diagnose problems ranging from engine starting difficulties to the need for engine overhaul. It is assumed that the user is equipped with basic hand tools and test equipment (tachometer, dwell meter, timing light, voltmeter, and ohmmeter).

Troubleshooting is divided into two sections. The first, *General Diagnosis*, is used to locate the problem area. In the second, *Specific Diagnosis*, the problem is systematically evaluated.

General Diagnosis

Problem: Symptom	*Begin at Specific Diagnosis, Number* ____
Engine Won't Start:	
Starter doesn't turn	1.1, 2.1
Starter turns, engine doesn't	2.1
Starter turns engine very slowly	1.1, 2.4
Starter turns engine normally	3.1, 4.1
Starter turns engine very quickly	6.1
Engine fires intermittently	4.1
Engine fires consistently	5.1, 6.1
Engine Runs Poorly:	
Hard starting	3.1, 4.1, 5.1, 8.1
Rough idle	4.1, 5.1, 8.1
Stalling	3.1, 4.1, 5.1, 8.1
Engine dies at high speeds	4.1, 5.1
Hesitation (on acceleration from standing stop)	5.1, 8.1
Poor pickup	4.1, 5.1, 8.1
Lack of power	3.1, 4.1, 5.1, 8.1
Backfire through the carburetor	4.1, 8.1, 9.1
Backfire through the exhaust	4.1, 8.1, 9.1
Blue exhaust gases	6.1, 7.1
Black exhaust gases	5.1
Running on (after the ignition is shut off)	3.1, 8.1
Susceptible to moisture	4.1
Engine misfires under load	4.1, 7.1, 8.4, 9.1
Engine misfires at speed	4.1, 8.4
Engine misfires at idle	3.1, 4.1, 5.1, 7.1, 8.4

Engine Noise Diagnosis

Problem: Symptom	Probable Cause
Engine Noises:①	
Metallic grind while starting	Starter drive not engaging completely
Constant grind or rumble	* Starter drive not releasing, worn main bearings
Constant knock	Worn connecting rod bearings
Knock under load	Fuel octane too low, worn connecting rod bearings
Double knock	Loose piston pin
Metallic tap	* Collapsed or sticky valve lifter, excessive valve clearance, excessive end play in a rotating shaft
Scrape	* Fan belt contacting a stationary surface
Tick while starting	S.U. electric fuel pump (normal), starter brushes
Constant tick	* Generator brushes, shreaded fan belt
Squeal	* Improperly tensioned fan belt
Hiss or roar	* Steam escaping through a leak in the cooling system or the radiator overflow vent
Whistle	* Vacuum leak
Wheeze	Loose or cracked spark plug

①—It is extremely difficult to evaluate vehicle noises. While the above are general definitions of engine noises, those starred (*) should be considered as possibly originating elsewhere in the car. To aid diagnosis, the following list considers other potential sources of these sounds.

Metallic grind:
Throwout bearing; transmission gears, bearings, or synchronizers; differential bearings, gears; something metallic in contact with brake drum or disc.

Metallic tap:
U-joints; fan-to-radiator (or shroud) contact.

Scrape:
Brake shoe or pad dragging; tire to body contact; suspension contacting undercarriage or exhaust; something non-metallic contacting brake shoe or drum.

Tick:
Transmission gears; differential gears; lack of radio suppression; resonant vibration of body panels; windshield wiper motor or transmission; heater motor and blower.

Squeal:
Brake shoe or pad not fully releasing; tires (excessive wear, uneven wear, improper inflation); front or rear wheel alignment (most commonly due to improper toe-in).

Hiss or whistle:
Wind leaks (body or window); heater motor and blower fan.

Roar:
Wheel bearings; wind leaks (body and window).

Index

Topic		Group
Battery	*	1
Cranking system	*	2
Primary electrical system	*	3
Secondary electrical system	*	4
Fuel system	*	5
Engine compression	*	6
Engine vaccuum	**	7
Secondary electrical system	**	8
Valve train	**	9
Exhaust system	**	10
Cooling system	**	11
Engine lubrication	**	12

* The engine need not be running
**The engine must be running

Sample Section

Test and Procedure	Results and Indications	Proceed to
4.1—Check for spark: Hold each spark plug wire approximately ¼" from ground with gloves or a heavy, dry rag. Crank the engine and observe the spark.	→ If no spark is evident:	→ **4.2**
	→ If spark is good in some cases:	→ **4.3**
	→ If spark is good in all cases:	→ **4.6**

Specific Diagnosis

This section is arranged so that following each test, instructions are given to proceed to another, until a problem is diagnosed.

1.1—Inspect the battery visually for case condition (corrosion, cracks) and water level.	If case is cracked, replace battery:	**1.4**
	If the case is intact, remove corrosion with a solution of baking soda and water (**CAUTION:** *do not get the solution into the battery*), and fill with water:	**1.2**
1.2—Check the battery cable connections: Insert a screwdriver between the battery post and the cable clamp. Turn the headlights on high beam, and observe them as the screwdriver is gently twisted to ensure good metal to metal contact. **Testing battery cable connections using a screwdriver**	If the lights brighten, remove and clean the clamp and post; coat the post with petroleum jelly, install and tighten the clamp:	**1.4**
	If no improvement is noted:	**1.3**

1.3—Test the state of charge of the battery using an individual cell tester or hydrometer.	If indicated, charge the battery. **NOTE:** *If no obvious reason exists for the low state of charge (i.e., battery age, prolonged storage), the charging system should be tested:*	**1.4**

Spec. Grav. Reading	Charged Condition
1.260–1.280	Fully Charged
1.230–1.250	Three Quarter Charged
1.200–1.220	One Half Charged
1.170–1.190	One Quarter Charged
1.140–1.160	Just About Flat
1.110–1.130	All The Way Down

State of battery charge

The effect of temperature on the specific gravity of battery electrolyte

1.4—Visually inspect battery cables for cracking, bad connection to ground, or bad connection to starter.	If necessary, tighten connections or replace the cables:	**2.1**

Tests in Group 2 are performed with coil high tension lead disconnected to prevent accidental starting.

2.1—Test the starter motor and solenoid: Connect a jumper from the battery post of the solenoid (or relay) to the starter post of the solenoid (or relay).	If starter turns the engine normally:	**2.2**
	If the starter buzzes, or turns the engine very slowly:	**2.4**
	If no response, replace the solenoid (or relay).	**3.1**
	If the starter turns, but the engine doesn't, ensure that the flywheel ring gear is intact. If the gear is undamaged, replace the starter drive.	**3.1**

Test and Procedure	Results and Indications	Proceed to
2.2—Determine whether ignition override switches are functioning properly (clutch start switch, neutral safety switch), by connecting a jumper across the switch(es), and turning the ignition switch to "start".	If starter operates, adjust or replace switch:	**3.1**
	If the starter doesn't operate:	**2.3**
2.3—Check the ignition switch "start" position: Connect a 12V test lamp between the starter post of the solenoid (or relay) and ground. Turn the ignition switch to the "start" position, and jiggle the key.	If the lamp doesn't light when the switch is turned, check the ignition switch for loose connections, cracked insulation, or broken wires. Repair or replace as necessary:	**3.1**
	If the lamp flickers when the key is jiggled, replace the ignition switch.	**3.3**

Checking the ignition switch "start" position

2.4—Remove and bench test the starter, according to specifications in the car section.	If the starter does not meet specifications, repair or replace as needed:	**3.1**
	If the starter is operating properly:	**2.5**
2.5—Determine whether the engine can turn freely: Remove the spark plugs, and check for water in the cylinders. Check for water on the dipstick, or oil in the radiator. Attempt to turn the engine using an 18″ flex drive and socket on the crankshaft pulley nut or bolt.	If the engine will turn freely only with the spark plugs out, and hydrostatic lock (water in the cylinders) is ruled out, check valve timing:	**9.2**
	If engine will not turn freely, and it is known that the clutch and transmission are free, the engine must be disassembled for further evaluation:	**Next Chapter**
3.1—Check the ignition switch "on" position: Connect a jumper wire between the distributor side of the coil and ground, and a 12V test lamp between the switch side of the coil and ground. Remove the high tension lead from the coil. Turn the ignition switch on and jiggle the key.	If the lamp lights:	**3.2**
	If the lamp flickers when the key is jiggled, replace the ignition switch:	**3.3**
	If the lamp doesn't light, check for loose or open connections. If none are found, remove the ignition switch and check for continuity. If the switch is faulty, replace it:	**3.3**

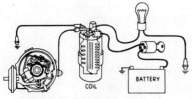

Checking the ignition switch "on" position

Test and Procedure	Results and Indications	Proceed to
3.2—Check the ballast resistor or resistance wire for an open circuit, using an ohmmeter.	On cars with point-type ignition systems, replace the resistor or resistance wire if the resistance is zero. On cars equipped with Solid-State Ignition, the resistance should be 1.35 ohms for 1975 and 1976 cars. The resistance should be 1.10 ohms for 1977 and later cars, except for California V8's which are equipped with the Dura-Spark I system and have no ballast resistors. If resistance is zero, replace the resistor or resistance wiring.	**3.3**
3.3—On point-type ignition systems, visually inspect the breaker points for burning, pitting or excessive wear. Gray coloring of the point contact surfaces is normal. Rotate the crankshaft until the contact heel rests on a high point of the distributor cam and adjust the point gap to specifications. On electronic ignition models, remove the distributor cap and visually inspect the armature. Ensure that the armature pin is in place, and that the armature is on tight and rotates when the engine is cranked. Make sure there are no cracks, chips or rounded edges on the armature.	If the breaker points are intact, clean the contact surfaces with fine emery cloth, and adjust the point gap to specifications. If the points are worn, replace them. On electronic systems, replace any parts which appear defective. If condition persists:	**3.4**
3.4—On point-type ignition systems, connect a dwell-meter between the distributor primary lead and ground. Crank the engine and observe the point dwell angle. On electronic ignition systems, conduct a stator (magnetic pickup assembly) test. See "Troubleshooting the Solid-State Ignition System".	On point-type systems, adjust the dwell angle if necessary. **NOTE:** *Increasing the point gap decreases the dwell angle and vice-versa.* If the dwell meter shows little or no reading; On electronic ignition systems, if the stator is bad, replace the stator. If the stator is good, proceed to the other tests in the solid-state ignition troubleshooting section.	**3.6** **3.5**
3.5—On point-type ignition systems, check the condenser for short: connect an ohmmeter across the condenser body and the pigtail lead. Checking the condenser for short OHMMETER	If any reading other than infinite is noted, replace the condenser:	**3.6**
3.6—Test the coil primary resistance: On point-type ignition systems, connect an ohmmeter across the coil primary terminals, and read the resistance on the low scale. Note whether an external ballast resistor or resistance wire is utilized. On electronic ignition systems, test the coil primary resistance. Connect an ohmmeter between the coil BAT terminal and socket #1 in the harness.	Coils utilizing ballast resistors or resistance wires should have approximately 1.0 ohms resistance. Coils with internal resistors should have approximately 4.0 ohms resistance. If values far from the above are noted, replace the coil. Resistance should be 1.0 to 2.0 ohms for early and Dura-Spark II systems, and 0.5 to 1.5 ohms for Dura-Spark I systems. If the coil is defective, replace the coil. Otherwise:	**4.1** **4.1**

Test and Procedure	Results and Indications	Proceed to
4.1—Check for spark: Hold each spark plug wire approximately ¼″ from ground with gloves or a heavy, dry rag. Crank the engine, and observe the spark.	If no spark is evident:	**4.2**
	If spark is good in some cylinders:	**4.3**
	If spark is good in all cylinders:	**4.6**
4.2—Check for spark at the coil high tension lead: Remove the coil high tension lead from the distributor and position it approximately ¼″ from ground. Crank the engine and observe spark. **CAUTION:** *This test should not be performed on cars equipped with transistorized ignition.*	If the spark is good and consistent:	**4.3**
	If the spark is good but intermittent, test the primary electrical system starting at 3.3:	**3.3**
	If the spark is weak or non-existent, replace the coil high tension lead, clean and tighten all connections and retest. If no improvement is noted:	**4.4**
4.3—Visually inspect the distributor cap and rotor for burned or corroded contacts, cracks, carbon tracks, or moisture. Also check the fit of the rotor on the distributor shaft (where applicable).	If moisture is present, dry thoroughly, and re-test per 4.1:	**4.1**
	If burned or excessively corroded contacts, cracks, or carbon tracks are noted, replace the defective part(s) and retest per 4.1:	**4.1**
	If the rotor and cap appear intact, or are only slightly corroded, clean the contacts thoroughly (including the cap towers and spark plug wire ends) and retest per 4.1: If the spark is good in all cases:	**4.6**
	If the spark is poor in all cases:	**4.5**
4.4—Check the coil secondary resistance: On point-type systems, connect an ohmmeter across the distributor side of the coil and the coil tower. Read the resistance on the high scale of the ohmmeter. On electronic ignition systems, connect an ohmmeter between socket #4 and the coil tower (see the charts). 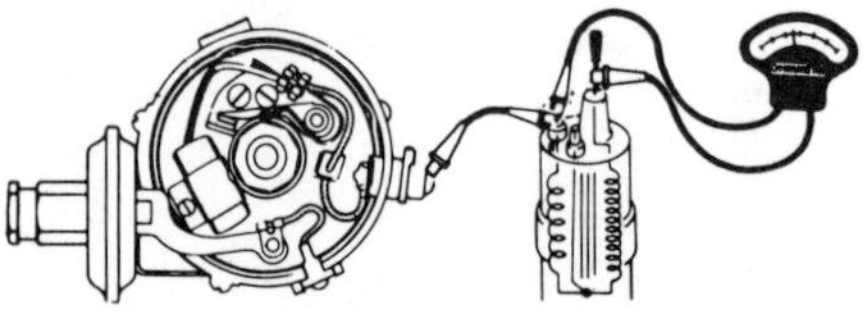	The resistance of a satisfactory coil should be between 4,000 and 10,000 ohms. If resistance is considerably higher (i.e. 40,000 ohms) replace the coil and retest per 4.1. **NOTE:** *this does not apply to high performance coils.* On electronic systems, resistance should be between 7,000 and 13,000 ohms. If not, replace the coil and retest per 4.1.	

Testing the coil secondary resistance

4.5—Visually inspect the spark plug wires for cracking or brittleness. Ensure that no two wires are positioned so as to cause induction firing (adjacent and parallel). Remove each wire, one by one, and check resistance with an ohmmeter.	Replace any cracked or brittle wires. If any of the wires are defective, replace the entire set. Replace any wires with excessive resistance (over 8000Ω per foot for suppression wire), and separate any wires that might cause induction firing.	**4.6**
4.6—Remove the spark plugs, noting the cylinders from which they were removed, and evaluate according to the chart below.	See following.	**See following.**

	Condition	Cause	Remedy	Proceed to
	Electrodes eroded, light brown deposits.	Normal wear. Normal wear is indicated by approximately .001″ wear per 1000 miles.	Clean and regap the spark plug if wear is not excessive: Replace the spark plug if excessively worn:	4.7
	Carbon fouling (black, dry, fluffy deposits).	If present on one or two plugs:		
		Faulty high tension lead(s).	Test the high tension leads:	4.5
		Burnt or sticking valve(s).	Check the valve train: (Clean and regap the plugs in either case.)	9.1
		If present on most or all plugs: Overly rich fuel mixture, due to restricted air filter, improper carburetor adjustment, improper choke or heat riser adjustment or operation.	Check the fuel system:	5.1
	Oil fouling (wet black deposits)	Worn engine components. **NOTE:** *Oil fouling may occur in new or recently rebuilt engines until broken in.*	Check engine vacuum and compression: Replace with new spark plug	6.1
	Lead fouling (gray, black, tan, or yellow deposits, which appear glazed or cinder-like).	Combustion by-products.	Clean and regap the plugs: (Use plugs of a different heat range if the problem recurs.)	4.7
	Gap bridging (deposits lodged between the electrodes).	Incomplete combustion, or transfer of deposits from the combustion chamber.	Replace the spark plugs:	4.7
	Overheating (burnt electrodes, and extremely white insulator with small black spots).	Ignition timing advanced too far.	Adjust timing to specifications:	8.2
		Overly lean fuel mixture.	Check the fuel system:	5.1
		Spark plugs not seated properly.	Clean spark plug seat and install a new gasket washer: (Replace the spark plugs in all cases.)	4.7

	Condition	Cause	Remedy	Proceed to
	Fused spot deposits on the insulator.	Combustion chamber blow-by.	Clean and regap the spark plugs:	4.7
	Pre-ignition (melted or severely burned electrodes, blistered or cracked insulators, or metallic deposits on the insulator).	Incorrect spark plug heat range.	Replace with plugs of the proper heat range:	4.7
		Ignition timing advanced too far.	Adjust timing to specifications:	8.2
		Spark plugs not being cooled efficiently.	Clean the spark plug seat, and check the cooling system:	11.1
		Fuel mixture too lean.	Check the fuel system:	5.1
		Poor compression.	Check compression:	6.1
		Fuel grade too low.	Use higher octane fuel:	4.7

Test and Procedure	Results and Indications	Proceed to
4.7—Determine the static ignition timing. Using the crankshaft pulley timing marks as a guide, locate top dead center on the compression stroke of the number one cylinder.	The rotor should be pointing toward the no. 1 tower in the distributor cap, and the armature spoke for that cylinder should be lined up with the stator.	4.8
4.8—Check coil polarity: Connect a voltmeter negative lead to the coil high tension lead, and the positive lead to ground (**NOTE:** *reverse the hook-up for positive ground cars*). Crank the engine momentarily. **Checking coil polarity**	If the voltmeter reads up-scale, the polarity is correct: If the voltmeter reads down-scale, reverse the coil polarity (switch the primary leads):	5.1 5.1
5.1—Determine that the air filter is functioning efficiently: Hold paper elements up to a strong light, and attempt to see light through the filter.	Clean permanent air filters in gasoline (or manufacturer's recommendation), and allow to dry. Replace paper elements through which light cannot be seen:	5.2
5.2—Determine whether a flooding condition exists: Flooding is identified by a strong gasoline odor, and excessive gasoline present in the throttle bore(s) of the carburetor.	If flooding is not evident: If flooding is evident, permit the gasoline to dry for a few moments and restart. If flooding doesn't recur: If flooding is persistent:	5.3 5.6 5.5
5.3—Check that fuel is reaching the carburetor: Detach the fuel line at the carburetor inlet. Hold the end of the line in a cup (not styrofoam), and crank the engine.	If fuel flows smoothly: If fuel doesn't flow (**NOTE:** *Make sure that there is fuel in the tank*), or flows erratically:	5.6 5.4

Test and Procedure	Results and Indications	Proceed to
5.4—Test the fuel pump: Disconnect all fuel lines from the fuel pump. Hold a finger over the input fitting, crank the engine (with electric pump, turn the ignition or pump on); and feel for suction.	If suction is evident, blow out the fuel line to the tank with low pressure compressed air until bubbling is heard from the fuel filler neck. Also blow out the carburetor fuel line (both ends disconnected):	**5.6**
	If no suction is evident, replace or repair the fuel pump: **NOTE:** *Repeated oil fouling of the spark plugs, or a no-start condition, could be the result of a ruptured vacuum booster pump diaphragm, through which oil or gasoline is being drawn into the intake manifold (where applicable).*	**5.6**
5.5—Check the needle and seat: Tap the carburetor in the area of the needle and seat.	If flooding stops, a gasoline additive (e.g., Gumout) will often cure the problem:	**5.6**
	If flooding continues, check the fuel pump for excessive pressure at the carburetor (according to specifications). If the pressure is normal, the needle and seat must be removed and checked, and/or the float level adjusted:	**5.6**
5.6—Test the accelerator pump by looking into the throttle bores while operating the throttle.	If the accelerator pump appears to be operating normally:	**5.7**
	If the accelerator pump is not operating, the pump must be reconditioned. Where possible, service the pump with the carburetor(s) installed on the engine. If necessary, remove the carburetor. Prior to removal:	**5.7**
5.7—Determine whether the carburetor main fuel system is functioning: Spray a commercial starting fluid into the carburetor while attempting to start the engine.	If the engine starts, runs for a few seconds, and dies:	**5.8**
	If the engine doesn't start:	**6.1**
5.8—Uncommon fuel system malfunctions: See below:	If the problem is solved:	**6.1**
	If the problem remains, remove and recondition the carburetor.	

Condition	Indication	Test	Usual Weather Conditions	Remedy
Vapor lock	Car will not re-start shortly after running.	Cool the components of the fuel system until the engine starts.	Hot to very hot	Ensure that the exhaust manifold heat control valve is operating. Check with the vehicle manufacturer for the recommended solution to vapor lock on the model in question.
Carburetor icing	Car will not idle, stalls at low speeds.	Visually inspect the throttle plate area of the throttle bores for frost.	High humidity, 32–40°F.	Ensure that the exhaust manifold heat control valve is operating, and that the intake manifold heat riser is not blocked.

Condition	Indication	Test	Usual Weather Conditions	Remedy
Water in the fuel	Engine sputters and stalls; may not start.	Pump a small amount of fuel into a glass jar. Allow to stand, and inspect for droplets or a layer of water.	High humidity, extréme temperature changes.	For droplets, use one or two cans of commercial gas dryer (Dry Gas) For a layer of water, the tank must be drained, and the fuel lines blown out with compressed air.

Test and Procedure	Results and Indications	Proceed to
6.1—Test engine compression: Remove all spark plugs. Insert a compression gauge into a spark plug port, crank the engine to obtain the maximum reading, and record.	If compression is within limits on all cylinders:	**7.1**
	If gauge reading is extremely low on all cylinders:	**6.2**
	If gauge reading is low on one or two cylinders: (If gauge readings are identical and low on two or more adjacent cylinders, the head gasket must be replaced.)	**6.2**

Testing compression
(© Chevrolet Div. G.M. Corp.)

Compression pressure limits
(© Buick Div. G.M. Corp.)

Maxi. Press. Lbs. Sq. In.	Min. Press. Lbs. Sq. In.	Maxi. Press. Lbs. Sq. In.	Min. Press. Lbs. Sq. In.	Max. Press. Lbs. Sq. In.	Min. Press. Lbs. Sq. In.	Max. Press. Lbs. Sq. In.	Min. Press. Lbs. Sq. In.
134	101	162	121	188	141	214	160
136	102	164	123	190	142	216	162
138	104	166	124	192	144	218	163
140	105	168	126	194	145	220	165
142	107	170	127	196	147	222	166
146	110	172	129	198	148	224	168
148	111	174	131	200	150	226	169
150	113	176	132	202	151	228	171
152	114	178	133	204	153	230	172
154	115	180	135	206	154	232	174
156	117	182	136	208	156	234	175
158	118	184	138	210	157	236	177
160	120	186	140	212	158	238	178

Test and Procedure	Results and Indications	Proceed to
6.2—Test engine compression (wet): Squirt approximately 30 cc. of engine oil into each cylinder, and retest per 6.1.	If the readings improve, worn or cracked rings or broken pistons are indicated:	**Next Chapter**
	If the readings do not improve, burned or excessively carboned valves or a jumped timing chain are indicated: **NOTE: A jumped timing chain is often indicated by difficult cranking.**	**7.1**
7.1—Perform a vacuum check of the engine: Attach a vacuum gauge to the intake manifold beyond the throttle plate. Start the engine, and observe the action of the needle over the range of engine speeds.	See below.	**See below**

	Reading	Indications	Proceed to
	Steady, from 17–22 in. Hg.	Normal:	**8.1**

Reading	Indications	Proceed to
Low and steady.	Late ignition or valve timing, or low compression:	**6.1**
Very low.	Vacuum leak:	**7.2**
Needle fluctuates as engine speed increases.	Ignition miss, blown cylinder head gasket, leaking valve or weak valve spring:	**6.1, 8.3**
Gradual drop in reading at idle.	Excessive back pressure in the exhaust system:	**10.1**
Intermittent fluctuation at idle.	Ignition miss, sticking valve:	**8.3, 9.1**
Drifting needle.	Improper idle mixture adjustment, carburetors not synchronized (where applicable), or minor intake leak. Synchronize the carburetors, adjust the idle, and retest. If the condition persists:	**7.2**
High and steady.	Early ignition timing:	**8.2**

Test and Procedure	Results and Indications	Proceed to
7.2—Attach a vacuum gauge per 7.1, and test for an intake manifold leak. Squirt a small amount of oil around the intake manifold gaskets, carburetor gaskets, plugs and fittings. Observe the action of the vacuum gauge.	If the reading improves, replace the indicated gasket, or seal the indicated fitting or plug: If the reading remains low:	**8.1** **7.3**
7.3—Test all vacuum hoses and accessories for leaks as described in 7.2. Also check the carburetor body (dashpots, automatic choke mechanism, throttle shafts) for leaks in the same manner.	If the reading improves, service or replace the offending part(s): If the reading remains low:	**8.1** **6.1**
8.1—Remove the distributor cap and check to make sure that the armature turns when the engine is cranked. Visually inspect the distributor components.	Clean, tighten or replace any components which appear defective.	**8.2**

Test and Procedure	Results and Indications	Proceed to
8.2—Connect a timing light (per manufacturer's recommendation) and check the dynamic ignition timing. Disconnect and plug the vacuum hose(s) to the distributor if specified, start the engine, and observe the timing marks at the specified engine speed.	If the timing is not correct, adjust to specifications by rotating the distributor in the engine: (Advance timing by rotating distributor opposite normal direction of rotor rotation, retard timing by rotating distributor in same direction as rotor rotation.)	**8.3**
8.3—Check the operation of the distributor advance mechanism(s): To test the mechanical advance, disconnect all but the mechanical advance, and observe the timing marks with a timing light as the engine speed is increased from idle. If the mark moves smoothly, without hesitation, it may be assumed that the mechanical advance is functioning properly. To test vacuum advance and/or retard systems, alternately crimp and release the vacuum line, and observe the timing mark for movement. If movement is noted, the system is operating.	If the systems are functioning: If the systems are not functioning, remove the distributor, and test on a distributor tester:	**8.4** **8.4**
8.4—Locate an ignition miss: With the engine running, remove each spark plug wire, one by one, until one is found that doesn't cause the engine to roughen and slow down.	When the missing cylinder is identified:	**4.1**
9.1—Evaluate the valve train: Remove the valve cover, and ensure that the valves are adjusted to specifications. A mechanic's stethoscope may be used to aid in the diagnosis of the valve train. By pushing the probe on or near push rods or rockers, valve noise often can be isolated. A timing light also may be used to diagnose valve problems. Connect the light according to manufacturer's recommendations, and start the engine. Vary the firing moment of the light by increasing the engine speed (and therefore the ignition advance), and moving the trigger from cylinder to cylinder. Observe the movement of each valve.	See below.	**See below**

Observation	Probable Cause	Remedy	Proceed to
Metallic tap heard through the stethoscope.	Sticking hydraulic lifter or excessive valve clearance.	Adjust valve. If tap persists, remove and replace the lifter:	**10.1**

Observation	Probable Cause	Remedy	Proceed to
Metallic tap through the stethoscope, able to push the rocker arm (lifter side) down by hand.	Collapsed valve lifter.	Remove and replace the lifter:	**10.1**
Erratic, irregular motion of the valve stem.*	Sticking valve, burned valve.	Recondition the valve and/or valve guide:	**Next Chapter**
Eccentric motion of the pushrod at the rocker arm.*	Bent pushrod.	Replace the pushrod:	**10.1**
Valve retainer bounces as the valve closes.*	Weak valve spring or damper.	Remove and test the spring and damper. Replace if necessary:	**10.1**

*—When observed with a timing light.

Test and Procedure	Results and Indications	Proceed to
9.2—Check the valve timing: Locate top dead center of the No. 1 piston, and install a degree wheel or tape on the crankshaft pulley or damper with zero corresponding to an index mark on the engine. Rotate the crankshaft in its direction of rotation, and observe the opening of the No. 1 cylinder intake valve. The opening should correspond with the correct mark on the degree wheel according to specifications.	If the timing is not correct, the timing cover must be removed for further investigation:	
10.1—Determine whether the exhaust manifold heat control valve is operating: Operate the valve by hand to determine whether it is free to move. If the valve is free, run the engine to operating temperature and observe the action of the valve, to ensure that it is opening.	If the valve sticks, spray it with a suitable solvent, open and close the valve to free it, and retest. If the valve functions properly: If the valve does not free, or does not operate, replace the valve:	**10.2** **10.2**
10.2—Ensure that there are no exhaust restrictions: Visually inspect the exhaust system for kinks, dents, or crushing. Also note that gasses are flowing freely from the tailpipe at all engine speeds, indicating no restriction in the muffler or resonator.	Replace any damaged portion of the system:	**11.1**

Test and Procedure	Results and Indications	Proceed to
11.1—Visually inspect the fan belt for glazing, cracks, and fraying, and replace if necessary. Tighten the belt so that the longest span has approximately ½″ play at its midpoint under thumb pressure.	Replace or tighten the fan belt as necessary:	**11.2**

Checking the fan belt tension

Test and Procedure	Results and Indications	Proceed to
11.2—Check the fluid level of the cooling system.	If full or slightly low, fill as necessary:	**11.5**
	If extremely low:	**11.3**
11.3—Visually inspect the external portions of the cooling system (radiator, radiator hoses, thermostat elbow, water pump seals, heater hoses, etc.) for leaks. If none are found, pressurize the cooling system to 14–15 psi.	If cooling system holds the pressure:	**11.5**
	If cooling system loses pressure rapidly, reinspect external parts of the system for leaks under pressure. If none are found, check dipstick for coolant in crankcase. If no coolant is present, but pressure loss continues:	**11.4**
	If coolant is evident in crankcase, remove cylinder head(s), and check gasket(s). If gaskets are intact, block and cylinder head(s) should be checked for cracks or holes. If the gasket(s) is blown, replace, and purge the crankcase of coolant:	**12.6**
	NOTE: *Occasionally, due to atmospheric and driving conditions, condensation of water can occur in the crankcase. This causes the oil to appear milky white. To remedy, run the engine until hot, and change the oil and oil - filter.*	
11.4— Check for combustion leaks into the cooling system: Pressurize the cooling system as above. Start the engine, and observe the pressure gauge. If the needle fluctuates, remove each spark plug wire, one by one, noting which cylinder(s) reduce or eliminate the fluctuation. 	Cylinders which reduce or eliminate the fluctuation, when the spark plug wire is removed, are leaking into the cooling system. Replace the head gasket on the affected cylinder bank(s).	

Radiator pressure tester

Test and Procedure	Results and Indications	Proceed to
11.5—Check the radiator pressure cap: Attach a radiator pressure tester to the radiator cap (wet the seal prior to installation). Quickly pump up the pressure, noting the point at which the cap releases.	If the cap releases within ± 1 psi of the specified rating, it is operating properly:	**11.6**
	If the cap releases at more than ± 1 psi of the specified rating, it should be replaced:	**11.6**

Testing the radiator pressure cap

Test and Procedure	Results and Indications	Proceed to
11.6—Test the thermostat: Start the engine cold, remove the radiator cap, and insert a thermometer into the radiator. Allow the engine to idle. After a short while, there will be a sudden, rapid increase in coolant temperature. The temperature at which this sharp rise stops is the thermostat opening temperature.	If the thermostat opens at or about the specified temperature:	**11.7**
	If the temperature doesn't increase: (If the temperature increases slowly and gradually, replace the thermostat.)	**11.7**
11.7—Check the water pump: Remove the thermostat elbow and the thermostat, disconnect the coil high tension lead (to prevent starting), and crank the engine momentarily.	If coolant flows, replace the thermostat and retest per 11.6:	**11.6**
	If coolant doesn't flow, reverse flush the cooling system to alleviate any blockage that might exist. If system is not blocked, and coolant will not flow, recondition the water pump.	—
12.1—Check the oil pressure gauge or warning light: If the gauge shows low pressure, or the light is on, for no obvious reason, remove the oil pressure sender. Install an accurate oil pressure gauge and run the engine momentarily.	If oil pressure builds normally, run engine for a few moments to determine that it is functioning normally, and replace the sender.	—
	If the pressure remains low:	**12.2**
	If the pressure surges:	**12.3**
	If the oil pressure is zero:	**12.3**
12.2—Visually inspect the oil: If the oil is watery or very thin, milky, or foamy, replace the oil and oil filter.	If the oil is normal:	**12.3**
	If after replacing oil the pressure remains low:	**12.3**
	If after replacing oil the pressure becomes normal:	—
12.3—Inspect the oil pressure relief valve and spring, to ensure that it is not sticking or stuck. Remove and thoroughly clean the valve, spring, and the valve body.	If the oil pressure improves:	—
	If no improvement is noted:	**12.4**

Oil pressure relief valve
((© British Leyland Motors)

Test and Procedure	Results and Indications	Proceed to
12.4—Check to ensure that the oil pump is not cavitating (sucking air instead of oil): See that the crankcase is neither over nor underfull, and that the pickup in the sump is in the proper position and free from sludge.	Fill or drain the crankcase to the proper capacity, and clean the pickup screen in solvent if necessary. If no improvement is noted:	**12.5**
12.5—Inspect the oil pump drive and the oil pump:	If the pump drive or the oil pump appear to be defective, service as necessary and retest per 12.1:	**12.1**
	If the pump drive and pump appear to be operating normally, the engine should be disassembled to determine where blockage exists:	**Next Chapter**
12.6—Purge the engine of ethylene glycol coolant: Completely drain the crankcase and the oil filter. Obtain a commercial butyl cellosolve base solvent, designated for this purpose, and follow the instructions precisely. Following this, install a new oil filter and refill the crankcase with the proper weight oil. The next oil and filter change should follow shortly thereafter (1000 miles).		

3

Engine and Engine Rebuilding

ENGINE ELECTRICAL

Ignition System

Three types of ignition systems are used in the Ford. A conventional system using breaker points and condenser is used on most 1968–73 models and on many early production 1974 Fords equipped with the 351 V8. A breakerless (solid state) ignition system using an armature and magnetic pickup coil assembly in the distributor and a solid state amplifier module located inline between the coil and distributor is installed in all 1975 and later models as standard equipment, and on most 1974 models except some early production 1974 Fords equipped with the 351 V8.

In 1977, an improved system with greater spark output was introduced. This system is known as Dura Spark and can be identified by the larger diameter distributor cap and larger (from 7 mm to 8 mm) plug wires. The Dura Spark system utilizes higher voltages up to 42,000 volts to allow wider spark plug gaps necessary to fire leaner fuel/air mixtures.

1979 LTD's sold in California and equipped with the 351 engine feature Ford's new Electronic Engine Control II (EEC II) system. See Chapter 2 for a description.

The first two systems employ a distributor which is driven by the camshaft at one-half crankshaft rpm, a high-voltage rotor, distributor cap and spark plug wiring, and an oil filled conventional type coil.

The two systems differ in the manner in which they convert electrical primary voltage (12 volts) from the battery into secondary voltage (20,000 volts or greater) to fire the spark plugs. In the conventional ignition system, the breaker points open and close as the moveable breaker arm rides the rotating distributor cam eccentric, thereby opening and closing the current to the ignition coil. When the points open, they interrupt the flow of primary current to the coil, causing a collapse of the magnetic field in the coil and creating a high-tension spark which is used to fire the spark plugs. In the breakerless system, a distributor shaft-mounted armature rotates past a magnetic pickup coil assembly causing fluctuations in the magnetic field generated by the pickup coil. These fluctuations in turn, cause the amplifier module to turn the ignition coil current off and on, creating the high-tension spark to fire the spark plugs. The amplifier module electronically controls the dwell, which is controlled mechanically in a conventional system by the duration that the points remain closed.

Both the conventional and breakerless ignition systems are equipped with dual ad-

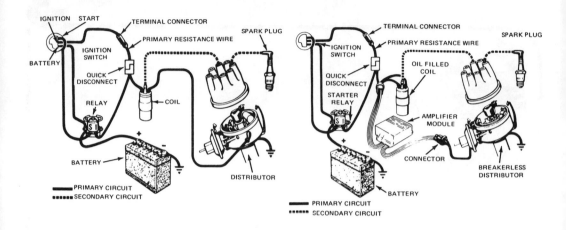

CONVENTIONAL   BREAKERLESS

Typical ignition systems

vance distributors. The vacuum advance unit governs ignition timing according to engine load, while the centrifugal advance unit governs ignition timing according to engine rpm. Centrifugal advance is controlled by spring-mounted weights contained in the distributor, located under the breaker point mounting plate on conventional systems and under the fixed base plate on breakerless sytems. As engine speed increases, centrifugal force moves the weights outward from the distributor shaft advancing the position of the distributor cam (conventional) or armature (breakerless), thereby advancing the ignition timing. Vacuum advance is controlled by a vacuum diaphragm which is mounted on the side of the distributor and attached to the breaker point mounting plate (conventional) or the magnetic pickup coil assembly (breakerless) via the vacuum advance link. Under light acceleration, the engine is operating under a low-load condition, causing the carburetor vacuum to act on the distributor vacuum diaphragm, moving the breaker point mounting plate (conventional) or pickup coil assembly (breakerless) opposite the direction of distributor shaft rotation, thereby advancing the ignition timing.

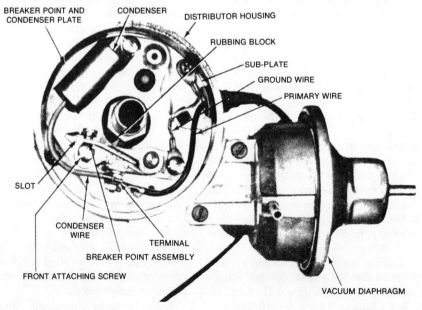

Distributor cap and rotor removed—conventional 6 cylinder distributor

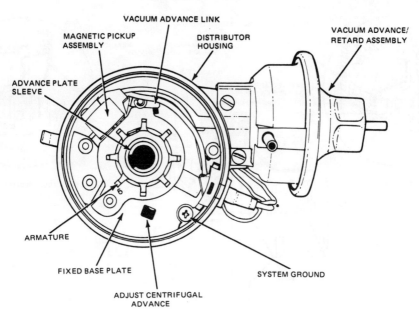

VACUUM ADVANCE LINK

MAGNETIC PICKUP ASSEMBLY

DISTRIBUTOR HOUSING

VACUUM ADVANCE/ RETARD ASSEMBLY

ADVANCE PLATE SLEEVE

ARMATURE

FIXED BASE PLATE

ADJUST CENTRIFUGAL ADVANCE

SYSTEM GROUND

Distributor cap and rotor removed—breaderless 8 cylinder distributor

The distributors on many models also incorporate a vacuum retard mechanism. The retard mechanism is contained in the rear part of the vacuum diaphragm chamber. When the engine is operating under high-vacuum conditions (deceleration or idle), intake manifold vacuum is applied to the retard mechanism. The retard mechanism moves the breaker point mounting plate (conventional) or pickup coil assembly (breakerless) in the direction of distributor rotation, thereby retarding the ignition timing. Ignition retard, under these conditions, reduces exhaust emissions of hydrocarbons, although it does reduce engine efficiency somewhat.

DISTRIBUTOR REMOVAL AND INSTALLATION

NOTE: *1979 LTD's sold in California with the 351 engine are equipped with the new EEC II system. The distributor is locked into place during assembly and should not be removed.*

1. On all V8 engines, remove the air cleaner assembly, taking note of the hose locations, to gain access to the distributor.

2. On models equipped with a conventional ignition system, disconnect the primary wire at the coil. On models equipped with breakerless ignition, disconnect the distributor wiring connector from the vehicle wiring harness.

3. Noting the position of the vacuum line(s) on the distributor diaphragm, discon-

nect the lines at the diaphragm. Unsnap the two distributor cap retaining clamps and remove the cap. Position the cap and ignition wires to one side.

4. Using chalk or paint, carefully mark the position of the distributor rotor in relation to the distributor housing and mark the position of the distributor housing in relation to the engine block. When this is done, you should have a line on the distributor housing directly in line with the tip of the rotor and another line on the engine block directly in line with the mark on the distributor housing. This is very important because the distributor must be reinstalled in the exact same location from which it was removed, if correct ignition timing is to be maintained.

5. Remove the distributor hold-down bolt and clamp. Remove the distributor from the engine.

NOTE: *Do not disturb the engine while the distributor is removed. If you attempt to start the engine with the distributor removed, you will have to retime the engine.*

6a. If the engine was cranked (disturbed) with the distributor removed, it will now be necessary to retime the engine. If the distributor has been installed incorrectly and the engine will not start, remove the distributor from the engine and start over again. Hold the distributor close to the engine and install the cap on the distributor in its normal position. Locate the No. 1 spark plug tower on the distributor cap. Scribe a mark on the

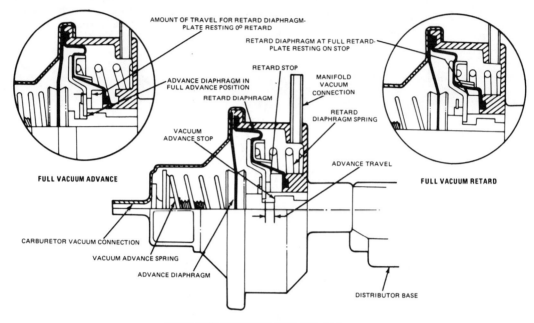

AMOUNT OF TRAVEL FOR RETARD DIAPHRAGM-
PLATE RESTING 0° RETARD

RETARD DIAPHRAGM AT FULL RETARD-
PLATE RESTING ON STOP

RETARD STOP

MANIFOLD
VACUUM
CONNECTION

ADVANCE DIAPHRAGM IN
FULL ADVANCE POSITION

RETARD DIAPHRAGM

RETARD
DIAPHRAGM SPRING

VACUUM
ADVANCE STOP

ADVANCE TRAVEL

FULL VACUUM ADVANCE

FULL VACUUM RETARD

CARBURETOR VACUUM CONNECTION

VACUUM ADVANCE SPRING

ADVANCE DIAPHRAGM

DISTRIBUTOR BASE

VACUUM ADVANCE AND RETARD DIAPHRAGMS AT REST

Dual diaphragm vacuum advance and retard mechanisms

body of the distributor directly below the No. 1 spark plug wire tower on the distributor cap. remove the distributor cap from the distributor and move the distributor and cap to one side. Remove the No. 1 spark plug and crank the engine over until the No. 1 cylinder is on its compression stroke. To accomplish this, place a wrench on the lower engine pulley and turn the engine slowly in a clockwise (6 cylinder) or counterclockwise (V8) direction until the TDC mark on the crankshaft damper aligns with the timing pointer. If you place your finger in the No. 1 spark plug hole, you will feel air escaping as the piston rises in the combustion chamber. On conventional ignition systems, the rotor must be at No. 1 firing position to install the distributor. On breakerless ignition systems, one of the armature segments must be aligned with the stator as shown in the accompanying illustration to install the distributor. Make sure that the oil pump intermediate shaft properly engages the distributor shaft. It may be necessary to crank the engine with the starter, after the distributor drive gear is partially engaged, in order to engage the oil pump intermediate shaft. Install, but do not tighten the retaining clamp and bolt. Rotate the distributor to advance the timing to a point where the armature tooth is aligned properly (breakerless ignition) or to a point where the points are just

starting to open (conventional ignition). Tighten the clamp.

b. If the engine was not cranked (disturbed) when the distributor was removed, position the distributor in the block with the rotor aligned with the mark previously scribed on the distributor body and the marks on the distributor body and cylinder block in alignment. Install the distributor hold-down bolt and clamp fingertight.

7. Install the distributor cap and wires.

8. On models equipped with conventional ignition connect the primary wire at the coil. On models equipped with breakerless ignition, connect the distributor wiring connector to the wiring harness.

9. Check the ignition timing as outlined in Chapter 2.

10. Install the air cleaner, if removed.

Charging System

The charging system is composed of the alternator, alternator regulator, charging system warning light, battery, and fuse link wire.

A failure of any component of the charging system can cause the entire system to stop functioning. Because of this, the charging system can be very difficult to troubleshoot when problems occur.

When the ignition key is turned on, cur-

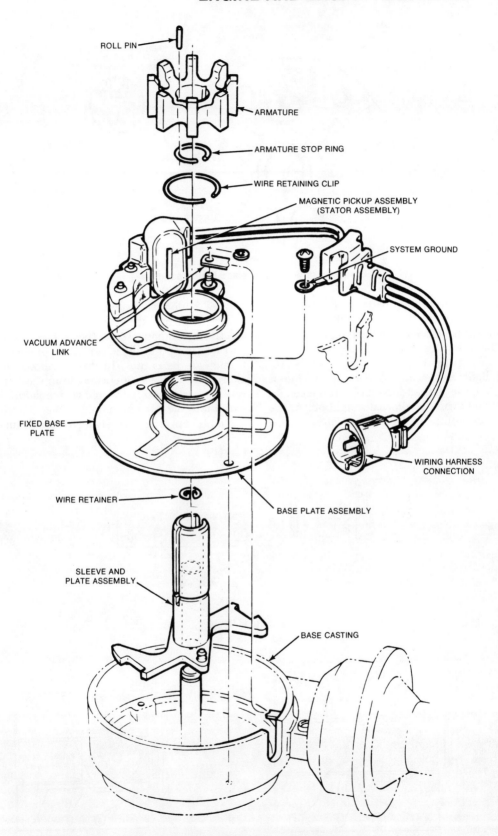

ROLL PIN

ARMATURE

ARMATURE STOP RING

WIRE RETAINING CLIP

MAGNETIC PICKUP ASSEMBLY
(STATOR ASSEMBLY)

SYSTEM GROUND

VACUUM ADVANCE
LINK

FIXED BASE
PLATE

WIRING HARNESS
CONNECTION

WIRE RETAINER

BASE PLATE ASSEMBLY

SLEEVE AND
PLATE ASSEMBLY

BASE CASTING

Breakerless V8 distributor disassembled

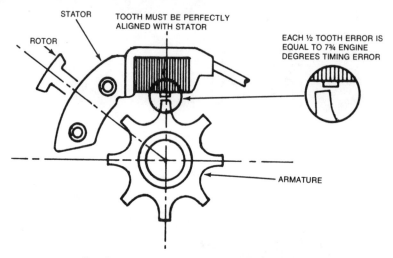

STATOR

TOOTH MUST BE PERFECTLY ALIGNED WITH STATOR

ROTOR

EACH ½ TOOTH ERROR IS EQUAL TO 7¾ ENGINE DEGREES TIMING ERROR

ARMATURE

Breakerless distributor static timing position

rent flows from the battery, through the charging system indicator light on the instrument panel, to the voltage regulator, and to the alternator. Since the alternator is not producing any current, the alternator warning light comes on. When the engine is started, the alternator begins to produce current and turns the alternator light off. As the alternator turns and produces current, that current is divided in two ways: part to the battery to charge the battery and power the electrical components of the vehicle, and part is returned to the alternator to enable it to increase its output. In this situation, the alternator is receiving current from the battery and from itself. A voltage regulator is wired into the current supply to the alternator to prevent it from receiving too much cur-

Firing Order

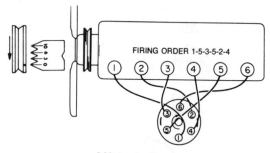

FIRING ORDER 1-5-3-5-2-4

240 cu. in. 6 cyl.

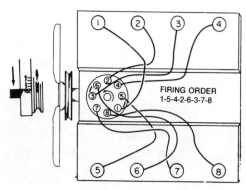

FIRING ORDER 1-5-4-2-6-3-7-8

V8 except 351, 400 cu. in.

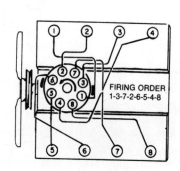

FIRING ORDER 1-3-7-2-6-5-4-8

V8 351, 400 cu. in.

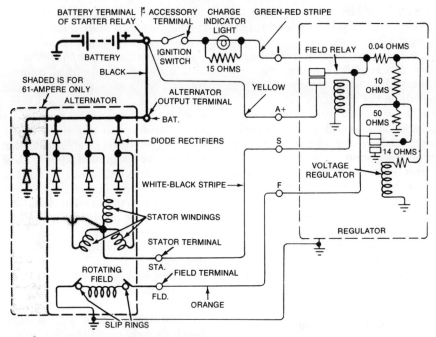

Alternator charging circuit w/indicator light—rear terminal type

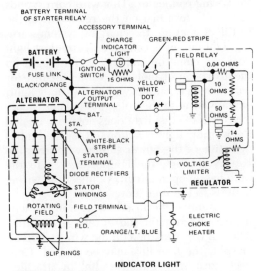

Alternator charging circuit w/indicator light—side terminal type

rent which would cause it to put out too much current. Conversely, if the voltage regulator does not allow the alternator to receive enough current, the battery will not be fully charged and will eventually go dead.

The battery is connected to the alternator at all times, whether the ignition key is turned on or not. If the battery were shorted to ground, the alternator would also be shorted. This would damage the alternator. To prevent this, a fuse link is installed in the wiring between the battery and the alternator on all 1970 and later models. If the battery is shorted, the fuse link is melted, protecting the alternator.

Since the alternator, the alternator regulator, the charging system warning light, the battery and the fuse link are all interconnected, the failure of one component can cause the others to become inoperative.

ALTERNATOR PRECAUTIONS

Several precautions must be observed with alternator equipped vehicles to avoid damaging the unit. They are as follows:

1. If the battery is removed for any reason, make sure that it is reconnected with the correct polarity. Reversing the battery connections may result in damage to the one-way rectifiers.

2. When utilizing a booster battery as a starting aid, always connect it as follows: positive to positive, and negative (booster battery) to good ground on the engine of the car being started.

3. Never use a fast charger as a booster to start cars with alternating-current (AC) circuits.

4. When servicing the battery with a fast charger, always disconnect the car battery cables.

5. Never attempt to polarize an alternator.

6. Avoid long soldering times when replacing diodes or transistors. Prolonged heat is damaging to alternators.

7. Do not use test lamps of more than 12 volts (V) for checking diode continuity.

8. Do not short across or ground any of the terminals on the alternator.

9. The polarity of the battery, alternator, and regulator must be matched and considered before making any electrical connections within the system.

10. Never separate the alternator on an open circuit. Make sure that all connections within the circuit are clean and tight.

11. Disconnect the battery terminals when performing any service on the electrical system. This will eliminate the possibility of accidental reversal of polarity.

12. Disconnect the battery ground cable if arc welding is to be done on any part of the car.

CHARGING SYSTEM TROUBLE-SHOOTING

There are many different types of charging system problems and most require expensive tools to diagnose. When one component of the system fails completely and the charging system warning light comes on, it is a little easier to locate the source of the problem. We will deal with only a complete failure of the system which causes the battery to go dead.

You will need two testing instruments for use in this section. They are both relatively cheap and readily available. The first is a current indicator. This device, when placed on a wire which has current passing through it, measures the current in amps. The other is a test light. This is simply a pointed screwdriver which contains a light bulb and has a ground wire attached to it. When the pointed end is touched to an electrical component that should have current running to it, and the ground wire is attached to a good ground, the light in the handle will come on to verify that current is indeed coming to the component.

This test works under three assumptions:

A. The battery is known to be good and fully charged;

B. The alternator belt is in good condition and adjusted to the proper tension;

C. All connections in the system are clean and tight.

NOTE: *In order for the current indicator to give a valid reading, the car must be equipped with battery cables which are of the same gauge size and quality as original equipment battery cables.*

1. Turn off all electrical components on the car. Make sure the doors of the car are closed. If the car is equipped with a clock, disconnect the clock by removing the lead wire from the rear of the clock. Disconnect the positive battery cable from the battery and connect the ground wire on a test light to the disconnected positive battery cable. Touch the probe end of the test light to the positive battery post. The test light should not light. If the test light does light, there is a short or open circuit on the car. See Chapter 5 for troubleshooting procedures for this problem.

2. Disconnect the voltage regulator wiring harness connector at the voltage regulator. Turn on the ignition key. Connect the wire on a test light to a good ground (engine bolt). Touch the probe end of a test light to the ignition wire connector into the voltage regulator wiring connector. This wire corresponds to the "I" terminal on the regulator. If the test light goes on, the charging system warning light circuit is complete. If the test light does not come on and the warning light on the instrument panel is on, either the resistor wire, which is parallel with the warning light, or the wiring to the voltage regulator, is defective. If the test light does not come on and the warning light is not on, either the bulb is defective or the power supply wire from the battery through the ignition switch to the bulb has an open circuit. Connect the wiring harness to the regulator.

3. Examine the fuse link wire in the wiring harness from the starter relay to the alternator. If the insulation on the wire is cracked or split, the fuse link may be melted. Connect a test light to the fuse link by attaching the ground wire on the test light to an engine bolt and touching the probe end of the light to the bottom of the fuse link wire where it splices into the alternator output wire. If the bulb in the test light does not light, the fuse link is melted.

4. Start the engine and place a current indicator on the positive battery cable. Turn off all electrical accessories and make sure the doors are closed. If the charging system is working properly, the gauge will show a charge of about 5 amps. If the system is not working properly, the gauge will show a draw

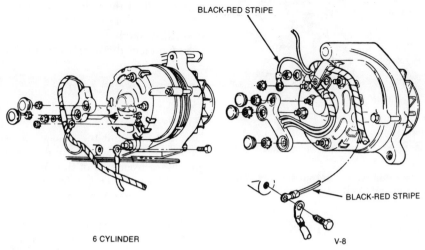

BLACK-RED STRIPE

BLACK-RED STRIPE

6 CYLINDER

V-8

1968–72 alternator wiring harness connections—typical Autolite except 65 ampere unit

of about 5 amps. A charge moves the needle toward the battery, a draw moves the needle away from the battery. Turn the engine off.

5. Disconnect the wiring harness from the voltage regulator at the regulator connector. Connect a male spade terminal (solderless connector) to each end of a jumper wire. Insert one end of the wire into the wiring harness connector which corresponds to the "A" terminal on the regulator. Insert the other end of the wire into the wiring harness connector which corresponds to the "F" terminal on the regulator. Position the connector with the jumper wire intalled so that it cannot contact any metal surface under the hood. Position a current indicator gauge on the positive battery cable. Have an assistant start the engine. Observe the reading on the current indicator. Have your assistant slowly raise the speed of the engine to about 2,000 rpm or until the current indicator needle

stops moving, whichever comes first. Do not run the engine for more than a short period of time in this condition. If the wiring harness connector or jumper wire becomes excessively hot during this test, turn off the engine and check for a grounded wire in the regulator wiring harness. If the current indicator shows a charge of about three amps less than the output of the alternator, the alternator is working properly. If the previous tests showed a draw, the voltage regulator is defective. If the gauge does not show the proper charging rate, the alternator is defective.

ALTERNATOR REMOVAL AND INSTALLATION

While internal alternator repairs are possible, they require special tools and training. Therefore, it is advisable to replace a defec-

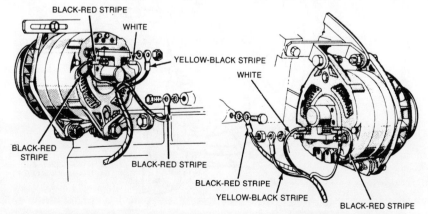

BLACK-RED STRIPE

WHITE

YELLOW-BLACK STRIPE

WHITE

BLACK-RED STRIPE

BLACK-RED STRIPE

BLACK-RED STRIPE

BLACK-RED STRIPE

YELLOW-BLACK STRIPE

BLACK-RED STRIPE

1968–72 alternator wiring harness connections—Leece-Neville 65 ampere unit

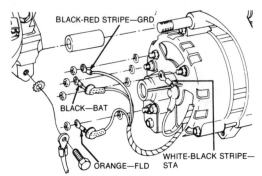

1968–72 alternator wiring harness connections —Autolite 65 ampere unit

tive alternator, or have it repaired by a qualified shop.

1. Disconnect the negative battery cable from the battery.

2. Disconnect the wires from the rear (rear terminal) or side (side terminal) of the alternator.

3. Loosen the alternator mounting bolts and remove the drive belt.

4. Remove the alternator mounting bolts and spacer (if equipped), and remove the alternator.

5. To install, position the alternator on its brackets and install the attaching bolts and spacer (if so equipped).

6. Connect the wires to the alternator.

7. Position the drive belt on the alternator

pulley. Adjust the belt tension as outlined in Chapter 1 under "Alternator Drive Belt Tension Adjustment."

8. Connect the negative battery cable.

VOLTAGE REGULATOR

The voltage regulator is a device which controls the output of the alternator. If the regulator did not limit the voltage output of the alternator, the excessive output could burn out the components of the electrical system. In addition, the regulator compensates for seasonal temperature changes as they affect voltage output.

Three types of regulators are used on 1968 and later Fords. An electro-mechanical Autolite (Motorcraft) unit is used with Autolite (Motorcraft) alternators. This unit is factory calibrated, permanently sealed, and cannot be adjusted. A Leece-Neville electromechanical unit was available through 1976 with the high-output alternator. This unit may be adjusted. A third transistorized Motorcraft unit is used on some 1974–79 models equipped with solid-state ignition. This unit may also be adjusted. The transistorized regulator is identical in appearance to the Motorcraft electro-mechanical unit, except where the sealed electro-mechanical unit has rivets holding down the regulator cover, the transistorized regulator has screws.

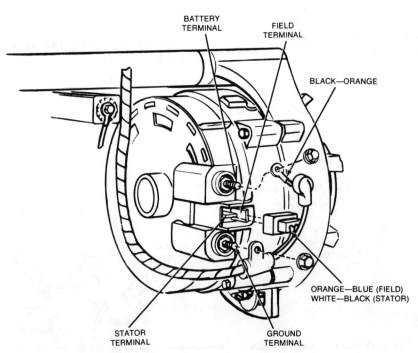

1972 and later alternator wiring harness connections—Autolite (Motorcraft) side terminal unit

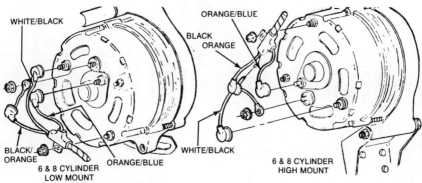

WHITE/BLACK

ORANGE/BLUE

BLACK
ORANGE

BLACK/
ORANGE

WHITE/BLACK

ORANGE/BLUE

6 & 8 CYLINDER
LOW MOUNT

6 & 8 CYLINDER
HIGH MOUNT

1973 and later Motorcraft alternator wiring harness connections—rear terminal units

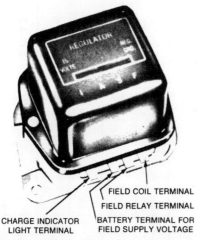

CHARGE INDICATOR
LIGHT TERMINAL

FIELD COIL TERMINAL

FIELD RELAY TERMINAL

BATTERY TERMINAL FOR
FIELD SUPPLY VOLTAGE

Autolite (Motorcraft) electro-mechanical regulator connections

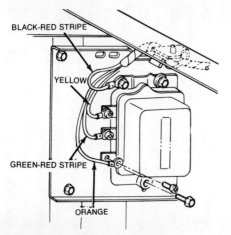

BLACK-RED STRIPE

YELLOW

GREEN-RED STRIPE

ORANGE

Leece-Neville regulator connections

VOLTAGE REGULATOR REMOVAL AND INSTALLATION

1. Remove the battery ground cable. On models with the regulator mounted behind the battery, it is necessary to remove the battery hold-down, and to move the battery.

2. Remove the regulator mounting screws.

3. Disconnect the regulator to the wiring harness.

4. Connect the new regulator to the wiring harness.

5. Mount the regulator to the regulator mounting plate. The radio suppression condenser mounts under one mounting screw; the ground lead under the other mounting screw. Tighten the mounting screws.

6. If the battery was moved to gain access to the regulator, position the battery and install the hold-down. Connect the battery ground cable, and test the system for proper voltage regulation.

TESTING

Autolite (Motorcraft) Electro-Mechanical and Motorcraft Transistor Units

Any electro-mechanical regulator which does not perform to specifications must be replaced. A transistorized regulator may be adjusted if not up to specifications as per the test. The accompanying illustration shows the voltage limiter adjustment screw location beneath the regulator cover.

Before proceeding with the test, make sure that the alternator drive belt tension is properly adjusted, the battery has a good charge (specific gravity of 1.250 or better), and that all charging system electrical connections are clean and tight. A voltmeter is needed for this test. The test is as follows:

1. Connect a voltmeter to the battery, with the positive lead to the battery positive terminal and the negative lead to the battery negative terminal. Turn off all electrical

Alternator and Regulator Specifications

| | ALTERNATOR | | | REGULATOR | | | | | | |
| | | | | | Field Relay | | | Regulator | | |
Year	Manufacturer	Field Current @ 12 V	Output (amps)	Manufacturer	Air Gap (in.)	Point Gap (in.)	Volts to Close	Air Gap (in.)	Point Gap (in.)	Volts @ 75°
'68	Autolite C6AF10300C	2.9	42	Autolite	①	①	4.2–9.0	①	①	13.5–15.3
	Autolite C6AF10300G	2.9	55	Autolite	①	①	4.2–9.0	①	①	13.5–15.3
	Autolite C6TF10300F	2.9	65	Autolite	①	①	4.2–9.0	①	①	13.5–15.3
	Leece-Neville	2.9	65	Leece-Neville	.012	.025	6.2–7.2	.047	.019	13.9–14.9
'69	Autolite (Orange tag)	2.9	42	Autolite	①	①	4.2–9.0	①	①	13.5–15.3
	Autolite (Red tag)	2.9	55	Autolite	①	①	4.2–9.0	①	①	13.5–15.3
	Autolite (Black tag)	2.9	65	Autolite	①	①	4.2–9.0	①	①	13.5–15.3
	Leece-Neville	2.9	65	Leece-Neville	.012	.025	6.2–7.2	.047	.019	13.9–14.9
'70–'75	Autolite② (Orange tag)	2.9	42	Autolite②	①	①	2.0–4.2	①	①	13.5–15.3
	Autolite② (Red tag)	2.9	55	Autolite②	①	①	2.0–4.2	①	①	13.5–15.3
	Autolite② (Green tag)	2.9	61	Autolite②	①	①	2.0–4.2	①	①	13.5–15.3
	Autolite② (Black tag)	2.9	65	Autolite②	①	①	2.0–4.2	①	①	13.5–15.3
	Autolite② (side terminal)	2.9	70	Motorcraft	①	①	2.5–4.0	①	①	13.5–15.3

	Leece-Neville	2.9	65	Leece-Neville	.012	.025	6.2–7.2	.047	.019	13.9–14.9
	Motorcraft (side terminal)	2.9	90	Motorcraft	①	①	2.5–4.0	①	①	13.5–15.3
'76–79	Motorcraft (Orange tag)	2.9	40	Motorcraft	①	①	2.0–4.2	①	①	13.5–15.3
	Motorcraft (Green tag)	2.9	60	Motorcraft	①	①	2.0–4.2	①	①	13.5–15.3
	Motorcraft (side terminal)	2.9	70	Motorcraft	①	①	2.5–4.0	①	①	13.5–15.3
	Motorcraft (side terminal)	2.9	90	Motorcraft	①	①	2.5–4.0	①	①	13.5–15.3

① Electro-mechanical regulator—not adjustable   ② Beginning 1974, the name Autolite has been changed to Motorcraft

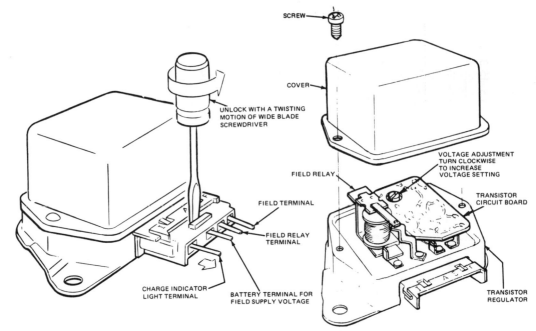

Motorcraft transistorized regulator adjustment

equipment. Check and record the voltmeter reading with the engine stopped.

2. Connect a tachometer to the engine, with the red (positive) lead to the distributor terminal on the ignition coil and the black (negative) lead to a good ground, such as an engine bolt.

3. Place the transmission in Neutral or Park and start the engine. Increase the engine speed to 1,800–2,200 rpm for 2–3 minutes to bring the engine and regulator to operating temperature. Check and record the voltmeter reading. It should now be 1 to 2 volts higher than the first reading. This is the regulated voltage reading. If the reading is less than 1 volt or greater than 2½ volts, the regulator must be replaced (electromechanical type) or adjusted (transistorized type).

4. If the reading is between 1 and 2 volts, turn on the headlights and heater blower to load the alternator. The voltage should not decrease more than ½ volt from the regulated voltage reading in Step 3. If the voltage drop is greater than ½ volt, the regulator should be replaced.

Leece-Neville Electro-Mechanical Unit

REGULATOR TEST

1. Connect a voltmeter to the battery post terminals.

2. Start the engine. Disconnect the regu-

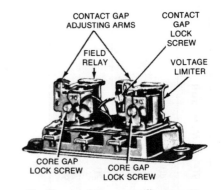

Leece-Neville regulator gap adjustments

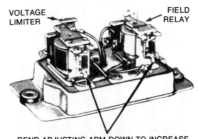

Leece-Neville regulator voltage adjustments

lator field (F) lead and connect it to the battery terminal of the regulator.

CAUTION: *Do not run the engine with the regulator wiring in this position any longer than necessary as excessive voltage could damage the alternator.*

3. Stop the engine. Disconnect the field (F) lead from the battery terminal and reconnect it to the field terminal on the regulator. If the voltmeter reads 15–20 volts or greater, the regulator is defective and must be replaced.

FIELD RELAY TEST

NOTE: *Make sure that the battery has a good charge (specific gravity of 1.250) for this test. Connect the voltmeter as in the "Regulator Test."*

1. Without turning on the engine, turn the ignition switch on and off several times. Each time the switch is turned on, a definite clicking sound should be heard in the regulator.

2. If no click is heard, check for battery voltage at the IGN terminal of the regulator with the ignition switch in the IGN position. With battery voltage at the IGN terminal and if no clicking is heard while operating the ignition switch, the field relay is defective necessitating replacement of the voltage regulator unit.

VOLTAGE ADJUSTMENT

Leece-Neville Electro-Mechanical Unit

1. Run the engine for 10–15 minutes to allow the regulator to reach operating temperature. Connect a voltmeter across the battery posts. Turn off all electrical equipment. Check the voltage at the battery. It should be 13.9–14.1 volts.

2. The voltage control adjustment (voltage limiter) is adjusted at the component closest to the F terminal. Remove the regulator cover. Voltage may be increased by raising the spring tension and decreased by lowering the spring tension. To adjust the spring tension, move the lower spring mounting tab.

NOTE: *Voltage will drop about ½ volt when the regulator cover is installed and should be compensated for in the adjustment.*

3. After making the adjustment, cycle the regulator by stopping and starting the engine. This will indicate if the adjustment is stable. If the voltage reading has changed, follow Steps 1 and 2 until the correct voltage is obtained.

Starting System

The battery is the first link in the chain of mechanisms which work together to provide cranking of the automobile engine. In most modern cars, the battery is a lead-acid electrochemical device consisting of six two-volt (2 V) subsections connected in series so the unit is capable of producing approximately 12 V of electrical pressure. Each subsection, or cell, consists of a series of positive and negative plates held a short distance apart in a solution of sulfuric acid and water. The two types of plates are of dissimilar metals. This causes a chemical reaction to be set up, and it is this reaction which produces current flow from the battery when its positive and negative terminals are connected to an electrical appliance such as a lamp or motor. The continued transfer of electrons would eventually convert the sulfuric acid in the electrolyte to water, and make the two plates identical in chemical composition. As electrical energy is removed from the battery, its voltage output tends to drop. Thus, measuring battery voltage and battery electrolyte composition are two ways of checking the ability of the unit to supply power. During the starting of the engine, electrical energy is removed from the battery. However, if the charging circuit is in good condition and the operating conditions are normal, the power removed from the battery will be replaced by the alternator which will force electrons back through the battery, reversing the normal flow, and restoring the battery to its original chemical state.

The battery and starting motor are linked by very heavy electrical cables designed to minimize resistance to the flow of current. Generally, the major power supply cable that leaves the battery goes directly to the starter, while other electrical system needs are supplied by a smaller cable. During starter operation, power flows from the battery to the starter and is grounded through the car's frame and the battery's negative ground strap.

The starting motor is a specially designed, direct current electric motor capable of producing a very great amount of power for its size. One thing that allows the motor to produce a great deal of power is its tremendous rotating speed. It drives the engine through a tiny pinion gear (attached to the starter's armature), which drives the very large flywheel ring gear at a greatly reduced speed. Another factor allowing it to produce so much power is that only intermittent operation is required of it. Thus, little allowance for air circulation is required, and the windings can be built into a very small space.

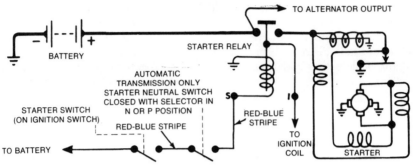

Positive engagement starter circuit

The starter solenoid is a magnetic device which employs the small current supplied by the starting switch circuit of the ignition switch. This magnetic action moves a plunger which mechanically engages the starter.

Positive engagement Ford starters, except those used with 429 and 460 V8 engines, employ a separate relay, mounted away from the starter, to switch the motor and solenoid current on and off, from the battery. The relay thus replaces the solenoid electrical switch, but does not eliminate the need for a solenoid mounted on the starter used to mechanically engage the starter drive gears. The relay is used to reduce the amount of current the starting switch must carry. On solenoid actuated starters installed in 429 and 460 V8 engines, the contacts in the solenoid take the place of the relay.

The starting switch circuit consists of the starting switch contained within the ignition switch, a transmission neutral safety switch or clutch pedal switch which prevents the car from being started in any gear but Neutral or

Park (automatic only), and the wiring necessary to connect these in series with the starter solenoid or relay.

A pinion, which is a small gear, is mounted to a one-way drive clutch. This clutch is splined to the starter armature shaft. When the ignition switch is moved to the "start" position, the solenoid plunger slides the pinion toward the flywheel ring gear via a collar and spring. If the teeth on the pinion and flywheel match properly, the pinion will engage the flywheel immediately. If the gear teeth butt one another, the spring will be compressed and will force the gears to mesh as soon as the starter turns far enough to allow them to do so. As the solenoid plunger reaches the end of its travel, it closes the contacts that connect the battery and starter and then the engine is cranked.

As soon as the engine starts, the flywheel ring gear begins turning fast enough to drive the pinion at an extremely high rate of speed. At this point, the one-way clutch begins allowing the pinion to spin faster than the

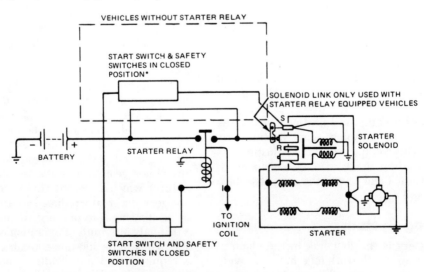

Solenoid actuated starter circuit—with and without starter relay

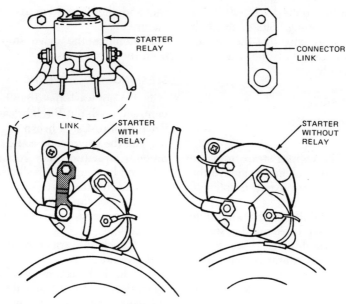

Solenoid connector link

starter shaft so that the starter will not operate at excessive speed. When the ignition switch is released from the starter position, the solenoid is de-energized, and a spring contained within the solenoid assembly pulls the gear out of mesh and interrupts the current flow to the starter.

STARTER

All Ford 6 cylinder models, and V8 models except the 429 and 460 V8 engines, use the positive engagement starter. This medium-duty unit uses a remote starter relay to open and close the circuit to the battery.

The starter installed in 429 and 460 V8 models is the solenoid actuated starter. This heavy-duty unit uses an outboard solenoid mounted atop the starter which has an internal electrical switch to open and close the circuit to the battery.

If, for some reason (such as an engine swap), a solenoid actuated starter is installed in a car originally equipped with a starter relay (any car not originally equipped with a 429 or 460 V8), a special connector link must be installed on the starter solenoid. This link connects the battery terminal with the solenoid operating windings. Therefore, when the key is turned to the Start position, the starter solenoid is actuated, sending battery current to the solenoid. The solenoid then operates the starter through the solenoid internal contacts. See the accompanying illustration for the proper installation of the connector link.

STARTER REMOVAL AND INSTALLATION

1. Disconnect the negative battery cable.
2. Raise the front of the car and install jackstands beneath the frame. Firmly apply the parking brake and place blocks in back of the rear wheels.
3. Disconnect the heavy starter cable at the starter. On solenoid actuated starters (429 and 460 V8 only), label and disconnect the wires from the solenoid.
4. Turn the front wheels fully to the right. On many models, it will be necessary to remove the two bolts retaining the steering idler arm to the frame to gain acess to the starter.
5. Remove the starter mounting bolts and remove the starter.
6. Reverse the above procedure to install.

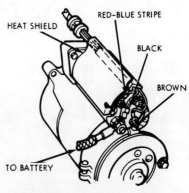

Solenoid actuated starter connections

Torque the mounting bolts to 15–20 ft lbs and the idler arm retaining bolts to 28–35 ft lbs (if removed). Make sure that the nut securing the heavy cable to the starter is snugged down tightly.

STARTER OVERHAUL

Solenoid Actuated Starter

DISASSEMBLY

1. Disconnect the copper strap from the starter terminal on the solenoid, remove the retaining screws and remove the solenoid from the drive housing.

2. Loosen the retaining screw and slide the brush cover band back on the starter frame for access to the brushes.

3. Remove the commutator brushes from their holders. Hold each spring away from the brush with a hook, while sliding the brush out of the holder.

4. Remove the through-bolts and separate the drive-end housing, starter frame and brush end plate assemblies.

5. Remove the solenoid plunger and shift fork assembly. If either the plunger or fork is to be replaced, they can be separated by removing the roll pin.

6. Remove the armature and drive assembly from the frame. Remove the drive stop ring and slide the drive assembly off the armature shaft.

7. Remove the drive stop ring retainer from the drive housing.

CLEANING AND INSPECTION

1. Do not wash the drive because the solvent will wash out the lubricant, causing the drive to slip. Use a brush or compressed air to clean the drive, field coils, armature, commutator, armature shaft front end plate, and rear end housing. Wash all other parts in solvent and dry the parts.

2. Inspect the armature windings for broken or burned insulation and unsoldered connections.

3. Check the armature for open circuits and grounds.

4. Check the commutator for run-out. Inspect the armature shaft and the two bearings for scoring and excessive wear. On a starter with needle bearings, apply a small amount of grease to the needles. If the commutator is rough, or more than 0.005 in. out-of-round, turn it down.

5. Check the brush holders for broken springs and the insulated brush holders for shorts to ground. Tighten any rivets that may be loose. Replace the brushes if worn to ¼ in. in length.

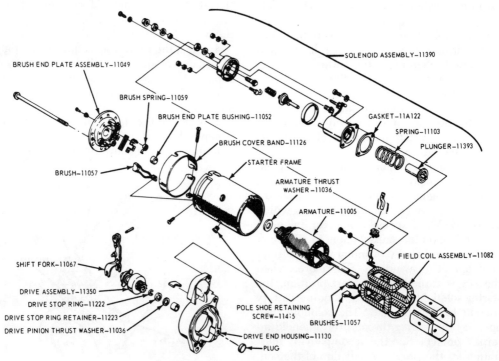

Solenoid actuated starter disassembled

6. Check the brush spring tension. Replace the springs if the tension is not within specified limits (80 ounces minimum).

7. Inspect the field coils for burned or broken insulation and continuity. Check the field brush connections and lead insulation. A brush kit is available. All other assemblies are to be replaced rather than repaired.

8. Examine the wear pattern on the starter drive teeth. The pinion teeth must penetrate to a depth greater than ½ the ring gear tooth depth, to eliminate premature ring gear and starter drive failure.

9. Replace starter drives and ring gears with milled, pitted or broken teeth or evidence of inadequate engagement.

ASSEMBLY

1. Install a small amount of Lubriplate® on the armature shaft splines. Install the drive assembly on the armature shaft and install a new stop ring.

2. Apply a small amount of Lubriplate on the shift lever pivot pin. Position the solenoid plunger and shift lever assembly in the drive housing.

3. Place a new retainer in the drive housing. Apply a small amount of Lubriplate to the drive end of the armature shaft. Place the armature and drive assembly into the drive housing. Be sure that the shift lever tangs properly engage the drive assembly.

4. Apply a small amount of Lubriplate on the commutator end of the armature shaft.

5. Position the frame and field assembly to the drive housing. Be sure that the frame is properly indexed to the drive housing assembly.

6. Position the brush plate assembly to the frame assembly. Be sure that the brush plate is properly indexed to the drive housing assembly.

7. Place the brushes in their holders. Pull each spring away from the holder with a hook to allow entry of the brush. Center the brush springs on the brushes. Press the insulated brush leads away from all other interior components to prevent possible shorts.

8. Position the rubber gasket between the solenoid mounting and the upper outside surface of the frame. Position the starter solenoid with the metal gasket (if used), and install the solenoid mounting screws.

9. Connect the copper strap to the starter terminal on the solenoid.

10. Position the cover band and tighten the retaining screw.

11. Connect the starter to a battery to check its operation.

BRUSH REPLACEMENT

Positive Engagement Starter

Replace the starter brushes when they are worn to ¼ in. Always install a complete set of new brushes.

1. Loosen and remove the brush cover band, gasket, and starter drive plunger lever cover. Remove the brushes from their holders.

2. Remove the two through-bolts from the starter frame.

3. Remove the drive end housing and the plunger lever return spring.

4. Remove the starter drive plunger lever pivot pin and lever, and remove the armature.

5. Remove the brush end plate.

6. Remove the ground brush retaining screws from the frame and remove the brushes.

7. Cut the insulated brush leads from the field coils, as close to the field connection point as possible.

8. Clean and inspect the starter motor.

9. Replace the brush end plate if the insulator between the field brush holder and the end plate is cracked or broken.

10. Position the new insulated field brushes lead on the field coil connection. Position and crimp the clip provided with the brushes to hold the brush lead to the connection. Solder the lead, clip, and connection together using rosin core solder. Use a 300-watt soldering iron.

11. Install the ground brush leads to the frame with the retaining screws.

12. Clean the commutator with 00 or 000 sandpaper.

13. Position the brush end plate to the starter frame, with the end plate boss in the frame slot.

14. Install the armature in the starter frame.

15. Install the starter drive gear plunger lever to the frame and starter drive assembly, and install the pivot pin.

16. Partially fill the drive end housing bearing bore with grease (approximately ¼ full). Position the return spring on the plunger lever, and the drive end housing to the starter frame. Install the through-bolts and tighten to specified torque (55 to 75 in. lbs). Be sure that the stop ring re-

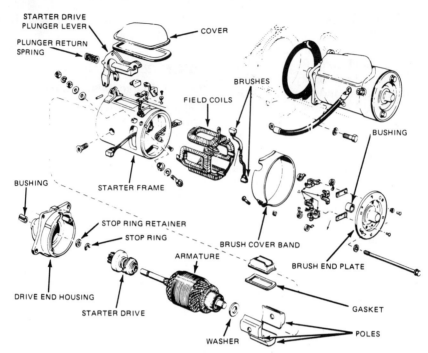

STARTER DRIVE
PLUNGER LEVER

PLUNGER RETURN
SPRING

COVER

BRUSHES

FIELD COILS

BUSHING

BUSHING

STARTER FRAME

STOP RING RETAINER

STOP RING

BRUSH COVER BAND

ARMATURE

BRUSH END PLATE

DRIVE END HOUSING

STARTER DRIVE

GASKET

WASHER

POLES

Positive engagement starter disassembled

tainer is seated properly in the drive end housing.

17. Install the commutator brushes in the brush holders. Center the brush springs on the brushes.

18. Position the plunger lever cover and brush cover band, with its gasket, on the starter. Tighten the band retaining screw.

19. Connect the starter to a battery to check its operation.

Solenoid Actuated Starter

Replace the starter brushes when they are worn to ¼ in. Always install a complete set of new brushes.

1. Disconnect the copper strap from the starter terminal on the solenoid.

2. Loosen the retaining screw and slide the brush cover band back on the starter frame for access to the brushes.

3. Remove the commutator brushes from their holders. Hold each spring away from the brush with a hook, while sliding the brush out of the holder.

4. Remove the through-bolts and separate the drive end housing, starter frame and brush end plate assemblies.

5. Remove the ground brush retaining screws from the frame and remove the brushes.

6. Cut the insulated brush leads from the field coils, as close to the field connection point as possible.

7. Clean and inspect the starter motor.

8. Replace the brush end plate, if the insulator between the field brush holder and the end plate is cracked or broken.

9. Position the new insulated field brushes' lead on the field coil connection. Position and crimp the clip provided with the brushes to hold the brush lead to the connection. Solder the lead, clip, and connection together, using rosin core solder. Use a 300-watt soldering iron.

10. Install the ground brush leads to the frame with the retaining screws.

11. Clean the commutator with 00 or 000 sandpaper.

12. Apply a small amount of lubriplate on the commutator end of the armature shaft.

13. Position the rubber gasket over the solenoid plunger lever, then position the frame to the end housing so that the wide slot in the frame clears the plunger lever and the end housing dowel is indexed with its frame slot.

14. Position the brush plate assembly to the frame assembly. Be sure that the brush plate is properly indexed to the frame. In-

stall the thorough-bolts, making certain that the insulated brush lead is not between the through-bolt and the frame, and tighten to 45 to 85 in. lbs.

15. Place the brushes in their holders. Pull each spring away from the holder with a hook to allow entry of the brush. Press the insulated brush leads away from all the other interior components to prevent possible shorts.

16. Slide the cover band into position and tighten the retaining screw.

17. Connect the copper strap to the starter terminal on the solenoid.

18. Connect the starter to a battery to check its operation.

STARTER DRIVE REPLACEMENT

All Except 429 and 460 V8 (Positive Engagement Type)

1. Remove the starter from the engine.
2. Remove the brush cover band.
3. Remove the starter drive plunger lever cover.
4. Loosen the thru-bolts just enough to allow removal of the drive end housing and the starter drive plunger lever return spring.
5. Remove the pivot pin which attaches the starter drive plunger lever to the starter frame and remove the lever.

6. Remove the stop ring retainer and stop-ring from the armature shaft.

7. Remove the starter drive from the armature shaft.

8. Inspect the teeth on the starter drive. If they are excessively worn, inspect the teeth on the ring gear of the flywheel. If the teeth on the flywheel are excessively worn, the flywheel ring gear should be replaced.

9. Apply a thin coat of white grease to the armature shaft, in the area in which the starter drive operates.

10. Install the starter drive on the armature shaft and install a new stop-ring.

11. Position the starter drive plunger lever on the starter frame and install the pivot pin. *Make sure the plunger lever is properly engaged with the starter drive.*

12. Install a new stop ring retainer on the armature shaft.

13. Fill the drive end housing bearing fore ¼ full with grease.

14. Position the starter drive plunger lever return spring and the drive end housing to the starter frame.

15. Tighten the starter thru-bolts to 55–75 in. lbs.

16. Install the starter drive plunger lever cover and the brush cover band on the starter.

17. Install the starter.

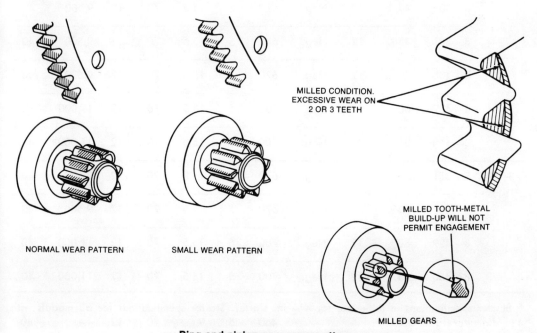

MILLED CONDITION. EXCESSIVE WEAR ON 2 OR 3 TEETH

NORMAL WEAR PATTERN

SMALL WEAR PATTERN

MILLED TOOTH-METAL BUILD-UP WILL NOT PERMIT ENGAGEMENT

MILLED GEARS

Ring and pinion gear wear patterns

Battery and Starter Specifications

Year	Engine No. Cyl Displacement (cu in.)	BATTERY Ampere Hour Capacity	Volts	Terminal Grounded	STARTER Lock Test Amps	Volts	Torque (ft lbs)	No-Load Test Amps	Volts	RPM	Brush Spring Tension (oz)
'68–'70	6	45	12	Neg.	670	5	15.5	70	12	9,500	40
	8—302, 351	55①	12	Neg.	670	5	15.5	70	12	9,500	40
	8—390	45②	12	Neg.	670	5	15.5	70	12	9,500	40
	8—428, 429	80	12	Neg.	700	5	15.5	70	12	11,000	40
'71	6	45③	12	Neg.	670	5	15.5	70	12	9,500	40
	8—302	45③	12	Neg.	670	5	15.5	70	12	9,500	40
	8—351	45②	12	Neg.	670	5	15.5	70	12	9,500	40
	8—390	55①	12	Neg.	670	5	15.5	70	12	9,500	40
	8—400	70④	12	Neg.	700	5	15.5	70	12	11,000	40
	8—429	80	12	Neg.	700	5	15.5	70	12	11,000	40
'72	6	45	12	Neg.	670	5	15.5	70	12	9,500	40
	8—302	45	12	Neg.	670	5	15.5	70	12	9,500	40
	8—351	45②	12	Neg.	670	5	15.5	70	12	9,500	40
	8—400	70④	12	Neg.	670	5	15.5	70	12	9,500	40
	8—429	80	12	Neg.	700	5	15.5	70	12	11,000	40
	8—460	85	12	Neg.	700	5	15.5	70	12	11,000	40
'73–'79	8—351	55②	12	Neg.	670	5	15.5	70	12	9,500	40
	8—400	70④	12	Neg.	670	5	15.5	70	12	9,500	40
	8—429	80	12	Neg.	700	5	15.5	70	12	11,000	40
	8—460	85	12	Neg.	700	5	15.5	70	12	11,000	40

• Starter specifications in table are for 4½ in. starter. Starter specifications for all models with 4 in. diameter starter are: 460   5   9   70   12   —   40

① 70 Amp with air conditioning   ③ 55 Amp with air conditioning
② 70 Amp with air conditioning   ④ 80 Amp with air conditioning

Battery

REMOVAL AND INSTALLATION

1. Loosen the battery cable bolts and spread the ends of the battery cable terminals.

2. Disconnect the negative battery cable first.

3. Disconnect the positive battery cable.

4. Remove the battery hold-down.

5. Wearing heavy gloves, remove the battery from under the hood. *Be careful not to tip the battery and spill acid on yourself or the car during removal.*

6. To install, wearing heavy gloves, place the battery in its holder under the hood. *Use care not to spill the acid.*

7. Install the battery hold-down.

8. Install the positive battery cable first.

9. Install the negative battery cable.

10. Apply a *light* coating of grease to the cable ends.

ENGINE MECHANICAL

A total of 10 different engines have been used in the full size Ford from 1968 to 1979. All of the engines are conventional cast-iron, overhead valve, water-cooled designs using hydraulic valve lifters. They fall into five basic engine families.

A 240 cubic inch six-cylinder engine is used in 1968–72 models. The unit is an inline design, with seven main bearings and timing gears (in lieu of a timing chain and sprockets). Unlike the sixes installed in the smaller Ford products, this six has a detachable intake manifold.

The second engine family includes the 302 and the 351 Windsor V8s. The 302 V8 is used in 1968–72 models and is used again starting in 1978. The 351W V8 is utilized from 1969 to 1974. These small and medium sized V8s are remarkably compact powerplants (the 302 measures a mere 20 in. across) using new thin-wall casting techniques. Both units have wedge-

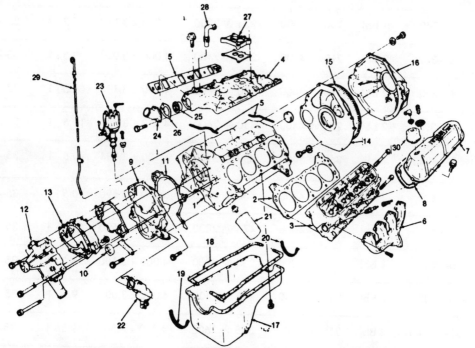

1. Cylinder block	11. Front cover gasket	21. Oil filter
2. Cylinder head gasket	12. Water pump	22. Fuel pump
3. Cylinder head	13. Water pump gasket	23. Distributor
4. Intake manifold	14. Rear cover plate	24. Thermostat housing
5. Intake manifold gasket	15. Flywheel	25. Thermostat
6. Exhaust manifold	16. Flywheel housing	26. Thermostat gasket
7. Valve cover	17. Oil pan	27. Carburetor spacer
8. Valve cover gasket	18. Oil pan gasket	28. Heater hose fitting
9. Front cover	19. Front main seal	29. Dipstick
10. Front cover seal	20. Rear main seal	30. Filler cap

Exploded view of stationary engine components—302, 351 Windsor V8

General Engine Specifications

Year	Engine No. Cyl Displace- ment (cu in.)	Carbu- retor Type	Advertised Horsepower @ rpm ■	Advertised Torque @ rpm (ft lbs) ■	Bore and Stroke (in.)	Advertised Compres- sion Ratio	Oil Pressure @ 2050 rpm
'68	6—240	1 bbl	150 @ 4000	234 @ 2200	4.000 x 3.180	9.2 : 1	35–60
	8—302	2 bbl	210 @ 4400	295 @ 2400	4.000 x 3.000	9.5 : 1	35–60
	8—390	2 bbl	270 @ 4400	390 @ 2600	4.050 x 3.784	9.5 : 1	35–60
	8—390	2 bbl	280 @ 4400	403 @ 2600	4.050 x 3.784	10.5 : 1	35–60
	8—390	4 bbl	315 @ 4600	427 @ 2800	4.050 x 3.784	10.5 : 1	35–60
	8—428	4 bbl	345 @ 4600	462 @ 2800	4.130 x 3.984	10.5 : 1	35–60
	8—428 PI	4 bbl	360 @ 5400	459 @ 3200	4.130 x 3.984	10.5 : 1	35–60
	8—429	4 bbl	360 @ 4600	480 @ 2800	4.360 x 3.590	10.5 : 1	35–60
'69	6—240	1 bbl	150 @ 4000	234 @ 2200	4.000 x 3.180	9.2 : 1	35–60
	8—302	2 bbl	210 @ 4400	295 @ 2400	4.000 x 3.000	9.5 : 1	35–60
	8—390	2 bbl	270 @ 4400	390 @ 2600	4.050 x 3.784	9.5 : 1	35–60
	8—390	2 bbl	280 @ 4400	430 @ 2600	4.050 x 3.784	10.5 : 1	35–60
	8—428 PI	4 bbl	360 @ 5400	459 @ 3200	4.130 x 3.984	10.5 : 1	35–60
	8—429	2 bbl	320 @ 4400	460 @ 2200	4.360 x 3.590	10.5 : 1	35–60
	8—429	4 bbl	360 @ 4600	476 @ 2800	4.360 x 3.590	11.0 : 1	35–60
'70	6—240	1 bbl	150 @ 4000	234 @ 2200	4.000 x 3.180	9.2 : 1	35–60
	8—302	2 bbl	210 @ 4400	295 @ 2400	4.000 x 3.000	9.5 : 1	35–60
	8—351 W	2 bbl	250 @ 4600	355 @ 2600	4.000 x 3.500	9.5 : 1	35–60
	8—390	2 bbl	270 @ 4400	390 @ 2600	4.050 x 3.784	9.5 : 1	35–60
	8—428 PI	4 bbl	360 @ 5400	459 @ 3200	4.130 x 3.984	10.5 : 1	35–60
	8—429	2 bbl	320 @ 4400	460 @ 2200	4.360 x 3.590	10.5 : 1	35–60
	8—429	4 bbl	360 @ 4600	476 @ 2800	4.360 x 3.590	11.0 : 1	35–60

General Engine Specifications (cont.)

Year	Engine No. Cyl Displacement (cu in.)	Carburetor Type	Advertised Horsepower @ rpm ■	Advertised Torque @ rpm (ft lbs) ■	Bore and Stroke (in.)	Advertised Compression Ratio	Oil Pressure @ 2050 rpm
'71	6—240	1 bbl	140 @ 4000	230 @ 2200	4.000 x 3.180	8.9 : 1	35–60
	8—302	2 bbl	210 @ 4600	296 @ 2600	4.000 x 3.000	9.0 : 1	35–60
	8—351 W	2 bbl	240 @ 4600	350 @ 2600	4.000 x 3.500	8.9 : 1	35–60
	8—390	2 bbl	255 @ 4400	376 @ 2600	4.050 x 3.784	9.5 : 1	35–60
	8—400	2 bbl	260 @ 4400	400 @ 2200	4.000 x 4.000	9.0 : 1	50–70
	8—429	2 bbl	320 @ 4400	460 @ 2200	4.360 x 3.590	10.5 : 1	35–75
	8—429	4 bbl	360 @ 4600	480 @ 2800	4.360 x 3.590	10.5 : 1	35–75
	8—429 PI	4 bbl	370 @ 5400	450 @ 3400	4.360 x 3.590	11.0 : 1	35–75
'72	6—240	1 bbl	103 @ 3800	170 @ 2200	4.000 x 3.180	8.5 : 1	35–60
	8—302	2 bbl	140 @ 4000	239 @ 2000	4.000 x 3.000	8.5 : 1	35–60
	8—351 W	2 bbl	153 @ 3800	266 @ 2000	4.000 x 3.500	8.3 : 1	35–60
	8—351 C	2 bbl	163 @ 3800	277 @ 2000	4.000 x 3.500	8.6 : 1	35–60
	8—400	2 bbl	172 @ 4000	298 @ 2200	4.000 x 4.000	8.4 : 1	50–70
	8—429	4 bbl	208 @ 4400	322 @ 2800	4.362 x 3.590	8.5 : 1	35–75
	8—429	4 bbl	212 @ 4400	327 @ 2600	4.362 x 3.590	8.5 : 1	35–75
	8—460	4 bbl	200 @ 4400	326 @ 2800	4.362 x 3.850	8.5 : 1	35–75
	8—460	4 bbl	212 @ 4400	342 @ 2800	4.362 x 3.850	8.5 : 1	35–75
'73	8—351 W	2 bbl	153 @ 3800	266 @ 2000	4.000 x 3.500	8.3 : 1	35–60
	8—351 C	2 bbl	163 @ 3800	277 @ 2000	4.000 x 3.500	8.6 : 1	35–60
	8—400	2 bbl	172 @ 4000	298 @ 2200	4.000 x 4.000	8.4 : 1	50–70
	8—429	4 bbl	208 @ 4400	322 @ 2800	4.362 x 3.590	8.5 : 1	35–75
	8—429	4 bbl	212 @ 4400	327 @ 2600	4.362 x 3.590	8.5 : 1	35–75

General Engine Specifications (cont.)

Year	Engine No. Cyl Displacement (cu in.)	Carburetor Type	Advertised Horsepower @ rpm ■	Advertised Torque @ rpm (ft lbs) ■	Bore and Stroke (in.)	Advertised Compression Ratio	Oil Pressure @ 2050 rpm
	8—460	4 bbl	200 @ 4400	326 @ 2800	4.362 x 3.850	8.5 : 1	35–75
	8—460	4 bbl	212 @ 4400	342 @ 2800	4.362 x 3.850	8.5 : 1	35–75
'74	8—351 W	2 bbl	162 @ 4000	275 @ 2200	4.000 x 3.500	8.2 : 1	45–65
	8—351 C	2 bbl	163 @ 4200	278 @ 2000	4.000 x 3.500	8.0 : 1	45–75
	8—400	2 bbl	170 @ 3400	330 @ 2000	4.000 x 4.000	8.0 : 1	45–75
	8—460	4 bbl	195 @ 3800	335 @ 2600	4.362 x 3.850	8.0 : 1	35–65
	8—460 PI	4 bbl	275 @ 4400	395 @ 2800	4.362 x 3.850	8.8 : 1	25–65
'75	8—351 M	2 bbl	148 @ 3800①	243 @ 2400②	4.000 x 3.500	8.0 : 1	45–75
	8—400	2 bbl	158 @ 3800③	276 @ 2000④	4.000 x 4.000	8.0 : 1	45–75
	8—460	4 bbl	218 @ 4000	369 @ 2600⑤	4.362 x 3.850	8.0 : 1	35–65
	8—460 PI	4 bbl	226 @ 4000	374 @ 2600	4.362 x 3.850	8.0 : 1	35–65
'76–'77	8—351 M	2 bbl	152 @ 3800	274 @ 1600	4.000 x 3.500	8.0 : 1	45–75
	8—400⑥	2 bbl	180 @ 3800	336 @ 1800	4.000 x 4.000	8.0 : 1	45–75
	8—460	4 bbl	202 @ 3800	352 @ 1600	4.362 x 3.850	8.0 : 1	35–65
	8—460 PI	4 bbl	202 @ 3800	352 @ 1600	4.362 x 3.850	8.0 : 1	35–65
'78	8—302	2 bbl	134 @ 3400	248 @ 1600	4.000 x 3.000	8.4 : 1	40–60
	8—351 W	2 bbl	144 @ 3200	277 @ 1600	4.000 x 3.500	8.3 : 1	40–60
	8—351 M	2 bbl	145 @ 3400	273 @ 1800	4.000 x 3.500	8.0 : 1	50–75
	8—400	2 bbl	160 @ 3800	314 @ 1800	4.000 x 4.000	8.0 : 1	50–75
	8—460	4 bbl	202 @ 4000	348 @ 2000	4.362 x 3.850	8.0 : 1	35–65
	8—460 PI	4 bbl	202 @ 3800	352 @ 1600	4.362 x 3.850	8.0 : 1	35–65

General Engine Specifications (cont.)

Year	Engine No. Cyl Displacement (cu in.)	Carburetor Type	Advertised Horsepower @ rpm ■	Advertised Torque @ rpm (ft lbs) ■	Bore and Stroke (in.)	Advertised Compression Ratio	Oil Pressure @ 2050 rpm
'79	8—302	VV	134 @ 3400	248 @ 1600	4.000 x 3.000	8.4 : 1	40–60
	8—351 W	2 bbl	144 @ 3200	277 @ 1600	4.000 x 3.500	8.3 : 1	40–60
	8—351 W Calif.	VV	139 @ 3200	270 @ 1600	4.000 x 3.500	8.3 : 1	40–60

■ Beginning 1972, horsepower and torque are SAE net figures. They are measured at the rear of the transmission with all accessories installed and operating. Since the figures vary when a given engine is installed in different models, some are representative rather than exact.

W Windsor Design
C Cleveland Design
M Modified Cleveland Design
PI Police Intercepter
VV Variable Venturi
① California cars—150 @ 3800 rpm
② California cars—244 @ 2800 rpm
③ California cars—144 @ 3600 rpm
④ California cars—255 @ 2200 rpm
⑤ California cars—367 @ 2600 rpm
⑥ California only—400 cu in. engine equipped with 4 bbl carburetor

Torque Specifications
All readings in ft lbs

Year	Engine No. Cyl Displacement (cu in.)	Cylinder Head Bolts	Rod Bearing Bolts	Main Bearing Bolts	Crankshaft Pulley Bolt	Flywheel to Crankshaft Bolts	MANIFOLD	
							Intake	Exhaust
'68	6—240	70–75	40–45	60–70	130–145	75–85	25	25
	8—302	65–70	19–24	60–70	70–90	75–85	21	15½
	8—390, 428, 429	80–90	40–45	95–105	70–90	75–85	33½	15½
'69	6—240	70–75	40–45	60–70	130–150	75–85	25	25
	8—302	65–72	19–24	60–70	70–90	75–85	24	14
	8—390, 428	80–90	40–45	95–105	70–90	75–85	33½	21
	8—429	130–140	40–45	95–105	70–90	75–85	27½	30½
'70	6—240	70–75	40–45	60–70	130–150	75–85	25	25
	8—302	65–72	19–24	60–70	70–90	75–85	24	14
	8—351	95–100	40–45	95–105	70–90	75–85	23–25	18–24

Torque Specifications (cont.)

All readings in ft lbs

Year	Engine No. Cyl Displacement (cu in.)	Cylinder Head Bolts	Rod Bearing Bolts	Main Bearing Bolts	Crankshaft Pulley Bolt	Flywheel to Crankshaft Bolts	MANIFOLD	
							Intake	Exhau
'70	8—390	80–90	①	95–105	70–90	75–85	32–35	18–24
	8—429	130–140	40–45	95–105	70–90	75–85	27½	30½
'71	6—240	70–75	40–45	60–70	130–150	75–85	25	25
	8—302	65–72	19–24	60–70	70–90	75–85	24	14
	8—351	95–100	40–45	95–105	70–90	75–85	23–25	18–24
	8—390	80–90	40–45	95–105	70–90	75–85	32–35	18–24
	8—400	95–105	40–45	95–105	70–90	75–85	27–33	12–16
	8—429	130–140	40–45	95–105	70–90	75–85	27½	30½
'72	6—240	70–75	40–45	60–70	130–150	75–85	23–28	23–28
	8—302	65–72	19–24	60–70	70–90	75–85	23–25	12–16
	8—351W	105–112	40–45	95–105	100–130	75–85	23–25	18–24
	8—351C, 400	95–105③	40–45④	⑤	70–90	75–85	⑥	12–16
	8—429, 460	130–140	40–45	95–105	70–90	75–85	25–30	28–33
'73–'79	8—351W	105–112	40–45	95–105	100–130	75–85	23–25	18–24
	8—351C, 351M, 400	95–105	40–45	⑤	70–90	75–85	⑥	12–16
	8—429, 460	130–140	40–45	95–105	70–90	75–85	25–30	28–33
	8—302	65–72	19–24	60–70	70–90	75–85	23–25	18–24

① 390—40–45; 428—53–58
  Tighten cylinder head bolts in 3 steps; the first 20 ft lbs less than maximum torque, the second 10 ft lbs less than maximum torque, and the third maximum torque
② 351C engine—12–16
③ 351 HO—120

④ 351 HO—40–45
⑤ ½ x 13 in. bolt—95–105
  ⅜ x 16 in. bolt—35–45
⑥ 5⁄16 in. bolt—21–25
  ⅜ in. bolt—27–23
  ¼ in. bolt—6–9

Valve Specifications

Year	Engine No. Cyl Displacement (cu in.)	Seat Angle (deg)	Face Angle (deg)	Spring Test Pressure (lbs @ in.)	Spring Installed Height (in.)	STEM TO GUIDE Clearance (in.)		Stem Diameter (in.)	
						Intake	Exhaust	Intake	Exhaust
'68	6—240	45	44	197 @ 1.30	$1\frac{11}{16}$	.0010–.0027	.0010–.0027	.3420	.3420
	8—302	45	44	180 @ 1.23	$1\frac{21}{32}$	.0010–.0027	.0015–.0032	.3420	.3415
	8—390	45	44	220 @ 1.38	$1\frac{13}{16}$	.0010–.0024	.0015–.0032	.3715	.3710
	8—427	①	②	268 @ 1.31	$1\frac{13}{16}$	.0010–.0024	.0020–.0034	.3715	.3705
	8—428	45	44	220 @ 1.38	$1\frac{13}{16}$	.0010–.0024	.0015–.0032	.3715	.3710
	8—429	45	44	253 @ 1.33	$1\frac{13}{16}$	.0010–.0027	.0010–.0027	.3420	.3420
'69	6—240	45	44	197 @ 1.30	$1\frac{11}{16}$	.0010–.0027	.0010–.0027	.3420	.3420
	8—302	45	44	180 @ 1.23	$1\frac{21}{32}$	.0010–.0027	.0015–.0032	.3420	.3415
	8—390	45	44	220 @ 1.38	$1\frac{13}{16}$	.0010–.0027	.0015–.0032	.3715	.3710
	8—429	45	44	251 @ 1.33	$1\frac{13}{16}$	.0010–.0027	.0010–.0027	.3420	.3420
'70	6—240	45	44	197 @ 1.30	$1\frac{11}{16}$	.0010–.0027	.0010–.0027	.3420	.3420
	8—302	45	44	180 @ 1.23	$1\frac{21}{32}$	.0010–.0027	.0015–.0032	.3420	.3415
	8—351	45	44	215 @ 1.34	$1\frac{25}{32}$	.0010–.0027	.0010–.0027	.3420	.3415

Valve Specifications (cont.)

Year	Engine No. Cyl Displacement (cu in.)	Seat Angle (deg)	Face Angle (deg)	Spring Test Pressure (lbs @ in.)	Spring Installed Height (in.)	STEM TO GUIDE Clearance (in.) Intake	Exhaust	Stem Diameter (in.) Intake	Exhaust
	8—390	①	44	220 @ 1.38	$1\frac{13}{16}$	.0010–.0027	.0015–.0032	.3715	.3710
	8—429	45	44	253 @ 1.33	$1\frac{13}{16}$	.0010–.0027	.0010–.0027	.3420	.3420
'71	6—240	45	44	197 @ 1.30	$1\frac{11}{16}$	.0010–.0027	.0010–.0027	.3420	.3420
	8—302	45	44	180 @ 1.23	$1\frac{21}{32}$	.0010–.0027	.0015–.0032	.3420	.3415
	8—351③	45	44	215 @ 1.34	$1\frac{25}{32}$	.0010–.0027	.0015–.0032	.3420	.3415
	8—351④	45	44	210 @ 1.42	$1\frac{13}{16}$	.0010–.0027	.0015–.0032	.3420	.3415
	8—390	①	44	220 @ 1.38	$1\frac{13}{16}$	.0010–.0027	.0015–.0032	.3715	.3710
	8—400	45	44	226 @ 1.39	$1\frac{13}{16}$	.0010–.0027	.0015–.0032	.3420	3415
	8—429	45	45	253 @ 1.33	$1\frac{13}{16}$	.0010–.0027	.0015–.0032	.3420	.3415
'72	6—240	45	44	197 @ 1.30	$1\frac{11}{16}$	.0010–.0027	.0010–.0027	.3420	.3420
	8—302	45	44	200 @ 1.31	$1\frac{11}{16}$	.0010–.0027	.0015–.0032	.3420	.3415
	8—351③	45	44	215 @ 1.34	$1\frac{25}{32}$	.0010–.0027	.0015–.0032	.3420	.3415
	8—351④	45	44	210 @ 1.42	$1\frac{13}{16}$	.0010–.0027	.0015–.0032	.3420	.3415

8—400	45	44	226 @ 1.39	1 13/16	.0010–.0027	.0015–.0032	.3420	.3415
8—429	45	45	229 @ 1.33	1 13/16	.0010–.0027	.0010–.0027	.3420	.3420
8—460	45	45	229 @ 1.33	1 13/16	.0010–.0027	.0010–.0027	.3420	.3420
'73–'74 8—351③	45	44	200 @ 1.34	1 25/32	.0010–.0027	.0015–.0032	.3420	.3415
8—351④	45	44	210 @ 142⑤	1 13/16	.0010–.0027	.0015–.0032	.3420	.3415
8—400	45	44	226 @ 1.39	1 13/16	.0010–.0027	.0015–.0032	.3420	.3415
8—429	45	45	229 @ 1.33	1 13/16	.0010–.0027	.0010–.0027	.3420	.3420
8—460	45	45	229 @ 1.33	1 13/16	.0010–.0027	.0010–.0027	.3420	.3420
'75–'77 8—351⑥	45	44	226 @ 1.39	1 13/16	.0010–.0027	.0015–.0032	.3420	.3415
8—400	45	44	226 @ 1.39	1 13/16	.0010–.0027	.0015–.0032	.3420	.3415
8—460	45	45	253 @ 1.33	1 13/16	.0010–.0027	.0010–.0027	.3420	.3420

Valve Specifications (cont.)

Year	Engine No. Cyl Displacement (cu in.)	Seat Angle (deg)	Face Angle (deg)	Spring Test Pressure (lbs @ in.)	Spring Installed Height (in.)	STEM TO GUIDE Clearance (in.) Intake	Exhaust	Stem Diameter (in.) Intake	Exhaust
'78–'79	8—302	45	44	⑦	1 11/16 ⑪	.0010–.0027	.0015–.0032	.3420	.3415
	8—351 W	45	44	⑩	1 13/16 ⑪	.0010–.0027	.0015–.0032	.3420	.3415
	8—351 M	44½–45	45½–45¾	226 @ 1.39	1 13/16	.0010–.0027	.0015–.0032	.3420	.3415
	8—400	44½–45	45½–45¾	226 @ 1.39	1 13/16	.0010–.0027	.0015–.0032	.3420	.3415
	8—460	44½–45	45½–45¾	⑧	1 13/16	.0010–.0027	.0010–.0027	.3420	.3420
	8—460 PI	44½–45	45½–45¾	⑨	1 13/16	.0010–.0027	.0010–.0027	.3420	.3420

① Intake valve seat angle 30°
  Exhaust valve seat angle 45°
② Intake valve face angle 29°
  Exhaust valve face angle 44°
③ Windsor heads
④ Cleveland heads
⑤ 1974 models—226 @ 1.39
⑥ Modified Cleveland heads
⑦ Intake: 200 @ 1.31, Exhaust: 200 @ 1.20
⑧ Intake: 240 @ 1.33, Exhaust: 253 @ 1.33
⑨ Intake: 315 @ 1.32, Exhaust: 315 @ 1.33
⑩ Intake: 200 @ 1.34, Exhaust: 200 @ 1.20
⑪ Exhaust: 1 5/8

Crankshaft and Connecting Rod Specifications

All measurements are given in inches

Year	Engine No. Cyl Displacement (cu in.)	CRANKSHAFT				CONNECTING ROD		
		Main Brg Journal Dia	Main Brg Oil Clearance	Shaft End-Play	Thrust on No.	Journal Diameter	Oil Clearance	Side Clearance
'68	6—240	2.3986–2.3990	.0008–.0024	.004–.008	5	2.1232–2.1246	.0007–.0028	.014–.020
	8—302	2.2486–2.2490	.0005–.0024	.004–.008	3	2.1232–2.1246	.0007–.0028	.014–.020
	8—390, 427, 428, 429	2.7488–2.7492	.0008–.0012	.004–.008	3	2.4384–2.4388	.0007–.0028	.014–.020
'69	6—240	2.3982–2.3990	.0005–.0015	.004–.008	5	2.1228–2.1236	.0008–.0015	.006–.013
	8—302	2.2482–2.2490	.0005–.0015	.004–.008	3	2.1228–2.1236	.0008–.0015	.010–.020
	8—390	2.7484–2.7492	.0013–.0025	.004–.010	3	2.4380–2.4388	.0008–.0015	.010–.020
	8—428	2.7484–2.7492	.0010–.0020	.004–.010	3	2.4380–2.4388	.0020–.0030	.010–.020
	8—429	2.9994–3.0002	.0005–.0015	.004–.008	3	2.4992–2.5000	.0008–.0015	.010–.020
'70	6—240	2.3982–2.3990	.0005–.0015	.004–.008	5	2.1228–2.1236	.0008–.0026	.006–.013
	8—302	2.2482–2.2490	.0005–.0015	.004–.008	3	2.1228–2.1236	.0008–.0026	.010–.020
	8—351	2.9994–2.3002	.0013–.0025	.004–.008	3	2.3103–2.3111	.0008–.0026	.010–.020
	8—390	2.7484–2.7492	.0005–.0025	.004–.008	3	2.4380–2.4388	.0008–.0026	.010–.020

Crankshaft and Connecting Rod Specifications (cont.)

All measurements are given in inches

Year	Engine No. Cyl Displacement (cu in.)	CRANKSHAFT				CONNECTING ROD		
		Main Brg Journal Dia	Main Brg Oil Clearance	Shaft End-Play	Thrust on No.	Journal Diameter	Oil Clearance	Side Clearance
'70	8—428	2.7484-2.7492	.0008-.0020	.004-.008	3	2.4380-2.4388	.0008-.0026	.010-.020
	8—429	2.9994-3.0002	.0005-.0025	.004-.008	3	2.4992-2.5000	.0008-.0026	.010-.020
'71	6—240	2.3982-2.3990	.0005-.0022	.004-.008	5	2.1228-2.1236	.0008-.0026	.006-.013
	8—302	2.2482-2.2490	.0005-.0024①	.004-.008	3	2.1228-2.1236	.0008-.0026	.010-.020
	8—351W	2.9994-3.0002	.0013-.0030	.004-.008	3	2.3103-2.3111	.0008-.0026	.010-.020
	8—351C	2.7484-2.7492	.0009-.0026	.004-.010	3	2.3103-2.3111	.0008-.0026	.010-.020
	8—390	2.7484-2.7492	.0008-.0020	.004-.008	3	2.4380-2.4388	.0010-.0030	.010-.020
	8—400	2.9994-3.0002	.0009-.0026	.004-.010	3	2.3103-2.3111	.0008-.0026	.010-.020
	8—429	2.9994-3.0002	.0005-.0025	.004-.008	3	2.4992-2.5000	.0008-.0028	.010-.020
'72	6—240	2.3982-2.3990	.0005-.0022	.004-.008	5	2.1228-2.1236	.0008-.0026	.006-.013
	8—302	2.2482-2.2490	.0005-.0024①	.004-.008	3	2.1228-2.1236	.0008-.0026	.010-.020
	8—351W	2.9994-3.0002	.0008-.0026	.004-.008	3	2.3103-2.3111	.0008-.0026	.010-.020
	8—351C	2.7484-2.7492	.0011-.0028	.004-.010	3	2.3103-2.3111	.0011-.0026	.010-.020

8—400	2.9994–3.0002	.0011–.0028	.004–.010	3	2.3103–2.3111	.0011–.0026	.010–.020
8—429	2.9994–3.0002	.0010–.0020②	.004–.008	3	2.4992–2.5000	.0008–.0028	.010–.020
8—460	2.9994–3.0002	.0010–.0020②	.004–.008	3	2.4992–2.5000	.0008–.0026	.010–.020
'73–'74 8—351W	2.9994–3.0002	.0008–.0026	.004–.008	3	2.3103–2.3111	.0008–.0026	.010–.020
8—351C	2.7484–2.7492	.0011–.0028	.004–.010	3	2.3103–2.3111	.0011–.0026	.010–.020
8—400	2.9994–3.0002	.0011–.0028	.004–.010	3	2.3103–2.3111	.0011–.0026	.010–.020
8—429	2.9994–3.0002	.0010–.0020②	.004–.008	3	2.4992–2.5000	.0008–.0028	.010–.020
8—460	2.9994–3.0002	.0010–.0020②	.004–.008	3	2.4992–2.5000	.0008–.0026	.010–.020
'75–'77 8—351M	2.9994–3.0002	.0009–.0026	.004–.008	3	2.3103–2.3111	.0008–.0026	.010–.020
8—400	2.9994–3.0002	.0009–.0026	.004–.008	3	2.3103–2.3111	.0008–.0026	.010–.020
8—460	2.9994–3.0002	.0009–.0027③	.004–.008	3	2.4992–2.5000	.0008–.0028	.010–.020
'78–'79 8—302	2.2482–2.2490	.0005–.0015④	.004–.008	3	2.1228–2.1236	.0008–.0015	.010–.020
8—351W	2.9994–3.0002	.0008–.0015	.004–.008	3	2.3103–2.3111	.0008–.0015	.010–.020
8—351M, 400	2.9994–3.0002	.0008–.0015	.004–.008	3	2.3103–2.3111	.0008–.0015	.010–.020
8—460	2.9994–3.0002	.0008–.0015	.004–.008	3	2.4992–2.5000	.0008–.0015	.010–.020

① #1—.0001–.0018
② #1—.010–.015
③ #1 bearing—.0004–.0022 in.
④ #1 bearing—.0001–.0015

Ring Gap

All measurements are given in inches

Year	Engine No. Cyl Displacement (cu in.)	Top Compression	Bottom Compression	Oil Control
1968–79	All	.010–.020	.010–.020	.015–.055①

1. 72–74 351 and 400 is .015–.069

Ring Side Clearance

All measurements are given in inches

Year	Engine	Top Compression	Bottom Compression	Oil Control
1968–1979	All	.002–.004	.002–.004	Snug

Piston Clearance

Year	Engine No. Cyl Displacement (cu in.)	Piston to Bore Clearance (in.)
1968–1979	All All	.0014–①.0022

1. 302 and 351W is .0018–.0026

shaped combustion chambers, individual stud-mounted rocker arms and trapezoidal-shaped valve covers.

The third engine family includes the 351 Cleveland, 351 Modified, and the 400 V8s. The 351C is used on 1972–74 models. The 351M, which is a modified Cleveland design, is used starting in 1975. The 400 V8 is installed in 1971–78 models. This family of engines is based on the smaller 302–351W series, but enjoys a higher volumetric efficiency quotient due to its larger valves and better breathing semi-hemispherical combustion chambers.

The fourth engine family includes the 390 and 428 cubic inch V8s. The 390 V8 may be found in 1968–71 models. The 428 V8 is used in 1968–70 models. These engines are the last examples of the "Y"-block design, first introduced in the mid-fifties. Identifying features of these engines are the shaft-mounted rocker arms, and an intake manifold that extends beneath the valve covers.

The last group of engines includes the 429 and 460 V8s. The 429 V8 is installed in 1969–73 models. The 460 V8 may be found in full size Fords starting in 1974. It was last used in 1978. This family of engines was introduced to replace the old "Y"-block series, and is also based on the smaller 302–351W design. Identifying features of these powerplants are their great bulk and the tunnel-port shaped configuration of the intake manifold.

For a definitive identification of all engines mentioned above, see the "Engine Code" chart in Chapter 1.

Engine Removal and Installation

Before setting out to tear out your engine, and tying up both yourself and your car for a length of time, there are a few preliminary steps that should be taken. Jot down those engine and transmission numbers (see Chapter 1) and make a trip to your parts dealer to order all those gaskets, hoses, belts, filters, etc. (i.e., exhaust manifold-to-head pipe flange gasket[s]) which are in need of replacement. This will help avoid last minute or weekend parts dashes that can tie up a car even longer. Also, have enough oil, antifreeze, transmission fluid, etc. (see "Capacities" chart) on hand for the job.

If the car is still running, have the engine, engine compartment, and underbody steam cleaned, or at least hosed off at one of those coin-operated, do-it-yourself car washes. The less dirt, the better. Have all of the necessary tools together. These should include a sturdy hydraulic jack and a pair of jackstands of sufficient capacity, a chain/pulley engine hoist of sufficient test strength, a wooden block and a small jack

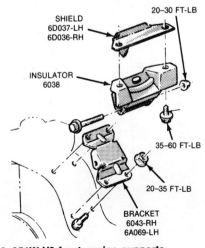

302, 351W V8 front engine supports

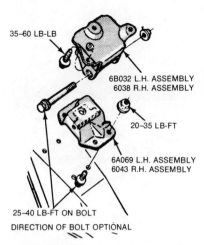

35–60 LB-LB

6B032 L.H. ASSEMBLY
6038 R.H. ASSEMBLY

20–35 LB-FT

6A069 L.H. ASSEMBLY
6043 R.H. ASSEMBLY

25–40 LB-FT ON BOLT
DIRECTION OF BOLT OPTIONAL

351C, 351M, 400 V8 front engine supports

to support the oil pan or transmission, a can of penetrating fluid to help loosen rusty nuts and bolts, a few jars or plastic containers to store and identify used engine hardware, and a punch or bottle of brush paint to matchmark adjacent parts to aid reassembly. Once you have all of your parts, tools, and fluids together, proceed with the task.

ENGINE REMOVAL

1. Scribe the hood hinge outline on the underside of the hood, disconnect the hood and remove.

2. Drain the entire cooling system and the engine oil.

3. Remove the air cleaner, disconnect the battery at the cylinder head. On automatic transmission-equipped cars, disconnect oil cooler lines at the radiator. Label and disconnect all emission control hoses and electrical leads.

4. Remove the upper and lower radiator hoses from the engine and, if the engine is equipped with a fan shroud, disconnect the shroud from the radiator and position it rearward. Remove the radiator from the car.

5. Remove the fan attaching screws and remove the fan, fan spacer and shroud from the engine as an assembly. Loosen and remove all drive belts.

6. Disconnect the heater hoses from the engine. If the vehicle is equipped with power steering, remove the pump from the engine and position it out of the way.

7. Remove the alternator mounting bolts and ground wire from the block and

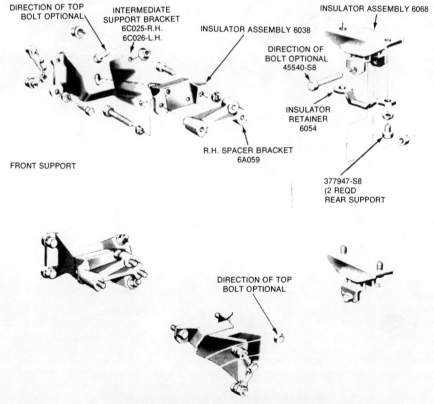

DIRECTION OF TOP
BOLT OPTIONAL

INTERMEDIATE
SUPPORT BRACKET
6C025-R.H.
6C026-L.H.

INSULATOR ASSEMBLY 6038

INSULATOR ASSEMBLY 6068

DIRECTION OF
BOLT OPTIONAL
45540-S8

INSULATOR
RETAINER
6054

FRONT SUPPORT

R.H. SPACER BRACKET
6A059

377947-S8
(2 REQD
REAR SUPPORT

DIRECTION OF TOP
BOLT OPTIONAL

Six-cylinder engine front and rear supports

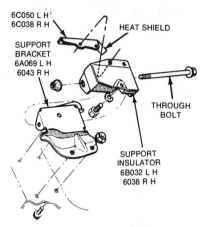

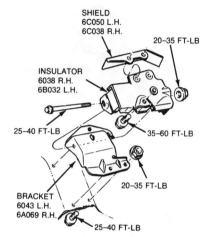

1969–71 429 V8 front engine supports

1973–78 429, 460 V8 front engine supports

remove the alternator. Disconnect the carburetor and kick-down linkage from the engine.

8. On models with power brakes, remove the vacuum line from the engine. On cars with air conditioning, remove the compressor mounting bracket from the engine and position the compressor out of the way without disconnecting the refrigerant lines.

NOTE: *If the compressor lines do not*

have enough slack to move the compressor out of the way without disconnecting the refrigerant lines, the air conditioning system must be evacuated, using the required tools, before the refrigerant lines can be disconnected.

CAUTION: *Evacuating the air conditioning system should be left to an expert.*

9. Disconnect fuel tank line at the fuel pump and plug the line.

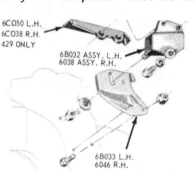

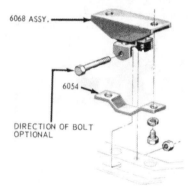

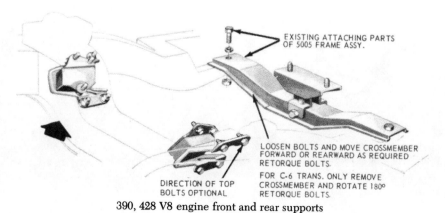

390, 428 V8 engine front and rear supports

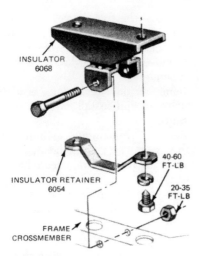

INSULATOR
6068

INSULATOR RETAINER
6054

40-60
FT-LB

20-35
FT-LB

FRAME
CROSSMEMBER

Rear engine support—All V8

10. Disconnect the coil primary wire at the coil. Disconnect wires at the oil pressure and water temperature-sending units.

11. Remove the starter and dust seal.

12. On a car equipped with a manual transmission, remove the clutch retracting spring. Disconnect the clutch equalizer shaft and arm bracket at the underbody rail and remove the arm bracket and equalizer.

13. Raise the car. Install jackstands beneath the frame. Remove the flywheel or converter housing upper retaining bolts through the access holes in the floor pan.

14. Disconnect the exhaust pipe or pipes at the exhaust manifold. Disconnect the right and left motor mount at the underbody bracket. Remove the flywheel or converter housing cover.

15. On a car with manual transmission remove the flywheel housing lower retaining bolts.

16. On a car with automatic transmission, disconnect throttle valve vacuum line at the intake manifold, disconnect the converter from the flywheel. Remove the converter housing lower retaining bolts. On a car with power steering, disconnect power steering pump from cylinder head. Remove the drive belt and wire steering pump out of the way.

17. Lower the car. Support the transmission and flywheel or converter housing with a jack.

18. Attach an engine lifting hook. Lift the engine up and out of the compartment and onto an adequate work stand.

ENGINE INSTALLATION

1. Place a new gasket over the studs of the exhaust manifold/s except on 390 and 428 engines.

2. Attach engine sling and lifting device. Then lift engine from work stand.

3. Lower the engine into the engine compartment. Be sure the exhaust manifold/s properly line up with the muffler inlet pipe/s and the dowels in the block engage the holes in the flywheel housing. On a car with automatic transmission, start the converter pilot into the crankshaft. On a car with manual transmission, start the transmission main drive gear into the clutch disc. If the engine hangs up after the shaft enters, rotate the crankshaft slowly (with transmission in gear) until the shaft and clutch disc splines mesh.

4. Install the flywheel or converter housing upper bolts.

5. Install engine support insulator to bracket retaining nuts. Disconnect engine lifting sling and remove lifting brackets.

6. Raise front of car. Connect exhaust line/s and tighten attachments.

7. Position dust seal and install starter.

8. On cars with manual transmissions, install remaining flywheel housing-to-engine bolts. Connect clutch release rod. Position the clutch equalizer bar and bracket and install retaining bolts. Install clutch pedal retracting spring.

9. On cars with automatic transmissions, remove the retainer holding the converter in the housing. Attach the converter to the flywheel. Install the converter housing inspection cover. Install the remaining converter housing retaining bolts.

10. Remove the support from the transmission and lower the car.

11. Connect engine ground strap and coil primary wire.

12. Connect water temperature gauge wire and the heater hose at coolant outlet housing. Connect accelerator rod at the bellcrank.

13. On cars with automatic transmission, connect the transmission filler tube bracket. Connect the throttle valve vacuum line.

14. On cars with power steering, install the drive belt and power steering pump bracket. Install the bracket retaining bolts. Adjust drive belt to proper tension.

15. Remove plug from the fuel tank line. Connect the flexible fuel line and the oil pressure sending unit wire.

16. Install the pulley, belt spacer, and fan. Adjust belt tension.

17. Install the alternator and the negative battery cable. Connect all emission control hoses and electrical leads disconnected to remove the engine.

18. In vehicles with power brakes, connect vacuum line at intake manifold. On cars with air conditioning, install compressor on mounting bracket.

19. Install radiator. Connect radiator hoses. Fill the cooling system.

20. On cars with automatic transmissions, connect oil cooler lines.

21. Install oil filter. Connect heater hose at water pump, after bleeding the system.

22. Bring crankcase to level with correct grade of oil. Run engine at fast idle and check for leaks. Install air cleaner and make final engine adjustments.

23. Install and adjust hood.

24. Road-test car.

Cylinder Head

REMOVAL AND INSTALLATION

Six-Cylinder

1. Drain coolant and remove air cleaner. Disconnect battery cable at cylinder head.

2. Disconnect exhaust pipe at manifold.

3. Disconnect accelerator retracting spring, choke control cable and accelerator rod at carburetor.

4. Disconnect fuel line and distributor control vacuum line at the carburetor.

5. Disconnect coolant tubes from carburetor spacer. Disconnect coolant and heater hoses.

6. Disconnect distributor control vacuum line at distributor and fuel inlet line at the filter. Remove lines as an assembly.

7. On an engine equipped with positive crankcase ventilation, disconnect the emission exhaust tube.

8. Disconnect spark plug wires at the plugs and the small wire from the temperature-sending unit. On an engine equipped with a Thermactor exhaust emission control system, disconnect the air pump hose at the air manifold assembly. Unscrew the tube nuts and remove the air manifold. Disconnect the anti-backfire valve air and vacuum lines at the intake manifold. On a car equipped with power brakes, disconnect the brake vacuum line at the intake manifold.

9. Remove the rocker arm cover.

10. Loosen the rocker arm stud nut so that the rocker arm can be rotated to one side. Remove valve pushrods and keep them in sequence.

11. Remove one cylinder head bolt from each end and install two $7/16$ in. x 14 guide studs.

12. Remove remaining cylinder head bolts, then remove cylinder head.

13. Prior to installation, clean head and block surfaces.

14. Apply sealer to both sides of head gasket. Position gasket over guide studs or dowel pins.

NOTE: *Apply gasket sealer only to steel shim head gaskets. Steel-asbestos composite head gaskets are to be installed without any sealer.*

15. Install new gasket on the exhaust pipe flange.

16. Lift the cylinder head over the guide studs and slide it carefully into place while guiding the exhaust manifold studs into the exhaust pipe flange.

17. Coat cylinder head attaching bolts with water-resistant sealer and install (but do not tighten), the head bolts.

18. Torque the head, in proper sequence, and in three progressive steps to 75 ft lbs.

19. Lubricate both ends of the pushrods and insert them in their original bores and sockets.

20. Lubricate valve stem tips and rocker arm pads.

21. Position the rocker arms and tighten the stud nuts enough to hold the pushrods in position. Adjust valve lash, as outlined later.

22. Do a preliminary, cold valve lash adjustment.

23. Install exhaust pipe-to-manifold nuts and lockwashers. Torque to 17–22 ft lbs.

24. Connect radiator and heater hoses. Connect coolant tubes at the carburetor spacer.

25. Connect distributor vacuum line and the carburetor fuel line. Connect battery cable to cylinder head.

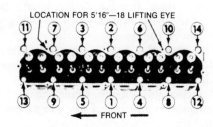

Cylinder head bolt torque sequence—six-cylinder

26. On engines equipped with positive crankcase ventilation, clean components thoroughly and install.

NOTE: *On engines equipped with a Thermactor exhaust emission control system, install the air manifold assembly on the cylinder head. Connect the air pump outlet hose to the air manifold. Connect the anti-backfire valve, air and vacuum lines to the intake manifold.*

27. Connect accelerator rod pull-back spring. Connect choke control cable and the accelerator rod at the carburetor.

28. Connect distributor control vacuum line at distributor. Connect carburetor fuel line at fuel filter.

29. Connect temperature sending unit wire at sending unit. Connect spark plug wires.

30. Completely fill and bleed the cooling system.

31. Run engine for a minimum of 30 minutes at 1,200 rpm to stabilize engine temperature. Then, check for coolant and oil leaks.

32. Adjust engine idle mixture speed. Check vale lash and adjust, if necessary.

33. Install valve rocker arm cover, then the air cleaner.

All V8

1. Drain the cooling system.

2. Remove the intake manifold and the carburetor as an assembly, following the procedures under "Intake Manifold Removal."

3. Disconnect the spark plug wires, marking them as to placement. Position them out of the way of the cylinder head. Remove the spark plugs.

4. Disconnect the resonator or muffler inlet pipe(s) at the exhaust manifold(s).

NOTE: *On some 351 and 400 engines, it may be necessary to remove the exhauust manifolds from the cylinder heads to gain access to the lower head bolts.*

5. Disconnect the battery ground cable at the cylinder head (if applicable).

6. Remove the rocker arm covers.

7. On cars with air conditioning, remove the mounting bolts and the drive belt, and position the compressor out of the way of the cylinder head. Remove the compressor upper mounting bracket from the cylinder head.

CAUTION: *If the compressor refrigerant lines do not have enough slack to permit repositioning of the compressor without first disconnecting the refrigerant lines, the air conditioning system will have to be evacuated by a trained air conditioning serviceman. Under no circumstances should an untrained person attempt to disconnect the air conditioning refrigerant lines.*

8. In order to remove the left cylinder head, on cars equipped with power steering, it may be necessary to remove the steering pump and bracket, remove the drive belt, and wire or tie the pump out of the way, but in such a way as to prevent the loss of its fluid.

9. In order to remove the right head it may be necessary to remove the alternator mounting bracket bolt and spacer, the ignition coil, and the air cleaner inlet duct from the right cylinder head.

10. In order to remove the left cylinder head on a car equipped with a Thermactor exhaust emission control system, disconnect the hose from the air manifold on the left cylinder head.

11. If the right cylinder head is to be removed on a car equipped with a Thermactor exhaust emission control system, remove the Thermactor air pump and its mounting bracket. Disconnect the hose from the air manifold on the right cylinder head.

12. On 390 and 428 engines, unbolt the rocker arm shafts from front to back, two turns at a time, and remove the rocker shaft and arm assembly. On all other V8 engines, loosen the rocker arm stud nuts enough to rotate the rocker arms to one side in order to facilitate the removal of the pushrods. On all V8 engines, remove the pushrods in sequence, so that they may be installed in their original positions. On all V8 engines except the 390 and 428 V8, remove the exhaust valve stem caps.

13. Remove the cylinder head attaching bolts, noting their positions. Lift the cylinder head off the block. Remove and discard the old cylinder head gasket.

14. Prior to installation, clean all surfaces where gaskets are to be installed. These include the cylinder head, intake manifold, rocker arm (valve) cover, and the cylinder block contact surfaces. If water in the crankcase indicates that the head was removed because of a blown head gasket, check the flatness of the cylinder head and engine block surfaces. The method for this checking is outlined in the "Engine Rebuilding" section under "Cylinder Head Reconditioning."

15. Position the new cylinder head gasket over the cylinder dowels on the block. Coat the head bolts with water-resistant sealer.

Position new gaskets on the muffler inlet pipes at the exhaust manifold flange.

16. Position the cylinder head to the block, and install the head bolts, each in its original position. On all engines on which the exhaust manifold has been removed from the head to facilitate removal, it is necessary to properly guide the exhaust manifold studs into the muffler inlet pipe flange when installing the head.

17. Following the cylinder head torque sequence diagrams, step-torque the cylinder head bolts in three stages. First, torque the bolts to 20 ft lbs less than the maximum figure listed in the "Torque Specifications" chart. Second, torque the bolts to 10 ft lbs less than the maximum figure. Finally, torque the bolts to the maximum figure in the chart. At this point, tighten the exhaust manifold-to-cylinder head attaching bolts to specifications.

18. Tighten the nuts on the exhaust manifold studs at the muffler inlet flanges to 18 ft lbs.

19. Clean and inspect the pushrods one at a time. Clean the oil passage within each pushrod with a suitable solvent and blow the passage out with compressed air. Check the ends of the pushrods for nicks, grooves, roughness, or excessive wear. Visually inspect the pushrods for straightness, and replace any bent ones. Do not attempt to straighten pushrods.

20. Install the pushrods in their original positions. Apply Lubriplate or a similar product to the valve stem tips and to the pushrod guides in the cylinder head. Install the exhaust valve stem caps.

21. On 390 and 428 V8 engines, the intake manifold and rocker arm and shaft assemblies must now be installed. When tightening down the rocker arm shaft assembly, make sure that the oil holes face downward, the identification notch faces downward and toward the front (right bank) or toward the rear (left bank), and that the crankshaft damper has the "XX" mark aligned with the pointer. The rocker arms bolts are tightened front to

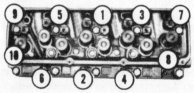

V8 cylinder head bolt torque sequence—351C head shown

rear, two turns at a time, to avoid bending pushrods.

22. On all V8 engines except the 390 and 428, apply white grease to the fulcrum seats and sockets. Turn the rocker arms to their proper positions and tighten the stud nuts enough to hold the rocker arms in position. Make sure that the lower ends of the pushrods have remained properly seated in the valve lifters.

23. On all V8 engines except the 390 and 428, perform a preliminary valve adjustment as described at the end of the "Cylinder Head" section of this chapter.

24. On all V8 engines, apply a coat of oil-resistant sealer to the upper side of the new valve cover gasket. Position the gasket on the valve cover with the cemented side of the gasket facing the valve cover. Install the valve covers and tighten the bolts to 3–5 ft lbs.

25. On all V8 engines except the 390 and 428 V8, install the intake manifold (and carburetor) as outlined under "Intake Manifold Installation."

26. Refer to Steps 7–11 (inclusive) of the "Removal" procedure and reverse the procedures if applicable to your car.

27. Refer to the "Belt Tension Adjustment" procedure in Chapter 1 and adjust all drive belts which were removed.

28. Refill the cooling system.

29. Connect the battery ground cable at the cylinder head (if applicable).

30. Install the spark plugs and connect the spark plug wires.

31. Start the engine and check for leaks.

32. With the engine running, check and adjust the carburetor idle speed and mixture as explained in Chapter 2.

33. With the engine running, listen for abnormal valve noises or irregular idle and correct them.

PRELIMINARY VALVE ADJUSTMENT

All engines used in full-size Ford products, from 1968 to the present, are equipped with hydraulic valve lifters. Valve systems with hydraulic valve lifters operate with zero clearance in the valve train, and because of this the rocker arms are nonadjustable. The only means by which valve system clearances can be altered is by installing 0.060 in. over- or undersize pushrods; but, because of the hydraulic lifter's natural ability to compensate for slack in the valve train, all components of the valve system should be checked for wear if there is excessive play in the system.

When a valve in the engine is in the closed position, the valve lifter is resting on the base circle of the camshaft lobe and the pushrod is in its lowest position. To remove this additional clearance from the valve train, the valve lifter expands to maintain zero clearance in the valve system. When a rocker arm is loosened or removed from the engine, the lifter expands to its fullest travel. When the rocker arm is reinstalled on the engine, the proper valve setting is obtained by tightening the rocker arm to a specified limit. But with the lifter fully expanded, if the camshaft lobe is on a high point it will require excessive torque to compress the lifter and obtain the proper setting. Because of this, when any component of the valve system has been removed, a preliminary valve adjustment procedure must be followed to ensure that when the rocker arm is reinstalled on the engine and tightened, the camshaft lobe for that cylinder is in the low position.

Six-Cylinder

1. Crank the engine until the TDC mark on the crankshaft damper is aligned with timing pointer on the cylinder front cover.
2. Scribe a mark on the damper at this point.
3. Scribe two more marks on the damper, each equally spaced from the first mark (see illustration).

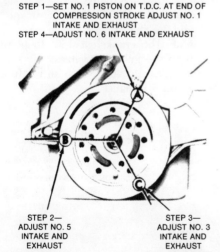

STEP 1—SET NO. 1 PISTON ON T.D.C. AT END OF COMPRESSION STROKE ADJUST NO. 1 INTAKE AND EXHAUST
STEP 4—ADJUST NO. 6 INTAKE AND EXHAUST

STEP 2—
ADJUST NO. 5
INTAKE AND
EXHAUST

STEP 3—
ADJUST NO. 3
INTAKE AND
EXHAUST

STEP 5—
ADJUST NO. 2
INTAKE AND
EXHAUST

STEP 6—
ADJUST NO. 4
INTAKE AND
EXHAUST

Position of crankshaft for preliminary valve adjustment—six-cylinder

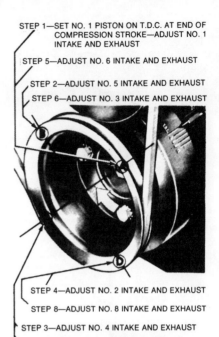

STEP 1—SET NO. 1 PISTON ON T.D.C. AT END OF COMPRESSION STROKE—ADJUST NO. 1 INTAKE AND EXHAUST
STEP 5—ADJUST NO. 6 INTAKE AND EXHAUST
STEP 2—ADJUST NO. 5 INTAKE AND EXHAUST
STEP 6—ADJUST NO. 3 INTAKE AND EXHAUST
STEP 4—ADJUST NO. 2 INTAKE AND EXHAUST
STEP 8—ADJUST NO. 8 INTAKE AND EXHAUST
STEP 3—ADJUST NO. 4 INTAKE AND EXHAUST
STEP 7—ADJUST NO. 7 INTAKE AND EXHAUST

Position of crankshaft for preliminary valve adjustment—1968–69 302 V8 without positive stop rocker arm stud

4. With the engine on TDC of the compression stroke, (mark A aligned with the pointer) back off the rocker arm adjusting nut until there is end-play in the pushrod. Tighten the adjusting nut until all clearance is removed, then tighten the adjusting nut one additional turn on 1969 and later models and ¾ of a turn on all 1968 models. To determine when all clearance is removed from the rocker arm, turn the pushrod with the fingers. When the pushrod can no longer be turned, all clearance has been removed.
5. Repeat this procedure for each valve, turning the crankshaft ⅓ turn to the next mark each time and following the engine firing order of 1-5-3-6-2-4.

1968–69 302 V8

NOTE: *This procedure for the early 302 engine is designed for engines in which the rocker arm mounting studs do not incorporate a positive stop shoulder on the mounting stud. These engines were originally equipped with this kind of stud. However, due to production differences, it is possible some early 302 engines may be encountered that are equipped with positive stop rocker arm mounting studs. Before following this procedure, verify that the rocker arm mounting studs do not incorporate a positive stop shoulder. On studs without a*

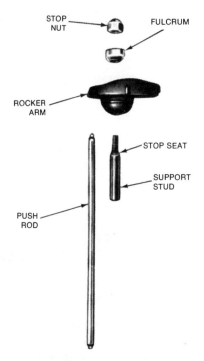

Positive stop rocker arm stud and nut

3. Scribe three more marks on the damper, dividing the damper into quarters (see illustration).

4. With mark A aligned with the timing pointer, adjust the valves on the No. 1 cylinder by backing off the adjusting nut until the pushrod has free play in it. Then, tighten the nut until there is no free play in the rocker arm. This can be determined by turning the pushrod while tightening the nut; when the pushrod can no longer be turned, all clearance has been removed. After the clearance has been removed. After the clearance has been removed, tighten the nut an addition ¾ of a turn.

5. Repeat this procedure for each valve, turning the crankshaft ¼ turn to the next mark each time and following the engine firing order of 1-5-4-2-6-3-7-8.

351, 400, 429, 460, and 1970–72 302 V8

1. Crank the engine until the No. 1 cylinder is at TDC of the compression stroke and the timing pointer is aligned with the mark on the crankshaft damper.

2. Scribe a mark on the damper at this point.

3. Scribe two additional marks on the damper (see illustration).

4. With the timing pointer aligned with mark A on the damper, tighten the following valves to the specified torque:

302, 429, and 460 No. 1, 7 and 8 Intake; No. 1, 5, and 4 Exhaust

351 and 400-No. 1, 4 and 8 Intake; No. 1, 3 and 7 Exhaust

5. Rotate the crankshaft 180° to point B and tighten the following valves:

302, 429, and 460 No. 5 and 4 Intake; No. 2 and 6 Exhaust

positive stop, the shank portion of the stud that is exposed just above the cylinder head is the same diameter as the threaded portion, at the top of the stud, to which the rocker arm retaining nut attaches. If the shank portion of the stud is of greater diameter than the threaded portion, this identifies it as a positive stop rocker arm stud and the procedure for the 351 engine should be followed.

1. Crank the engine until the No. 1 cylinder is at TDC of the compression stroke and the timing pointer is alinged with the mark on the crankshaft damper.

2. Scribe a mark on the damper at this point.

With No. 1 at TDC at end of compression stroke make a chalk mark at points B and C approximately 90 degrees apart.

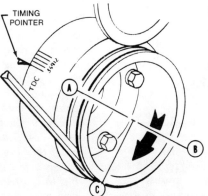

POSITION A – No. 1 at TDC at end of compression stroke.
POSITION B – Rotate the crankshaft 180 degrees (one half revolution) clockwise from POSITION A.
POSITION C – Rotate the crankshaft 270 degrees (three quarter revolution) clockwise from POSITION B.

Position of crankshaft for preliminary valve adjustment—1969–75 302, 351, 400, 429 and 460 V8

351 and 400-No. 3 and 7 Intake; No. 2 and 6 Exhaust

6. Rotate the crankshaft 270° to point C and tighten the following valves:

302, 429, and 460 No. 2, 3, and 6 Intake; No. 7, 3 and 8 Exhaust

351 and 400-No. 2, 5 and 6 Intake; No. 4, 5 and 8 Exhaust

7. Rocker arm tightening specifications are: 302 and 351W—tighten nut until it contacts the rocker shoulder, then torque to 18–20 ft lbs; 351C and 400—tighten bolt to 18–25 ft lbs; 429 and 460—tighten nut until it contacts rocker shoulder, then torque to 18–22 ft lbs.

VALVE GUIDES

Ford Motor Company engines use integral valve guides. Mercury and Ford dealers offer valves with oversize stems for worn guides. To fit these, enlarge valve guide bores with valve guide reamers to an oversize that cleans up wear. If a large oversize is required it is best to approach that size in stages by using a series of reamers of increasing diameter. This helps to maintain the concentricity of the guide bore with the valve seat. The correct valve guide-to-stem clearance is at front of this section. As an alternative, some local automotive machine shops will fit replacement guides that use standard stem valves.

CYLINDER HEAD OVERHAUL

See the "Engine Rebuilding" section at the end of this chapter for all decarbonizing and cylinder head overhaul operations.

NOTE: *When valve guides become worn, the excessive clearance between the valve and the head can allow the valve to tap on the cylinder head and emit a noise very similar to the noise a defective valve lifter emits. When checking the valve system to locate a noise, and the lifters are not defective and no excessive clearances exist in the valve train, the valve guides should be checked for wear.*

Frequently valves become bent or warped, or their seats become blocked with carbon or other material. Left unattended, these situations can cause burnt valves, damaged cylinder heads and other expensive trouble. To detect leaking valves early, perform this test whenever the cylinder head is removed.

1. After removing head, replace spark plugs. Removing spark plugs before removing heads eliminates breakage.

2. Place head on bench with valves, springs, retainers, and keys installed—combustion chambers up.

3. Pour enough non-flammable solvent into each combustion chamber to completely cover both valves. Watch combustion chambers for two minutes for any leakage.

Rocker Arms

390 and 428 V8 engines utilize shaft-mounted rocker arm assemblies. Removal and installation procedures for these rocker arm assemblies are included under the "Cylinder Head Removal and Installation" procedure. Remember that the oil holes must always face downward and that the large rocker shaft retaining bolt is always the second from the front of the engine. In all cases, the torque sequence for the rocker shaft retaining bolts is from the front to the rear of the engine, two turns at a time. Torque the retaining bolts to 40–45 ft lbs.

The 240 six-cylinder and all other V8 engines are equipped with individual stud-mounted rocker arms. Use the following procedure to remove the rocker arms:

1. Disconnect the choke heat chamber air hose, the air cleaner and inlet duct assembly, the choke heat tube, PCV valve and hose and the EGR hoses (if so equipped).

2. On models so equipped, disconnect the Thermactor by-pass valve and air supply hoses.

3. Label and disconnect the spark plug wires at the plugs. Remove the plug wires from the looms.

4. Remove the valve cover attaching bolts and remove the cover(s).

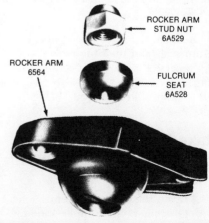

Valve rocker arm and related parts—240 six, 302 V8, 351W V8

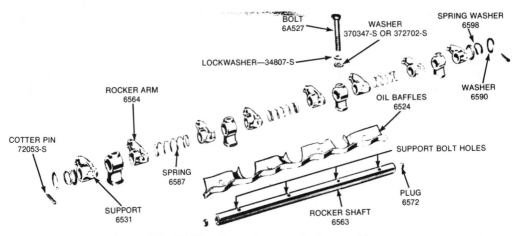

390, 428 V8 valve rocker arm shaft assembly

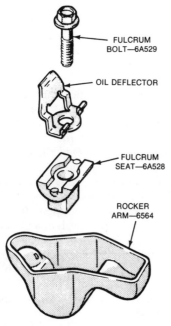

Valve rocker arm and related parts—351C, 351M, 400, 429, 460 V8

5. Remove the valve rocker arm stud nut, fulcrum seat, and then the rocker arm.

6. Reverse the above procedure to install, taking care to adjust the valve lash as outlined under "Preliminary Valve Adjustment."

Intake Manifold

REMOVAL AND INSTALLATION

All V8

1. Drain the cooling system.

2. Disconnect the upper radiator hose and water pump by-pass hose from the thermostat housing. Disconnect the water tem-

perature sending unit wire. Remove the heater hose from the automatic choke housing and disconnect the hose from the intake manifold.

3. Remove the air cleaner. Disconnect the automatic choke heat chamber air inlet hose at the inlet tube near the right valve cover. Remove the crankcase ventilation hose and intake duct assembly. On all models so equipped, disconnect the Thermactor air hose from the check valve at the rear of the intake manifold and loosen the hose clamp at the bracket. Remove the air hose and Thermactor air by-pass valve from the bracket and position it to one side.

4. Remove all carburetor linkage and automatic transmission kick-down linkage that attaches to the manifold. Disconnect the fuel line, choke heat tube, and any vacuum lines from the carburetor or intake manifold, marking them for installation.

5. Disconnect the distributor vacuum hoses from the distributor. Remove the distributor cap and mark the relative position of the rotor on the distributor housing. Disconnect the spark plug wires at the spark plugs and the primary and secondary wires from the coil. Remove the distributor hold-down bolt and remove the distributor.

6. If equipped with air conditioning, remove the brackets retaining the compressor to the intake manifold.

7. On 390 and 428 engines, remove the valve covers the rocker arm assemblies and the pushrods. The rocker arms should be removed by backing off each of the four bolts two turns at a time, from front to back. Keep the pushrods in order so that they can be installed in their original positions.

8. Remove the manifold attaching bolts.

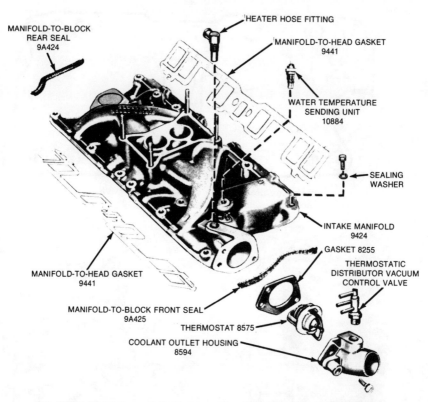

302, 351W V8 intake manifold assembly—390, 428, 429, 460 V8 similar

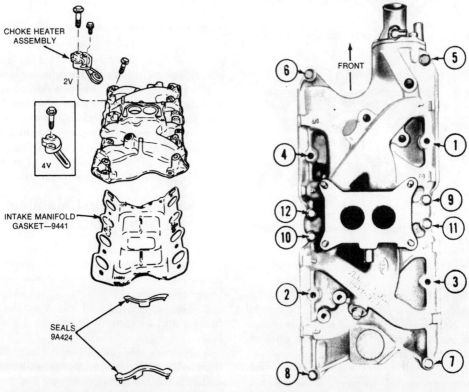

351C, 351M, 400 V8 intake manifold assembly

Intake manifold torque sequence—302 V8

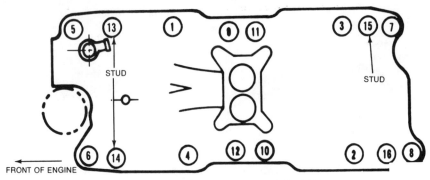

Intake manifold torque sequence—351W V8

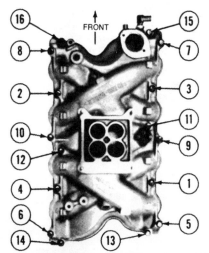

Intake manifold torque sequence—429, 460 V8

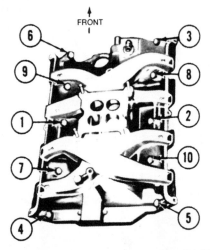

Intake manifold torque sequence—390, 428 V8

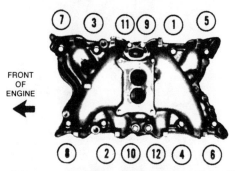

Intake manifold torque sequence—351C, 351M, 400 V8

Lift off the intake manifold and carburetor as an assembly.

NOTE: *If it is necessary to pry the manifold to loosen it from the engine, be careful not to damage any gasket sealing surfaces. Always discard all old gaskets and attaching bolt sealing washers.*

9. Clean all gasket surfaces and firmly cement new gaskets in place, using non-hardening sealer. Make sure that the gaskets interlock with the seal tabs, and that the gasket holes align with those in the cylinder heads.

10. Reverse the above procedure to install, taking care to run a finger around the seal area on the installed manifold to make sure that the seals did not slip out during installation. Finally, torque the intake manifold bolts in the proper sequence, and recheck the torque after the engine is warm.

Intake and Exhaust Manifold

REMOVAL AND INSTALLATION

Six-Cylinder

1. Remove the air cleaner. Remove the carburetor linkage and kick down linkage from the engine.

2. Disconnect the fuel line from the carburetor and all vacuum lines from the manifolds.

3. Remove the negative battery cable, then remove the alternator mounting bolts and remove the alternator from the engine with the wires attached.

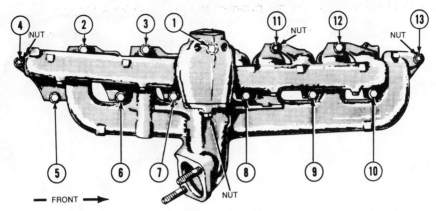

Intake and exhaust manifold torque sequence—six cylinder

4. Disconnect the muffler inlet pipe from the engine.

5. Remove the manifold attaching parts from the engine, and remove the two manifolds as an assembly.

6. To separate the manifolds, remove the carburetor and then remove the nuts which secure the manifolds together.

7. Clean all gasket areas and reverse above procedure to install; using all new gaskets. Torque to specifications listed in the "Torque Specifications" chart.

Exhaust Manifold

REMOVAL AND INSTALLATION

All V8

1. On the right exhaust manifold, remove the air cleaner and intake duct assembly.

2. Disconnect the automatic choke heat chamber air inlet hose from the inlet tube near the right valve cover. Remove the automatic choke heat tube.

3. Remove the nuts or bolts retaining the heat stove to the exhaust manifold and remove the stove.

4. Disconnect the exhaust manifold(s) from the muffler inlet pipe(s).

5. Remove the manifold retaining bolts and washers and the manifold(s).

6. Reverse the above procedure to install, using new inlet pipe gaskets. Torque the exhaust manifold retaining bolts to specifications, in sequence from the centermost bolt outward. Start the engine and check for exhaust leaks.

Timing Gear Cover

REMOVAL AND INSTALLATION

Six-Cylinder

1. Drain the cooling system and the crankcase.

2. Remove the radiator from the car.

3. Loosen and remove all engine drive belts.

4. On vehicles with power steering, disconnect the pump mounting bracket from the cylinder front cover and position the pump and bracket out of the way.

5. On models with air conditioning, remove the condenser mounting bolts and position the condenser out of the way. *Do not disconnect the refrigerant lines.*

6. Disconnect and remove the fan and fan spacer.

7. Remove any accessory drive pulleys from the crankshaft damper. Remove the capscrew and washer from the crankshaft end; then, using a puller, remove the crankshaft damper.

8. Remove the alternator adjusting arm bolt and position the arm out of the way. Remove the dipstick.

9. Remove the bolts retaining the timing cover to the block. Remove the front cover and accessory drive belt idler pulley assembly (if so equipped), and discard the gasket.

10. Reverse the above procedure to in-

TOOL—T64T-6316-A

TOOL—T58P-6316-B OR -A

Removing crankshaft damper—six-cylinder and 390, 428 V8

stall, using a new gasket. Torque the timing cover bolts to 15–20 ft lbs.

Timing Gear Cover and Chain
REMOVAL AND INSTALLATION
All V8

1. Drain the cooling system and crankcase.

2. Disconnect the negative battery cable.

3. If equipped with a fan shroud, disconnect it from the radiator and position it rearward.

4. Remove the radiator. Remove the fuel pump.

5. Remove the fan attaching bolts, remove the fan, fan spacer and shroud from the engine.

6. Loosen and remove all engine drive belts.

7. Remove the power steering pump mounting bracket and position the pump and bracket out of the way.

8. If equipped with air conditioning, remove the compressor and condenser and position them out of the way. *Do not disconnect the refrigerant lines.*

9. Disconnect the alternator adjusting arm from the engine and position it out of the way.

10. If equipped with Thermactor, remove the pump from the engine.

11. Disconnect the heater hose and by-pass hose from the water pump.

12. Remove any accessory drive pulleys from the crankshaft damper and remove the crankshaft front bolt and washer.

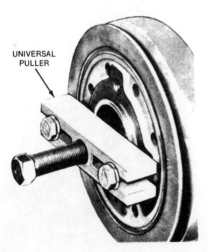

UNIVERSAL PULLER

Removing crankshaft damper—V8 except 390, 428 V8

TIMING MARKS

Aligning timing marks—all V8

13. Using a puller, remove the crankshaft damper from the engine.

14. On 390 and 428 V8, use a suitable tool to pull the crankshaft sleeve away from the cylinder front cover. Remove the sleeve from the engine.

15. Remove the front cover attaching bolts and the front oil pan bolts.

16. Remove the cover from the engine.

17. Remove the crankshaft front oil slinger.

18. To check timing chain free-play, rotate the crankshaft in a clockwise direction until all slack is removed from the left-side of the chain. Scribe a mark on the engine parallel to the present position of the chain. Next, rotate the crankshaft in a counterclockwise direction to remove all the slack from the right-side of the chain. Force the left-side of the chain outward with the fingers and measure the distance between the present position of the chain and the reference mark on the engine. If the distance exceeds ½ in., replace the chain and sprockets.

19. To replace the chain and sprockets, crank the engine until the timing marks are aligned as shown in the illustration.

20. Remove the camshaft sprocket attaching bolt and remove the chain and sprockets from the engine by sliding them forward as an assembly.

TOOL—T52L-6306-AEE or 6306-AJ

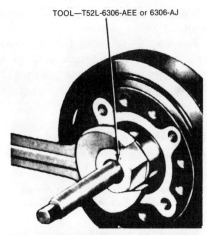

Installing crankshaft damper—all engines

FUEL PUMP ECCENTRIC   DOWEL

CRANKSHAFT FRONT OIL SLINGER

Fuel pump eccentric and front oil slinger installed—all V8 except 390, 428 V8

21. To install, position the chain and sprockets on the engine, making sure that the timing marks on the sprockets are aligned.

22. Clean all gasket surfaces. Trim away the exposed portion of the oil pan gasket flush with the front of the block.

23. Cut and position the required portion of a new gasket to the oil pan, applying sealer to both sides of it.

24. Reinstall the front cover, applying oil-resistant sealer to the new gasket.

25. Install the components that were removed from the engine by reversing the removal procedure.

Timing Gear and Camshaft

REMOVAL AND INSTALLATION

Six-Cylinder

1. Remove the timing case cover.

2. Mark the location of the grille center support and hood lock assembly in relation to the radiator support. Remove the grille, center support, and hood lock as an assembly.

3. Remove the air cleaner and valve cover.

4. Disconnect the fuel pump outlet line and remove the fuel pump from the engine.

5. Loosen the rocker arm nuts and position the rocker arms to the side so the pushrods can be removed. Keep the pushrods in order so that they can be returned to their original location in the engine.

6. Remove the pushrod cover from the side of the engine, and, using a magnet, remove the lifters from their bores. Keep the lifters in order so that they can be returned to their original location in the engine.

7. Rotate the engine until the timing marks are aligned on the timing gears.

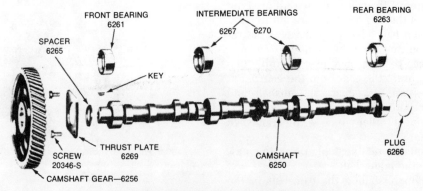

Six-cylinder camshaft and related parts

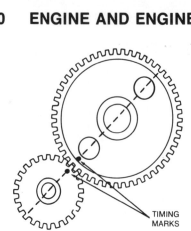

Aligning timing marks—six-cylinder

TOOL—T64T-6306-A

TOOL—T65L-6306-A
Installing camshaft timing gear

TIMING MARKS

TOOL—T52L-6316-FEE
OR 6316-FF
Removing crankshaft timing gear

8. Remove the camshaft thrust plate screws.

9. Remove the camshaft by pulling it out the front of the engine. Use care not to damage the camshaft lobes or journals while removing the cam from the engine.

10. Place the camshaft/gear assembly in a press and press the cam from the gear.

11. Position new gear on camshaft and press into position.

12. Using a puller, remove the crankshaft timing gear.

13. Using a suitable tool, press the new gear onto the crankshaft.

14. Before installing the camshaft in the engine, coat the lobes with lubriplate and the

journals and all valve train components with heavy oil.

15. Reverse above procedure to install, following recommended torque settings and performing preliminary valve adjustment before starting engine.

Camshaft

REMOVAL AND INSTALLATION

All V8

1. Remove the intake manifold.

2. Remove the cylinder front cover, timing chain and sprockets as outlined previously.

3. Remove the rocker arm covers.

4. On 390 and 428 engines it is necessary

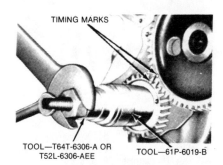

CAMSHAFT THRUST PLATE

CAMSHAFT GEAR   SCREW
Camshaft thrust plate screw locations—six-cylinder

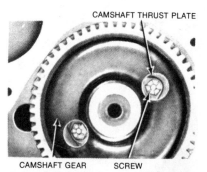

TIMING MARKS

TOOL—T64T-6306-A OR
T52L-6306-AEE   TOOL—61P-6019-B
Installing crankshaft timing gear

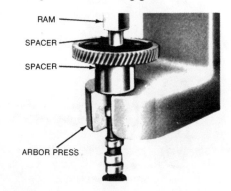

RAM

SPACER

SPACER

ARBOR PRESS

Removing camshaft from gear in press

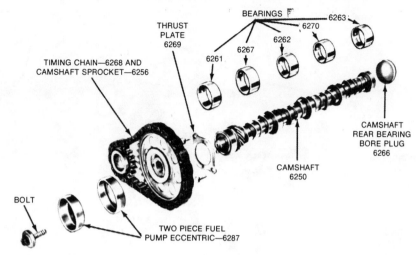

BEARINGS

6263

6270

THRUST
PLATE
6269

6262

6267

TIMING CHAIN—6268 AND
CAMSHAFT SPROCKET—6256

6261

CAMSHAFT
REAR BEARING
BORE PLUG
6266

CAMSHAFT
6250

BOLT

TWO PIECE FUEL
PUMP ECCENTRIC—6287

V8 camshaft and related parts—351C, 351M, 400 V8 shown; others similar

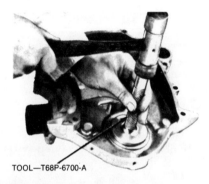

TOOL—T68P-6700-A

Installing front oil seal

to remove the rocker arm shafts to remove the intake manifold. On all other engines with individual rocker arms, loosen the rocker arm fulcrum bolts and rotate the rocker arms to the side.

5. Remove the pushrods and lifters and keep them in order so that they can be installed in their original location.

6. Remove the camshaft thrust plate and washer if so equipped. Remove the camshaft from the front of the engine. On certain engine/chassis combinations it may be necessary to remove the grille to gain adequate clearance to remove the camshaft. Use care not to damage the camshaft lobes or journals while removing the cam from the engine.

7. Before installing the camshaft in the engine, coat the lobes with lubriplate and the journals and all valve train components with heavy oil.

8. Reverse above procedure to install.

9. On all engines with individually mounted rocker arms, a preliminary valve

adjustment must be performed before starting the engine.

TIMING GEAR COVER OIL SEAL REPLACEMENT

All Engines

It is a recommended procedure to replace the cover seal any time that the timing (front) cover is removed.

1. With the cover removed from the engine, drive the old seal from the rear of the cover with a pin punch. Clean out the recess in the cover.

2. Coat the new seal with grease (to ease installation) and drive it into the cover until it is fully seated. Check the seal after installation to be sure that the spring is properly positioned in the seal.

Pistons and Connecting Rods

REMOVAL AND INSTALLATION

1. Drain crankcase and remove oil pan. Remove oil baffle tray if so equipped.

2. Drain cooling system and remove cylinder head or heads.

3. Remove any ridge and/or deposits from the upper end of cylinder bores with a ridge reamer.

4. Check rods and pistons for identification numbers and, if necessary, number them.

5. Remove connecting rod capnuts and caps. Push the rods away from the crankshaft and install caps and nuts loosely to their respective rods.

6. Push pistons and rod assemblies up and out of the cylinders.

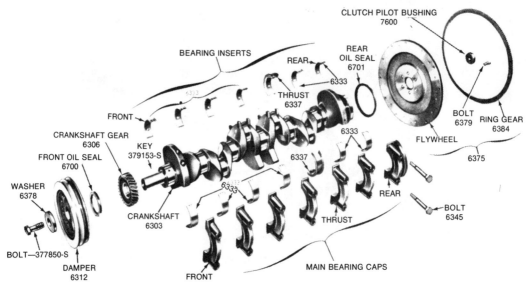

Crankshaft and related parts—six-cylinder

7. Prior to installation, lightly coat pistons, rings and cylinder walls with light engine oil.

8. With bearing caps removed, install pieces of protective rubber hose on bearing cap bolts.

9. Install each piston in its respective bore, using thread guards on each assembly.

Guide the rod bearing into place on the crankcase journal.

10. Remove thread guards from connecting rods and install lower half of bearing and cap. Check clearances.

11. Install oil pan.

12. Install cylinder head.

13. Refill crankcase and cooling system.

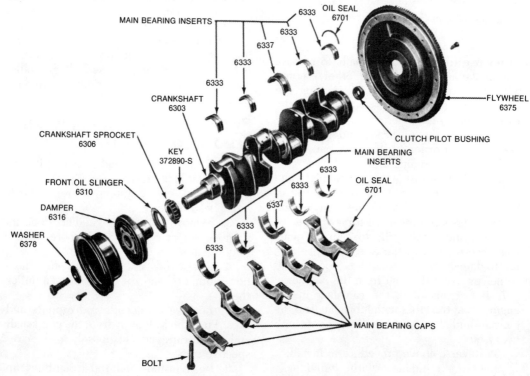

Crankshaft and related parts—351C, 351M, 400 V8 shown; others similar

14. Start engine, bring to operating temperature and check for leaks.

PISTON RING REPLACEMENT

Before replacing rings, inspect cylinder bores.

1. If cylinder bore is in satisfactory condition, place each ring in bore in turn and square it in bore with head of piston. Measure ring gap. If ring gap is greater than limit, get new ring. If ring gap is less than limit, file end of ring to obtain correct gap.

2. Check ring side clearance by installing rings on piston, and inserting feeler gauge to correct dimension between ring and lower land. Gauge should slide freely around ring circumference without binding. Any wear will form a step on lower land. Replace any pistons having high steps. Before checking ring side clearance be sure ring grooves are clean and free of carbon, sludge, or grit.

3. Space ring gaps at equidistant intervals around piston circumference. Be sure to install piston in its original bore. Install short lengths of rubber tubing over connecting rod bolts to prevent damage to rod journal. Install ring compressor over rings on piston. Lower piston rod assembly into bore until

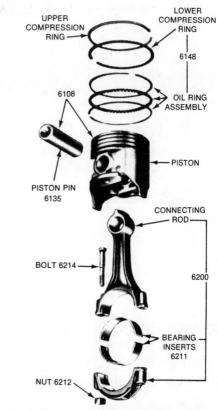

Typical piston, connecting rod and related parts

Piston and Connecting Rod Positioning

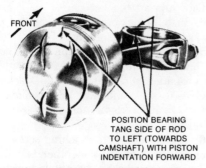

Correct piston and rod position—six-cylinder

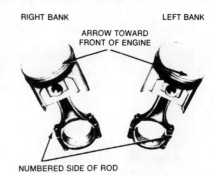

Correct piston and rod position—351C, 351M, 400 V8

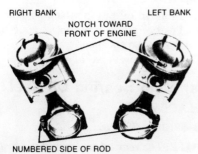

Correct piston and rod position—302, 351W, 429 and 460 V8

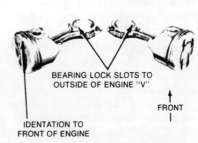

Correct piston and rod position—390, 428 V8

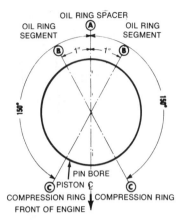

Piston ring spacing

ring compressor contacts block. Using wooden handle of hammer, pushpiston into bore while guiding rod onto journal.

ENGINE LUBRICATION

Oil Pan

REMOVAL AND INSTALLATION

Six-Cylinder

1. Drain crankcase and cooling system.

2. Disconnect upper hose at outlet elbow and lower hose at radiator. Remove the radiator.

3. Disconnect flexible fuel line at fuel pump.

4. With automatic transmission, disconnect kick-down rod at bellcrank assembly. On car with manual transmission, disconnect clutch linkage.

5. Raise car on hoist.

6. Disconnect starter cable at starter. Remove retaining bolts and remove starter.

7. Remove nuts on both engine front support insulator-to-support brackets.

8. Remove bolt and insulator, rear support insulator-to-crossmember and insulator-to-transmission extension housing.

9. Raise transmission, remove support insulator, lower transmission to crossmember.

10. Raise engine with transmission jack and place 3 in. thick wood blocks between both front support insulators and intermediate support brackets.

11. Remove oil pan retaining bolts and oil pump mounting bolts. With oil pump in pan, rotate crankshaft as needed to remove pan.

12. Install in reverse of above.

1968–69 302, 351 V8

1. Remove oil level dipstick. Drain oil pan.

2. Disconnect stabilizer bar from lower control arms, and pull ends down.

3. Remove oil pan attaching bolts and position pan on front crossmember.

4. Remove one oil inlet tube bolt and loosen the other to position tube out of way to remove pan.

5. Turn crankshaft as required for clearance to remove pan.

6. Install in reverse of above.

All 390, 428, 400, 429, 460 V8, 1970–79 302, 351 V8

1. Raise car and place safety stands in position. Drain oil from crankcase. On 429 V8s, disconnect the negative battery cable. On 1970–71 429 V8s, remove bolt attaching vacuum line retaining clip to upper right side of converter housing.

2. Disconnect stabilizer bar links and pull ends down. On models equipped with a fan shroud, remove the shroud from the radiator and position it rearward over the fan. On automatic transmission equipped cars, position oil cooler lines aside.

3. Remove nuts and lockwashers from engine front support insulator-to-intermediate support bracket.

4. Install block of wook on jack and position jack under leading edge of pan.

5. Raise engine approximately 1¼ in. and insert a 1 in. block between insulators and crossmember. Remove floor jack. On 351C, 400, 429, and 460 V8s, remove the starter. On 1972–78 429 and 460 V8s remove the oil filter.

6. Remove oil pan attaching screws and lower pan to frame crossmember.

7. Turn crankshaft to obtain clearance between crankshaft counterweight and rear of pan.

8. Remove oil pump attaching bolts.

9. Position tube and screen out of the way and remove the pan.

10. Install in reverse of above.

Rear Main Bearing Oil Seal

REPLACEMENT

1968–69 302, 351 V8

NOTE: *The rear oil seal originally installed in these engines is a rope (fabric) type seal. However, all service replacements are of the rubber type. To remove the rope type seal and install the rubber type, the following procedure is used.*

1. Drain the crankcase and remove the oil pan.

2. Remove the lower half of the rear main bearing cap and, after removing the old seal from the cap, drive out the pin in the bottom of the seal groove with a punch.

3. Loosen all main bearing caps and allow the crankshaft to lower slightly.

NOTE: *The crankshaft should not be allowed to drop more than* $1/32$ *in.*

4. With a 6 in. length of $3/16$ in. brazing rod, drive up on either exposed end of the top half of the oil seal. When the opposite end of the seal starts to protrude, have a helper grasp it with pliers and gently pull while the driven end is being tapped.

5. After removing both halves of the rope seal and the retaining pin from the lower half of the bearing cap, follow Steps 4 through 10 of the following procedure for 1970–76 engines to install the rubber seal.

1968–69 390, 428, 429 V8 and all 1970–79 Engines

NOTE: *The rear oil seal installed in these engines is a rubber type seal.*

1. Loosen all main bearing cap bolts, lowering crankshaft slightly but not more than $1/32$ in.

2. Remove rear main cap, and remove upper and lower halves of seal. On block half of seal, use seal removing tool or insert a small metal screw into end of seal with which to draw it out.

3. Clean seal grooves with solvent and dip replacement seal in clean engine oil.

4. Install upper seal half in its groove in block with lip toward front of engine by rotating it on seal journal of crankshaft until approximately $3/8$ in. protrudes below parting surface.

5. Tighten other main caps and torque to specification.

6. Install lower seal half in rear main cap with lip to front and approximately $3/8$ in. of seal proturdes to mate with upper seal.

7. Install rear main cap and torque.

8. Dip side seals in engine oil and install them. Tap seals in last half inch if necessary. Do not cut protruding ends of seals.

1968–69 Six-Cylinder

If the rear main bearing oil seal is the only operation involved, it can be replaced in the car according to the following procedure.

NOTE: *If the oil seal is being replaced in conjunction with a rear main bearing replacement, the enine must be removed from the car.*

1. Remove the starter.

2. On cars equipped with automatic transmissions, remove the transmission. On cars equipped with manual transmissions, re-

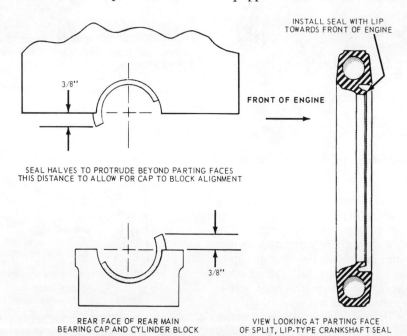

SEAL HALVES TO PROTRUDE BEYOND PARTING FACES
THIS DISTANCE TO ALLOW FOR CAP TO BLOCK ALIGNMENT

INSTALL SEAL WITH LIP
TOWARDS FRONT OF ENGINE

FRONT OF ENGINE

REAR FACE OF REAR MAIN
BEARING CAP AND CYLINDER BLOCK

VIEW LOOKING AT PARTING FACE
OF SPLIT, LIP-TYPE CRANKSHAFT SEAL

Installing split-type rubber rear oil seal

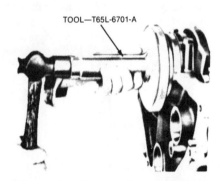

FROM FORWARD FACE OF SLINGER GROOVE TO REAR FACE OF BLOCK

REAR FACE OF BLOCK

APPLY 1/16" DIA. BEAD OF C3AZ-19562-A, B (OR EQUIVALENT) SEALER IN SHADED AREA OF CYLINDER BLOCK PRIOR TO ASSEMBLY OF BEARING CAP - (BOTH SIDES) DO NOT PERMIT SEALER TO GET ON I.D. OF SPLIT LIP SEAL

APPLY 1/16" DIA. BEAD OF C3AZ-19562-A, B (OR EQUIVALENT) SEALER AS INDICATED ON BEARING CAP - (BOTH SIDES)

LEAVE 1/8" GAP FOR SEALER EXPANSION

NOTE: CLEAN SURFACES PRIOR TO APPLICATION OF SEALER. USE FORD SPOT REMOVER. B7A-19521-A, OR EQUIVALENT.

Applying silicone sealer to rear main bearing cap and block

TOOL—T65L-6701-A

Installing crankshaft rear oil seal—1968–69 six-cylinder

move the transmission, clutch, flywheel and engine rear cover plate.

3. With an awl, punch holes in the main bearing oil seal, on opposite sides of the crankshaft and just above the bearing cap to cylinder block split line. Insert a sheet metal screw in each hole. With two large screwdrivers, pry the oil seal out.

4. Clean the oil recess in the cylinder block, main bearing cap and the crankshaft sealing surface.

5. Lubricate the entire oil seal. Then, install and drive the seal into its seat 0.005 in. below the face of the cylinder block with Ford tool T-65L-6701-A, or a socket of the proper diameter.

6. The remaining procedure is the reverse of removal.

Oil Pump

REMOVAL AND INSTALLATION

1. Remove the oil pan as outlined under the previous applicable "Oil Pan Removal and Installation" procedure.

2. On 302 and 351W V8 applications, remove the oil pump inlet tube and screen assembly.

3. Remove the oil pump attaching bolts,

OIL PUMP

OIL PUMP SCREEN

INLET TUBE

Typical oil pump and inlet tube installed—390, 428 V8 shown

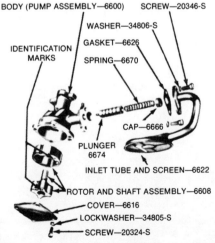

BODY (PUMP ASSEMBLY—6600)   SCREW—20346-S

WASHER—34806-S

IDENTIFICATION MARKS

GASKET—6626

SPRING—6670

CAP—6666

PLUNGER 6674

INLET TUBE AND SCREEN—6622

ROTOR AND SHAFT ASSEMBLY—6608

COVER—6616

LOCKWASHER—34805-S

SCREW—20324-S

Typical oil pump disassembled—six-cylinder shown

Lower the oil pump, gasket, and intermediate driveshaft from the crankcase. If not already removed, remove and clean the inlet tube and screen assembly.

4. To install, prime the oil pump by filling either the inlet or outlet port with engine oil. Rotate the pump shaft to distribute the oil within the pump body.

5. Position the intermediate driveshaft into the distributor socket. With the shaft firmly seated in the socket, the stop on the shaft should contact the roof of the crankcase. Remove the shaft and position the stop as necessary.

6. Insert the intermediate driveshaft into the oil pump. Using a new gasket, install the pump and shaft as an assembly. Do not attempt to force the pump into position if it will not seat readily. If necesary, rotate the intermediate driveshaft hex into a new position so that it will mesh with the distributor shaft.

7. Torque the oil pump attaching bolts to 12–15 ft lbs on the six-cylinder engines, 22–32 ft lbs on the 302 and 351 W V8, 25–35 ft lbs on the 351C, 351M and 400 V8, and 20–25 ft lbs on the 390, 428, 429, and 460 V8.

8. Clean and install the inlet tube and screen assembly.

9. Install the oil pan as previously outlined under "Oil Pan Removal and Installation."

ENGINE COOLING

All Ford engines are water-cooled by a solution of water and ethylene glycol antifreeze. In addition to the freeze protection properties of the antifreeze solution, the solution has a higher boiling point than plain water, thereby preventing overheating in many cases, and contains anticorrosion and water pump lubrication additives.

The coolant circulates via the rotating motion of the water pump. It passes from the radiator, through the lower radiator hose, past the water pump, through the cooling passages of the engine, past the thermostat (if open), through the upper radiator hose and back into the radiator. As the hot coolant passes through the radiator, outside air is drawn through the radiator cooling fins by the engine fan. Heat is exchanged prior to the coolant's recirculation through the engine. Heat is supplied to the car's interior by by-passing a portion of the coolant through the heater core.

When the engine is cold, the thermostat, located in a housing between the top of the engine and the upper radiator hose, is closed and prevents the coolant from passing into the radiator. This causes the coolant in the engine to heat quickly, thereby shortening the time needed for the engine to reach its normal operating temperature. When the coolant reaches a predetermined temperature, the thermostat opens and the normal cooling cycle resumes.

Later models are equipped with a coolant recovery or constant full system. These systems use a plastic recovery reservoir and a non-vented radiator cap to contain coolant expansion. When adding coolant to these systems, add coolant to the reservoir only, not the radiator.

On models equipped with automatic transmission, the lower section (down-flow) or left-side (crossflow) of the radiator contains an automatic transmission fluid cooler. Oil from the transmission is transported by a pair of metal hydraulic lines, under pressure, to the radiator's bottom (or left) section, where it is cooled.

Radiator

Removal and Installation

1. Drain the cooling system.

2. Disconnect the upper and lower hoses at the radiator.

3. On cars with automatic transmissions, disconnect the oil cooler lines at the radiator.

4. On vehicles with a fan shroud, remove the shroud retaining screws and position the shroud out of the way.

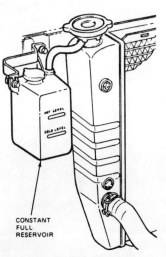

CONSTANT
FULL
RESERVOIR

Constant-full cooling system

5. Remove the radiator attaching bolts and lift out the radiator.

6. If a new radiator is to be installed, transfer the petcock from the old radiator to the new one. On cars with automatic transmissions, transfer the oil cooler line fittings from the old radiator to the new one.

7. Position the radiator and install, but do not tighten, the radiator support bolts. On cars with automatic transmissions, connect the oil cooler lines. Then tighten the radiator support bolts.

8. On vehicles with a fan shroud, reinstall the shroud.

9. Connect the radiator hoses. Close the radiator petcock. Then fill and bleed the cooling system.

10. Start the engine and bring to operating temperature. Check for leaks.

11. On cars with automatic transmissions, check the cooler lines for leaks and interference. Check the transmission fluid level.

Water Pump

REMOVAL AND INSTALLATION

1. Drain the cooling system.

2. On 351C, 351M, and 400 V8 engines, disconnect the negative battery cable.

3. If equipped with a fan shroud, remove the shroud attaching bolts and position the shroud over the fan.

4. Remove the fan and spacer from the water pump shaft. Remove the shroud, if so equipped.

5. Remove the air conditioning drive belt and idler pulley, if so equipped. Remove the alternator, power steering and Thermactor drive belts, if so equipped. Remove the power steering pump attaching bolts, if so equipped, and position it to one side (leaving it connected).

6. Remove all accessory brackets which attach to the water pump. Remove the water pump pulley.

7. Disconnect the lower radiator hose, heater hose, and the water pump by-pass hose at the water pump.

8. Remove the bolts attaching the water pump and gasket. Discard the old gasket.

9. Clean all gasket surfaces. On the 429 and 460 V8, remove the water pump backing plate and replace the gasket.

NOTE: *The 240 six-cylinder engine originally had a one-piece gasket for the cylinder front cover and the water pump. Trim away the old gasket at the edge of the cylinder cover and replace with a service gasket.*

10. Coat both sides of a new gasket with water-resistant sealer and place it on the front cover. Install the water pump and tighten the attaching bolts diagonally, in rotation, to 12–15 ft lbs (302, 351, 400 V8), 15–20 ft lbs (240 Six, 429, 460 V8), or 20–25 ft lbs (390, 428 V8).

11. Connect the lower radiator hose, heater hose, and water pump by-pass hose at the water pump.

12. Install all accessory brackets attaching to the water pump. Install the pump pulley on the pump shaft.

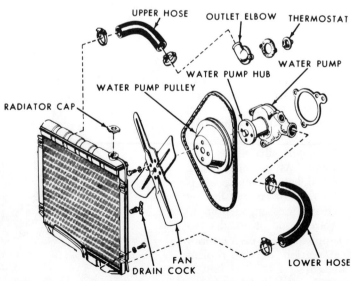

Cooling system and related parts—typical V8 with downflow radiator

13. Install the power steering pump and drive belt, if so equipped. Install the alternator, air conditioning, and Thermactor drive belts, if so equipped. Install the air conditioning idler pulley backet, if so equipped. Adjust the drive belt tension of all accessory drive belts as outlined in Chapter 1.

14. Position the fan shroud, if so equipped, over the water pump pulley. Install the spacer and fan. Install the shroud attaching bolts, if so equipped.

15. Fill and bleed the cooling system. Operate the engine until normal running temperature is reached. Check for leaks.

Thermostat

REMOVAL AND INSTALLATION

1. Open the drain cock an drain the radiator so that the coolant level is below the coolant outlet elbow which houses the thermostat.

2. Remove the outlet elbow retaining bolts and position the elbow clear of the intake manifold or cylinder head sufficiently to provide access to the thermostat.

3. Remove the thermostat and old gasket. The thermostat must be rotated counterclockwise for removal.

4. Clean the mating surfaces of the outlet

Installing thermostat

elbow and the engine to remove all old gasket material and sealer. Coat the new gasket material and sealer. Coat the new gasket with water-resistant sealer and install it on the engine. Install the thermostat in the outlet elbow. The thermostat must be rotated clockwise to lock it in position.

5. Install the outlet elbow and retaining bolts on the engine. Torque the bolts to 12–15 ft lbs.

6. Refill the radiator. Run the engine at operating temperature and check for leaks. Recheck the coolant level.

Engine Rebuilding

This section describes, in detail, the procedures involved in rebuilding a typical engine. The procedures specifically refer to an inline engine, however, they are basically identical to those used in rebuilding engines of nearly all design and configurations. Procedures for servicing atypical engines (i.e., horizontally opposed) are described in the appropriate section, although in most cases, cylinder head reconditioning procedures described in this chapter will apply.

The section is divided into two sections. The first, Cylinder Head Reconditioning, assumes that the cylinder head is removed from the engine, all manifolds are removed, and the cylinder head is on a workbench. The camshaft should be removed from overhead cam cylinder heads. The second section, Cyl-

Torque (ft. lbs.)*

Bolt Diameter (inches)	U.S./Bolt Grade (SAE) 1 and 2	5	6	8	Wrench Size (inches) Bolt	Wrench Size (inches) Nut	Bolt Diameter (mm)	Metric/Bolt Grade 5D	8G	10K	12K	Wrench Size (mm) Bolt and Nut
$1/4$	5	7	10	10.5	$3/8$	$7/16$	6	5	6	8	10	10
$5/16$	9	14	19	22	$1/2$	$9/16$	8	10	16	22	27	14
$3/8$	15	25	34	37	$9/16$	$5/8$	10	19	31	40	49	17
$7/16$	24	40	55	60	$5/8$	$3/4$	12	34	54	70	86	19
$1/2$	37	60	85	92	$3/4$	$13/16$	14	55	89	117	137	22
$9/16$	53	88	120	132	$7/8$	$7/8$	16	83	132	175	208	24
$5/8$	74	120	167	180	$15/16$	1	18	111	182	236	283	27
$3/4$	120	200	280	296	$1 1/8$	$1 1/8$	22	182	284	394	464	32
$7/8$	190	302	440	473	$1 5/16$	$1 5/16$	24	261	419	570	689	36
1	282	466	660	714	$1 1/2$	$1 1/2$						

*—Torque values are for lightly oiled bolts. CAUTION: Bolts threaded into aluminum require much less torque.

inder Block Reconditioning, covers the block, pistons, connecting rods and crankshaft. It is assumed that the engine is mounted on a work stand, and the cylinder head and all accessories are removed.

Procedures are identified as follows:

Unmarked—Basic procedures that must be performed in order to successfully complete the rebuilding process.

Starred (*)—Procedures that should be performed to ensure maximum performance and engine life.

Double starred (**)—Procedures that may be performed to increase engine performance and reliability. These procedures are usually reserved for extremely heavy-duty or competition usage.

In many cases, a choice of methods is also provided. Methods are identified in the same manner as procedures. The choice of method for a procedure is at the discretion of the user.

The tools required for the basic rebuilding procedure should, with minor exceptions, be those included in a mechanic's tool kit. An accurate torque wrench, and a dial indicator (reading in thousandths) mounted on a universal base should be available. Bolts and nuts with no torque specification should be tightened according to size (see chart). Special tools, where required, all are readily available from the major tool suppliers (i.e., Craftsman, Snap-On, K-D). The services of a competent automotive machine shop must also be readily available.

When assembling the engine, any parts that will be in frictional contact must be pre-lubricated, to provide protection on initial start-up. Vortex Pre-Lube, STP, or any product specifically formulated for this purpose may be used. NOTE: *Do not use engine oil.* Where semi-permanent (locked but removable) installation of bolts or nuts is desired, threads should be cleaned and coated with Loctite. Studs may be permanently installed using Loctite Stud and Bearing Mount.

Aluminum has become increasingly popular for use in engines, due to its low weight and excellent heat transfer characteristics. The following precautions must be observed when handling aluminum engine parts:

—Never hot-tank aluminum parts.

—Remove all aluminum parts (identification tags, etc.) from engine parts before hot-tanking (otherwise they will be removed during the process).

—Always coat threads lightly with engine oil or anti-seize compounds before installation, to prevent seizure.

—Never over-torque bolts or spark plugs in aluminum threads. Should stripping occur, threads can be restored according to the following procedure, using Heli-Coil thread inserts:

Tap drill the hole with the stripped threads to the specified size (see chart). Using the specified tap (NOTE: *Heli-Coil tap sizes refer to the size thread being replaced, rather than the actual tap size*), tap the hole for the Heli-

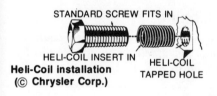

STANDARD SCREW FITS IN

HELI-COIL INSERT IN

**Heli-Coil installation
(© Chrysler Corp.)**

HELI-COIL
TAPPED HOLE

NOTCH

HELI-COIL
INSERT

COIL INSTALLATION TOOL

Heli-Coil and installation tool

Heli-Coil Specifications

	Heli-Coil Insert		Drill	Tap	Insert. Tool	Extracting Tool
Thread Size	Part No.	Insert Length (In.)	Size	Part No.	Part No.	Part No.
1/2 -20	1185-4	3/8	17/64(.266)	4 CPB	528-4N	1227-6
5/16-18	1185-5	15/32	Q(.332)	5 CPB	528-5N	1227-6
3/8 -16	1185-6	9/16	X(.397)	6 CPB	528-6N	1227-6
7/16-14	1185-7	21/32	29/64(.453)	7 CPB	528-7N	1227-16
1/2 -13	1185-8	3/4	33/64(.516)	8 CPB	528-8N	1227-16

Coil. place the insert on the proper installation tool (see chart). Apply pressure on the insert while winding it clockwise into the hole, until the top of the insert is one turn below the surface. Remove the installation tool, and break the installation tang from the bottom of the insert by moving it up and down. If the Heli-Coil must be removed, tap the removal tool firmly into the hole, so that it engages the top thread, and turn the tool counter-clockwise to extract that insert.

Snapped bolts or studs may be removed, using a stud extractor (unthreaded) or Vise-Grip pliers (threaded). Penetrating oil (e.g., Liquid Wrench) will often aid in breaking frozen threads. In cases where the stud or bolt is flush with, or below the surface, proceed as follows:

Drill a hole in the broken stud or bolt, approximately ¹/₂ its diameter. Select a screw extractor (e.g., Easy-Out) of the proper size, and tap it into the stud or bolt. Turn the extractor counter-clockwise to remove the stud or bolt.

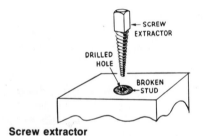

Screw extractor

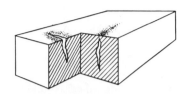

Magnaflux indication of cracks

Magnaflux and Zyglo are inspection techniques used to locate material flaws, such as stress cracks. Magnafluxing coats the part with fine magnetic particles, and subjects the part to a magnetic field. Cracks cause breaks in the magnetic field, which are outlined by the particles. Since Magnaflux is a magnetic process, it is applicable only to ferrous materials. The Zyglo process coats the material with a fluorescent dye penetrant, and then subjects it to blacklight inspection, under which cracks glow brightly. Parts made of any material may be tested using Zyglo. While Magnaflux and Zyglo are excellent for general inspection, and locating hidden defects, specific checks of suspected cracks may be made at lower cost and more readily using spot check dye. The dye is sprayed onto the suspected area, wiped off, and the area is then sprayed with a developer. Cracks then will show up brightly. Spot check dyes will only indicate surface cracks; therefore, structural cracks below the surface may escape detection. When questionable, the part should be tested using Magnaflux or Zyglo.

Cylinder Head Reconditioning

NOTE: *This engine rebuilding section is a guide to accepted engine rebuilding procedures. Every effort is made to illustrate the engine(s) used by this manufacturer; but, occasionally, typical examples of standard engine rebuilding practice are illustrated.*

Procedure	Method
Identify the valves: 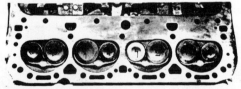 **Valve identification**	Invert the cylinder head, and number the valve faces front to rear, using a permanent felt-tip marker.
Remove the rocker arms:	Remove the rocker arms with shaft(s) or balls and nuts. Wire the sets of rockers, balls and nuts together, and identify according to the corresponding valve.

Procedure	Method
Remove the valves and springs:	Using an appropriate valve spring compressor (depending on the configuration of the cylinder head), compress the valve springs. Lift out the keepers with needlenose pliers, release the compressor, and remove the valve, spring, and spring retainer.

Check the valve stem-to-guide clearance:

Clean the valve stem with lacquer thinner or a similar solvent to remove all gum and varnish. Clean the valve guides using solvent and an expanding wire-type valve guide cleaner. Mount a dial indicator so that the stem is at 90° to the valve stem, as close to the valve guide as possible. Move the valve off its seat, and measure the valve guide-to-stem clearance by moving the stem back and forth to actuate the dial indicator. Measure the valve stems using a micrometer, and compare to specifications, to determine whether stem or guide wear is responsible for excessive clearance.

Checking the valve stem-to-guide clearance

De-carbon the cylinder head and valves:

Chip carbon away from the valve heads, combustion chambers, and ports, using a chisel made of hardwood. Remove the remaining deposits with a stiff wire brush. **NOTE: *Ensure that the deposits are actually removed, rather than burnished.***

Removing carbon from the cylinder head

Hot-tank the cylinder head:

Have the cylinder head hot-tanked to remove grease, corrosion, and scale from the water passages. **NOTE: *In the case of overhead cam cylinder heads, consult the operator to determine whether the camshaft bearings will be damaged by the caustic solution.***

Degrease the remaining cylinder head parts:

Using solvent (i.e., Gunk), clean the rockers, rocker shaft(s) (where applicable), rocker balls and nuts, springs, spring retainers, and keepers. Do not remove the protective coating from the springs.

Check the cylinder head for warpage:

1 & 3 CHECK DIAGONALLY
2 CHECK ACROSS CENTER

Place a straight-edge across the gasket surface of the cylinder head. Using feeler gauges, determine the clearance at the center of the straight-edge. Measure across both diagonals, along the longitudinal centerline, and across the cylinder head at several points. If warpage exceeds .003″ in a 6″ span, or .006″ over the total length, the cylinder head must be resurfaced. **NOTE: *If warpage exceeds the manufacturers maximum tolerance for material removal, the cylinder head must be replaced.*** When milling the cylinder heads of V-type engines, the intake manifold mounting position is altered, and must be corrected by milling the manifold flange a proportionate amount.

Checking the cylinder head for warpage

Procedure	Method

** Porting and gasket matching:

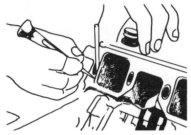

Marking the cylinder head for gasket matching

Port configuration before and after gasket matching

** Coat the manifold flanges of the cylinder head with Prussian blue dye. Glue intake and exhaust gaskets to the cylinder head in their installed position using rubber cement and scribe the outline of the ports on the manifold flanges. Remove the gaskets. Using a small cutter in a hand-held power tool (i.e., Dremel Moto-Tool), gradually taper the walls of the port out to the scribed outline of the gasket. Further enlargement of the ports should include the removal of sharp edges and radiusing of sharp corners. Do not alter the valve guides. **NOTE:** *The most efficient port configuration is determined only by extensive testing. Therefore, it is best to consult someone experienced with the head in question to determine the optimum alterations.*

** Polish the ports:

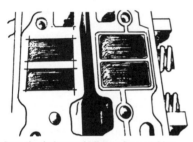

Relieved and polished ports

** Using a grinding stone with the above mentioned tool, polish the walls of the intake and exhaust ports, and combustion chamber. Use progressively finer stones until all surface imperfections are removed. **NOTE:** *Through testing, it has been determined that a smooth surface is more effective than a mirror polished surface in intake ports, and vice-versa in exhaust ports.*

---

* Knurling the valve guides:

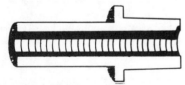

Cut-away view of a knurled valve guide

* Valve guides which are not excessively worn or distorted may, in some cases, be knurled rather than replaced. Knurling is a process in which metal is displaced and raised, thereby reducing clearance. Knurling also provides excellent oil control. The possibility of knurling rather than replacing valve guides should be discussed with a machinist.

Replacing the valve guides: **NOTE:** *Valve guides should only be replaced if damaged or if an oversize valve stem is not available.*

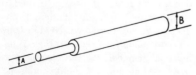

A-VALVE GUIDE I.D.
B-SLIGHTLY SMALLER THAN VALVE GUIDE O.D.

Valve guide removal tool

Depending on the type of cylinder head, valve guides may be pressed, hammered, or shrunk in. In cases where the guides are shrunk into the head, replacement should be left to an equipped machine shop. In other cases, the guides are replaced as follows: Press or tap the valve guides out of the head using a stepped drift (see illustration). Determine the height above the boss that the guide must extend, and obtain a stack of washers, their I.D. similar to the guide's O.D., of that height. Place the stack of washers on the guide, and insert the guide into the boss. **NOTE:** *Valve*

Procedure	Method

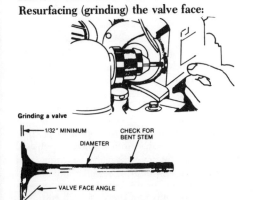

A-VALVE GUIDE I.D.
B-LARGER THAN THE VALVE GUIDE O.D.
Valve guide installation tool (with washers used during installation)

guides are often tapered or beveled for installation. Using the stepped installation tool (see illustration), press or tap the guides into position. Ream the guides according to the size of the valve stem.

Replacing valve seat inserts:

Replacement of valve seat inserts which are worn beyond resurfacing or broken, if feasible, must be done by a machine shop.

Resurfacing (grinding) the valve face:

Grinding a valve

1/32" MINIMUM — DIAMETER — CHECK FOR BENT STEM — VALVE FACE ANGLE — THIS LINE PARALLEL WITH VALVE HEAD — FOR DIMENSIONS, REFER TO SPECIFICATIONS
Critical valve dimensions

Using a valve grinder, resurface the valves according to specifications. **CAUTION:** *Valve face angle is not always identical to valve seat angle.* A minimum margin of $1/32''$ should remain after grinding the valve. The valve stem tip should also be squared and resurfaced, by placing the stem in the V-block of the grinder, and turning it while pressing lightly against the grinding wheel.

Resurfacing the valve seats using reamers:

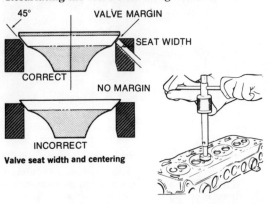

45° — VALVE MARGIN — SEAT WIDTH
CORRECT
NO MARGIN
INCORRECT
Valve seat width and centering

Reaming the valve seat

Select a reamer of the correct seat angle, slightly larger than the diameter of the valve seat, and assemble it with a pilot of the correct size. Install the pilot into the valve guide, and using steady pressure, turn the reamer clockwise. **CAUTION:** *Do not turn the reamer counter-clockwise.* Remove only as much material as necessary to clean the seat. Check the concentricity of the seat (see below). If the dye method is not used, coat the valve face with Prussian blue dye, install and rotate it on the valve seat. Using the dye marked area as a centering guide, center and narrow the valve seat to specifications with correction cutters. **NOTE:** *When no specifications are available, minimum seat width for exhaust valves should be* $5/64''$, *intake valves* $1/16''$. After making correction cuts, check the position of the valve seat on the valve face using Prussian blue dye.

* Resurfacing the valve seats using a grinder:

Grinding a valve seat

Select a pilot of the correct size, and a coarse stone of the correct seat angle. Lubricate the pilot if necessary, and install the tool in the valve guide. Move the stone on and off the seat at approximately two cycles per second, until all flaws are removed from the seat. Install a fine stone, and finish the seat. Center and narrow the seat using correction stones, as described above.

Procedure	*Method*
Checking the valve seat concentricity:	Coat the valve face with Prussian blue dye, install the valve, and rotate it on the valve seat. If the entire seat becomes coated, and the valve is known to be concentric, the seat is concentric.

Checking the valve seat concentricity using a dial gauge

* Install the dial gauge pilot into the guide, and rest the arm on the valve seat. Zero the gauge, and rotate the arm around the seat. Run-out should not exceed .002".

* **Lapping the valves:** NOTE: *Valve lapping is done to ensure efficient sealing of resurfaced valves and seats. Valve lapping alone is not recommended for use as a resurfacing procedure.*

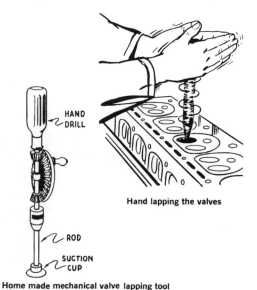

Hand lapping the valves

* Invert the cylinder head, lightly lubricate the valve stems, and install the valves in the head as numbered. Coat valve seats with fine grinding compound, and attach the lapping tool suction cup to a valve head (**NOTE: *Moisten the suction cup*).** Rotate the tool between the palms, changing position and lifting the tool often to prevent grooving. Lap the valve until a smooth, polished seat is evident. Remove the valve and tool, and rinse away all traces of grinding compound.

** Fasten a suction cup to a piece of drill rod, and mount the rod in a hand drill. Proceed as above, using the hand drill as a lapping tool. **CAUTION: *Due to the higher speeds involved when using the hand drill, care must be exercised to avoid grooving the seat.*** Lift the tool and change direction of rotation often.

HAND DRILL

ROD

SUCTION CUP

Home made mechanical valve lapping tool

Check the valve springs:

NOT MORE THAN 5/64"

CLOSED COIL END DOWNWARD

Checking the valve spring free length and squareness

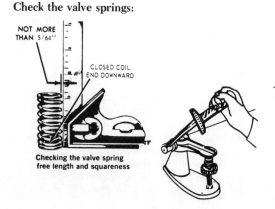

Checking the valve spring tension

Place the spring on a flat surface next to a square. Measure the height of the spring, and rotate it against the edge of the square to measure distortion. If spring height varies (by comparison) by more than $1/16$" or if distortion exceeds $1/16$", replace the spring.

** In addition to evaluating the spring as above, test the spring pressure at the installed and compressed (installed height minus valve lift) height using a valve spring tester. Springs used on small displacement engines (up to 3 liters) should be ± 1 lb of all other springs in either position. A tolerance of ± 5 lbs is permissible on larger engines.

Procedure	Method

* Install valve stem seals:

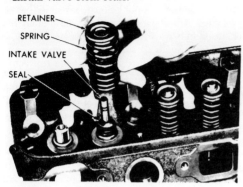

RETAINER
SPRING
INTAKE VALVE
SEAL

Valve stem seal installation

* Due to the pressure differential that exists at the ends of the intake valve guides (atmospheric pressure above, manifold vacuum below), oil is drawn through the valve guides into the intake port. This has been alleviated somewhat since the addition of positive crankcase ventilation, which lowers the pressure above the guides. Several types of valve stem seals are available to reduce blow-by. Certain seals simply slip over the stem and guide boss, while others require that the boss be machined. Recently, Teflon guide seals have become popular. Consult a parts supplier or machinist concerning availability and suggested usages. **NOTE:** *When installing seals, ensure that a small amount of oil is able to pass the seal to lubricate the valve guides; otherwise, excessive wear may result.*

Install the valves:

Lubricate the valve stems, and install the valves in the cylinder head as numbered. Lubricate and position the seals (if used, see above) and the valve springs. Install the spring retainers, compress the springs, and insert the keys using needlenose pliers or a tool designed for this purpose. **NOTE:** *Retain the keys with wheel bearing grease during installation.*

Checking valve spring installed height:

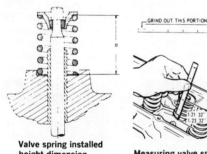

GRIND OUT THIS PORTION

Valve spring installed
height dimension

Measuring valve spring
installed height

Measure the distance between the spring pad and the lower edge of the spring retainer, and compare to specifications. If the installed height is incorrect, add shim washers between the spring pad and the spring. **CAUTION:** *Use only washers designed for this purpose.*

** CC'ing the combustion chambers:

** Invert the cylinder head and place a bead of sealer around a combustion chamber. Install an apparatus designed for this purpose (burette mounted on a clear plate; see illustration) over the combustion chamber, and fill with the specified fluid to an even mark on the burette. Record the burette reading, and fill the combustion chamber with fluid. (**NOTE:** *A hole drilled in the plate will permit air to escape.*) Subtract the burette reading, with the combustion chamber filled, from the previous reading, to determine combustion chamber volume in cc's. Duplicate this procedure in all combustion chambers on the cylinder head,

Procedure	Method

CC'ing the combustion chamber

and compare the readings. The volume of all combustion chambers should be made equal to that of the largest. Combustion chamber volume may be increased in two ways. When only a small change is required (usually), a small cutter or coarse stone may be used to remove material from the combustion chamber. **NOTE:** *Check volume frequently.* Remove material over a wide area, so as not to change the configuration of the combustion chamber. When a larger change is required, the valve seat may be sunk (lowered into the head). **NOTE:** *When altering valve seat, remember to compensate for the change in spring installed height.*

Inspect the rocker arms, balls, studs, and nuts (where applicable):

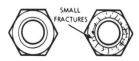

Stress cracks in
rocker nuts

Visually inspect the rocker arms, balls, studs, and nuts for cracks, galling, burning, scoring, or wear. If all parts are intact, liberally lubricate the rocker arms and balls, and install them on the cylinder head. If wear is noted on a rocker arm at the point of valve contact, grind it smooth and square, removing as little material as possible. Replace the rocker arm if excessively worn. If a rocker stud shows signs of wear, it must be replaced (see below). If a rocker nut shows stress cracks, replace it. If an exhaust ball is galled or burned, substitute the intake ball from the same cylinder (if it is intact), and install a new intake ball. **NOTE:** *Avoid using new rocker balls on exhaust valves.*

Replacing rocker studs:

Reaming the stud bore for oversize rocker studs

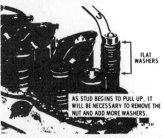

Extracting a pressed in rocker stud

In order to remove a threaded stud, lock two nuts on the stud, and unscrew the stud using the lower nut. Coat the lower threads of the new stud with Loctite, and install.

Two alternative methods are available for replacing pressed in studs. Remove the damaged stud using a stack of washers and a nut (see illustration). In the first, the boss is reamed .005–.006″ oversize, and an oversize stud pressed in. Control the stud extension over the boss using washers, in the same manner as valve guides. Before installing the stud, coat it with white lead and grease. To retain the stud more positively, drill a hole through the stud and boss, and install a roll pin. In the second method, the boss is tapped, and a threaded stud installed. Retain the stud using Loctite Stud and Bearing Mount.

Procedure	Method

Inspect the rocker shaft(s) and rocker arms (where applicable):

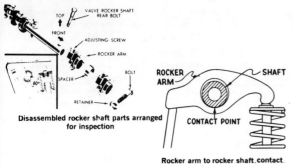

Disassembled rocker shaft parts arranged for inspection

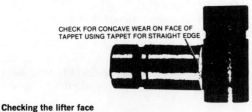

Rocker arm to rocker shaft contact

Remove rocker arms, springs and washers from rocker shaft. NOTE: *Lay out parts in the order they are removed.* Inspect rocker arms for pitting or wear on the valve contact point, or excessive bushing wear. Bushings need only be replaced if wear is excessive, because the rocker arm normally contacts the shaft at one point only. Grind the valve contact point of rocker arm smooth if necessary, removing as little material as possible. If excessive material must be removed to smooth and square the arm, it should be replaced. Clean out all oil holes and passages in rocker shaft. If shaft is grooved or worn, replace it. Lubricate and assemble the rocker shaft.

Inspect the camshaft bushings and the camshaft (overhead cam engines):

See next section.

Inspect the pushrods:

Remove the pushrods, and, if hollow, clean out the oil passages using fine wire. Roll each pushrod over a piece of clean glass. If a distinct clicking sound is heard as the pushrod rolls, the rod is bent, and must be replaced.

* The length of all pushrods must be equal. Measure the length of the pushrods, compare to specifications, and replace as necessary.

Inspect the valve lifters:

CHECK FOR CONCAVE WEAR ON FACE OF TAPPET USING TAPPET FOR STRAIGHT EDGE

Checking the lifter face

Remove lifters from their bores, and remove gum and varnish, using solvent. Clean walls of lifter bores. Check lifters for concave wear as illustrated. If face is worn concave, replace lifter, and carefully inspect the camshaft. Lightly lubricate lifter and insert it into its bore. If play is excessive, an oversize lifter must be installed (where possible). Consult a machinist concerning feasibility. If play is satisfactory, remove, lubricate, and reinstall the lifter.

* Testing hydraulic lifter leak down:

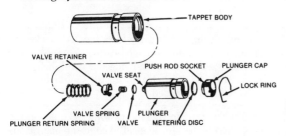

Exploded view of a typical hydraulic lifter

Submerge lifter in a container of kerosene. Chuck a used pushrod or its equivalent into a drill press. Position container of kerosene so pushrod acts on the lifter plunger. Pump lifter with the drill press, until resistance increases. Pump several more times to bleed any air out of lifter. Apply very firm, constant pressure to the lifter, and observe rate at which fluid bleeds out of lifter. If the fluid bleeds very quickly (less than 15 seconds), lifter is defective. If the time exceeds 60 seconds, lifter is sticking. In either case, recondition or replace lifter. If lifter is operating properly (leak down time 15–60 seconds), lubricate and install it.

Cylinder Block Reconditioning

Procedure	Method

Checking the main bearing clearance:

PLASTI-GAGE

Installing Plastigage on lower bearing shell

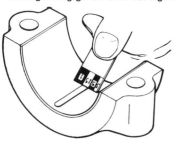

Measuring Plastigage to determine bearing clearance

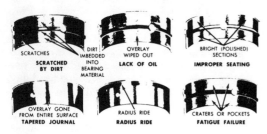

SCRATCHES   DIRT   OVERLAY   BRIGHT (POLISHED) IMBEDDED   WIPED OUT   SECTIONS
SCRATCHED   INTO   **LACK OF OIL**   **IMPROPER SEATING**
BY DIRT   BEARING   MATERIAL

OVERLAY GONE   RADIUS RIDE   CRATERS OR POCKETS
FROM ENTIRE SURFACE
TAPERED JOURNAL   **RADIUS RIDE**   **FATIGUE FAILURE**

Causes of bearing failure

Invert engine, and remove cap from the bearing to be checked. Using a clean, dry rag, thoroughly clean all oil from crankshaft journal and bearing insert. **NOTE:** *Plastigage is soluble in oil; therefore, oil on the journal or bearing could result in erroneous readings.* Place a piece of Plastigage along the full length of journal, reinstall cap, and torque to specifications. Remove bearing cap, and determine bearing clearance by comparing width of Plastigage to the scale on Plastigage envelope. Journal taper is determined by comparing width of the Plastigage strip near its ends. Rotate crankshaft 90° and retest, to determine journal eccentricity. **NOTE:** *Do not rotate crankshaft with Plastigage installed.* If bearing insert and journal appear intact, and are within tolerances, no further main bearing service is required. If bearing or journal appear defective, cause of failure should be determined before replacement.

* Remove crankshaft from block (see below). Measure the main bearing journals at each end twice (90° apart) using a micrometer, to determine diameter, journal taper and eccentricity. If journals are within tolerances, reinstall bearing caps at their specified torque. Using a telescope gauge and micrometer, measure bearing I.D. parallel to piston axis and at 30° on each side of piston axis. Subtract journal O.D. from bearing I.D. to determine oil clearance. If crankshaft journals appear defective, or do not meet tolerances, there is no need to measure bearings; for the crankshaft will require grinding and/or undersize bearings will be required. If bearing appears defective, cause for failure should be determined prior to replacement.

Checking the connecting rod bearing clearance:

Connecting rod bearing clearance is checked in the same manner as main bearing clearance, using Plastigage. Before removing the crankshaft, connecting rod side clearance also should be measured and recorded.

* Checking connecting rod bearing clearance, using a micrometer, is identical to checking main bearing clearance. If no other service is required, the piston and rod assemblies need not be removed.

Procedure	Method
Removing the crankshaft:  Connecting rod matching marks	Using a punch, mark the corresponding main bearing caps and saddles according to position (i.e., one punch on the front main cap and saddle, two on the second, three on the third, etc.). Using number stamps, identify the corresponding connecting rods and caps, according to cylinder (if no numbers are present). Remove the main and connecting rod caps, and place sleeves of plastic tubing over the connecting rod bolts, to protect the journals as the crankshaft is removed. Lift the crankshaft out of the block.
Remove the ridge from the top of the cylinder:  Cylinder bore ridge	In order to facilitate removal of the piston and connecting rod, the ridge at the top of the cylinder (unknown area; see illustration) must be removed. Place the piston at the bottom of the bore, and cover it with a rag. Cut the ridge away using a ridge reamer, exercising extreme care to avoid cutting too deeply. Remove the rag, and remove cuttings that remain on the piston. **CAUTION:** *If the ridge is not removed, and new rings are installed, damage to rings will result.*
Removing the piston and connecting rod: 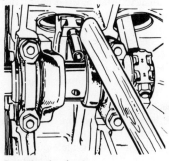 Removing the piston	Invert the engine, and push the pistons and connecting rods out of the cylinders. If necessary, tap the connecting rod boss with a wooden hammer handle, to force the piston out. **CAUTION:** *Do not attempt to force the piston past the cylinder ridge* (see above).
Service the crankshaft:	Ensure that all oil holes and passages in the crankshaft are open and free of sludge. If necessary, have the crankshaft ground to the largest possible undersize.
	** Have the crankshaft Magnafluxed, to locate stress cracks. Consult a machinist concerning additional service procedures, such as surface hardening (e.g., nitriding, Tuftriding) to improve wear characteristics, cross drilling and chamfering the oil holes to improve lubrication, and balancing.
Removing freeze plugs:	Drill a small hole in the center of the freeze plugs. Thread a large sheet metal screw into the hole and remove the plug with a slide hammer.
Remove the oil gallery plugs:	Threaded plugs should be removed using an appropriate (usually square) wrench. To remove soft, pressed in plugs, drill a hole in the plug, and thread in a sheet metal screw. Pull the plug out by the screw using a slide hammer.

Procedure	Method
Hot-tank the block:	Have the block hot-tanked to remove grease, corrosion, and scale from the water jackets. **NOTE:** *Consult the operator to determine whether the camshaft bearings will be damaged during the hot-tank process.*
Check the block for cracks:	Visually inspect the block for cracks or chips. The most common locations are as follows: 　　Adjacent to freeze plugs. 　　Between the cylinders and water jackets. 　　Adjacent to the main bearing saddles. 　　At the extreme bottom of the cylinders. Check only suspected cracks using spot check dye (see introduction). If a crack is located, consult a machinist concerning possible repairs.
	** Magnaflux the block to locate hidden cracks. If cracks are located, consult a machinist about feasibility of repair.
Install the oil gallery plugs and freeze plugs:	Coat freeze plugs with sealer and tap into position using a piece of pipe, slightly smaller than the plug, as a driver. To ensure retention, stake the edges of the plugs. Coat threaded oil gallery plugs with sealer and install. Drive replacement soft plugs into block using a large drift as a driver.
	* Rather than reinstalling lead plugs, drill and tap the holes, and install threaded plugs.

Check the bore diameter and surface:

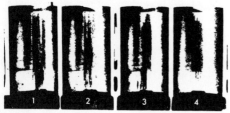

1, 2, 3 Piston skirt seizure resulted in this pattern. Engine must be rebored
4. Piston skirt and oil ring seizure caused this damag Engine must be rebored

5, 6 Score marks caused by a split piston skirt. Damage is not serious enough to warrant reboring
7. Ring seized longitudinally, causing a score mark 1 3/16" wide, on the land side of the piston groove. The honing pattern is destroyed and the cylinder must be rebored

Visually inspect the cylinder bores for roughness, scoring, or scuffing. If evident, the cylinder bore must be bored or honed oversize to eliminate imperfections, and the smallest possible oversize piston used. The new pistons should be given to the machinist with the block, so that the cylinders can be bored or honed exactly to the piston size (plus clearance). If no flaws are evident, measure the bore diameter using a telescope gauge and micrometer, or dial gauge, parallel and perpendicular to the engine centerline, at the top (below the ridge) and bottom of the bore. Subtract the bottom measurements from the top to determine taper, and the parallel to the centerline measurements from the perpendicular measurements to determine eccentricity. If the measurements are not within specifications, the cylinder must be bored or honed, and an oversize piston installed. If the measurements are within specifications the cylinder may be used as is, with only finish honing (see below). **NOTE:** *Prior to submitting the block for boring, perform the following operation(s).*

Procedure	*Method*

8. Result of oil ring seizure. Engine must be rebored

9. Oil ring seizure here was not serious enough to warrant reboring. The honing marks are still visible

Cylinder wall damage

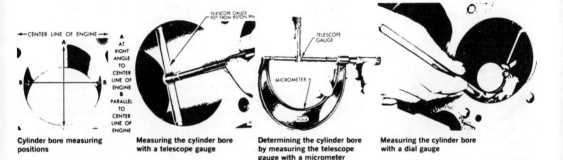

Cylinder bore measuring positions

Measuring the cylinder bore with a telescope gauge

Determining the cylinder bore by measuring the telescope gauge with a micrometer

Measuring the cylinder bore with a dial gauge

Procedure	Method
Check the block deck for warpage:	Using a straightedge and feeler gauges, check the block deck for warpage in the same manner that the cylinder head is checked (see Cylinder Head Reconditioning). If warpage exceeds specifications, have the deck resurfaced. **NOTE:** *In certain cases a specification for total material removal (Cylinder head and block deck) is provided. This specification must not be exceeded.*
* Check the deck height:	The deck height is the distance from the crankshaft centerline to the block deck. To measure, invert the engine, and install the crankshaft, retaining it with the center main cap. Measure the distance from the crankshaft journal to the block deck, parallel to the cylinder centerline. Measure the diameter of the end (front and rear) main journals, parallel to the centerline of the cylinders, divide the diameter in half, and subtract it from the previous measurement. The results of the front and rear measurements should be identical. If the difference exceeds .005″, the deck height should be corrected. **NOTE:** *Block deck height and warpage should be corrected concurrently.*

Procedure	Method

Check the cylinder block bearing alignment:

Checking main bearing saddle alignment

Remove the upper bearing inserts. Place a straightedge in the bearing saddles along the centerline of the crankshaft. If clearance exists between the straightedge and the center saddle, the block must be align-bored.

Clean and inspect the pistons and connecting rods:

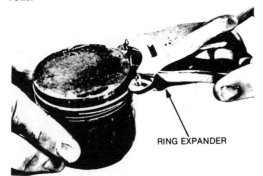

RING EXPANDER

Removing the piston rings

Ring Groove Cleaner

Cleaning the piston ring grooves

Connecting rod length checking dimension

Using a ring expander, remove the rings from the piston. Remove the retaining rings (if so equipped) and remove piston pin. **NOTE:** *If the piston pin must be pressed out, determine the proper method and use the proper tools; otherwise the piston will distort.* Clean the ring grooves using an appropriate tool, exercising care to avoid cutting too deeply. Thoroughly clean all carbon and varnish from the piston with solvent. **CAUTION:** *Do not use a wire brush or caustic solvent on pistons.* Inspect the pistons for scuffing, scoring, cracks, pitting, or excessive ring groove wear. If wear is evident, the piston must be replaced. Check the connecting rod length by measuring the rod from the inside of the large end to the inside of the small end using calipers (see illustration). All connecting rods should be equal length. Replace any rod that differs from the others in the engine.

* Have the connecting rod alignment checked in an alignment fixture by a machinist. Replace any twisted or bent rods.

* Magnaflux the connecting rods to locate stress cracks. If cracks are found, replace the connecting rod.

Fit the pistons to the cylinders:

90°

Measuring the piston for fitting (© Buick Div.)

Using a telescope gauge and micrometer, or a dial gauge, measure the cylinder bore diameter perpendicular to the piston pin, 2½″ below the deck. Measure the piston perpendicular to its pin on the skirt. The difference between the two measurements is the piston clearance. If the clearance is within specifications or slightly below (after boring or honing), finish honing is all that is required. If the clearance is excessive, try to obtain a slightly larger piston to bring clearance within specifications. Where this is not possible, obtain the first oversize piston, and hone (or if necessary, bore) the cylinder to size.

Procedure	Method
Assemble the pistons and connecting rods:  Installing piston pin lock rings	Inspect piston pin, connecting rod small end bushing, and piston bore for galling, scoring, or excessive wear. If evident, replace defective part(s). Measure the I.D. of the piston boss and connecting rod small end, and the O.D. of the piston pin. If within specifications, assemble piston pin and rod. **CAUTION:** *If piston pin must be pressed in, determine the proper method and use the proper tools; otherwise the piston will distort.* Install the lock rings; ensure that they seat properly. If the parts are not within specifications, determine the service method for the type of engine. In some cases, piston and pin are serviced as an assembly when either is defective. Others specify reaming the piston and connecting rods for an oversize pin. If the connecting rod bushing is worn, it may in many cases be replaced. Reaming the piston and replacing the rod bushing are machine shop operations.
Clean and inspect the camshaft: 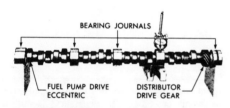 Checking the camshaft for straightness (© Chevrolet Motor Div. G.M. Corp.) Camshaft lobe measurement	Degrease the camshaft, using solvent, and clean out all oil holes. Visually inspect cam lobes and bearing journals for excessive wear. If a lobe is questionable, check all lobes as indicated below. If a journal or lobe is worn, the camshaft must be reground or replaced. **NOTE:** *If a journal is worn, there is a good chance that the bushings are worn.* If lobes and journals appear intact, place the front and rear journals in V-blocks, and rest a dial indicator on the center journal. Rotate the camshaft to check straightness. If deviation exceeds .001″, replace the camshaft. * Check the camshaft lobes with a micrometer, by measuring the lobes from the nose to base and again at 90° (see illustration). The lift is determined by subtracting the second measurement from the first. If all exhaust lobes and all intake lobes are not identical, the camshaft must be reground or replaced.
Replace the camshaft bearings: 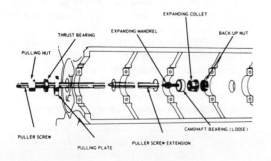 Camshaft removal and installation tool (typical)	If excessive wear is indicated, or if the engine is being completely rebuilt, camshaft bearings should be replaced as follows: Drive the camshaft rear plug from the block. Assemble the removal puller with its shoulder on the bearing to be removed. Gradually tighten the puller nut until bearing is removed. Remove remaining bearings, leaving the front and rear for last. To remove front and rear bearings, reverse position of the tool, so as to pull the bearings in toward the center of the block. Leave the tool in this position, pilot the new front and rear bearings on the installer, and pull them into position. Return the tool to its original position and pull remaining bearings into position. **NOTE:** *Ensure that oil holes align when installing bearings.* Replace camshaft rear plug, and stake it into position to aid retention.

Procedure	Method
Finish hone the cylinders: 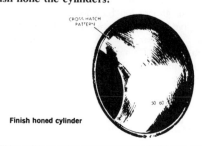 Finish honed cylinder	Chuck a flexible drive hone into a power drill, and insert it into the cylinder. Start the hone, and move it up and down in the cylinder at a rate which will produce approximately a 60° cross-hatch pattern (see illustration). **NOTE:** *Do not extend the hone below the cylinder bore.* After developing the pattern, remove the hone and re-check piston fit. Wash the cylinders with a detergent and water solution to remove abrasive dust, dry, and wipe several times with a rag soaked in engine oil.
Check piston ring end-gap:  Checking ring end-gap	Compress the piston rings to be used in a cylinder, one at a time, into that cylinder, and press them approximately 1″ below the deck with an inverted piston. Using feeler gauges, measure the ring end-gap, and compare to specifications. Pull the ring out of the cylinder and file the ends with a fine file to obtain proper clearance. **CAUTION:** *If inadequate ring end-gap is utilized, ring breakage will result.*
Install the piston rings:  Checking ring side clearance 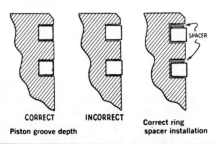 CORRECT INCORRECT Piston groove depth Correct ring spacer installation	Inspect the ring grooves in the piston for excessive wear or taper. If necessary, recut the groove(s) for use with an overwidth ring or a standard ring and spacer. If the groove is worn uniformly, overwidth rings, or standard rings and spacers may be installed without recutting. Roll the outside of the ring around the groove to check for burrs or deposits. If any are found, remove with a fine file. Hold the ring in the groove, and measure side clearance. If necessary, correct as indicated above. **NOTE:** *Always install any additional spacers above the piston ring.* The ring groove must be deep enough to allow the ring to seat below the lands (see illustration). In many cases, a "go-no-go" depth gauge will be provided with the piston rings. Shallow grooves may be corrected by recutting, while deep grooves require some type of filler or expander behind the piston. Consult the piston ring supplier concerning the suggested method. Install the rings on the piston, lowest ring first, using a ring expander. **NOTE:** *Position the ring markings as specified by the manufacturer (see car section).*
Install the camshaft:	Liberally lubricate the camshaft lobes and journals, and slide the camshaft into the block. **CAUTION:** *Exercise extreme care to avoid damaging the bearings when inserting the camshaft.* Install and tighten the camshaft thrust plate retaining bolts.

Procedure	Method

Check camshaft end-play:

Checking camshaft
end-play with a
feeler gauge

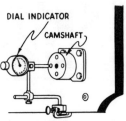

DIAL INDICATOR

CAMSHAFT

Checking camshaft end-play with a
dial indicator

Using feeler gauges, determine whether the clearance between the camshaft boss (or gear) and backing plate is within specifications. Install shims behind the thrust plate, or reposition the camshaft gear and retest end-play.

* Mount a dial indicator stand so that the stem of the dial indicator rests on the nose of the camshaft, parallel to the camshaft axis. Push the camshaft as far in as possible and zero the gauge. Move the camshaft outward to determine the amount of camshaft end-play. If the end-play is not within tolerance, install shims behind the thrust plate, or reposition the camshaft gear and retest.

Install the rear main seal (where applicable):

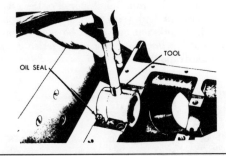

OIL SEAL

TOOL

Seating the rear
main seal

Position the block with the bearing saddles facing upward. Lay the rear main seal in its groove and press it lightly into its seat. Place a piece of pipe the same diameter as the crankshaft journal into the saddle, and firmly seat the seal. Hold the pipe in position, and trim the ends of the seal flush if required.

Install the crankshaft:

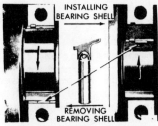

INSTALLING
BEARING SHELL

REMOVING
BEARING SHELL

Removal and installation of upper bearing insert using a
roll-out pin (© Buick Div. G.M. Corp.)

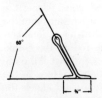

60°

¾"

Home made bearing roll-out pin

Thoroughly clean the main bearing saddles and caps. Place the upper halves of the bearing inserts on the saddles and press into position. **NOTE:** *Ensure that the oil holes align.* Press the corresponding bearing inserts into the main bearing caps. Lubricate the upper main bearings, and lay the crankshaft in position. Place a strip of Plastigage on each of the crankshaft journals, install the main caps, and torque to specifications. Remove the main caps, and compare the Plastigage to the scale on the Plastigage envelope. If clearances are within tolerances, remove the Plastigage, turn the crankshaft 90°, wipe off all oil and retest. If all clearances are correct, remove all Plastigage, thoroughly lubricate the main caps and bearing journals, and install the main caps. If clearances are not within tolerance, the upper bearing inserts may be removed, without removing the crankshaft, using a bearing roll out pin (see illustration). Roll in a bearing that will provide proper clearance, and retest. Torque all main caps, excluding the thrust bearing cap, to specifications. Tighten the thrust bearing cap finger tight. To properly align the thrust bearing, pry the crankshaft the extent of its axial travel several

Procedure	Method

times, the last movement held toward the front of the engine, and torque the thrust bearing cap to specifications. Determine the crankshaft end-play (see below), and bring within tolerance with thrust washers.

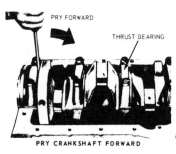
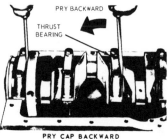

PRY CRANKSHAFT FORWARD   PRY CAP BACKWARD   TIGHTEN CAP

Aligning the thrust bearing

Measure crankshaft end-play:

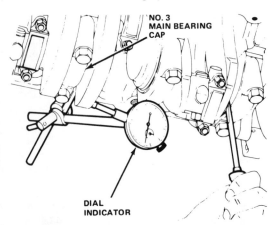

Checking crankshaft end-play with a dial indicator

Mount a dial indicator stand on the front of the block, with the dial indicator stem resting on the nose of the crankshaft, parallel to the crankshaft axis. Pry the crankshaft the extent of its travel rearward, and zero the indicator. Pry the crankshaft forward and record crankshaft end-play. **NOTE:** *Crankshaft end-play also may be measured at the thrust bearing, using feeler gauges (see illustration).*

Checking crankshaft end-play with a feeler gauge

Install the pistons:

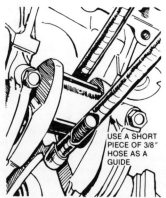

Tubing used as guide when installing a piston

Press the upper connecting rod bearing halves into the connecting rods, and the lower halves into the connecting rod caps. Position the piston ring gaps according to specifications (see car section), and lubricate the pistons. Install a ring compresser on a piston, and press two long (8″) pieces of plastic tubing over the rod bolts. Using the plastic tubes as a guide, press the pistons into the bores and onto the crankshaft with a wooden hammer handle. After seating the rod on the crankshaft journal, remove the tubes and install the cap finger tight. Install the remaining pistons in the same manner. Invert the engine and check the bearing clearance at two points (90° apart) on each journal with Plastigage. **NOTE:** *Do not turn the crankshaft with Plastigage installed.* If clearance is within tolerances, remove *all* Plastigage, thoroughly lubricate the journals, and torque the

Procedure	Method

Installing a piston

rod caps to specifications. If clearance is not within specifications, install different thickness bearing inserts and recheck. **CAUTION:** *Never shim or file the connecting rods or caps.* Always install plastic tube sleeves over the rod bolts when the caps are not installed, to protect the crankshaft journals.

Check connecting rod side clearance:

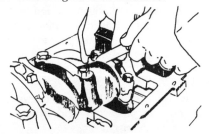

Checking connecting rod side clearance

Determine the clearance between the sides of the connecting rods and the crankshaft, using feeler gauges. If clearance is below the minimum tolerance, the rod may be machined to provide adequate clearance. If clearance is excessive, substitute an unworn rod, and recheck. If clearance is still outside specifications, the crankshaft must be welded and reground, or replaced.

Inspect the timing chain:

Visually inspect the timing chain for broken or loose links, and replace the chain if any are found. If the chain will flex sideways, it must be replaced. Install the timing chain as specified. **NOTE:** *If the original timing chain is to be reused, install it in its original position.*

Check timing gear backlash and runout:

Checking camshaft gear backlash

Checking camshaft gear runout

Mount a dial indicator with its stem resting on a tooth of the camshaft gear (as illustrated). Rotate the gear until all slack is removed, and zero the indicator. Rotate the gear in the opposite direction until slack is removed, and record gear backlash. Mount the indicator with its stem resting on the edge of the camshaft gear, parallel to the axis of the camshaft. Zero the indicator, and turn the camshaft gear one full turn, recording the runout. If either backlash or runout exceed specifications, replace the worn gear(s).

Completing the Rebuilding Process

Following the above procedures, complete the rebuilding process as follows:

Fill the oil pump with oil, to prevent cavitating (sucking air) on initial engine start up. Install the oil pump and the pickup tube on the engine. Coat the oil pan gasket as necessary, and install the gasket and the oil pan. Mount the flywheel and the crankshaft vibrational damper or pulley on the crankshaft. NOTE: *Always use new bolts when installing the flywheel.* Inspect the clutch shaft pilot bushing in the crankshaft. If the bushing is excessively worn, remove it with an expanding puller and a slide hammer, and tap a new bushing into place.

Position the engine, cylinder head side up. Lubricate the lifters, and install them into their bores. Install the cylinder head, and torque it as specified in the car section. Insert the pushrods (where applicable), and install the rocker shaft(s) (if so equipped) or position the rocker arms on the pushrods. If solid lift-ers are utilized, adjust the valves to the "cold" specifications.

Mount the intake and exhaust manifolds, the carburetor(s), the distributor and spark plugs. Adjust the point gap and the static ignition timing. Mount all accessories and install the engine in the car. Fill the radiator with coolant, and the crankcase with high quality engine oil.

Break-in Procedure

Start the engine, and allow it to run at low speed for a few minutes, while checking for leaks. Stop the engine, check the oil level, and fill as necessary. Restart the engine, and fill the cooling system to capacity. Check the point dwell angle and adjust the ignition timing and the valves. Run the engine at low to medium speed (800–2500 rpm) for approximately ½ hour, and retorque the cylinder head bolts. Road test the car, and check again for leaks.

Follow the manufacturer's recommended engine break-in procedure and maintenance schedule for new engines.

4

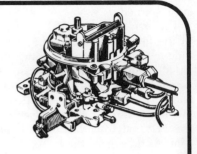

Emission Controls and Fuel System

EMISSION CONTROLS

There are three basic sources of automotive pollution in the modern internal combustion engine. They are the crankcase with its accompanying blow-by vapors, the fuel system with its evaporation of unburned gasoline, and the combustion chambers with their resulting exhaust emissions. Pollution arising from the incomplete combustion of fuel generally falls into three categories; hydrocarbons (HC), carbon monoxide (CO), and oxides of nitrogen (NO_x).

Positive Crankcase Ventilation System

All 1968 and later Fords are equipped with a positive crankcase ventilation (PCV) system to control crankcase blow-by vapors. The system consists of a PCV valve and oil separator mounted on top of the valve cover, a nonventilated oil filter cap, and a pair of hoses supplying filtered intake air to the valve cover and delivering the crankcase vapors from the valve cover to the intake manifold (six-cylinder) or carburetor (V8).

The system functions as follows:

When the engine is running, a small portion of the gases which are formed in the combustion chamber leak by the piston rings

and enter the crankcase. Since these gases are under pressure, they tend to escape from the crankcase and enter the atmosphere. If these gases are allowed to remain in the crankcase for any period of time, they contaminate the engine oil and cause sludge to build up in the crankcase. If the gases are allowed to escape into the atmosphere, they pollute the air, with unburned hydrocarbons. The job of the crankcase emission control equipment is to recycle these gases back into

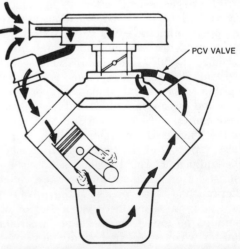

Positive crankcase ventilation system operation —V8

the engine combustion chamber where they are reburned.

The crankcase (blow-by) gases are recycled in the following way: as the engine is running, clean, filtered air is drawn through the air filter and into the crankcase. As the air passes through the crankcase, it picks up the combustion gases and carries them out of the crankcase, through the oil separator, through the PCV valve, and into the induction system. As they enter the intake manifold, they are drawn into the combustion chamber where they are reburned.

The most critical component in the system is the PCV valve. This valve controls the amount of gases which are recycled into the combustion chamber. At low engine speeds, the valve is partially closed, limiting the flow of the gases into the intake manifold. As engine speed increases, the valve opens to admit greater quantities of the gases into the intake manifold. If the valve should become blocked or plugged, the gases will be prevented from escaping from the crankcase by the normal route. Since these gases are under pressure, they will find their own way out of the crankcase. This alternate route is usually a weak oil seal or gasket in the engine. As the gas escapes by the gasket, it also creates an oil leak. Besides causing oil leaks, a clogged PCV valve also allows these gases to remain in the crankcase for an extended period of time, promoting the formation of sludge in the engine.

Fuel Evaporative Control System

1970 Fords manufactured for sale in California, and all 1971–77 models nationwide are equipped with a fuel evaporative control system to prevent the evaporation of unburned gasoline. The 1970 system consists of a sealed fuel tank filler cap, an expansion area at the top of the gas tank, a combination vapor separator and expansion tank assembly, a 3-way vapor control valve, a carbon canister located in the engine compartment which stores these vapors, and the hoses which connect this equipment. The 1971 and later system consists of a special-vacuum/pressure relief filler cap, and expansion area at the top of the fuel tank, a foam-filled vapor separator mounted on top of the fuel tank, a carbon canister which stores fuel vapors and hoses which connect this equipment. On both systems, the carburetor fuel bowl vapors are re-

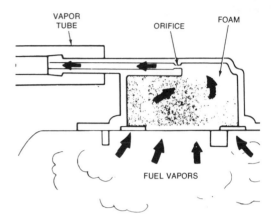

Fuel vapors entering vapor separator

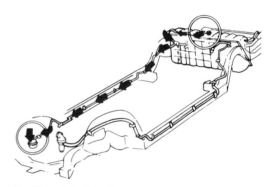

Routing of fuel tank vapors

tained within the fuel bowl until the engine is started, at which point they are internally vented into the engine for burning.

The system functions as follows:

Changes in atmospheric temperature cause the gasoline in fuel tanks to expand or contract. If this expansion and consequent vaporization takes places in a conventional fuel tank, the fuel vapors escape through the filler cap or vent hose and pollute the atmosphere. The fuel evaporative emission control system prevents this by routing the gasoline vapors to the engine where they are burned.

As the gasoline in the fuel tank of a parked car begins to expand due to heat, the vapor that forms moves to the top of the fuel tank. The fuel tanks on all 1970 and later cars are enlarged so that there exists an area representing 10–20% of the total fuel tank volume above the level of the fuel tank filler tube where these gases may collect. The vapors then travel upward into the vapor separator which prevents liquid gasoline from escaping from the fuel tank. The fuel vapor is then drawn through the vapor separator outlet hose, through the 3-way vapor control valve

(1970 only), then to the charcoal canister in the engine compartment. The vapor enters the canister, passes through a charcoal filter, and then exits through the canister's grated bottom. As the vapor passes through the charcoal, it is cleansed by hydrocarbons, so that the air that passes out of the bottom of the canister is free of pollutants.

When the engine is started, vacuum from the carburetor draws fresh air into the canister. As the entering air passes through the charcoal in the canister, it picks up the hydrocarbons that were deposited there by the fuel vapors. This mixture of hydrocarbons and fresh air is then carried through a hose to the air cleaner. In the carburetor, it combines with the incoming air/fuel mixture and enters the combustion chambers of the engine where it is burned.

On both systems, there still remains the problem of allowing air into the tank to replace the gasoline displaced during normal use and the problem of relieving excess pressure from the fuel tank should it reach a dangerous level. On 1970 systems, the 3-way control valve accomplishes this. On 1971 and later systems, the special filler cap performs this task. Under normal circumstances, the filler cap functions as a check valve, allowing air to enter the tank to replace the fuel consumed. At the same time it prevents vapors from escaping from the cap. In case of severe pressure within the tank, the filler cap valve opens, venting the pollutants to the atmosphere.

Thermactor System

All 1968 models equipped with manual transmission, the 1969 428 Police Interceptor engine, all 1974 models manufactured for sale in California, and all 1975–79 models are equipped with a Thermactor emission control system.

The Thermactor emission control system makes use of a belt-driven air pump to inject fresh air into the hot exhaust stream through the engine exhaust ports. The result is the extended burning of those fumes which were not completely ignited in the combustion chamber, and the subsequent reduction of some of the hydrocarbon and carbon monoxide content of the exhaust emissions into harmless carbon dioxide and water.

The Thermactor system is composed of the following components:

1. Air supply pump (belt-driven)
2. Air by-pass valve
3. Check valves
4. Air manifolds (internal or external)
5. Air supply tubes (on external manifolds only).

Air for the Thermactor system is cleaned by means of a centrifugal filter fan mounted on the air pump driveshaft. The air filter does not require a replaceable element.

To prevent excessive pressure, the air pump is equipped with a pressure relief valve which uses a replaceable plastic plug to control the pressure setting.

The Thermactor air pump has sealed bear-

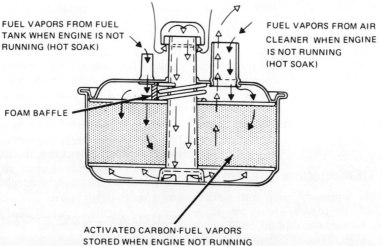

FLOW OF FRESH AIR TO PURGE STORED FUEL VAPORS WHEN ENGINE IS RUNNING

FUEL VAPORS TO AIR CLEANER TO BE BURNED WHEN ENGINE IS RUNNING

FUEL VAPORS FROM FUEL TANK WHEN ENGINE IS NOT RUNNING (HOT SOAK)

FUEL VAPORS FROM AIR CLEANER WHEN ENGINE IS NOT RUNNING (HOT SOAK)

FOAM BAFFLE

ACTIVATED CARBON-FUEL VAPORS STORED WHEN ENGINE NOT RUNNING

Cross-section of charcoal canister

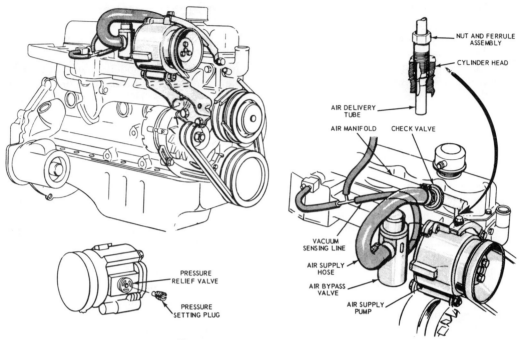

Thermactor installation—240 six

ings which are lubricated for the life of the unit, and pre-set rotor vane and bearing clearances, which do not require any periodic adjustments.

The air supply from the pump is controlled by the air by-pass valve, sometimes called a dump valve. During deceleration, the air by-pass valve opens, momentarily diverting the air supply through a silencer and into the atmosphere, thus preventing backfires within the exhaust system.

A check valve is incorporated in the air inlet side of the air manifolds. Its purpose is to prevent exhaust gases from backing up into the Thermactor system. This valve is especially important in the event of drive belt failure, and during deceleration, when the air by-pass valve is dumping the air supply.

The air manifolds and air supply tubes channel the air from the Thermactor air pump into the exhaust ports of each cylinder, thus completing the cycle of the Thermactor system.

Improved Combustion System

All 1968 Fords equipped with automatic transmission, all 1969 models except the 428 Police Interceptor engine, and all 1970 and later models (regardless of other exhaust emission control equipment) are equipped with the Improved Combustion (IMCO) System. The IMCO System controls emissions arising from the incomplete combustion of the air/fuel mixture in the cylinders. The IMCO system incorporates a number of modifications to the distributor spark control system, the fuel system, and the internal design of the engine.

Internal engine modifications include the following: elimination of surface irregularities and crevices as well as a low surface area-to-volume ratio in the combustion chambers, a high-velocity intake manifold combined with short exhaust ports, selective valve timing and a higher temperature and capacity cooling system.

Modifications to the fuel system include the following: recalibrated carburetors to achieve a leaner air/fuel mixture, more precise calibration of the choke mechanism, the installation of idle mixture limiter caps and a heated air intake system.

Modifications to the distributor spark control system include the following: a modified centrifugal advance curve, the use of dual diaphragm distributors in most applications, a ported vacuum switch, a deceleration valve and a spark delay valve.

HEATED AIR INTAKE SYSTEM

The heated air intake portion of the air cleaner consists of a thermostat (all 1968–72

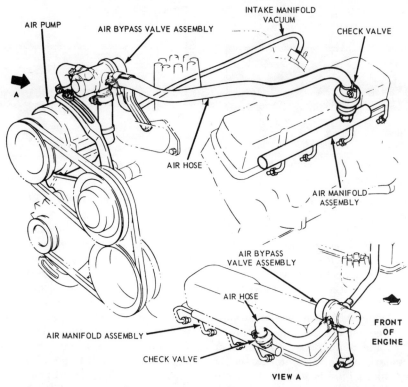

Thermactor installation—302, 351, 400, 460 V8, except 1975–76 models

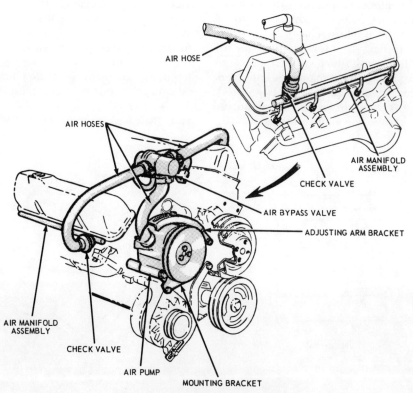

Thermactor installation—390, 428 V8

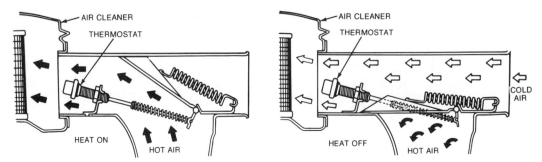

AIR CLEANER

THERMOSTAT

HEAT ON

HOT AIR

AIR CLEANER

THERMOSTAT

COLD AIR

HEAT OFF

HOT AIR

Temperature-operated duct and valve assembly

models except the 351C land 400 V8), or bimetal switch and vacuum motor (all 1973–79 and all 351C and 400 V8), and a spring-loaded temperature control door in the snorkel of the air cleaner. The temperature control door is located between the end of the air cleaner snorkel which draws in air from the engine compartment and the duct that carries heated air up from the exhaust manifold. When underhood temperature is below 90° F, the temperature control door blocks off underhood air from entering the air cleaner and allows only heated air from the exhaust manifold to be drawn into the air cleaner. When underhood temperature rises above 130° F, the temperature control door blocks off heated air from the exhaust manifold and allows only underhood air to be drawn into the air cleaner.

By controlling the temperature of the engine intake air this way, exhaust emissions are lowered and fuel economy is improved. In addition, throttle plate icing is reduced, and cold weather driveability is improved from the necessary leaner mixtures.

DUAL DIAPHRAGM DISTRIBUTORS

Dual diaphragm distributors are installed in most 1968 and later models and appear in many different engine/transmission/equipment combinations. The best way to tell if you have one is to take a look at your distributor vacuum capsule on the side of the distributor. One vacuum hose running from the vacuum capsule indicates a single diaphragm distributor. Two vacuum hoses means that you have a dual diaphragm unit.

The dual distributor diaphragm is a two-chambered housing which is mounted on the side of the distributor. The outer side of the housing is a distributor vacuum advance mechanism, connected to the carburetor by a vacuum hose. The purpose of the vacuum advance is to advance ignition timing according to the conditions under which the engine is operating. This device has been used on automobiles for many years now and its chief advantage is economical engine operation. The second side of the dual diaphragm is the side that has been added to help control

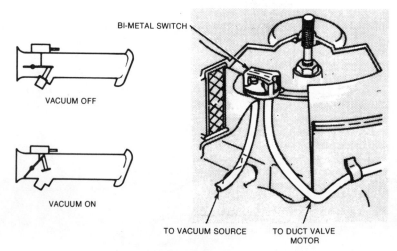

BI-METAL SWITCH

VACUUM OFF

VACUUM ON

TO VACUUM SOURCE

TO DUCT VALVE MOTOR

Vacuum-operated duct and valve assembly

engine exhaust emissions at idle and during deceleration.

The inner side of the dual diaphragm is connected by a vacuum hose to the intake manifold. When the engine is idling or decelerating, intake manifold vacuum is high and carburetor vacuum is low. Under these conditions, intake manifold vacuum, applied to the inner side of the dual diaphragm, retards ignition timing to promote more complete combustion of the air fuel mixture in the engine combustion chambers.

PORTED VACUUM SWITCH (DISTRIBUTOR VACUUM CONTROL VALVE)

The distributor vacuum control valve is a temperature-sensitive valve which screws into the water jacket of the engine. Three vacuum lines are attached to the vacuum control valve: one which runs from the carburetor to the control valve, one which runs from the control valve to the distributor vacuum advance (outer) chamber, and one which runs from the intake manifold to the distributor vacuum control valve.

During normal engine operation, vacuum from the carburetor passes through the top nipple on the distributor control valve, through the valve to the second nipple on the valve, and out the second nipple on the valve to the distributor vacuum advance chamber. When the engine is idling however, carburetor vacuum is very low, so that there is little, if any, vacuum in the passageways described above.

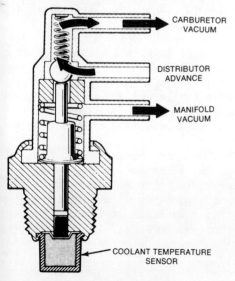

CARBURETOR VACUUM

DISTRIBUTOR ADVANCE

MANIFOLD VACUUM

COOLANT TEMPERATURE SENSOR

Ported vacuum switch operation

If the engine should begin to overheat while idling, a check ball inside the distributor vacuum control which normally blocks off the third nipple of the valve (intake manifold vacuum) moves upward to block off the first nipple (carburetor vacuum). This applies intake manifold vacuum (third nipple) to the distributor vacuum advance chamber (second nipple). Since intake manifold vacuum is very high while the engine is idling, ignition timing is advanced by the application of intake manifold vacuum to the distributor vacuum advance chamber. This raises the engine idle speed and helps to cool the engine.

DECELERATION VALVE

Some IMCO-equipped 1968–72 engines are equipped with a distributor vacuum advance control valve (deceleration valve) which is used with dual-diaphragm distributors to further aid in controlling ignition timing. The deceleration valve is in the vacuum line which runs from the outer (advance) diaphragm to the carburetor—the normal vacuum supply for the distributor. During deceleration, the intake manifold vacuum rises causing the deceleration valve to close off the carburetor vacuum source and connect the intake manifold vacuum source to the distributor advance diaphragm. The increase in vacuum provides maximum ignition timing advance, thus providing more complete fuel combustion, and decreasing exhaust system backfiring.

SPARK DELAY VALVE

The spark delay valve is a plastic, spring-loaded, color-coded valve which is installed in the vacuum line to the distributor advance diaphragm on many 1971 and later models. Under heavy throttle applications, the valve will close, blocking normal carburetor vacuum to the distributor. After the designated period of closed time, the valve opens, restoring the carburetor vacuum to the distributor.

Distributor Modulator (Dist-o-vac) System

1970 models equipped with automatic transmission and the 240, 302, or 390 2 bbl engines, and 1971 models equipped with automatic transmission and the 240, 390 2 bbl, or 429 4 bbl engines are equipped with a Dist-O-Vac spark control system. This sys-

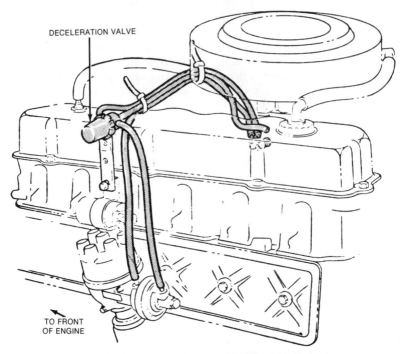

DECELERATION VALVE

TO FRONT
OF ENGINE

Deceleration valve installation—240 six

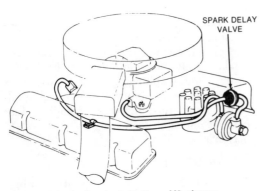

SPARK DELAY
VALVE

Spark delay valve installation—V8 shown

tem is used in conjunction with all of the IMCO system equipment except the deceleration valve.

The three components of the Dist-O-Vac system are the speed sensor, the thermal switch, and the electronic control module. The electronic control module consists of two sub-assemblies: the electronic control amplifier and the three-way solenoid valve.

The speed sensor, a small unit mounted in the speedometer cable, contains a rotating magnet and a stationary winding which is insulated from ground. The magnet, which rotates with the speedometer cable, generates a small voltage which increases directly with speed. This voltage is directed to the electronic control amplifier.

The thermal switch consists of a bimetallic-element switch which is mounted in the right door pillar and senses the temperature of the air. The switch is closed at 58° F or lower, and open at temperatures about 58° F. This switch is also connected to the electronic control amplifier.

Within the electronic control module case, there is a printed circuit board and an electronic amplifier. The speed sensor and thermal switch are connected to this assembly. The thermal switch is the dominant circuit. When the temperature of the outside air is 58° F or lower, the circuit is closed, so that regardless of speed, the electronic control amplifier will not trigger the three-way solenoid valve. At temperatures above 58° F, however, the thermal switch circuit is open, allowing the circuit from the speed sensor to take over and control the action of the solenoid valve.

The three-way solenoid valve is located within the electronic control module and below the printed circuit board of the amplifier. It is vented to the atmosphere at the top, and connected at the bottom of the carburetor spark port (small hose) and the primary (advance) side of the dual-diaphragm distributor (large hose). The large hose is also channeled through the temperature-sensing valve. The small hose is equipped with an air

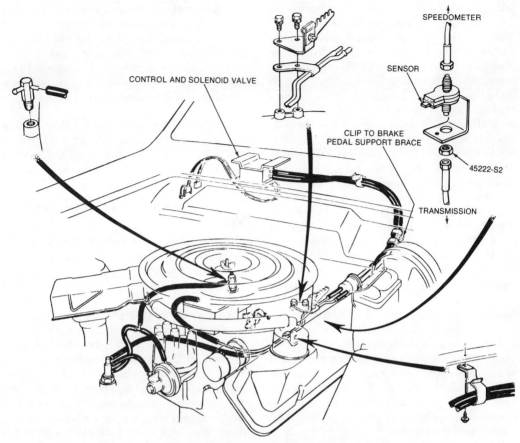

Typical Dist-O-Vac system installation

bleed to provide a positive airflow in the direction of the carburetor. The air bleed purges the hose of vacuum, thus assuring that raw gasoline will not be drawn through the hose and into the distributor diaphragm.

When the thermal switch is closed (air temperature 58° F or lower), or when it is open and the speed sensor is not sending out a strong enough voltage signal (speeds below approximately 35 mph), the amplifier will not activate the solenoid valve and the valve is in the closed position, blocking the passage of air from the small tube through the large tube. With the valve in this position, the larger hose is vented to the atmosphere through the top opening in the three-way valve assembly. Consequently, no vacuum is being supplied to the primary diaphragm on the distributor, and, therefore, no vacuum advance.

When the air temperature is above 58° F and/or the speed of the car is sufficient to generate the required voltage (35 mph or faster), the valve opens, blocking the vent to the atmosphere while opening the vacuum

line from the carburetor spark port to the primary diaphragm of the distributor.

Electronic Spark Control

1972 Fords manufactured for sale in California equipped with a 351C or 400 V8, and all 1972 Fords equipped with the 429 Police Interceptor engine, use the electronic spark control system.

Electronic Spark Control is a system which blocks off carburetor vacuum to the distributor vacuum advance mechanism under certain temperature and speed conditions. The Electronic Spark Control System consists of four components: a temperature sensor, a speed sensor, an amplifier, and a distributor modulator vacuum valve. The system serves to prevent ignition timing advance (by blocking off carburetor vacuum from the distributor vacuum advance mechanism) until the car reaches a speed of 35 mph when the ambient temperature is over 65° F.

The temperature sensor, which is mounted on the front face of the left door pillar, monitors the outside air temperature and relays this information to the amplifier. The amplifier, which is located under the instrument panel, controls the distributor modulator vacuum valve. The modulator valve, which is attached to the ignition coil mounting bracket, is connected into the carburetor vacuum line to the distributor, and is normally open. If the temperature of the outside air is below 48° F, the contacts in the temperature sensor are open and no signal is sent to the amplifier. Since no signal is sent to the amplifier, the amplifier does not send a signal to the distributor modulator valve, and the vacuum passage from the carburetor to the distributor vacuum advance remains open. When the outside temperature rises to 65° F or above, the contacts in the temperature sensor close, and a signal is sent to the amplifier. The amplifier relays the message to the distributor modulator, which closes to block the vacuum passage to the distributor, preventing ignition timing advance.

When the ambient temperature is 65° F or above, ignition timing advance is prevented until the amplifier receives a signal from the speed sensor that the speed of the vehicle has reached 35 mph, and the distributor modulator vacuum valve can be opened to permit ignition timing advance.

The speed sensor is a miniature generator which is connected to the speedometer cable of the car. As the speedometer cable turns, the inside of the speed sensor turns with the speedometer cable. As the speed of the car increases, a rotating magnet in the speed sensor induces an electronic current in the stationary windings in the speed sensor. This current is sent to the amplifier. As the speed of the vehicle increases, the amount of current sent to the amplifier by the speed sensor increases proportionately. When the car reaches a speed of 35 mph, the amplifier signals the distributor modulator vacuum valve to open, allowing carburetor vacuum to be sent to the distributor vacuum advance chamber. This permits the ignition timing to advance.

It should be noted that this system operates only when the ambient temperature is 65° F or above, and then only when the speed of the car is below 35 mph.

Transmission Regulated Spark System

1972 Fords equipped with the 240 Six or the 351W V8 and automatic transmission use a transmission regulated spark control system.

The transmission regulated spark control system (TRS) differs from the Dist-O-Vac and ESC systems in that the speed sensor and amplifier are replaced by a switch on the transmission. The switch is activated by a mechanical linkage which opens the switch when the transmission is shifted into High gear. The switch, when opened, triggers the opening of the vacuum lines to the distributor, thus providing vacuum advance. So, in short, the TRS system blocks vacuum advance to the distributor only when the outside temperature is above 65° F and the transmission is in First or Second gear.

Exhaust Gas Recirculation System

All 1973 and later models are equipped with an exhaust gas recirculation (EGR) system to control oxides of nitrogen.

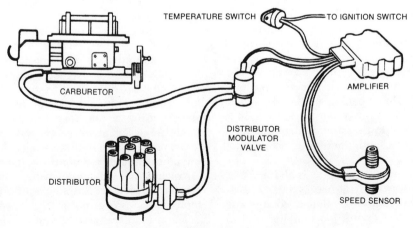

Electronic spark control system schematic

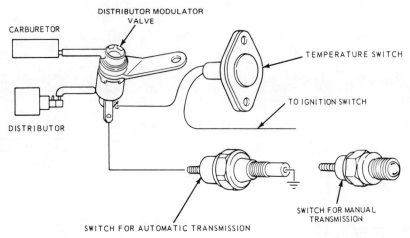

Transmission regulated spark control system schematic

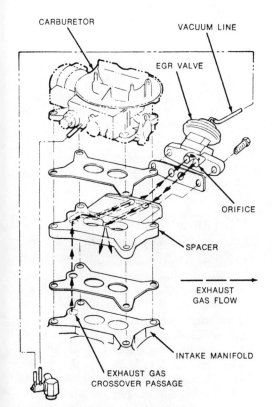

Spacer entry EGR valve operation

On V8 engines, exhaust gases travel through the exhaust gas crossover passage in the intake manifold. On spacer entry equipped engines, a portion of these gases are diverted into a spacer which is mounted under the carburetor. On floor entry models, a regulated portion of exhaust gases enters the intake manifold through a pair of small holes drilled in the floor of the intake mani-

fold riser. The EGR control valve, which is attached to the rear of the spacer or intake manifold, consists of a vacuum diaphragm with an attached plunger which normally blocks off exhaust gases from entering the intake manifold.

On all models, the EGR valve is controlled by a vacuum line from the carburetor which passes through a ported vacuum switch. The EGR ported vaccum switch provides vacuum to the EGR valve at coolant temperatures above 125° F. The vacuum diaphragm then opens the EGR valve permitting exhaust gases to flow through the carburetor spacer and enter the combustion chambers. The exhaust gases are relatively oxygen-free, and tend to dilute the combustion charge. This lowers peak combustion temperature thereby reducing oxides of nitrogen.

On some models equipped with a 351C, 400, 429 or 460 V8, an EGR subsystem, consisting of a speed sensor and control amplifier, prevents exhaust gases from entering the combustion mixture when the car is traveling 65 mph or faster.

Delay Vacuum By-pass (DVB) System

All 1973 Fords equipped with the 351C, 400, 429, or 460 V8 manufactured before March 15, 1973 are equipped with the Delay Vacuum By-pass spark control system. This system provides two paths by which carburetor vacuum can reach the distributor vacuum advance. The system consists of a spark delay valve, a check valve, a solenoid vacuum valve, and an ambient temperature switch.

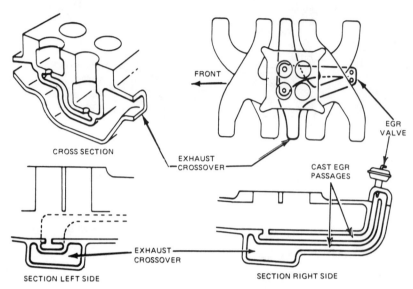

Floor entry EGR valve operation

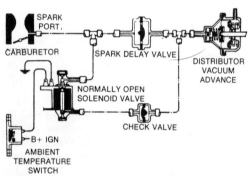

Delay vacuum by-pass system schematic

When the ambient temperature is below 49° F, the temperature switch contacts are open and the vacuum solenoid is open (de-energized). Under these conditions, vacuum will flow from the carburetor, through the open solenoid, and to the distributor. Since the spark delay valve resists the flow of carburetor vacuum, the vacuum will always flow through the vacuum solenoid when it is open, since this is the path of least resistance. When the ambient temperature rises above 60° F, the contacts in the temperature switch (which is located in the door post) close. This passes ignition switch current to the solenoid, energizing the solenoid. This blocks one of the two vacuum paths. All distributor vacuum must now flow through the spark delay valve. When carburetor vacuum rises above a certain level on acceleration, a rubber valve in the spark delay valve blocks vacuum from passing through the valve for from 5 to 30 seconds. After this time delay has elapsed, normal vacuum is supplied to the distributor. When the vacuum solenoid is closed, (temperature above 60°), the vacuum line from the solenoid to the distributor is vented to atmosphere. To prevent the vacuum that is passing through the spark delay valve from escaping through the solenoid into the atmosphere, a one-way check valve is installed in the vacuum line from the solenoid to the distributor.

Cold Temperature Actuated Vacuum (CTAV) System

This system is installed on some 1973 models manufactured after March 15, 1973 and many 1974 models to control distributor spark advance. It is basically a refinement of the DVB or TAV spark control systems with the temperature switch relocated in the air cleaner and a latching relay added to maintain a strong vacuum signal at the distributor, whether it be EGR port or spark port carburetor vacuum, and to keep the system from intermittently switching vacuum signals when the intake air is between 49 and 60° F. When the temperature switch closes at 60° F, the latching relay (normally off) is energized and stays on until the ignition switch is turned off. The latching relay then overrides the temperature switch and forces the solenoid valve to keep the spark port vacuum system closed and open the EGR port vacuum system. This prevents full vacuum advance, once the engine is warmed-up, thereby lowering emissions.

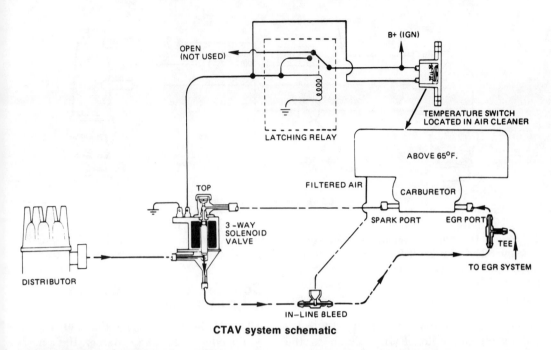

CTAV system schematic

EGR/Coolant Spark Control (CSC) System

The EGR/CSC system is used on most 1974 and later models. It regulates both distributor spark advance and the EGR valve opera-

tion according to coolant temperature by sequentially switching vacuum signals.

The major EGR/CSC system components are:

1. 95° F EGR-PVS valve;
2. Spark Delay Valve (SDV);

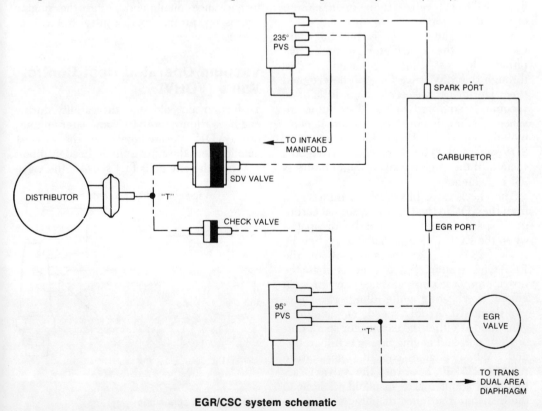

EGR/CSC system schematic

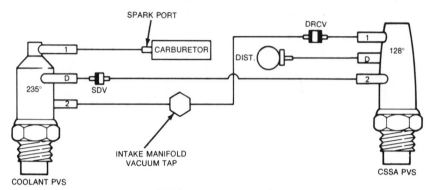

CSSA system schematic

3. Vacuum check valve.

When the engine coolant temperature is below 82° F, the EGR-PVS valve admits carburetor EGR port vacuum (occurring at about 2,500 rpm) directly to the distributor advance diaphragm, through the one-way check valve.

At the same time, the EGR-PVS valve shuts off carburetor EGR vacuum to the EGR valve and transmission diaphragm.

When engine coolant temperature is 95° F and above, the EGR-PVS valve is actuated and directs carburetor EGR vacuum to the EGR valve and transmission instead of the distributor. At temperatures between 82–95° F, the EGR-PVS valve may be open, closed, or in mid-position.

The SDV valve delays carburetor spark vacuum to the distributor advance diaphragm by restricting the vacuum signal through the SDV valve for a predetermined time. During normal acceleration, little or no vacuum is admitted to the distributor advance diaphragm until acceleration is completed, because of (1) the time delay of the SDV valve and (2) the re-routing of EGR port vacuum if the engine coolant temperature is 95° F or higher.

The check valve blocks off vacuum signal from the SDV to the EGR-PVS so that carburetor spark vacuum will not be dissipated when the EGR-PVS is actuated above 95° F.

The 235° F PVS is not part of the EGR/CSC system, but is connected to the distributor vacuum advance to prevent engine overheating while idling (as on previous models). At idle speed, no vacuum is generated at either the carburetor spark port or EGR port and engine timing is fully retarded. When engine coolant temperature reaches 235° F, however, the valve is actuated to admit intake manifold vacuum to the distributor advance diaphragm. This ad-

vances the engine timing and speeds up the engine. The increase in coolant flow and fan speed lowers engine temperature.

Cold Start Spark Advance (CSSA) System

All 1975–78 Fords using the 460 V8 are equipped with the CSSA System. It is a modification of the existing spark control system to aid in cold start driveability. The system uses a coolant temperature sensing vacuum switch located on the thermostat housing. When the engine is cold (below 125° F), it permits full manifold vacuum to the distributor advance diaphragm. After the engine warms up, normal spark control (retard) resumes.

Vacuum Operated Heat Control Valve (VOHV)

To further aid cold start driveability during engine warmup, most 1975 and later engines use a VOHV located between the exhaust manifold and the exhaust inlet (header) pipe.

When the engine is first started, the valve

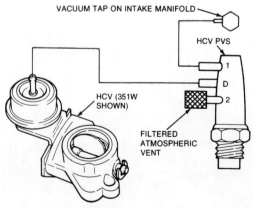

VOHV system schematic

is closed, blocking exhaust gases from exiting from one bank of cylinders. These gases are then diverted back through the intake manifold crossover passage under the carburetor. The result is quick heat to the carburetor and choke.

The VOHV is controlled by a ported vacuum switch which uses manifold vacuum to keep the vacuum motor on the valve closed until the coolant reaches a predetermined "warm-up" value. When the engine is warmed-up, the PVS shuts off vacuum to the VOHV, and a strong return spring opens the VOHV butterfly.

Catalytic Reactor (Converter) System

Starting in 1975, all Fords are equipped with a catalytic converter system to meet applicable Federal and California emission control standards. California models are equipped with two converters, while models sold in the 49 states have only one unit. Starting in 1979, models sold in all 50 states are equipped with two converters.

Catalytic converters convert noxious emissions of hydrocarbons (HC) and carbon monoxide (CO) into harmless carbon dioxide and water. The reaction takes place inside the reactor(s) at great heat using platinum or palladium metals as the catalyst. The units are installed in the exhaust system ahead of the mufflers. They are designed, if the engine is properly tuned, to last 50,000 miles before replacement.

Electronic Engine Control II System (EEC II)

Starting in 1979, the EEC II system is installed on all California LTD's equipped with the 351 V8.

The system is based on the Versailles EEC I system introduced in 1978, but certain components have been altered to improve reliability and performance. The EEC II system controls spark timing, EGR, and air/fuel ratio. A solid state microcomputer interprets information sent by seven sensors, and uses this information to control ignition timing, EGR flow, air/fuel mixture, thermactor air flow, and various cold engine functions. The system utilizes a three-way catalytic converter, and a closed loop feedback variable venturi carburetor. With the EEC II system, Ford has ushered in a new era of sophisticated and complicated emission controls. Diagnosis and/or repair of any part of the system requires extensive training, and elaborate test equipment. If you suspect a problem in your EEC II system, you will have to see your dealer.

NOTE: *See chapter 2 for further details of the EEC II system.*

Component Service

POSITIVE CRANKCASE VENTILATION SYSTEM

1. Remove the PCV system components, filler cap, PCV valve, hoses, tubes, fittings, etc. from the engine.
2. Soak the rubber ventilation hose(s) in a low volatility petroleum base solvent.
3. Clean the rubber ventilation hose(s) by passing a suitable cleaning brush through them.
4. Thoroughly wash the rubber hoses in a low volatility petroleum base solvent and dry with compressed air.
5. Thoroughly wash the crankcase breather cap, if so equipped, in a low volatility petroleum base solvent and shake dry. Do not dry with compressed air; damage to the filtering media may result.
6. Thoroughly clean tubes, fittings, connections to assure unobstructed flow of emission gases.
7. Install new PCV valve and re-install previously removed hoses, tubes, fittings, etc. to their proper location.
8. Replace any system component that shows signs of damage, wear or deterioration as required.
9. Replace any hose or tube that cannot be cleaned satisfactorily.

FUEL EVAPORATIVE CONTROL SYSTEM

Except for 1970 models manufactured for sale in California, the only service performed on the evaporative control system is the replacement of the charcoal (carbon) canister at the intervals listed in the maintenance schedule in Chapter 1. The above mentioned California registered 1970 Fords require replacement of the 3-way vent valve once a year or every 12,000 miles. The procedure is as follows.

1. Working under the vehicle, disconnect two hoses from the control valve. Remove the vent valve cover.
2. Remove two attaching bolts and re-

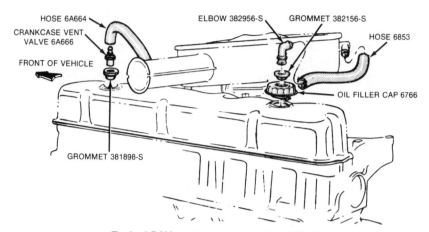

Typical PCV system components—240 six

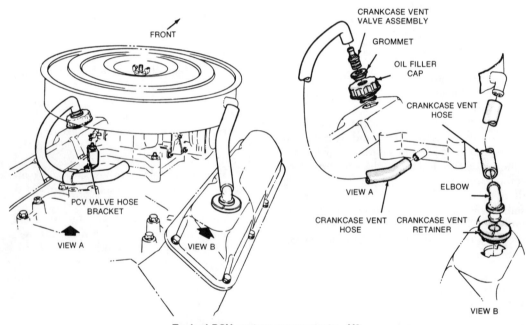

Typical PCV system components—V8

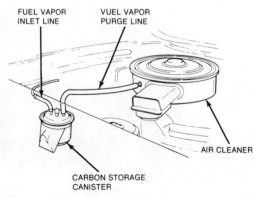

Charcoal (carbon) canister location

move the valve from the crossmember of the rear of the gas tank.

3. To install, position the valve to the crossmember and install two attaching bolts.

4. Connect the two hoses to the valve assembly. Install the cover.

EXHAUST GAS RECIRCULATION SYSTEM

EGR Valve Cleaning

Remove the EGR valve for cleaning. Do not strike or pry on the valve diaphragm housing or supports, as this may damage the valve operating mechanism and/or change the valve calibration. Check orifice hole in the EGR valve body for deposits. A small hand drill of no more than 0.060 in. diameter may be used to clean the hole if plugged. Extreme care must be taken to avoid enlarging the hole or damaging the surface of the orifice plate.

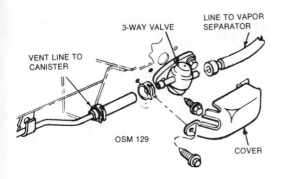

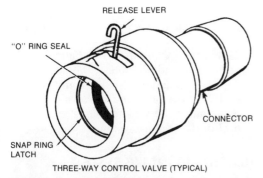

THREE-WAY CONTROL VALVE (TYPICAL)

Evaporative control 3-way valve location (1970 California models only)

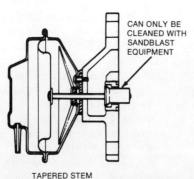

Cleaning EGR valve orifice

VALVES WHICH CANNOT BE DISASSEMBLED

Valves which are riveted or otherwise permanently assembled should be replaced if highly contaminated; they cannot be cleaned.

VALVES WHICH CAN BE DISASSEMBLED

Separate the diaphragm section from the main mounting body. Clean the valve plates, stem, and the mounting plate, using a small power-driven rotary type wire brush. Take care not to damage the parts. Remove deposits between stem and valve disc by using a steel blade or shim approximately 0.028 in. thick in a sawing motion around the stem shoulder at both sides of the disc.

The poppet must wobble and move axially before reassembly.

Clean the cavity and passages in the main body of the valve with a power-driven rotary wire brush. If the orifice plate has a hole less than 0.450 in. it must be removed for cleaning. Remove all loosened debris using shop compressed air. Reassemble the diaphragm section on the main body using a new gasket between them. Torque the attaching screws to specification. Clean the orifice plate and the counterbore in the valve body. Reinstall the orifice plate using a small amount of contact cement to retain the plate in place during assembly of the valve to the carburetor spacer. Apply cement to only outer edges of the orifice plate to avoid restriction of the orifice.

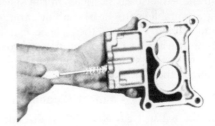

Cleaning EGR spacer machined holes

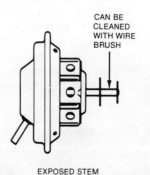

EGR valve comparison

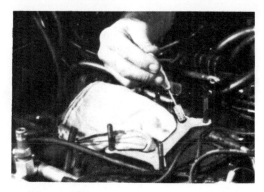

Cleaning EGR exhaust gas entry port in intake manifold

Cleaning EGR spacer exhaust passages

EGR Supply Passages and Carburetor Space Cleaning

Remove the carburetor and carburetor spacer on engines so equipped. Clean the supply tube with a small power-driven rotary type wire brush or blast cleaning equipment. Clean the exhaust gas passages in the spacer using a suitable wire brush and/or scraper. The machined holes in the spacer can be cleaned by using a suitable round wire brush. Hard encrusted material should be probed loose first, then brushed out.

EGR Exhaust Gas Channel Cleaning

Clean the exhaust gas channel, where applicable, in the intake manifold, using a suitable carbon scraper. Clean the exhaust gas entry port in the intake manifold by hand passing a suitable drill bit thru the holes to auger out the deposits. Do not use a wire brush. The manifold riser bore(s) should be suitably plugged during the above action to prevent any of the residue from entering the induction system.

Component Replacement

PCV VALVE

Disconnect the ventilation hose at the oil filler cap on V8 applications and pull out the PCV valve from its grommet. On six-cylinder engines, disconnect the ventilation hose from its connection at the front of the valve cover and pull out the PCV valve from its grommet. Clean out all of the passageways in the hoses and fittings with a kerosene-soaked rag. Install a new PCV valve in its grommet and connect the ventilation hose.

EVAPORATIVE CONTROL CHARCOAL CANISTER

Loosen and remove the canister mounting bolts from the mounting bracket. Disconnect the purge hose from the air cleaner and the feed hose from the fuel tank. Discard the old canister and install a new unit. Make sure that the hoses are connected properly.

PORTED VACUUM SWITCH (DISTRIBUTOR VACUUM CONTROL VALVE)

1. Drain about one gallon of coolant out of the radiator.
2. Tag the vacuum hoses that attach to the control valve and disconnect them.
3. Unscrew and remove the control valve.
4. Install the new control valve.
5. Connect the vacuum hoses.
6. Fill the cooling system.

HEATED AIR INTAKE SYSTEM

Temperature Operated Duct and Valve Assembly

1. Remove the hex-head cap screws which secure the air intake duct and valve assembly to the air cleaner.
2. Remove the air intake duct and valve assembly from the engine.
3. If the duct and valve assembly was removed because of a suspected temperature malfunction, check the operation of the thermostat and valve plate assembly. Refer to the Air Intake Duct test for the proper procedure.
4. If inspection reveals that the valve plate is sticking or the thermostat is malfunctioning, remove the thermostat and valve plates as follows:
   a. Detach the valve plate tension spring from the valve plate using long-nose pliers. Loosen the thermostat locknut and unscrew the thermostat from the mounting bracket. Grasp the valve plate and withdraw it from the duct.
5. Install the air intake duct and valve assembly on the shroud tube.
6. Connect the air intake duct and valve

assembly to the air cleaner and tighten the hex-head retaining cap screws.

7. If it was necessary to disassemble the thermostat and air duct and valve, assemble the unit as follows:

a. Install the valve plate. Install the locknut on the thermostat, and screw the thermostat into the mounting bracket. Install the valve plate tension spring on the valve plate and duct.

b. Check the operation of the thermostat and air duct assembly. Refer to the Air Intake Duct Test for the proper procedure. Tighten the locknut.

8. Install the vacuum override motor (if applicable) and check for proper operation.

Vacuum Operated Duct and Valve Assembly

1. Disconnect the vacuum hose at the vacuum motor.

2. Remove the hex head cap screws which secure the air intake duct and valve assembly to the air cleaner.

3. Remove the duct and valve assembly from the engine.

4. Position the duct and valve assembly to the air cleaner and heat stove tube. Install the attaching cap screws.

5. Connect the vacuum line at the vacuum motor.

SPARK DELAY VALVE

1. Locate the spark delay valve in the distributor vacuum line and disconnect it from the line.

2. Install a new spark delay valve in the line, making sure that the black end of the valve is connected to the line from the carburetor and the color coded end is connected to the line from the spark delay valve to the distributor.

DIST-O-VAC AND ESC TEMPERATURE SENSOR

1. Open the right door and remove the two screws which attach the temperature sensor to the right door pillar.

2. Disconnect the lead wires from the temperature sensor.

3. Connect the lead wires to the new sensor.

4. Position the sensor on the door pillar and install the attaching screws.

DIST-O-VAC AND ESC SPEED SENSOR

1. Disconnect the lead wires from the sensor.

2. Disconnect the speed sensor from the speedometer cable.

3. Position the O-rings on both ends of the new speed sensor.

4. Connect both ends of the speedometer cable to the speed sensor.

5. Connect the lead wires to the speed sensor.

ESC AMPLIFIER

1. Locate the amplifier under the instrument panel, near the glove compartment.

2. Disconnect the wiring harness from the amplifier.

3. Remove the two amplifier attaching screws and remove the amplifier.

4. Position a new amplifier under the instrument panel and connect the wiring harness to it.

5. Install the two amplifier attaching screws.

ESC DISTRIBUTOR VACUUM MODULATOR VALVE

1. Tag the hoses that attach to the modulator and disconnect them from the amplifier.

2. Disconnect the lead wires from the modulator.

3. Remove the No. 2 left front valve cover bolt (six-cylinder) or the inboard left front valve cover bolt and remove the modulator.

4. Position the new modulator on the valve cover and install the attaching bolt.

5. Connect the wires and hoses to the modulator.

THERMACTOR AIR PUMP

1. Disconnect the air outlet hose at the air pump.

2. Loosen the pump belt tension adjuster.

3. Disengage the drive belt.

4. Remove the mounting bolt and air pump.

5. To install, position the air pump on the mounting bracket and install the mounting bolt.

6. Place drive belt in pulleys and attach the adjusting arm to the air pump.

7. Adjust the drive belt tension to specifications and tighten the adjusting arm and mounting bolts.

8. Connect the air outlet hose to the air pump.

THERMACTOR AIR PUMP FILTER FAN

1. Loosen the air pump adjusting arm bolt and mounting bracket bolt to relieve drive belt tension.

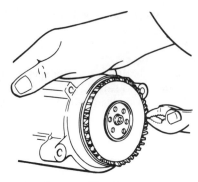

Thermactor air pump filter fan removal

2. Remove drive pulley attaching bolts and pull drive pulley off the air pump shaft.

3. Pry the outer disc loose; then, pull off the centrifugal filter fan with slip-joint pliers. CAUTION: *Do not attempt to remove the metal drive hub.*

4. Install a new filter fan by drawing it into position, using the pulley and bolts as an installer. Draw the fan evenly by alternately tightening the bolts, making certain that the outer edge of the fan slips into the housing.

NOTE: *A slight interference with the housing bore is normal. After a new fan is installed, it may squeal upon initial operation, until its outer diameter sealing lip has worn in, which may require 20 to 30 miles of operation.*

THERMACTOR CHECK VALVE

1. Disconnect the air supply hose at the valve. (Use a 1¼ in. crowfoot wrench, the valve has a standard, right-hand pipe thread.)

2. Clean the threads on the air manifold adaptor (air supply tube on 302 V8 engine) with a wire brush. Do not blow compressed air through the check valve in either direction.

3. Install the check valve and tighten.

4. Connect the air supply hose.

THERMACTOR AIR BY-PASS VALVE

1. Disconnect the air and vacuum hoses at the air by-pass valve body.

2. Position the air by-pass valve, and connect the respective hoses.

FUEL SYSTEM

Troubleshooting the Fuel System

The Problem	Is Caused By	What to Do
Engine cranks, but won't start (or is hard to start) when cold	• Empty fuel tank • Incorrect starting procedure • Defective fuel pump • No fuel in carburetor • Clogged fuel filter • Engine flooded • Defective choke	• Check for fuel in tank • Follow correct procedure • Check pump output— • Check for fuel in the carburetor • Replace fuel filter • Wait 15 minutes; try again— • Check choke plate
Engine cranks, but is hard to start (or does not start) when hot—(presence of fuel is assumed)	• Defective choke	• Check choke plate
Rough idle or engine runs rough	• Dirt or moisture in fuel • Clogged air filter • Faulty fuel pump	• Replace fuel filter • Replace air filter • Check fuel pump output—
Engine stalls or hesitates on acceleration	• Dirt or moisture in the fuel • Dirty carburetor • Defective fuel pump • Incorrect float level, defective accelerator pump	• Replace fuel filter • Clean the carburetor— • Check fuel pump output— • Have carburetor checked

Troubleshooting the Fuel System (cont.)

The Problem	Is Caused By	What to Do
Poor gas mileage	• Clogged air filter • Dirty carburetor • Defective choke, faulty carburetor adjustment	• Replace air filter • Clean carburetor— • Have carburetor checked
Engine is flooded (won't start accompanied by smell of raw fuel)	• Improperly adjusted choke or carburetor	• Wait 15 minutes and try again, without pumping gas pedal • If it won't start, have carburetor checked

Mechanical Fuel Pump

A single-action mechanical fuel pump, driven by the camshaft, is used on all models except the Police Interceptor 429 and 460 V8. The mechanical fuel pump is located at the lower left-side of the engine block on six-cylinder models, and at the lower left-side of the cylinder front cover on V8 models. The Police Interceptor engines use an electrical fuel pump located in the fuel tank beneath the vapor separator. The tank must be removed for electrical fuel pump service.

All mechanical fuel pumps, except those used on 1968–71 428 and 429 Police Interceptor engines are permanently sealed and cannot be disassembled. The only replaceable component of the permanently sealed type is the rocker arm spring. The police interceptor fuel pumps (both electrical and mechanical) are rebuildable. Refer to the accompanying illustrations for disassembly.

On all models, the fuel is filtered by a one-piece filter, located at the carburetor fuel inlet. See Chapter 1 for fuel filter maintenance.

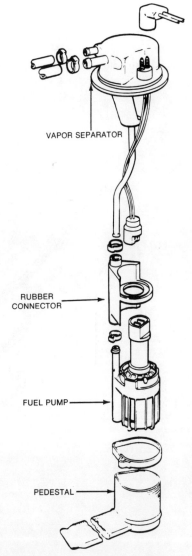

Electric fuel pump and related parts

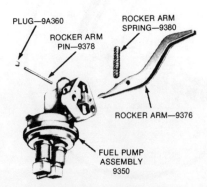

Carter permanently-sealed fuel pump—V8

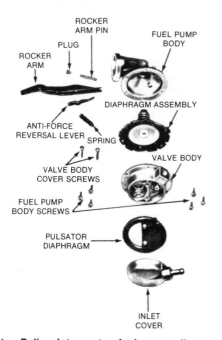

ROCKER
ARM PIN

PLUG

ROCKER
ARM

FUEL PUMP
BODY

DIAPHRAGM ASSEMBLY

ANTI-FORCE
REVERSAL LEVER

SPRING

VALVE BODY
COVER SCREWS

VALVE BODY

FUEL PUMP
BODY SCREWS

PULSATOR
DIAPHRAGM

INLET
COVER

Carter Police Interceptor fuel pump disassembled

REMOVAL AND INSTALLATION

1. Disconnect the plug and inlet and outlet lines from the fuel pump.

2. Remove the fuel pump retaining bolts and carefully pull the pump and old gasket away from the block.

3. Discard the old gasket. Clean the mating surfaces on the block and position a new gasket on the block, using oil-resistant sealer.

4. Mount the fuel pump and gasket to the engine block, being careful to insert the pump lever (rocker arm) in the engine block, aligning it correctly above the camshaft lobe.

NOTE: *If resistance is felt while positioning the fuel pump on the block, the camshaft lobe is probably on the high position. To ease installation, connect a remote engine starter switch to the engine and "tap" the switch until resistance fades.*

5. While holding the pump securely against the block, install the retaining bolts. On six-cylinder engines, torque the bolts to 12–15 ft lbs, and on V8s, 20–24 ft lbs.

6. Unplug and reconnect the fuel lines at the pump.

7. Start the engine and check for fuel leaks. Also check for oil leaks where the fuel pump attaches to the block.

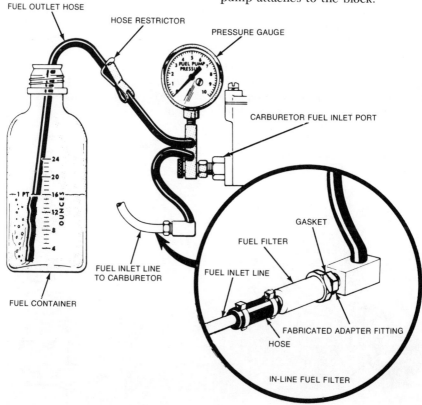

FUEL OUTLET HOSE

HOSE RESTRICTOR

PRESSURE GAUGE

CARBURETOR FUEL INLET PORT

GASKET

FUEL FILTER

FUEL INLET LINE

FUEL INLET LINE
TO CARBURETOR

FUEL CONTAINER

FABRICATED ADAPTER FITTING

HOSE

IN-LINE FUEL FILTER

Typical fuel pump pressure and capacity text equipment

TESTING AND ADJUSTMENT

No adjustments may be made to the fuel pump. Before removing and replacing the old fuel pump, the following test may be made while the pump is still installed on the engine.

CAUTION: *To avoid accidental ignition of fuel during the test, first remove the coil high-tension wire from the distributor and the coil.*

1. If a fuel pressure gauge is available, connect the gauge to the engine and operate the engine until the pressure stops rising. Stop the engine and take the reading. If the reading is within the specifications given in the "Tune-Up Specifications" chart in Chapter 2, the malfunction is not in the fuel pump. Also check the pressure drop after the engine is stopped. A large pressure drop below the minimum specification indicates leaky valves. If the pump proves to be satisfactory, check the tank and inlet line.

2. If a fuel pressure gauge is not available, disconnect the fuel line at the pump outlet, place a vessel beneath the pump outlet, and crank the engine. A good pump will force the fuel out of the outlet in steady spurts. A worn diaphragm spring may not provide proper pumping action.

3. As a further test, disconnect and plug the fuel line from the tank at the pump, and hold your thumb over the pump inlet. If the pump is functioning properly, suction should be felt on your thumb. No suction indicates that the pump diaphragm is leaking, or that the diaphragm linkage is worn.

4. Check the crankcase for gasoline. A ruptured diaphragm may leak fuel into the engine.

Electric Choke

Starting in 1973, all Fords use an electrically-assisted choke to reduce exhaust emissions of carbon monoxide during warmup. The system consists of a choke cap, a thermostatic spring, a bimetal sensing disc (switch) and a ceramic positive temperature coefficient (PTC) heater.

The choke is powered from the center tap of the alternator, so that current is constantly applied to the temperature sensing disc. The system is grounded through the carburetor body. At temperatures below approximately 60° F, the switch is open and no current is supplied to the ceramic heater, thereby resulting in normal unassisted thermostatic spring choking action. When the temperature rises above about 60° F, the temperature sensing disc closes and current is supplied to the heater, which in turn, acts on the thermostatic spring. Once the heater starts, it causes the thermostatic spring to pull the choke plate(s) open within 1½ minutes, which is sooner than it would open if non-assisted.

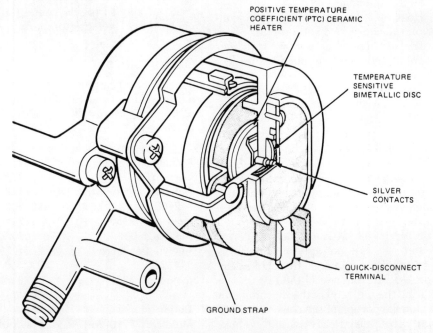

POSITIVE TEMPERATURE COEFFICIENT (PTC) CERAMIC HEATER

TEMPERATURE SENSITIVE BIMETALLIC DISC

SILVER CONTACTS

QUICK-DISCONNECT TERMINAL

GROUND STRAP

Electric choke components

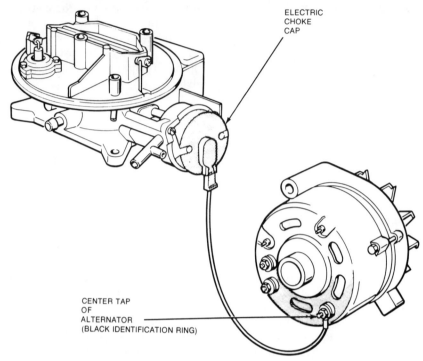

ELECTRIC
CHOKE
CAP

CENTER TAP
OF
ALTERNATOR
(BLACK IDENTIFICATION RING)

Electric choke wiring

ELECTRIC CHOKE OPERATIONAL TEST

1. Detach the electrical lead from the choke cap.

2. Use a jumper lead to connect the terminal on the choke cap and the wire terminal, so that the electrical circuit is still completed.

3. Start the engine.

4. Hook up a test light between the connector on the choke lead and ground.

5. The test light should glow. If it does not, current is not being supplied to the electrically-assisted choke.

6. Connect the test light between the terminal on the alternator and the terminal on the choke cap. If the light now glows, replace the lead, since it is not passing current to the choke assist.

CAUTION: *Do not ground the terminal on the alternator while performing Step 6.*

7. If the light still does not glow, the fault lies somewhere in the electrical system. Check the system out.

If the electrically-assisted choke receives power but still does not appear to be functioning properly, reconnect the choke lead and proceed with the rest of the test.

8. Tape the bulb end of the thermometer to the metallic portion of the choke housing.

9. If the electrically-assisted choke operates below 55° F, it is defective and must be replaced.

10. Allow the engine to warm up to between 80 and 100° F; at these temperatures the choke should operate for about 1½ minutes.

11. If it does not operate for this length of time, check the bimetallic spring to see if it is connected to the tang on the choke lever.

12. If the spring is connected and the choke is not operating properly, replace the cap assembly.

Carburetors

Nine different carburetors have been used on full size Fords from 1968 to the present. The carburetors are installed as per the following usage chart:

Autolite 1101	1968–69 240 Six
Carter YF	1968–72 240 Six
Autolite (Motorcraft) 2100	1968–74 302, 351, 390, 400, 429 V8
Motorcraft 2150	1975–79 351, 400
Autolite 4100	1968–69 428PI V8
Autolite (Motorcraft) 4300	1968–74, 390, 428, 429, 460 V8
Motorcraft 4350	1975–78 400 V8 and 460 V8
Carter Thermo-Quad®	1974 460 V8
Motorcraft 2700 Variable Venturi (VV)	1979 49 states 302 and all 1979 California models

Motorcraft 7200 Variable Venturi (VV)

1979 California 351 with EEC II (The 7200 VV is essentially the 2700 VV operating in conjunction with the rest of the EEC II system.)

In accordance with Federal emissions regulations, all carburetors are equipped with idle mixture screw limiter caps. These caps are installed to prevent tampering with the carburetor fuel mixture screws so that the engine cannot be adjusted to a richer idle mixture.

Most models are equipped with a throttle solenoid positioner. The purpose of a throttle solenoid is to prevent the engine from running on (dieseling) after the ignition is turned off. Dieseling is a common occurrence with many cars using emission control systems that require a leaner fuel mixture, a higher operating temperature, and a higher curb idle speed. The throttle solenoid prevents running-on and dieseling by closing the throttle plate(s) after the key is turned off, thereby shutting off the air and gas to the overheated combustion chamber.

THROTTLE SOLENOID (ANTI-DIESELING SOLENOID) TEST

1. Turn the ignition key on and open the throttle. The solenoid plunger should extend (solenoid energize).
2. Turn the ignition off. The plunger should retract, allowing the throttle to close.

NOTE: *With the antidieseling solenoid deenergized, the carburetor idle speed adjusting screw must make contact with the throttle shaft to prevent the throttle plates from jamming in the throttle bore when the engine is turned off.*

3. If the solenoid is functioning properly and the engine is still dieseling, check for one of the following:

  a. High idle or engine shut off speed;
  b. Engine timing not set to specification;
  c. Binding throttle linkage;
  d. Too low an octane fuel being used.

Correct any of these problems as necessary.

4. If the solenoid fails to function as outlined in Steps 1–2, disconnect the solenoid leads; the solenoid should de-energerize. If it does not, it is jammed and must be replaced.

5. Connect the solenoid to a 12 V power source and to ground. Open the throttle so that the plunger can extend. If it does not, the solenoid is defective.

6. If the solenoid is functioning correctly and no other source of trouble can be found, the fault probably lies in the wiring between the solenoid and the ignition switch or in the ignition switch itself. Remember to reconnect the solenoid when finished testing.

NOTE: *On some 1970–71 models, dieseling may occur when the engine is turned off because of feedback through the alternator warning light circuit. A diode kit is available from Ford to cure this problem. A failure of this diode may also lead to a similar problem.*

CARBURETOR REMOVAL AND INSTALLATION

1. Remove the air cleaner.
2. Disconnect the throttle cable or rod at the throttle lever. Disconnect the distributor vacuum line, exhaust gas recirculation line (1973 and later models), inline fuel filter, choke heat tube and the positive crankcase ventilation hose at the carburetor.
3. Disconnect the throttle solenoid (if so equipped) and electric choke assist (1973 and later models) at their connectors. Remove the wires to the carburetor on the 7200 VV.
4. Remove the carburetor retaining nuts. Lift off the carburetor carefully, taking care not to spill any fuel. Remove the carburetor mounting gasket and discard it. Remove the carburetor mounting spacer, if so equipped, from the intake manifold.
5. Prior to installation, clean the gasket mounting surfaces of the intake manifold, spacer (if so equipped), and carburetor. When using a spacer, use two new gaskets, sandwiching the spacer between the gaskets. If a spacer is not used, only one new carburetor mounting gasket is required.
6. Place the new gasket(s) and spacer (if so equipped) on the carburetor mounting studs. Position the carburetor on top of the gasket and hand tighten the retaining nuts. Then tighten the nuts in a criss-cross pattern to 10–15 ft lbs.
7. Connect the throttle linkage, the distributor vacuum line, exhaust gas recirculation line (1973 and later models), inline fuel filter, choke heat tube, positive crankcase ventilation hose, throttle solenoid (if so equipped) and electric-choke assist (1973 and later models).
8. Adjust the curb idle speed, the idle fuel mixture and the accelerator pump stroke

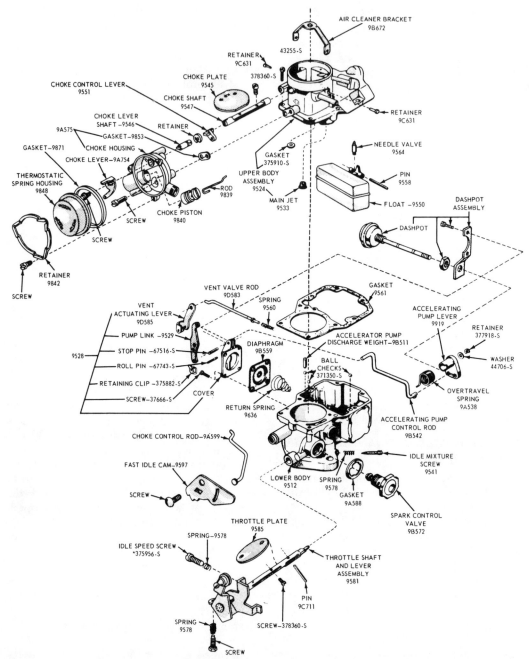

Exploded view—Autolite 1101-IV

(Autolite-Motorcraft 2 and 4 barrel carburetors only).

OVERHAUL

All except 7200 VV

NOTE: *The 7200 VV carburetor used on those vehicles equipped with the EEC II system is electronically controlled, and an integral part of a sophisticated emission control system. Do not attempt to overhaul this carburetor.*

Efficient carburetion depends greatly on careful cleaning and inspection during overhaul, since dirt, gum, water, or varnish in or on the carburetor parts are often responsible for poor performance.

Overhaul your carburetor in a clean, dustfree area. Carefully disassemble the carburetor, referring often to the exploded views. Keep all similar and lookalike parts segregated during the disassembly and cleaning to avoid accidental interchange during assembly. Make a note of all jet sizes.

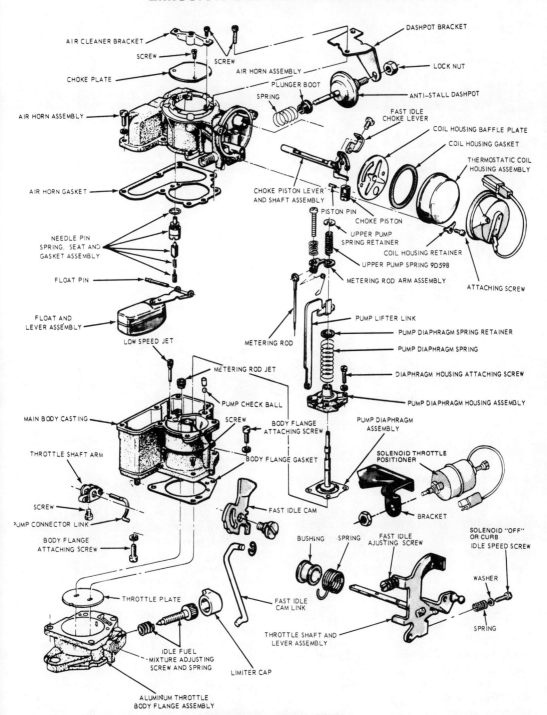

Exploded view—Carter YF-IV

When the carburetor is disassembled, wash all parts (except diaphragms, electric choke units, pump plunger, and any other plastic, leather, fiber, or rubber parts) in clean carburetor solvent. Do not leave parts in the solvent any longer than is necessary to sufficiently loosen the deposits. Excessive cleaning may remove the special finish from the float bowl and choke valve bodies, leaving these parts unfit for service. Rinse all parts in clean solvent and blow them dry with compressed air or allow them to air dry. Wipe clean all cork, plastic, leather, and fiber parts with a clean, lint-free cloth.

Blow out all passages and jets with compressed air and be sure that there are no restrictions or blockages. Never use wire or similar tools to clean jets, fuel passages, or air

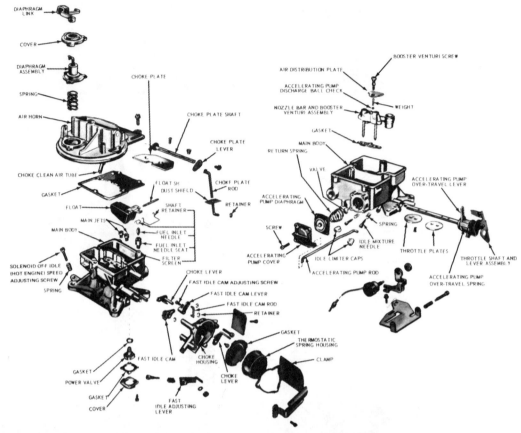

Exploded view—Autolite (Motorcraft) 2100-2V

bleeds. Clean all jets and valves separately to avoid accidental interchange.

Check all parts for wear or damage. If wear or damage is found, replace the defective parts. Especially check the following:

1. Check the float needle and seat for wear. If wear is found, replace the complete assembly.

2. Check the float hinge pin for wear and the float(s) for dents or distortion. Replace the float if fuel has leaked into it.

3. Check the throttle and choke shaft bores for wear or an out-of-round condition. Damage or wear to the throttle arm, shaft, or shaft bore will often require replacement of the throttle body. These parts require a close tolerance of fit; wear may allow air leakage, which could affect starting and idling.

NOTE: *Throttle shafts and bushings are not included in overhaul kits. They can be purchased separately.*

4. Inspect the idle mixture adjusting needles for burrs or grooves. Any such condition requires replacement of the needle, since you will not be able to obtain a satisfactory idle.

5. Test the accelerator pump check valves. They should pass air one way but not the other. Test for proper seating by blowing and sucking on the valve. Replace the valve if necessary. If the valve is satisfactory, wash the valve again to remove breath moisture.

6. Check the bowl cover for warped surfaces with a straightedge.

7. Closely inspect the valves and seats for wear and damage, replacing as necessary.

8. After the carburetor is assembled, check the choke valve for freedom of operation.

Carburetor overhaul kits are recommended for each overhaul. These kits contain all gaskets and new parts to replace those which deteriorate most rapidly. Failure to replace all parts supplied with the kit (especially gaskets) can result in poor performance later.

Some carburetor manufacturers supply overhaul kits of three basic types: minor repair; major repair; and gasket kits. Basically, they contain the following:

Minor Repair Kits:
    All gaskets
    Float needle valve

Volume control screw
All diaphragms
Spring for the pump diaphragm
Major Repair Kits:
    All jets and gaskets
    All diaphragms
    Float needle valve
    Volume control screw
    Pump ball valve

Float
Complete intermediate rod
Intermediate pump lever
Some cover hold-down screws and washers
Gasket Kits:
    All gaskets
After cleaning and checking all components, reassemble the carburetor, using new

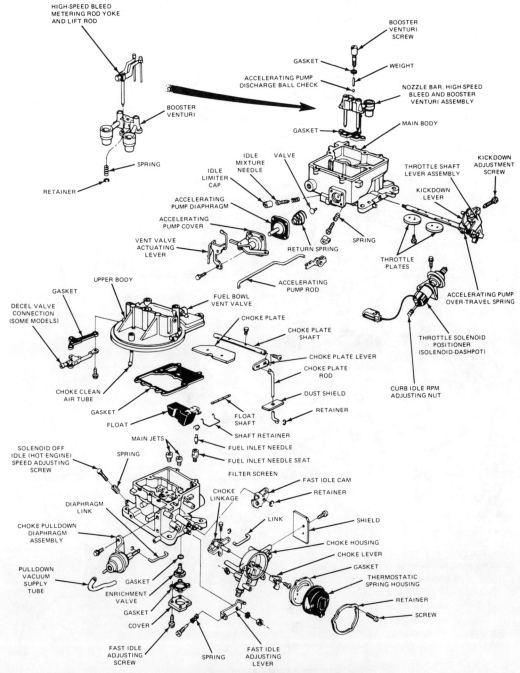

Exploded view—Motorcraft 2150-2V

parts and referring to the exploded view. When reassembling, make sure that all screws and jets are tight in their seats, but do not overtighten as the tips will be distorted. Tighten all screws gradually, in rotation. Do not tighten needle valves into their seats; uneven jetting will result. Always use new gaskets. Be sure to adjust the float level when reassembling.

AUTOMATIC CHOKE HOUSING ADJUSTMENT

All except VV carburetors

By rotating the spring housing of the automatic choke, the reaction of the choke to engine temperature can be controlled. To adjust, remove the air cleaner assembly, loosen the thermostatic spring housing retaining

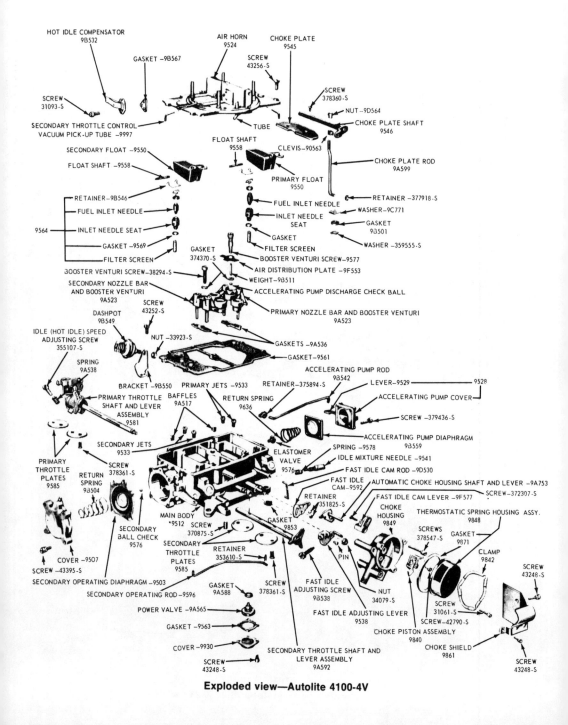

Exploded view—Autolite 4100-4V

screws and set the spring housing to the specified index mark. The marks are shown in the accompanying illustration. After adjusting the setting, tighten the retaining screws and replace the air cleaner assembly to the carburetor.

CHOKE PLATE PULL-DOWN CLEARANCE ADJUSTMENT

Autolite 1101

1. Remove the air cleaner assembly.
2. Remove the choke cover and thermo-

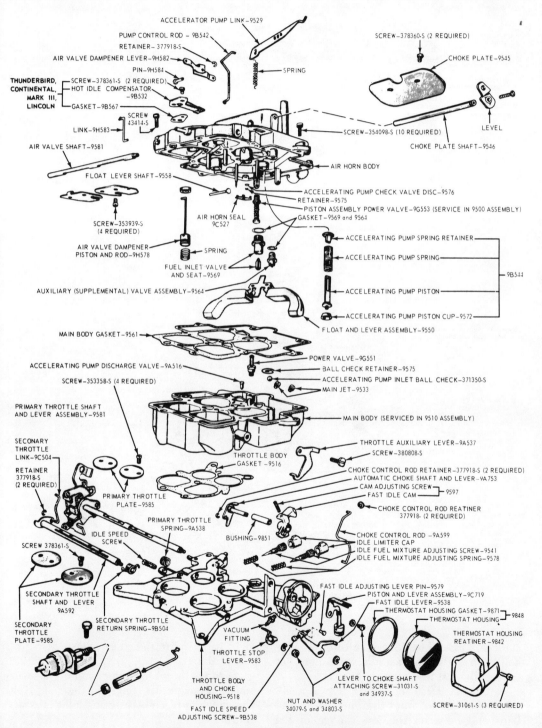

ACCELERATOR PUMP LINK—9529
PUMP CONTROL ROD—9B542
RETAINER—377918-S
AIR VALVE DAMPENER LEVER—9H582
PIN—9H584
SCREW—378361-S (2 REQUIRED)
THUNDERBIRD, CONTINENTAL, MARK III, LINCOLN
HOT IDLE COMPENSATOR—9B532
GASKET—9B567
SCREW 43414-S
LINK—9H583
AIR VALVE SHAFT—9581
FLOAT LEVER SHAFT—9558
SCREW—353939-S (4 REQUIRED)
AIR VALVE DAMPENER PISTON AND ROD—9H578
SPRING
FUEL INLET VALVE AND SEAT—9569
AUXILIARY (SUPPLEMENTAL) VALVE ASSEMBLY—9564
AIR HORN SEAL 9C527
MAIN BODY GASKET—9561
ACCELERATING PUMP DISCHARGE VALVE—9A516
SCREW—353358-S (4 REQUIRED)
PRIMARY THROTTLE SHAFT AND LEVER ASSEMBLY—9581
SECONARY THROTTLE LINK—9C504
RETAINER 377918-S (2 REQUIRED)
PRIMARY THROTTLE PLATE—9585
IDLE SPEED SCREW
SCREW 378361-S
BUSHING—9851
PRIMARY THROTTLE SPRING—9A538
SECONDARY THROTTLE SHAFT AND LEVER 9A592
SECONDARY THROTTLE PLATE—9585
SECONDARY THROTTLE RETURN SPRING—9B504
VACUUM FITTING
THROTTLE STOP LEVER—9583
THROTTLE BODY AND CHOKE HOUSING—9518
FAST IDLE SPEED ADJUSTING SCREW—9B538
NUT AND WASHER 34079-S and 34803-S

SCREW—378360-S (2 REQUIRED)
CHOKE PLATE—9545
LEVEL
SCREW—354098-S (10 REQUIRED)
CHOKE PLATE SHAFT—9546
AIR HORN BODY
ACCELERATING PUMP CHECK VALVE DISC—9576
RETAINER—9575
PISTON ASSEMBLY POWER VALVE—9G553 (SERVICE IN 9500 ASSEMBLY)
GASKET—9569 and 9564
ACCELERATING PUMP SPRING RETAINER
ACCELERATING PUMP SPRING
9B544
ACCELERATING PUMP PISTON
ACCELERATING PUMP PISTON CUP—9572
FLOAT AND LEVER ASSEMBLY—9550
POWER VALVE—9G551
BALL CHECK RETAINER—9575
ACCELERATING PUMP INLET BALL CHECK—371350-S
MAIN JET—9533
MAIN BODY (SERVICED IN 9510 ASSEMBLY)
THROTTLE AUXILIARY LEVER—9A537
SCREW—380808-S
THROTTLE BODY GASKET—9516
CHOKE CONTROL ROD RETAINER—377918-S (2 REQUIRED)
AUTOMATIC CHOKE SHAFT AND LEVER—9A753
CAM ADJUSTING SCREW
FAST IDLE CAM—9597
CHOKE CONTROL ROD REATINER 377918- (2 REQUIRED)
CHOKE CONTROL ROD—9A599
IDLE LIMITER CAP
IDLE FUEL MIXTURE ADJUSTING SCREW—9541
IDLE FUEL MIXTURE ADJUSTING SPRING—9578
FAST IDLE ADJUSTING LEVER PIN—9579
PISTON AND LEVER ASSEMBLY—9C719
FAST IDLE LEVER—9538
THERMOSTAT HOUSING GASKET—9871
THERMOSTAT HOUSING
9848
THERMOSTAT HOUSING REATINER—9842
LEVER TO CHOKE SHAFT ATTACHING SCREW—31031-S and 34937-S
SCREW—31061-S (3 REQUIRED)

Exploded view—Autolite (Motorcraft) 4300-4V

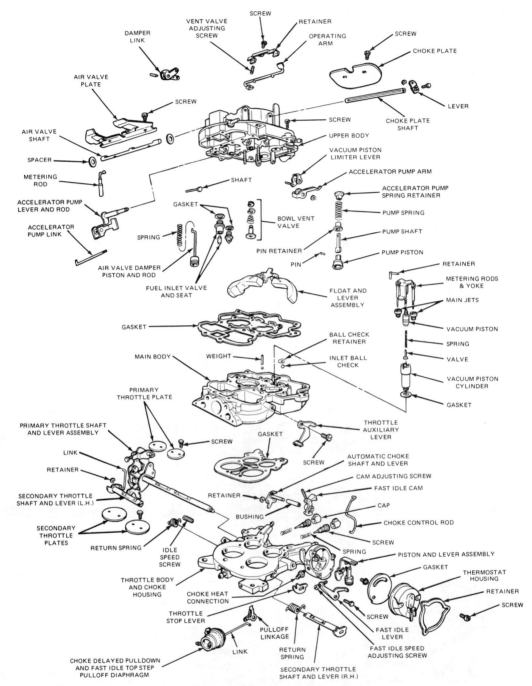

Exploded view—Motorcraft 4350-4V

static coil assembly. Block the throttle valve half open so that the fast idle screw does not contact the fast idle cam.

3. Bend a 0.036 in. wire gauge at a 90° angle about ⅛ in. from the end. Insert the bent end between the lower edge of the choke piston slot and the upper edge of the

right-hand slot in the choke housing (see the illustration).

4. Move the piston lever counterclockwise until the gauge fits snugly in the slot. Hold the gauge in place by exerting light pressure on the lever.

5. Insert a drill or gauge of the specified

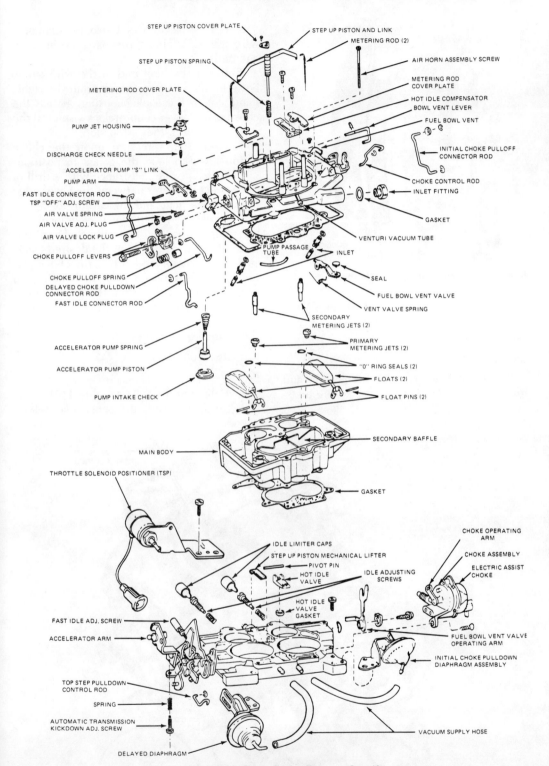

Exploded view—Carter Thermo-Quad®

thickness (see "Carburetor Specifications" chart) between the lower edge of the choke plate and the air horn wall.

6. To adjust, carefully bend the choke pis-

ton link (in an S or Z-shaped bend) until the choke plate clearance is that of the drill gauge.

7. After adjustment, install the choke

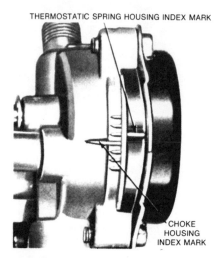

Automatic choke housing adjustment

cover and adjust as outlined under "Automatic Choke Housing Adjustment." Install the air cleaner.

Carter YF

1. Remove the carburetor air cleaner, and remove the choke thermostatic spring housing.

2. Bend a section of 0.026 in. diameter wire at a 90° angle approximately ⅛ in. from one end.

3. Insert the bent end of the wire gauge between the choke piston slot and the right-hand slot in the choke housing. Rotate the choke piston lever counterclockwise until the guage is snug in the piston slot.

4. Exert light pressure upon the choke piston lever to hold the gauge in position. Check the specified clearance with a drill of the correct diameter between the lower edge of the choke plate and the carburetor bore.

5. Choke plate pull-down clearance may be adjusted by bending the choke piston lever as required to obtain the desired clearance. It is recommended that the choke piston lever be removed prior to bending, in order to prevent distorting the piston link.

6. Install the choke thermostatic spring housing and gasket, and set the housing to the proper specification.

Autolite 2100, 4100

1968–69

1. Follow Steps 1–5 "Autolite 1101."

2. To adjust, turn the choke plate clevis

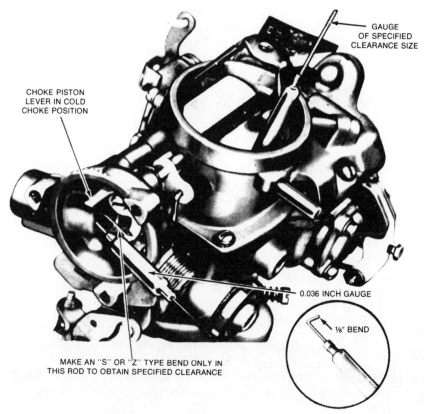

Adjusting choke plate pull-down—Autolite 1101

adjusting nut (see the illustration) as required until the choke plate clearance is that of the drill gauge.

3. After adjustment, install the choke

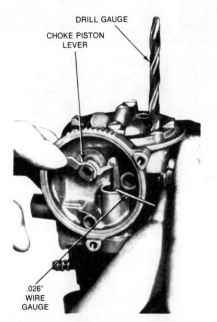

Adjusting choke plate pull-down—Carter YF

cover and adjust as outlined under "Automatic Choke Housing Adjustment." Install the air cleaner.

Autolite (Motorcraft) 2100

1970–74

1. Remove the air cleaner.

2. With the engine at its normal operating temperature, loosen the choke thermostatic spring housing retaining screws, and set the housing 90° in the rich direction.

3. Disconnect and remove the choke heat tube from the choke housing.

4. Turn the fast idle adjusting screw outward one full turn.

5. Start the engine. Use a drill of the specified diameter to check the clearance between the lower edge of the choke plate and the air horn wall.

6. To adjust the clearance, turn the diaphragm stopscrew (located on the underside of the choke diaphragm housing). Turning clockwise will decrease the clearance; counterclockwise will increase it.

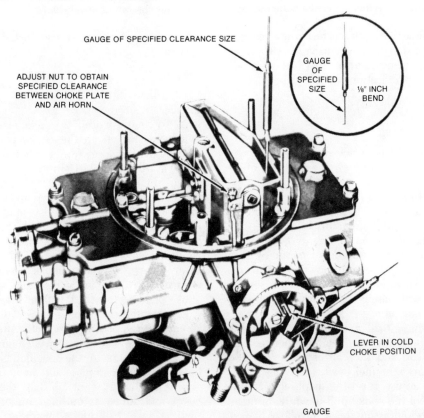

Adjusting choke plate pull-down—Autolite 2100, 4100—1968–69

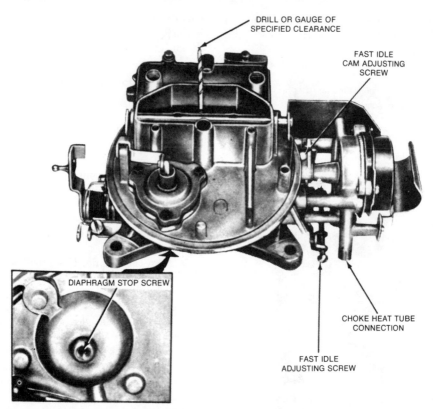

DRILL OR GAUGE OF
SPECIFIED CLEARANCE

FAST IDLE
CAM ADJUSTING
SCREW

DIAPHRAGM STOP SCREW

CHOKE HEAT TUBE
CONNECTION

FAST IDLE
ADJUSTING SCREW

Adjusting choke plate pull-down—Autolite (Motorcraft) 2100—1970-74

7. Connect the choke heat tube, and set the choke thermostatic spring housing to the proper specification. Adjust the fast idle speed to specifications.

Motorcraft 2150

1. Remove the air cleaner assembly.
2. Set the throttle on the top step of the fast idle cam.
3. Noting the position of the choke housing cap, loosen the retaining screws and rotate the cap 90 degrees in the rich (closing) direction.
4. Activate the pull-down motor by manually forcing the pull-down control diaphragm link in the direction of applied vacuum or by applying vacuum to the external vacuum tube.
5. Using a drill gauge of the specified diameter, measure the clearance between the choke plate and the center of the air horn wall nearest the fuel bowl.
6. To adjust, reset the diaphragm stop on the end of the choke pull-down diaphragm.
7. After adjusting, reset the choke housing cap to the specified notch. Check and reset

fast idle speed, if necessary. Install the air cleaner.

Autolite (Motorcraft) 4300, 4350

1. Follow Steps 1–5 under "Autolite 1101."
2. To adjust loosen the hex head screw (left-hand thread) on the choke plate shaft and pry the link away from the tapered shaft. Using a drill gauge 0.010 in. thinner than the specified clearance (to allow for tolerances in the linkage), insert the gauge between the lower edge of the choke plate and the air horn wall. Hold the choke plate against the gauge and maintain a light pressure in a counterclockwise direction on the choke lever. Then, with the choke piston snug against the 0.036 in. wire gauge and the choke plate against the 0.010 in. smaller drill gauge, tighten the hex head screw (left-hand thread) on the choke plate shaft. After tightening the hex head screw, make a final check using a drill gauge of the specified clearance between the choke plate and air horn.
3. After adjustment, install the choke cover and adjust as outlined under "Automatic Choke Housing Adjustment." Install the air cleaner.

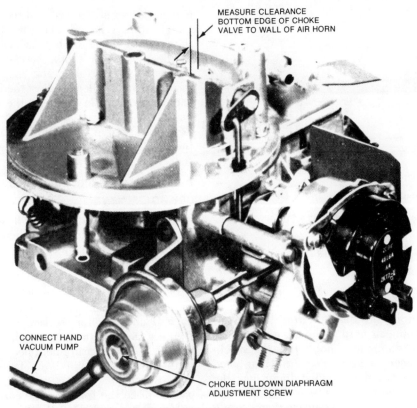

Adjusting choke plate pull-down—Motorcraft 2150

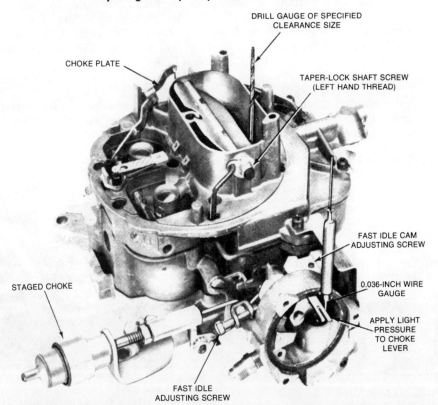

Choke plate pull-down and fast idle cam adjustment—Autolite (Motorcraft) 4300, 4350 similar

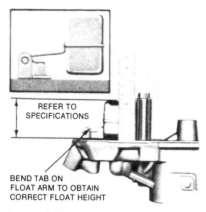

Float level adjustment—Autolite 1101

FLOAT LEVEL ADJUSTMENT

Autolite 1101

1. Remove the carburetor air horn and gasket from the carburetor.

2. Measure the distance from the gasket surface of the air horn to the top of the float. If the measurement is not within the specified tolerance, bend the float arm tab as necessary to obtain the specified dimension. Be careful not to exert any pressure on the fuel inlet needle, as this will damage it and result in an improper fuel level within the float bowl.

3. Install the carburetor air horn to the main body of the carburetor, using a new gasket.

Carter YF

The float level is adjusted dry in the following manner: Remove the carburetor air horn and gasket from the carburetor. Using a gauge made to the proper dimension, invert the air horn assembly and check the clearance be-

tween the top of the float and the bottom of the air horn. When checking the float level, the air horn should be held at eye level and the float lever arm should be resting on the pin of the needle valve. The float lever arm may be bent in order to adjust the float clearance. However, do not bend the tab at the end of the float arm, as this will prevent the float from bottoming in the fuel bowl when the bowl is empty. Using a new gasket, install the carburetor air horn.

Autolite (Motorcraft) 2100, 2150, 4100

DRY ADJUSTMENT

This preliminary setting of the float level adjustment must be done with the carburetor removed from the engine.

1. Remove the air horn and see that the float is raised and the fuel inlet needle is seated. Check the distance between the top surface of the main body (with the gasket removed) and the top surface of the float. Depress the float tab to seat the fuel inlet needle. Take a measurement near the center of the float, at a point ⅛ in. from the free end. If you are using a prefabricated float gauge, place the gauge in the corner of the enlarged end section of the fuel bowl. The gauge should touch the float near the end, but not on the end radius.

2. If necessary, bend the tab on the end of the float to bring the setting within the specified limits.

WET ADJUSTMENT

1. Bring the engine to its normal operating temperature, park the car on as nearly

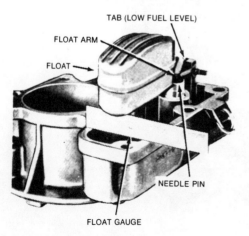

Float level adjustment—Carter YF

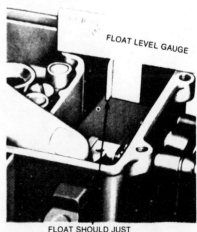

Dry float level adjustment—Autolite 2100, 2150, 4100

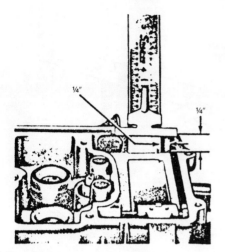

Wet float level adjustment—Autolite 2100, 2150, 4100

level a surface as possible, and stop the engine.

2. Remove the air cleaner assembly from the carburetor.

3. Remove the air horn retaining screws and the carburetor identification tag. Leave the air horn and gasket in position on the carburetor main body. Start the engine, let it idle for several minutes, rotate the air horn out of the way, and remove the gasket to provide access to the float assembly.

4. With the engine idling, use a standard depth scale to measure the vertical distance from the top machined surface of the carburetor main body to the level of the fuel bowl. This measurement must be made at least ¼ in. away from any vertical surface in order to assure an accurate reading.

5. Stop the engine before making any adjustment to the float level. Adjustment is accomplished by bending the float tab (which contacts the fuel inlet valve) up or down as required to raise or lower the fuel level. After making an adjustment, start the engine, and allow it to idle for several minutes before repeating the fuel level check. Repeat as necessary until the proper fuel level is attained.

6. Reinstall the air horn with a new gasket and secure it with the screws. Include the installation of the identification tag in its proper location.

7. Check the idle speed, fuel mixture, and dashpot adjustments. Install the air cleaner assembly.

Autolite (Motorcraft) 4300, 4350

1. Refer to the illustration for details of construction of a tool for checking the parallel setting of the dual pontoons.

2. Install the gauge on the carburetor and set it to the specified height.

3. Check the clearance and alignment of the pontoons to the gauge. Both pontoons should just barely touch the gauge for the

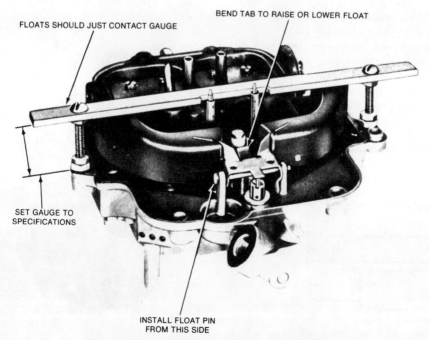

Float setting with fabricated gauge—4300, 4350

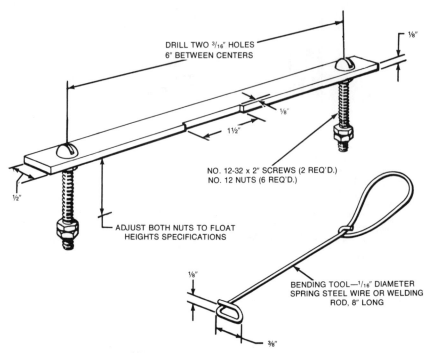

Float gauge and bending tool details—4300, 4350

proper setting. Pontoons may be aligned if necessary by slightly twisting them.

4. To adjust the float level, bend the primary needle tab down to raise the float and up to lower it.

Carter Thermo-Quad®

1. Taking note of their placement, disconnect all linkages and rods which connect the bowl cover to the carburetor body.

2. Remove the 10 screws retaining the bowl cover to the body.

3. Using legs to protect the throttle valves, remove the bowl cover. Invert the bowl cover, taking care not to lose any of the small parts.

4. With the bowl cover inverted and the floats resting on the seated needle, measure

the distance between the bowl cover (new gasket installed) to the bottom side of each float.

5. If not to specifications, bend the float lever to suit.

NOTE: *Never allow the lip of the float to be pressed against the needle when adjusting the float height.*

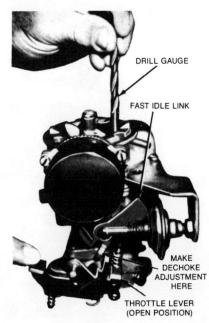

Dechoke clearance adjustment—Carter YF

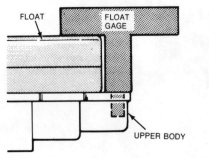

Float setting with rebuilding kit gauge—4300, 4350

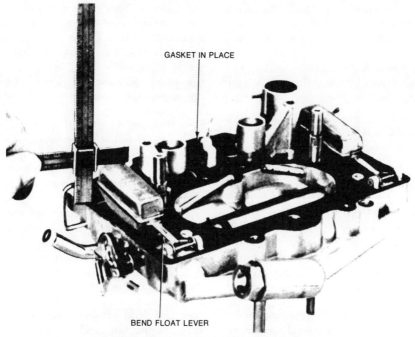

GASKET IN PLACE

BEND FLOAT LEVER

Checking float height—Carter Thermo-Quad®

DRILL OR GAUGE OF SPECIFIED SIZE

THROTTLE WIDE OPEN

Checking dechoke clearance—Autolite (Motorcraft) 4300, 4350

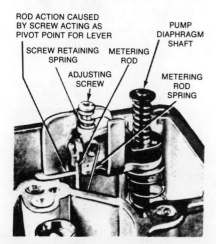

ROD ACTION CAUSED BY SCREW ACTING AS PIVOT POINT FOR LEVER

SCREW RETAINING SPRING   METERING ROD

ADJUSTING SCREW

PUMP DIAPHRAGM SHAFT

METERING ROD SPRING

Metering rod adjustment—Carter YF

6. Reverse Steps 1–3 to install. Make sure that the float pin does not protrude past the edge of the bowl cover.

DECHOKE CLEARANCE ADJUSTMENT

Carter YF

1. Remove the carburetor air cleaner.
2. Hold the throttle plate to the full open position while closing the choke plate as far as possible without forcing it. Use a drill of the proper diameter (see "Carburetor Specifications" chart) to check the clearance between the choke plate and air horn.
3. Adjust as necessary by bending the pawl on the fast idle speed lever. Bend forward to increase clearance and backward to decrease clearance.

Autolite (Motorcraft) 4300, 4350

1. Remove the air cleaner assembly.
2. Remove the automatic choke spring housing from the carburetor.
3. With the throttle plate wide open and the choke plate closed as far as possible without forcing it, insert a drill gauge of the specified diameter between the choke plate and air horn.
4. To adjust, bend the arm on the choke trip lever. Bend downward to increase clearance and upward to decrease clearance. After adjusting, recheck the clearance.

5. Install the automatic choke housing, taking care to engage the thermostatic spring with the tang on the choke lever and shaft assembly.

6. Adjust the automatic choke setting. Install the air cleaner. Adjust the idle speed and dashpot, if so equipped.

METERING ROD ADJUSTMENT

Carter YF

With the carburetor air horn and gasket removed from the carburetor, unscrew the idle speed adjusting screw until the throttle plate is tightly closed in the throttle bore. Press downward on the end of the diaphragm shaft until the metering rod arm contacts the lifter link at the diaphragm stem. With the metering rod in the preceding position, turn the rod adjustment screw (see the accompanying illustration) until the metering rod just bottoms in the body casting. Turn the metering rod adjusting screw one additional turn in the clockwise direction. Install the carburetor air horn along with a new gasket.

ACCLERATOR PUMP STROKE ADJUSTMENT

Autolite (Motorcraft) 2100, 2150, 4100

In order to keep the exhaust emission level of the engine within the specified limits, the accelerating pump stroke has been preset at the factory. The additional holes are provided for differing engine-transmission-body applications only. The primary throttle shaft lever (overtravel lever) has four holes and the accelerating pump link two holes to control the pump stroke. The accelerating pump operating rod should be in the overtravel lever hole number listed in the "Carburetor Specifications" chart, and in the inboard hole (hole closest to the pump plunger) in the accelerating pump link. If the pump stroke has been changed from the specified settings, use the following procedure to correct the stroke.

1. Release the operating rod from the retaining clip by pressing the tab end of the clip toward the rod while pressing the rod away from the clip until it disengages.

2. Position the clip over the specified hole (see "Carburetor Specifications" chart) in the overtravel lever. Press the ends of the clip together and insert the operating rod through the clip and the overtravel lever. Release the clip to engage the rod.

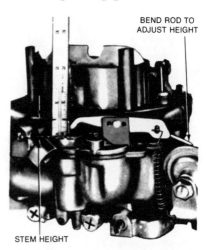

Accelerator pump stroke and piston stem height—Autolite (Motorcraft) 4300

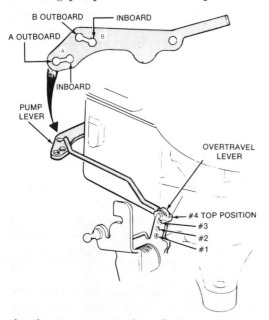

Accelerator pump stroke adjustment—Autolite (Motorcraft) 2100, 2150, 4100

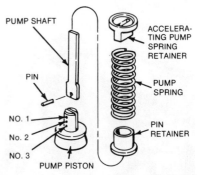

Accelerator pump stroke adjustment—Motorcraft 4350

Autolite (Motorcraft) 4300

The pump stroke is preset at the factory to limit exhaust emissions. The additional holes in the operating arm are provided for different engine applications. The stroke should not be changed from the specified hole (see "Carburetor Specifications" chart).

The only adjustments possible are the pump stroke and pump stem height. To change the pump stroke, merely remove the pivot pin and reposition it in the specified hole. To adjust the pump stem height, bend the operating rod at the angles, taking care not to cause binds in the system.

Motorcraft 4350

The acclerator pump adjustment is preset at the factory for reduced exhaust emissions. Adjustment is provided only for different engine installations. The adjustment is internal, with three piston-to-shaft pin positions in the pump piston.

To check that the shaft pin is located in the specified piston hole, remove the carburetor air horn and invert it. Disconnect the acclerator pump from the operating arm by pressing downward on the spring and sliding the arm out of the pump shaft slot. Disassemble the spring and nylon keeper retaining the adjustment pin. If the pin is not in its specified hole, remove it, reposition the shaft to the correct hole in the piston assembly and reinstall the pin. Then, slide the nylon retainer over the pin and position the spring on the shaft. Finally, compress the spring on the shaft and install the pump on the pump arm.

NOTE: *Under no circumstances should you adjust the stroke of the acclerator pump by turning the vacuum limiter lever adjusting nut. This adjustment is preset at the factory and modification could result in poor cold driveability.*

ANTI-STALL DASHPOT ADJUSTMENT

All Carburetors

Having made sure that the engine idle speed and mixture are correct and that the engine is at normal operating temperature, loosen the anti-stall dashpot locking nut (see accompanying illustration). With the throttle held closed, depress the plunger with a screwdriver blade and measure the clearance between the throttle lever and the plunger tip. If the clearance is not as specified in the "Carburetor Specifications" chart, turn the dashpot until the proper clearance is ob-

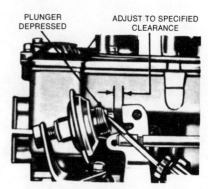

PLUNGER DEPRESSED   ADJUST TO SPECIFIED CLEARANCE

Typical anti-stall dashpot adjustment

tained between the throttle lever and the plunger tip. After tightening the locking nut, recheck the adjustment.

FAST IDLE CAM INDEX SETTING

Carter YF

1. Position the fast idle screw on the kickdown step of the fast idle cam against the shoulder of the high step.

2. Adjust by bending the choke plate connecting rod to obtain the specified clearance between the lower edge of the choke plate and the carburetor bore.

Autolite (Motorcraft) 2100, 4100

1968–72

1. Loosen the choke thermostatic spring housing retaining screws and position the housing 90° in the rich direction.

2. Position the fast idle speed screw at the kick-down step of the fast idle cam. This kickdown step is identified by a small "V" stamped in the side of the casting.

3. Be sure that the fast idle cam is in the kick-down position while checking or adjusting the fast idle cam clearance. Check the clearance between the lower edge of the choke plate and the wall of the air horn by inserting a drill of the specified diameter between them. Adjustment may be accomplished by turning the fast idle cam adjusting screw clockwise to increase or counterclockwise to decrease the clearance.

4. Set the choke thermostatic spring housing to specifications, and adjust the antistall dashpot, idle speed, and fuel mixture.

Motorcraft 2100, 2150

1973 AND LATER

1. Loosen the choke thermostatic spring housing retaining screws and rotate the housing 90° in the rich direction.

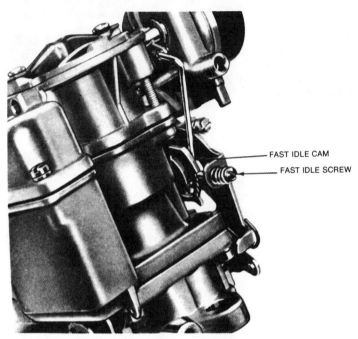

Fast idle cam index setting—Carter YF

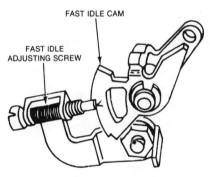

CONVENTIONAL ONE-PIECE FAST IDLE LEVER

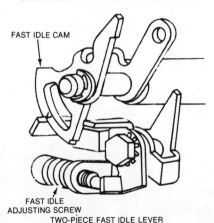

TWO-PIECE FAST IDLE LEVER
FOR 351-C AND 400 ENGINES

Fast idle cam index setting—Autolite (Motorcraft) 2100

2. Position the fast idle speed screw or lever on the high step of the cam.

3. Depress the choke pull-down diaphragm against the diaphragm stop screw thereby placing the choke in the pull-down position.

4. While holding the choke pull-down diaphragm depressed, slightly open the throttle and allow the fast idle cam to fall.

5. Close the throttle and check the position of the fast idle cam or lever. When the fast idle cam is adjusted correctly, the screw should contact the "V" mark on the cam. Adjustment is accomplished by rotating the fast idle cam adjusting screw as needed.

Autolite (Motorcraft) 4300, 4350

1. Loosen the choke thermostatic spring housing retaining screws and position the housing 90° in the rich direction.

2. Position the fast idle speed screw at the kick-down step of the fast idle cam. This kick-down step is identified by a small "V" stamped in the side of the casting.

3. Be sure that the fast idle cam is in the kick-down position while checking or adjusting the fast idle cam clearance. Check the clearance between the lower edge of the choke plate and the wall of the air horn by inserting a drill of the specified diameter between them. Adjustment may be accomplished by turning the fast idle cam

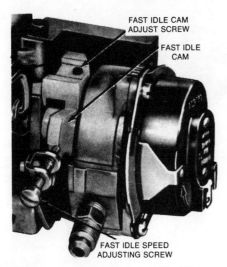

FAST IDLE CAM
ADJUST SCREW

FAST IDLE
CAM

FAST IDLE SPEED
ADJUSTING SCREW

Fast idle cam index setting—Autolite (Motorcraft) 4300, 4350

adjusting screw clockwise to increase or counterclockwise to decrease the clearance.

4. Set the choke thermostatic spring housing to specifications, and adjust the antistall dashpot, idle speed, and fuel mixture.

Motorcraft Variable Venturi 2700VV

For 1977, Ford's new 2700VV (variable venturi) carburetor is available on California cars equipped with the 302 V8. Since the design of this carburetor differs considerably from the other carburetors in the Ford lineup, an explanation of the differences in both theory and operation is presented here. Complete adjustment and repair instructions are also included in this section.

In exterior appearance, the variable venturi carburetor is generally similar to conventional carburetors and, like a conventional carburetor, it uses a normal float and fuel bowl system. However, the similarity ends there. In place of a normal choke plate and fixed area venturis, the 2700VV carburetor has a pair of small oblong castings in the top of the upper carburetor body where you would normally expect to see the choke plate. These castings slide back and forth across the top of the carburetor in response to fuel-air demands. Their movement is controlled by a spring-loaded diaphragm valve regulated by a vacuum signal taken below the venturis in the throttle bores. As the throttle is opened, the strength of the vacuum signal increases, opening the venturis and allowing more air to enter the carburetor.

Fuel is admitted into the venturi area by means of tapered metering rods that fit into the main jets. These rods are attached to the venturis, and, as the venturis open or close in response to air demand, the fuel needed to maintain the proper mixture increases or decreases as the metering rods slide in the jets. In comparison to a conventional carburetor with fixed venturis and a variable air supply, this system provides much more precise control of the fuel-air supply during all modes of operation. Because of the variable venturi principle there are fewer fuel metering systems and fuel passages. The only auxiliary fuel metering systems required are an idle trim, accelerator pump (similar to a conventional carburetor), starting enrichment, and cold running enrichment.

NOTE: *Adjustment, assembly and disassembly of this carburetor require special tools for some of the operations. These tools are available from your Ford dealer. Do not attempt any operations on this carburetor without first checking to see if you need the special tools for that particular operation. The adjustment and repair procedures given here mention when and if you will need the special tools.*

ADJUSTMENTS

Before making any adjustments, set the brake and block the wheels. Make sure the engine is at normal operating temperature.

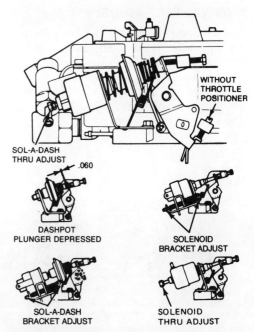

WITHOUT
THROTTLE
POSITIONER

SOL-A-DASH
THRU ADJUST

.060

DASHPOT
PLUNGER DEPRESSED

SOLENOID
BRACKET ADJUST

SOL-A-DASH
BRACKET ADJUST

SOLENOID
THRU ADJUST

Various throttle positioners

CURB IDLE SPEED

2700 VV carburetors may have a vacuum operated throttle modulator (VOTM) in conjunction with a solenoid, a VOTM alone, or neither of these devices. Vehicles without air conditioning should not be equipped with either a solenoid or a VOTM. Vehicles with air conditioning may have either a solenoid in conjunction with a VOTM or simply the VOTM. On all models equipped with automatic parking brake release, disconnect the vacuum line at the parking brake and plug it.

Vehicles with no Solenoid or VOTM

1. Place the transmission in drive.
2. Turn the throttle stop adjusting screw until the correct idle speed is obtained.
3. Cycle the throttle to check the idle. If the idle falls to within plus or minus 50 rpm of the specified speed, leave it alone.

Vehicles with both a Solenoid and VOTM

1. Place the transmission in drive, turn the air conditioner on, and make sure the cold enrichment rod is fully seated.
2. Disconnect the electro-magnetic clutch.
3. Turn the screw at the rear of the solenoid/VOTM to adjust the idle speed.
4. Cycle the throttle to check the repeatability to within plus or minus 50 rpm.

NOTE: *The procedure is the same for a carburetor equipped with only a VOTM.*

INTERNAL VENT ADJUSTMENT

This adjustment must be checked whenever the curb idle speed is adjusted. After you have set the curb idle, place an .010 feeler gauge between the accelerator pump stem and the pump operating link. Turn the adjusting nut until there is just a slight drag when the gauge is removed.

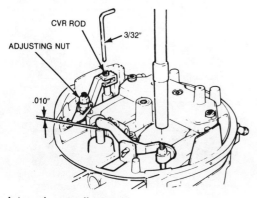

CVR ROD
3/32"
ADJUSTING NUT
.010"

Internal vent adjustment

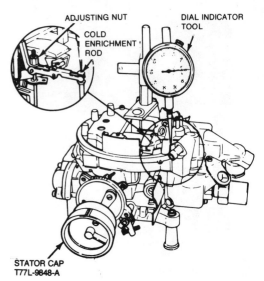

ADJUSTING NUT
COLD ENRICHMENT ROD
DIAL INDICATOR TOOL
STATOR CAP
T77L-9848-A

Cold enrichment metering rod adjustment

COLD ENRICHMENT METERING ROD

NOTE: *This procedure requires special tools.*

Remove the choke cap, after noting its position so that you will be able to return it to the correct setting. Install a dial indicator with the tip of the indicator on the top of the enrichment rod and adjust the dial to zero. The cold enrichment rod is seated by installing the stator cap as a weight. After installing the cap in place of the choke cap, raise it slightly and let it drop. This should seat the cold enrichment rod. The dial indicator should still read zero. If it does not, repeat the procedure. Remove the stator cap and reinstall it in the choke cap's original position. The index mark on the stator cap should be in the same relative position as the index mark on the choke cap. The dial indicator should now read to specification. If it does not, turn the adjusting nut clockwise to increase or counterclockwise to decrease rod height. Reinstall the choke cap in its original position.

CONTROL VACUUM

You will need a tachometer, a vacuum gauge and some allen wrenches for this adjustment. With the engine at curb idle and a tachometer hooked up, turn the venturi valve diaphragm adjusting screw clockwise until the valve is completely closed. Connect a vacuum gauge to the vacuum tap on the venturi valve cover. Turn the venturi bypass adjusting screw to reach the specified vacuum setting. Then turn the venturi valve diaphragm adjusting screw counterclockwise until the

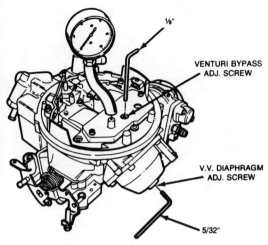

Control vacuum adjustment

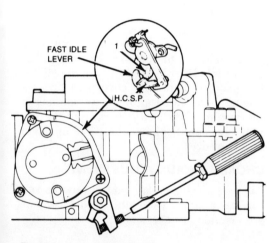

Fast idle speed adjustment

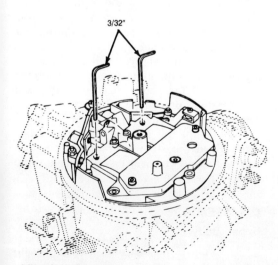

Idle trim adjustment

vacuum drops to the specified setting. In order to get the vacuum to drop, you must rev the engine once or twice. After you get the vacuum right, check and reset the curb idle if necessary.

FAST IDLE SPEED

With the engine idling, EGR disconnected and the vacuum line plugged, make sure the fast idle lever is on the specified step of the fast idle cam. Turn the fast idle adjusting screw clockwise to increase speed and counterclockwise to decrease speed.

IDLE TRIM ADJUSTMENT

NOTE *Idle trim is adjusted at the factory and should not be altered.*

Idle trim is adjusted with a $3/32$-inch allen wrench. Remove the air cleaner cover and locate the adjusting holes in the top of the carburetor. Turn the air adjusting screws clockwise to enrich, counterclockwise to lean out.

FUEL LEVEL ADJUSTMENT

Remove the carburetor upper body. Remove the old gasket and install a new one. Fabricate a gauge to the specified dimension. Turn the upper body upside down and place the fuel level gauge on the cast surface, not on the gasket. Measure the vertical distance from the cast surface to the bottom of the float. If it needs adjustment, bend the float operating lever away from the fuel inlet needle to decrease the setting and toward the needle to increase the setting.

FLOAT DROP ADJUSTMENT

You will need to fabricate a gauge for this adjustment, also. With the upper body in the

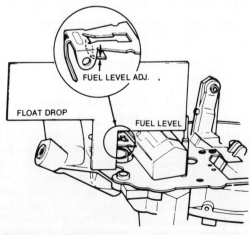

Fuel level adjustment

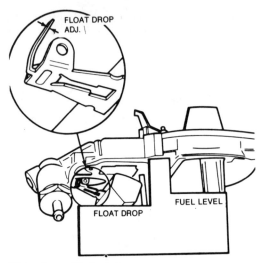

Float drop adjustment

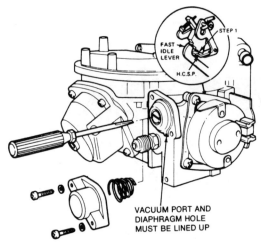

High cam speed positioner adjustment

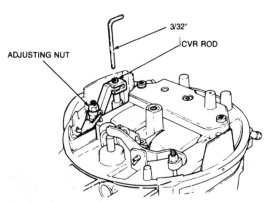

Control vacuum regulator adjustment

upright position, measure the distance between the cast surface of the upper body and the bottom of the float. To adjust, bend the stop tab on the float lever away from the hinge pin to increase the setting and toward the hinge pin to decrease the setting.

CONTROL VACUUM REGULATOR (CVR) ADJUSTMENT

NOTE: *The cold enrichment metering rod adjustment must be set before making this adjustment.*

Cycle the throttle to set the fast idle speed cam and then rotate the choke cap 180 degrees clockwise (rich). Press down on the CVR rod. If it moves downward, it is not seated and must be adjusted. To adjust, turn the rod clockwise until the adjusting nut just begins to rise. Then turn the adjusting screw clockwise in one-quarter turn increments until the rod is fully seated (no down travel). Reset the choke cap to the original setting.

HIGH CAM SPEED POSITIONER (HCSP) ADJUSTMENT

Holding the throttle closed, place the HCSP in the corner of the specified cam step (counting the highest step as the first). Place the fast idle lever in the corner of the HCSP. Remove the diaphragm cover and turn the assembly clockwise until it just bottoms on the casting, then turn it back until the vacuum port and diaphragm hole line up. Reinstall the cover.

CHOKE LINKAGE ADJUSTMENT

There is no choke plate on the variable venturi carburetor. Therefore, no adjustments are possible or necessary.

Overhaul

NOTE: *Special tools are required. Also, rebuilding kits include specific procedures. Read them carefully before attempting any carburetor overhaul.*

It will be easier and you will avoid damaging the carburetor if you make a carburetor stand out of four bolts. The following is a step-by-step procedure. However, many components can be serviced or replaced without completely disassembling the carburetor. Read the steps over carefully before you begin and you will probably save some time.

DISASSEMBLY

Upper Body

1. Remove the fuel inlet fitting, fuel filter, gasket and spring.

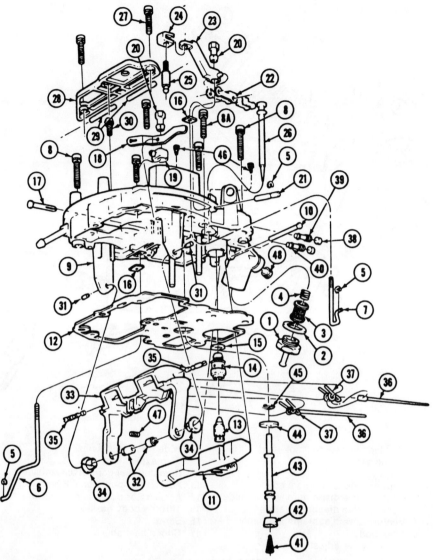

1.	Fuel inlet fitting	17.	Pin	33. Venturi valve
2.	Fuel inlet fitting gasket	18.	Accelerator pump link	34. Venturi valve pivot pin bushing
3.	Fuel filter	19.	Accelerator pump swivel	35. Metering rod pivot pin
4.	Fuel filter spring	20.	Nut	36. Metering rod
5.	Retaining E-ring	21.	Choke hinge pin	37. Metering rod spring
6.	Accelerator pump rod	22.	Cold enrichment rod lever	38. Cup plug
7.	Choke control rod	23.	Cold enrichment rod swivel	39. Main metering jet assembly
8.	Screw	24.	Control vacuum regulator	40. O-ring
8A.	Screw		adjusting nut	41. Accelerator pump return spring
9.	Upper body	25.	Control vacuum regulator	42. Accelerator pump cup
10.	Float hinge pin	26.	Cold enrichment rod	43. Accelerator pump plunger
11.	Float assembly	27.	Screw	44. Internal vent valve
12.	Float bowl gasket	28.	Venturi valve cover plate	45. Retaining E-ring
13.	Fuel inlet valve	29.	Roller bearing	46. Idle trim screw
14.	Fuel inlet seat	30.	Venturi air bypass screw	47. Venturi valve limiter adjusting screw
15.	Fuel inlet seat gasket	31.	Venturi valve pivot plug	48. Pipe plug
16.	Dust seal	32.	Venturi valve pivot pin	

2700 VV upper body

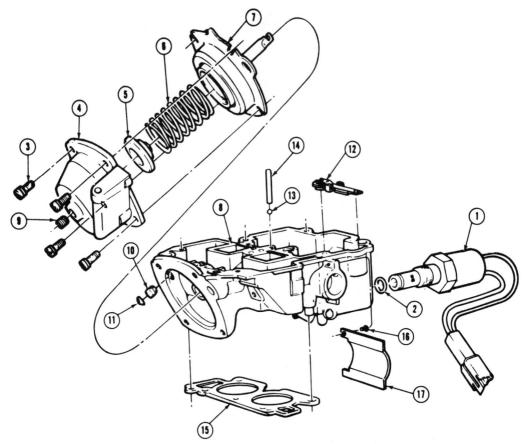

1. Cranking enrichment solenoid
2. O-ring seal
3. Screw
4. Venturi valve diaphragm cover
5. Venturi valve diaphragm spring guide
6. Venturi valve diaphragm spring
7. Venturi valve diaphragm assembly
8. Main body
9. Venturi valve adjusting screw
10. Wide open stop screw
11. Plug expansion
12. Cranking fuel control assembly
13. Accelerator pump check ball
14. Accelerator pump check ball weight
15. Throttle body gasket
16. Screw
17. Choke heat shield

2700 VV main body

2. Remove the screw retaining the upper body assembly and remove the upper body.

3. Remove the float hinge pin and float assembly.

4. Remove the fuel inlet valve, seat and gasket.

5. Remove the accelerator pump rod and the choke control rod.

6. Remove the accelerator pump link retaining pin and the link.

7. Remove the accelerator pump swivel and the retaining nut.

8. Remove the E-ring on the choke hinge pin and slide the pin out of the casting.

9. Remove the cold enrichment rod adjusting nut, lever and swivel; remove the control vacuum nut and regulator as an assembly.

10. Remove the cold enrichment rod.

11. Remove the venturi valve cover plate and roller bearings. Remove the venturi air bypass screw.

12. Using special tool T77P-9928-A, press the tapered plugs out of the venturi valve pivot pins.

13. Remove the venturi valve pivot pins, bushings and the venturi valve.

14. Remove the metering rod pivot pins, springs and metering rods. Be sure to mark the rods so that you know on which side they belong. Also, keep the venturi valve blocked open when working on the jets.

15. Using tool T77L-9533-B, remove the cup plugs.

16. Using tool T77L-9533-A, turn each main metering jet clockwise, counting the number of turns, until they bottom in the casting. You will need to know the number of

turns when you reassemble the carburetor. Remove the jets and mark them so that you know on which side they belong. Don't lose the O-rings.

17. Remove the accelerator pump plunger assembly.

18. Remove the idle trim screws. Remove the venturi valve limiter adjusting screw.

19. To assemble the upper body, reverse the order.

Main Body

1. Remove the cranking enrichment solenoid and the O-ring seal.

2. Remove the venturi valve cover, spring guide, and spring. Remove the venturi valve.

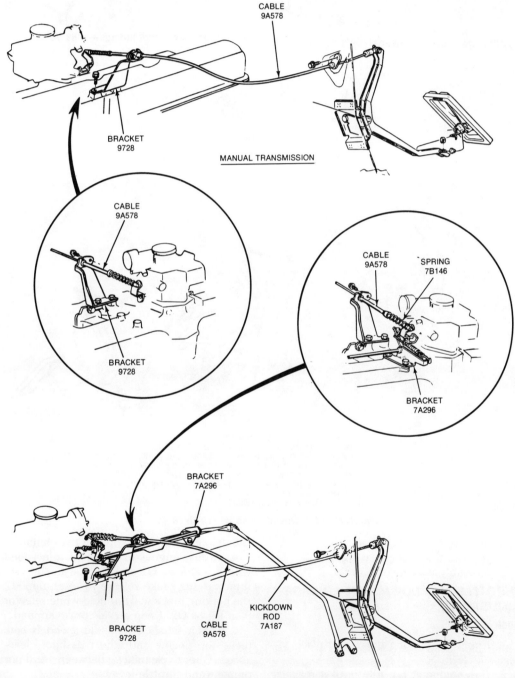

Throttle and downshift linkage—1971–72 six-cylinder

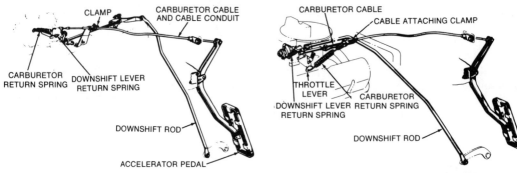

Throttle and downshift linkage—1968 six-cylinder

Throttle and downshift linkage—1968 V8

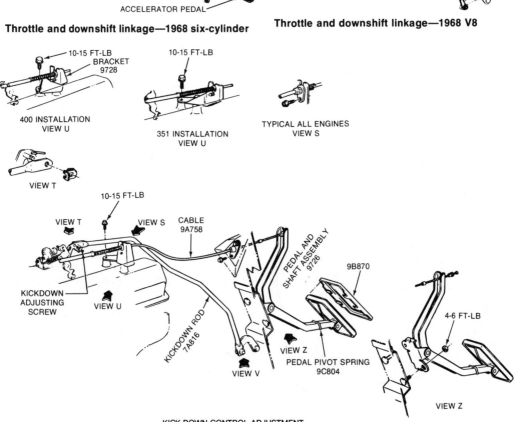

KICK-DOWN CONTROL ADJUSTMENT
A. WITH THE CARBURETOR HELD AT W.O.T. POSITION AND THE KICKDOWN ROD 7A186 HELD DOWNWARD AGAINST THE "THROUGH DETENT" STOP, ADJUST THE KICKDOWN LEVER ADJUSTING SCREW ON CARBURETOR TO OBTAIN .01 TO .08 CLEARANCE BETWEEN ADJUSTING SCREW AND THROTTLE ARM SHAFT LEVER TAB.
B. RETURN SYSTEM TO IDLE-NEUTRAL

Throttle and downshift linkage—1973–76 V8

3. Remove the throttle body.

4. Remove the choke heat shield.

5. Assembly is in reverse order.

THROTTLE AND DOWNSHIFT LINKAGE ADJUSTMENT

1968 Models

1. Apply the parking brake and place selector lever in N.

2. Run engine at fast idle until it reaches normal operating temperature. Then, slow it down to normal idle.

3. Connect a tachometer to the engine.

4. Adjust engine to specified idle speed with selector in D1 or D2. Due to the vacuum parking brake release (if so equipped), the parking brake will not hold while selector is in D1 or D2. Keep service brake applied.

5. When satisfied that idle speed is correct, stop engine and adjust dashpot clearance. Check clearance between dashpot plunger and throttle lever.

6. With engine stopped, disconnect carburetor return spring from throttle lever and

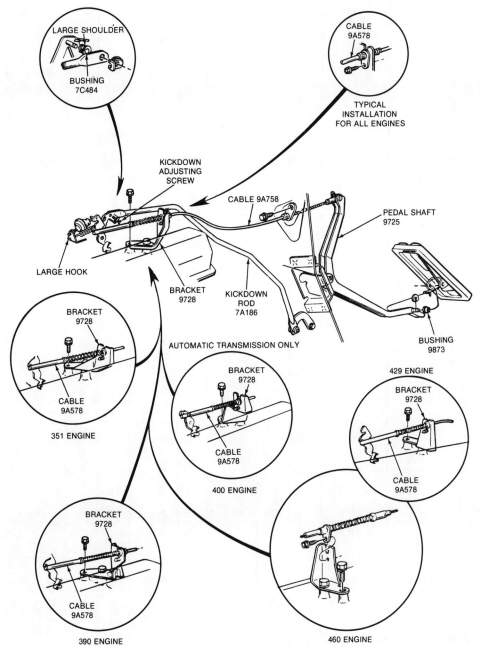

1971–72 V8 throttle linkage adjustment

loosen accelerator cable conduit attaching clamp.

7. With accelerator pedal to floor and throttle lever wide open, slide cable conduit to rear (to left on six-cylinder engine) to remove slack from cable. Tighten clamp.

8. Disconnect downshift lever return spring and hold throttle lever wide open. Depress downshift rod to "through detent stop." Set downshift lever adjusting screw against throttle lever.

9. Connect carburetor return spring and downshift lever return spring.

1969–79 Models

1. Disconnect downshift lever return spring.

2. Hold throttle shaft lever wide open, and hold downshift rod against "through detent stop."

3. Adjust downshift screw to provide 0.050–0.070 in. clearance between screw

Carburetor Specifications

Year	Fuel Level (in.) Dry	Float Adj Wet	Fast Idle Cam Index Setting (in.)	Anti-Stall Dashpot Adj (in.)	Accelerator Pump Operating Rod Position (in overtravel lever)	Dechoke Clearance Adjustment (in.)	Automatic Choke Thermostatic Spring Housing Adj	Choke Plate Pull-Down Clearance Adj (in.)
					Autolite 1101			
'68–'69	1 3/32	—		0.080		15/16	3 Lean	0.200
					Carter YF			
'68	7/32		0.0035	0.100		0.250	Index	0.280
'69	7/32		0.0035	None		0.250	Index	0.280
'70	3/8		Man. 0.029 Auto. 0.035	Auto. 7/64		0.250	Man.—Index Auto.—1 lean	0.225
'71	3/8		Man. 0.190 Auto. 0.200	Auto. 0.100		0.250	Index	Man. 0.200 Auto. 0.230
'72	3/8		0.220	0.100		0.250	1 Lean	0.230
					Autolite (Motorcraft) 2100			
'68	302—3/8 390—31/64	3/4 7/8	302 MT—0.110 302 AT—0.120 390 MT—0.170 390 AT—0.100	1/8	302—2 390—3	0.060	302 MT—Index 302 AT—1 Lean 390 All—Index	302 MT—0.120 302 AT—0.140 390 MT—0.210 390 AT—0.100

Year									
'69	302—³⁄₈, 351, 390,—³¹⁄₆₄, 429	³⁄₄	302 All—0.110 351, 390, 429 AT—0.100 390 MT—0.170	⅛	302 MT—3 302 AT—2 351, 390,—3 429	0.060	⅛	302 MT—2 Rich 302 AT—Index 351, 429—2 Rich 390 MT—1 Rich 390 AT—2 Rich	302 MT—0.130 302, 351 AT—0.120 390 MT—0.210 390, 429 AT—0.130
'70	⁷⁄₁₆	13⁄16	302 All—0.130 351 MT—0.190 351 AT—0.170 390 MT—0.170 390, 429 AT—0.160	AT—⅛	302, 351 MT—3 302 AT—2 351 AT—4 390, 429—3	0.060		302 All—1 Rich 351 All—2 Lean 390 MT—1 Rich 390 AT—2 Rich 429 All—2 Rich	302 All—0.150 351 MT—0.230 390 MT—0.210 351, 390 AT—0.200 429 All—0.200
'71	⁷⁄₁₆	13⁄16	302 MT—0.150 351 MT—0.190 302, 351 AT—0.130 390, 400,—0.160 429	351 AT, 400 AT—⅛ 429 AT	302 MT—3 302 AT—2 351, 390, 400, 429,—3	0.060		302, 351 MT—1 Rich 302, 351 AT—Index 390 AT—Index 400, 429 AT—1 Rich	302 MT—0.170 302 AT—0.150 351 MT—0.220 351, 400 AT—0.190 390, 429 AT—0.200
'72	⁷⁄₁₆	13⁄16	302, 351W—0.130 351C—0.160 400—0.150	302, 351W—⅛	302 All—2 351 All—3 400 (49 states)—4 400 (Calif.)—3	302, 400—0.060 351C, 351W—0.030		302, 351C—1 Rich 351W, 400—Index	302 All—0.150 351 W All—0.140 351C All—0.190 400 (49 states)—0.180 400 (Calif.)—0.170
'73	⁷⁄₁₆	13⁄16	See procedure	None	All—3	—		351W—2 Rich 351C, 400—3 Rich	0.160①

Carburetor Specifications (cont.)

Year	Fuel Level (in.) Dry	Float Adj Wet	Fast Idle Cam Index Setting (in.)	Anti-Stall Dashpot Adj (in.)	Accelerator Pump Operating Rod Position (in overtravel lever)	Dechoke Clearance Adjustment (in.)	Automatic Choke Thermostatic Spring Housing Adj	Choke Plate Pull-Down Clearance Adj (in.)
Autolite (Motorcraft) 2100								
'74	7/16	13/16	See procedure	None	351W, 351C—2 / 400—3	—	351W—2 Rich / 351C, 400—3 Rich	0.160①
Motorcraft 2150								
'75	7/16	13/16	See procedure	None	②	—	3 Rich	0.125
'76–'77	7/16	13/16	See procedure	None	#2	—	③	0.160
'78–'79	7/16	13/16	See procedure	None	#2	—	③	0.160
Autolite 4100								
'68–'69	Primary 17/32 / Secondary 11/16	Primary 20/32 / Secondary 1 1/16	0.120	3/32–1/8	#3	0.060	2 Rich	0.140
Autolite (Motorcraft) 4300								
'68	25/32		0.100	3/32	#3	0.300	MT—1 Rich / AT—2 Rich	MT—0.120 / AT—0.140
'69	25/32		MT—0.220 / AT—0.160	MT—3/32	#2	0.300	MT—Index / AT—1 Rich	MT—0.270 / AT—0.230

'70	428 PI—1.0 429—$^{25}/_{32}$	428 PI—0.120 429 MT—0.220	428 PI—0.080 429—0.070	428 PI—#3 429—#2	0.300	428 PI—2 Rich 429—Index	428 PI—0.160 429 MT—0.250 429 AT—0.220
'71	$^{49}/_{64}$	0.170	$^{1}/_{16}$	#2	0.300	Index	0.220
'72	$^{49}/_{64}$	429 AT—0.200 429 PI—0.190	None	#1	0.300	429 AT—2 Rich 429 PI—Index	429 AT—0.220 429 PI—0.215
'73	429, 460 AT —.76 460 PI—.88	429 AT—0.200 460 AT—0.190 460 PI—0.200	None	#1	0.300	Index	429, 460 AT— 0.210 460 PI—0.200
'74	$^{3}/_{4}$	0.200	None	#1	0.300	Index	460 PI—0.200 460 PI—0.230
			Motorcraft 4350				
'75	460-4V—$^{15}/_{16}$ 460 PI—$^{31}/_{32}$	0.160	None	#1	0.300	2 Rich	Initial—0.160 Delayed—0.190
'76-78	460-4V—1.0 460-PI—0.96	460 4V—0.140 460-PI—0.160	None	#2	0.300	2 Rich	Initial—0.140 Delayed— 0.190④
			Carter Thermo-Quad®				
'74	1$^{1}/_{16}$	0.099	None	Inner	0.130	Index	0.250

① Overrich choke setting—increase in steps of 0.020 in.
Lean choke setting—decrease clearance in steps of 0.020 in.

② D50E-BA, CA—3
D5AE-AA, EA—3
D50E-GA; D5ME-BA, FA—2

③ D6WE-AA—3 Rich
D6AE-HA, D6ME-AA—3 Rich
D6WE-BA—2 Rich

④ 460 PI—Initial—0.160
Delayed—0.210

Specifications—2700 VV
Carburetor

Throttle bore diameter	$1\frac{9}{16}$
Venturi diameter	Variable
Fuel inlet system	
Floatsetting (dry) $\pm \frac{1}{32}$	$1\frac{3}{64}$
Float drop $\pm \frac{1}{32}$	$1\frac{15}{32}$
Main metering system	
Metering rod ident.	144
Venturi valve limiter	$6\frac{1}{64}$
Wide open throttle stop	1 inch
Control vacuum (in. H_2O)	5.0
Spring preload vacuum (in. H_2O)	4.7
Pump system	
Internal vent	.010
Pump weight material	Aluminum
Choke system	
Bimetal identification	7-40 MF
Cap setting	Index
Fast idle cam set	INR @ 3rd Step
Cam Identification	4 Step
Cold enrichment rod setting	.125 $\pm$ .005
Cold enrichment rod ident.	7

and throttle shaft lever on 1969–72 models and 0.010–0.080 in. on 1973–76 models. On 240 cu. in. engine, tighten locknut.

4. Connect downshift lever return spring.

Fuel Tank

REMOVAL AND INSTALLATION

1. Raise the car in the air and support it with safety stands.

2. Remove the fuel from the tank. There should be a drain located in the bottom of the tank.

3. Remove all the hoses and lines from the tank.

4. Remove the filler neck attachment.

5. Remove the fuel tank retaining bolts and remove the tank.

6. Installation is the reverse of removal.

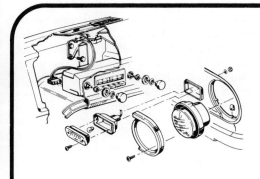

Chassis Electrical

UNDERSTANDING BASIC ELECTRICITY

For any electrical system to operate there must be a complete circuit. This means that the power flow from the battery must make a complete circle. When an electrical component is operating, power flows from the battery to the component, passes through the component causing the component to perform its function, then returns to the battery through the ground of the circuit. This ground is usually (but not always) the metal part of the car upon which the electrical component is mounted.

Perhaps the easiest way to visualize this is to think of connecting a light bulb, with two wires attached to it, to your car battery. The battery in your car has two posts, negative and positive. If one of the two wires attached to the light bulb was attached to the negative post and the other wire was attached to the positive post, you would have a complete circuit. Current from the battery would flow out one post, through the wire attached to it, and then to the light bulb, causing it to light. It would then leave the light bulb, travel through the other wire and return to the other post of the battery. The normal automative circuit differs from this simple cir-

cuit in two ways. First, instead of having a return wire from the bulb to the battery, the light bulb returns the current to the battery through the chassis of the vehicle. Since the negative battery cable is attached to the chassis and the chassis is made of electrically conductive metal, the chassis of the vehicle can serve as a ground wire to complete the circuit. Second, most automotive circuits contain switches to turn components on and off as required.

There are many types of switches, but the most common simply serves to prevent the passage of current when it is turned off. Since the switch is a part of the complete circuit, when the switch is turned off it breaks the circuit.

Some electrical components which require a large amount of current also have a relay in their circuit. A relay is simply an electrically operated switch, operated remotely by a control switch. The purpose of the relay is to avoid the current loss induced by routing the heavy current carrier circuit to the remote switch location. The horn circuit uses a relay.

Did you ever notice how your instrument panel lights get brighter the faster your car goes? That happens because your alternator (which supplies the battery) puts out more current at speeds above idle. This is a very normal thing, however it is possible for larger surges of current to pass through the electrical system of your car. If such a surge were to reach an electrical component it would be burnt out. To prevent this, fuses are connected into the current supply wires of most of the major electrical systems of your car. When an electrical current of more power than a component is designed to operate on tries to pass through that component's fuse, the fuse blows (melts) and breaks the circuit to the component, saving it from destruction.

The fuse also protects the component from damage if the power supply wire to the component is grounded before the current reaches the component. Every complete circuit from a power source must include a component which is using the power. Let's go back to the earlier example of the light bulb with two attached wires being hooked to a battery. If you were to disconnect the light bulb from the wires and touch the two wires together (don't try it), the result would be a display of sparks. A similar thing happens (on a smaller scale) when the power supply wire to a component or the electrical component itself becomes grounded before the normal ground connection for the circuit. To prevent damage to the system, the fuse for the circuit blows to interrupt the circuit and protect the components from damage. Because grounding a wire from a power source makes a complete circuit (less the required component to use the power), this phenomenon is called a short circuit. The most common causes of a short circuit are the insulation on a wire breaking or rubbing through to expose the current carrying core of the wire to the metal parts of the car, or a shorted switch.

Some electrical systems on the car are protected by a circuit breaker. A circuit breaker is basically a self-repairing fuse. When either of the above described events takes place in a system which is protected by a circuit breaker, the circuit breaker opens the circuit in the same way that a fuse does. However, when the short is removed from the circuit or the surge subsides, the circuit breaker resets itself and does not have to be replaced as a fuse does.

Since 1970, all models have incorporated a fuse link in the charging system. The fuse link is a short length of insulated wire, several gauge sizes smaller than the system it protects. The fuse link melts if a booster battery is wired into the system incorrectly, or if a component of the electrical system is shorted to ground. When the fuse link melts, it leaves an open circuit in the charging system and, consequently, the alternator will not charge the battery. A melted fuse link can be identified by bare wire ends or bubbled insulation. It is located in the engine wire harness on or near the starter solenoid, and is marked "fuse link" on 1970–71 models. The procedure for replacing the fuse link is in this chapter.

HEATER

Non-Air Conditioned Cars
BLOWER MOTOR REMOVAL AND INSTALLATION
1968–72 Models

1. Disconnect the negative battery cable.
2. Disconnect the blower motor wire leads under the hood.
3. Remove any parts mounted on the inside of the right fender apron.
4. Raise the vehicle on a hoist and remove the right front wheel.
5. Remove the fender apron-to-fender attaching bolts and lower the fender apron.
6. Insert a block of wood between the apron and the fender to gain working space.
7. Reach inside the fender apron and remove the blower motor mounting plate attaching screws.
8. Remove the blower motor, wheel and mounting plate from inside the fender as an assembly.
9. Reverse above procedure to install.

1973–78 Models

1. Disconnect the blower motor lead wire.
2. Remove the mounting screw from the black ground wire location at the upper cowl. Remove both wires from the clip.
3. Remove the right front tire and wheel.
4. In order to get to the blower motor, an access hole must be cut out in the right front fender apron. The pattern for this hole has been outlined on the apron by the factory. It appears as a beaded line.
5. A small indentation or drill dimple is present ½ in. from the centerline of the bead. Drill a 1 in. diameter hole at this drill dimple. Be careful not to damage the heater case by overdrilling.
6. Using aircraft snips, cut along the bead to create the opening. Do not use a saber saw.
7. Remove the blower motor mounting

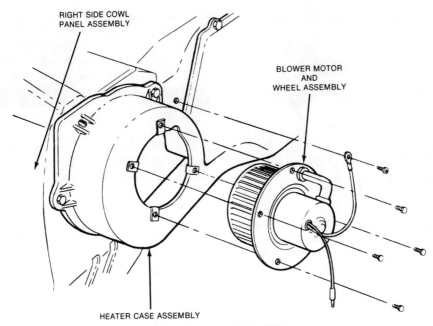

RIGHT SIDE COWL
PANEL ASSEMBLY

BLOWER MOTOR
AND
WHEEL ASSEMBLY

HEATER CASE ASSEMBLY

Typical blower motor installation

plate screws and disconnect the cooler tube from the motor.

8. Remove the motor and wheel assembly out of the heater case and out through the access hole.

9. To install, reverse the removal procedure. Apply rope sealer to the motor mounting plate. Obtain a cover plate from your local Ford parts department, drill 8, ⅛ in. holes in the fender apron and install the cover plate.

1979 Models

1. Disconnect the battery ground cable.

2. Disconnect the blower motor ground wire and the engine ground wire.

3. Disconnect the wiring harness connections.

4. Remove the blower motor cooling tube.

5. Remove the four retaining screws from the mounting plate.

6. Remove the blower motor and wheel assembly. It will be necessary to turn the assembly slightly to the right and follow the contour of the wheel well.

7. Installation is the reverse of removal.

HEATER CORE REMOVAL AND INSTALLATION

All Except 1979

On cars not equipped with air conditioning, the heater core is located in the left-side of

the case on the engine side of the dash panel. To remove:

1. Partially drain cooling system.

2. Remove heater hoses at core.

3. Remove retaining screws, core cover and seal from plenum.

4. Remove core from plenum.

5. Install in reverse of above, applying a thin coat of silicone to the pads.

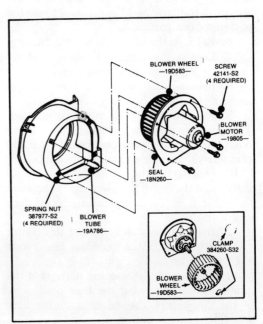

BLOWER WHEEL
—19D583—

SCREW
42141-S2
(4 REQUIRED)

BLOWER
MOTOR
—19805—

SEAL
—18N260—

SPRING NUT
387977-S2
(4 REQUIRED)

BLOWER
TUBE
—19A786—

CLAMP
384260-S32

BLOWER
WHEEL
—19D583—

1979 blower motor removal

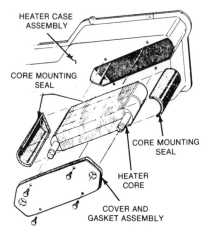

HEATER CASE ASSEMBLY

CORE MOUNTING SEAL

CORE MOUNTING SEAL

HEATER CORE

COVER AND GASKET ASSEMBLY

Heater core removal—typical of non-air conditioned cars

1979 Models

1. It is necessary to remove the plenum assembly to reach the heater core on 1979 models. Drain the coolant from the system.

2. Disconnect the negative battery cable.

3. Disconnect the heater hoses from the heater core tubes. Plug the tubes to prevent leakage.

4. Remove the one bolt located beneath the wiper motor that attaches the left side of the plenum to the dash. Remove the nut that retains the upper left corner of the heater case.

5. Disconnect the control system vacuum supply hose from the vacuum source and push the hose and the grommet into the passenger compartment.

6. Remove the glove compartment.

7. Loosen the right still plate, and remove the right side cowl trim panel.

8. Remove the attaching bolt on the lower right side of the instrument panel.

9. Remove the instrument panel pad. There are five screws attaching the lower edge, one screw on each outboard end, and two screws near the defroster openings.

10. Disengege the temperature control cable from the top of the plenum. Disconnect the cable from the temperature blend door crank arm.

11. Remove the clip attaching the center register bracket to the plenum, and rotate the bracket up to the right.

12. Disconnect the vacuum harness at the multiple connector near the floor duct.

13. Disconnect the white vacuum hose from the vacuum motor.

14. Remove the two screws attaching the passenger's side air duct to the plenum. It may be necessary to remove the two screws which attach the lower panel door vacuum motor to the mounting bracket to gain access.

15. Remove the one plastic fastener retaining the floor air distribution duct to the left end of the plenum, and remove the duct.

16. Remove the two nuts from the lower flange of the plenum.

17. Move the plenum rearward and rotate the top of the plenum down and out from under the instrument panel.

18. Once the plenum is removed, remove the heater core cover and remove the heater core.

19. Installation is the reverse of removal.

HEATER

Air Conditioned Cars

BLOWER MOTOR REMOVAL AND INSTALLATION

1968 Models

1. Take off the protective cover from the engine firewall. Disconnect the negative battery cable.

2. Take out the mounting plate-to-evaporator housing attaching screws.

3. Disconnect the motor wires.

4. Lift out the motor assembly.

5. Reverse above procedure to install.

1969–72 Models

1. Remove the battery.

2. Remove the right front wheel.

3. Remove the vacuum tank bolts and fender apron bolts.

4. Move the fender apron inboard.

5. Remove the blower motor attaching screws and vent hose.

6. Pry upward on the hood hinge and remove the blower.

7. Reverse the above procedure to install.

1973–79 Models

The procedure is the same as that outlined for 1973–77 non-air conditioned cars.

HEATER CORE REMOVAL AND INSTALLATION

1968 Models

1. Drain the cooling system and raise the front of the vehicle.

2. Remove the right front wheel and tire.

3. To gain access to the core, remove the

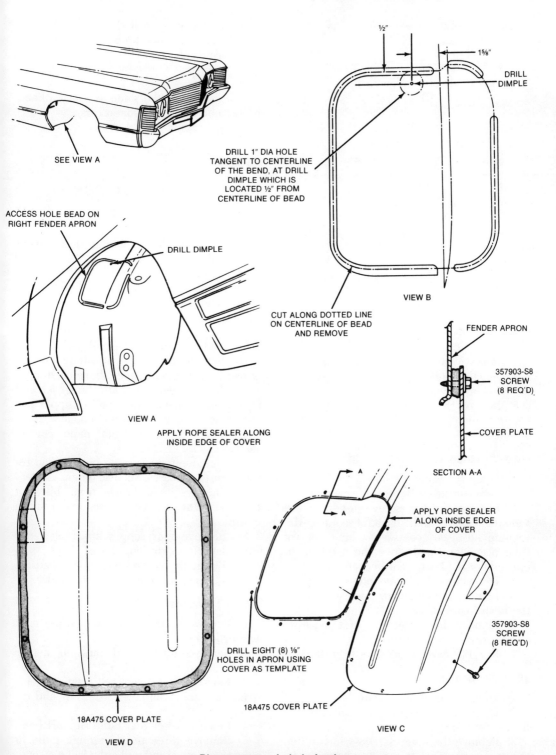

½"

1⅝"

DRILL DIMPLE

DRILL 1" DIA HOLE TANGENT TO CENTERLINE OF THE BEND, AT DRILL DIMPLE WHICH IS LOCATED ½" FROM CENTERLINE OF BEAD

SEE VIEW A

ACCESS HOLE BEAD ON RIGHT FENDER APRON

DRILL DIMPLE

VIEW A

VIEW B

CUT ALONG DOTTED LINE ON CENTERLINE OF BEAD AND REMOVE

FENDER APRON

357903-S8 SCREW (8 REQ'D)

COVER PLATE

SECTION A-A

APPLY ROPE SEALER ALONG INSIDE EDGE OF COVER

APPLY ROPE SEALER ALONG INSIDE EDGE OF COVER

A

A

357903-S8 SCREW (8 REQ'D)

DRILL EIGHT (8) ⅛" HOLES IN APRON USING COVER AS TEMPLATE

18A475 COVER PLATE

18A475 COVER PLATE

VIEW D

VIEW C

Blower access hole in fender

two upper bolts and the bolts around the wheel well retaining the inner fender apron. Pull the apron down and block it in this position.

4. Disconnect the heater hoses.

5. Remove the water valve retaining screws and position the valve to one side.

6. Remove the core housing-to-dash retaining screws and the core housing from the car.

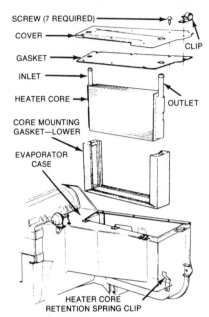

SCREW (7 REQUIRED)
COVER
CLIP
GASKET
INLET
HEATER CORE
OUTLET
CORE MOUNTING GASKET—LOWER
EVAPORATOR CASE
HEATER CORE RETENTION SPRING CLIP

Heater core removal—air conditioned cars

7. Remove the core from the housing by removing the retaining screws and separating the housing halves.

8. Reverse the above procedure to install, taking care to seal the housing halves together.

1969–72 Models

1. Drain the cooling system.

2. Remove the carburetor air cleaner.

3. Remove the two screws retaining the vacuum manifold to the dash. Disconnect the vacuum hoses as necessary, taking note of their placement, and move the manifold to one side of the heater core cover.

4. Disconnect the heater hoses.

5. Remove the seven attaching screws and the heater core cover.

6. Remove the heater core and pad from the housing.

7. Reverse above procedure to install.

1973–78 Models

1. Drain the cooling system.

2. Disconnect the heater hoses at the heater core tubes.

3. Remove the seven screws which retain the core cover plate to the core housing and lift off the plate.

4. Pull the heater core and mounting gasket up out of the case. Remove the core mounting gasket.

5. Reverse the above procedure to install, taking care to ensure that the core and gasket seat firmly forward of the core retention

spring in the case. Fill the cooling system with the recommended mixture of water and antifreeze (coolant).

1979 Models

The procedure is the same as that outlined for 1979 non-air conditioned cars.

RADIO

REMOVAL AND INSTALLATION

1968 Models

1. Disconnect battery.

2. Remove the moldings from wind shield pillars.

3. Unsnap mouldings from right-side of instrument panel pad.

4. Remove two pop off access cover from cluster area.

5. Remove four screws attaching right half of pad to instrument panel.

6. Remove two screws attaching left side of pad to instrument panel above cluster.

7. Remove one screw attaching each end of instrument panel lower pad to upper pad and remove upper pad from vehicle.

8. Pull all knobs from radio control shafts.

9. Remove ten retaining buttons and remove lens and mask from instrument cluster.

10. Remove two screws from blackout cover at right of speedometer and remove cover.

11. Remove four screws attaching radio front plate to instrument cluster.

12. Pull radio out and disconnect leads.

13. Reverse procedure to install radio.

1969–70 Models

1. Remove radio knobs and wiper and washer knobs.

2. Remove lighter and pull off heater switch knobs.

3. Remove ten screws retaining instrument panel trim cover assembly and remove.

4. Remove lower rear radio support bolt.

5. Remove three nuts retaining radio in instrument panel and pull radio half-way out.

6. Disconnect all leads and remove radio.

7. Reverse procedure to install radio.

1971–79 Models

NOTE: *For the 1979 all-electronic radio, perform step 6 first.*

1. Disconnect the negative battery cable.

2. Remove the radio knobs and the nuts retaining the radio cover bezel.

3. Remove the bezel and the nut retaining the fader control to the bezel.

4. Remove the upper and lower radio support brackets and bolts.

5. Disconnect all leads from the radio.

6. Remove the two nuts retaining the radio to the instrument panel and remove the radio.

7. Reverse above procedure to install.

WINDSHIELD WIPERS

MOTOR REMOVAL AND INSTALLATION

1. Disconnect the negative battery cable.

2. Remove the wiper arm and blade assemblies from the pivots shafts.

3. On 1968–70 models, remove the cowl grille. On 1971–72 and 1977 models, remove the left side cowl grille.

4. Disconnect the wiper links at the wiper output pin by removing the retaining clip.

5. Disconnect the wire leads from the motor.

6. On 1968 models, remove the motor and bracket attaching bolts from the engine side of the firewall and remove the motor from the car. On 1969–78 models, remove the motor attaching bolts from under the dash and remove the motor. On 1979 models, remove the motor attaching bolts from the dash panel extension.

7. Reverse above procedure to install.

NOTE: *Before installing the wiper arms and blades, operate the wiper motor to ensure that the pivot shafts are in the Park position when the arms and blades are installed.*

WIPER LINKAGE REMOVAL AND INSTALLATION

1. Disconnect the battery ground cable.

2. Remove the wiper arms and blades from the pivots as an assembly.

3. Remove the cowl grille from the car.

4. Disconnect the linkage arm from the drive arm by removing the clip.

5. Remove the pivot attaching screws from the cowl and remove the pivot from the cowl.

NOTE: *On 1969–72 models, to remove the left wiper transmission, it is first necessary to loosen the attaching screws on the right wiper arm pivot.*

INSTRUMENT CLUSTER

CLUSTER REMOVAL AND INSTALLATION

1968 Models

1. Disconnect battery.

2. Remove right and left windshield mouldings.

3. Pry moulding from right-side of in-

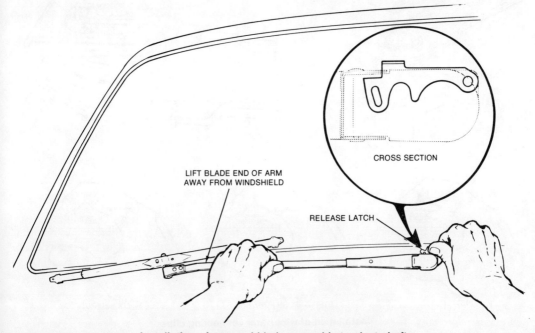

Installation of arm and blade assembly to pivot shaft

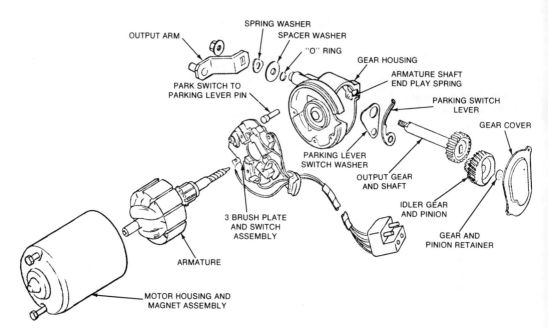

Wiper motor disassembled

strument panel pad covering the pad retaining screws.

4. Pry off two access covers located above the speedometer lens and on underside of pad.

5. Remove screws retaining instrument panel pad, and remove pad.

6. Remove radio knobs.

7. Remove button clips retaining instrument cluster mask and lens, and remove mask and lens.

8. Disconnect speedometer cable.

9. Remove screws retaining instrument panel lower pad and remove pad.

10. Remove screws from clock retainer and clock and position clock forward.

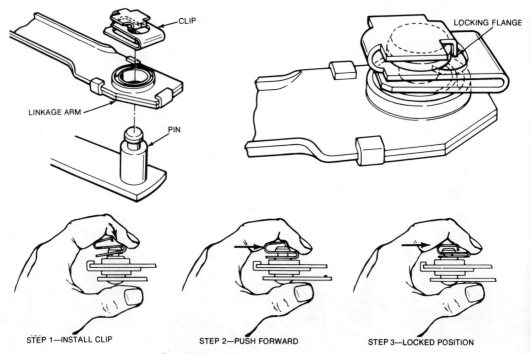

Installation of wiper arm connecting clips

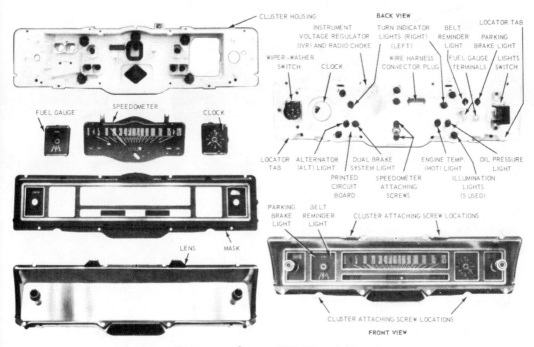

Instrument cluster—1969-72 models

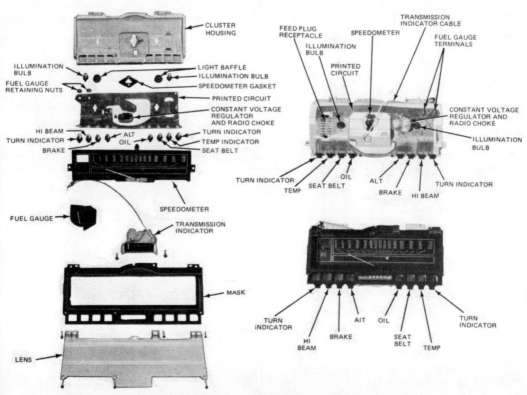

Instrument cluster—1973-77 models

11. Remove plate under speedometer and two rubber spacers and screws retaining speedometer assembly.

12. Reverse procedure to install.

1969-72 Models

1. Disconnect negative battery cable. Remove upper part of instrument panel by re-

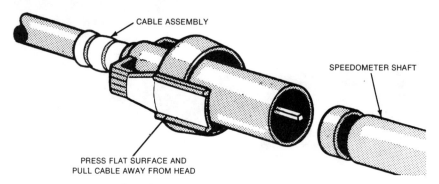

CABLE ASSEMBLY

SPEEDOMETER SHAFT

PRESS FLAT SURFACE AND
PULL CABLE AWAY FROM HEAD

Speedometer cable quick disconnect

moving screws along lower edge, two screws in each of the defroster registers, and disconnecting the radio speaker.

2. Remove cluster opening finish panels from each side of instrument cluster.

3. Disconnect plugs to printed circuit, radio, heater and A/C fan, windshield wipers and washers, and any other electrical connection to cluster.

4. Disconnect heater and A/C control cables and speedometer cable.

5. Remove all knobs from instrument panel if required.

6. Remove instrument cluster trim cover.

7. Remove mounting screws and remove cluster.

8. Reverse procedure to install.

1973–79 Models

1. Disconnect the negative battery cable.
2. Remove the steering column cover.

3. Disconnect the speedometer cable cable and the wire plugs to the printed circuit.

4. Remove the cluster trim cover.

5. Remove the screw attaching the transmission selector lever indicator cable to the column.

6. Remove the instrument cluster retaining screws and lift the cluster from the instrument panel.

7. Reverse the above procedure to install, taking care to ensure that the selector pointer is aligned.

SEATBELT SYSTEM

All 1974–75 Ford vehicles are equipped with the Federally-required starter interlock system. The purpose of this system is to force the wearing of seat belts.

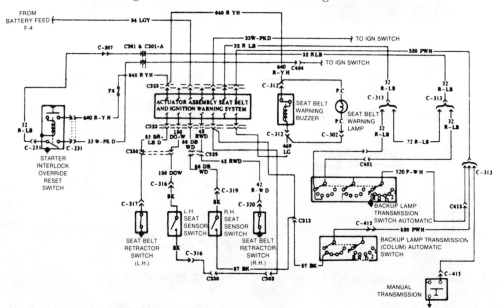

Seat belt/starter interlock system circuit—1974

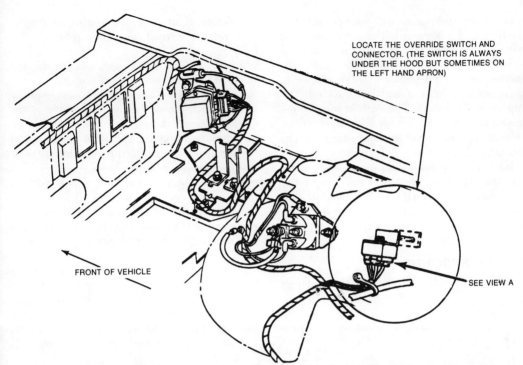

LOCATE THE OVERRIDE SWITCH AND CONNECTOR. (THE SWITCH IS ALWAYS UNDER THE HOOD BUT SOMETIMES ON THE LEFT HAND APRON)

FRONT OF VEHICLE

SEE VIEW A

CAUTION: Set the parking brake and remove the ignition key before any rework is performed. (If the no. 640 circuit is accidentally spliced into the no. 32 or no. 33 circuits, the car will start in gear)

1. Cut the no. 32 and no. 33 circuits
2. On the wiring harness end, splice the no. 32 and no. 33 circuits together. Use a B9A-14487-A butt connector on a 16 to 18 gage wire or a B9A-14487-B connector on a 10 to 14 gage wire
3. Tape the complete splice to water proof the connection
4. Reattach the connector to the override switch to prevent rattling
5. Test the rework by setting the car brakes, buckle up the seat belt and turn the key to on. If the starter cranks in the on position and in any gear the wires have been crossed. (Recheck the rework)
6. The buzzer function can be deleted by removing the buzzer from the connector and taping the connector to the harness to prevent rattling
7. The sequential seat belt warning light feature can be deleted by removing the bulb from its socket. This can only be done on previously sold vehicles. The light cannot be disconnected on a new and unsold car even if the purchaser so requests

NOTE: If the no. 32 and no. 33 circuit terminals contain two wires, cut and splice all wires from the no. 32 and no. 33 circuits into one butt connector.

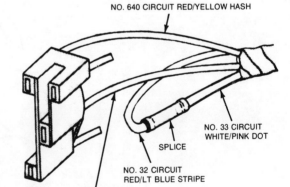

NO. 640 CIRCUIT RED/YELLOW HASH

NO. 33 CIRCUIT WHITE/PINK DOT

SPLICE

NO. 32 CIRCUIT RED/LT BLUE STRIPE

NO. 57 CIRCUIT BLACK (T-BIRD, MARK IV, LINCOLN ONLY)

VIEW A

STARTER INTERLOCK DELETION – ALL VEHICLES SO EQUIPPED – 1974-75

The system includes a warning light and buzzer (as in late 1972 and 1973), weight sensors in the front seats, switches in the outboard front seat belt retractors, and an electronic control module. The center front is tied into the warning light and buzzer system, but not into the starter interlock.

The electronic control module requires that the driver and right front passenger first sit down, then pull out their seat belts. If this is not done, the starter will not operate, but the light and buzzer will. The sequence must be followed each time the engine is started unless the driver and passenger have remained seated and buckled. If the seat belts have been pulled out and left buckled, the engine will not start. The switches in the retractors must be cycled for each start. If the belts are released after the start, the light and buzzer will operate.

If the system should fail, preventing starting, the interlock by-pass switch under the hood can be used. This switch permits one start without interference from the interlock system. This by-pass switch can also be used for servicing purposes.

TROUBLESHOOTING

If the starter will not crank or the warning buzzer will not shut off, perform the following checks:

Problem: Front seat occupant sits on a pre-buckled seat belt.

Solution: Unbuckle the prebuckled belt, fully retract, extract, and then rebuckle the belt.

Problem: The front seat occupants are buckled, but the starter will not crank.

Solution: The unoccupied seat sensor switch stuck closed before the seat was occupied. Reset the unoccupied seat sensor switches by applying and then releasing 50 lbs or more of weight to the seat directly over the seat sensor switches.

Problem: Starter will not crank with a heavy parcel on the front seat.

Solution: Buckle the seat belt around the parcel somewhere else in the car. Unbuckle the seat belt when the parcel is removed from the front seat.

Problem: Starter will not crank due to starter interlock system component failure.

Solution: An emergency starter interlock overide switch is located under the hood on the fender apron. Depress the red push button on the switch and release it. This will

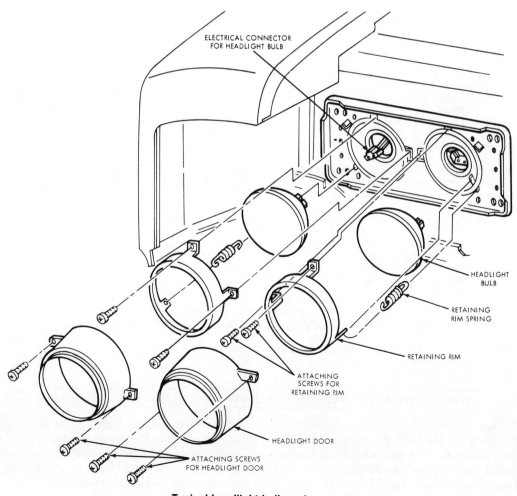

Typical headlight bulb replacement

allow one complete cycle of the ignition key from Off to Start and back to Off. Do not tape the button down as this will result in deactivation of the override feature.

LIGHTING

Headlights

REMOVAL AND INSTALLATION

1. Remove the headlight door mounting screws and the headlight door.
2. Remove the three screws that hold the headlight retainer to the adjusting ring, and remove the retainer.
3. Pull the headlight forward and disconnect the wire plug. Remove the headlight.
4. Attach a new headlight to the wiring plug.
5. Install the new light in the housing and replace the retainer ring.
6. Reinstall the headlight door.

Fuses and Flashers

The fuses and flashers are located under the instrument panel on all models.

CIRCUIT PROTECTION

Fuse Link

The fuse link is a short length of insulated wire contained in the alternator wiring harness, between the alternator and the starter relay. The fuse link is several wire gauge sizes smaller than the other wires in the harness. If a booster battery is connected incorrectly to the car battery or if some component of the charging system is shorted to ground, the fuse link melts and protects the alternator. The fuse link is attached to the starter relay. The insulation on the wire reads: FUSE LINK. A melted fuse link can usually be identified by cracked or bubbled insulation. If it is difficult to determine if the fuse link is melted, connect a test light to both ends of the wire. If the fuse link is not melted, the test light will light showing that an open circuit does not exist in the wire.

FUSE LINK REPLACEMENT

Fuse links originally installed in your car are black on 1970–71 models and the color of the circuit being protected on 1972 and later models. Service replacements are green or black, depending on usage. Black service re-

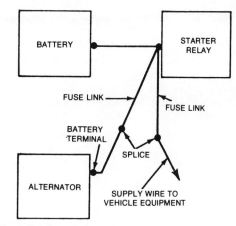

Fuse link location

placements are used with cars using 38 and 42 amp alternators, and green service replacements on cars using 55 or 61 amp alternators. All 1972 and later models use color coded flags molded on the wire or on the terminal insulator to identify the wire gauge of the link. Color identification is as follows: Red-18 gauge wire, orange-16 gauge wire, green-14 gauge wire, blue-20 gauge wire.

1. Disconnect the negative battery cable.
2. Disconnect the eyelet of the fuse link from the starter relay.
3. Cut the other end of the fuse link from the wiring harness at the splice.
4. Connect the eyelet end of a new fuse link to the starter relay.

NOTE: *Use only an original equipment type fuse link. Under no conditions should standard wire be substituted.*

5. Splice the open end of the new fuse link into the wiring harness.
6. Solder the splice with rosin-core solder and wrap the splice with electrical tape. This slice must be soldered.
7. Connect the negative battery cable.
8. Start the engine, to check to see that the new connections complete the circuit.

WIRING DIAGRAMS

NOTE: *Wiring diagrams have been left out of this book. As cars have become more complex, and available with longer and longer option lists, wiring diagrams have grown in size and complexity also. It has become virtually impossible to provide a readable reproduction in a reasonable number of pages. Information on ordering wiring diagrams from the vehicle manufacturer can be found in the owners manual.*

6

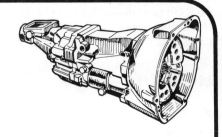

Clutch and Transmission

MANUAL TRANSMISSION

A 3-speed manual transmission is standard equipment on 1968–71 models. All forward gears are fully synchronized, helical-cut and in constant mesh. A column-mounted shifter is used with this transmission. On 1972 and later models, the 3-speed manual transmission is no longer available.

A 4-speed manual transmission is available as an option on 1968 models using the 390 and 428 V8 engines, and on 1969 models equipped with the 429 V8. This heavy-duty unit is also synchronized in all forward gears. On 1970 and later models, the 4-speed transmission is no longer available. This transmission used a floor-mounted shifter.

MANUAL TRANSMISSION LINKAGE ADJUSTMENT

Column Shift

1. Place the gearshift lever in the Neutral position.

2. Loosen the two gearshift adjustment nuts on the shift linkage.

3. Insert a $^3/_{16}$ in. alignment tool through the First and Reverse lever, the Second and Third gear shift lever, and the two holes in the lower casing. An alignment tool can be fabricated from $^3/_{16}$ in. rod bent to an L

shape. The extension that is to be inserted into the levers should be 1 in. in length from the elbow.

4. Manipulate the levers so that the alignment tool will move freely through the alignment holes.

5. Tighten the two gearshift rod adjustment nuts.

6. Remove the tool and check linkage operation.

Floor Shift

1. Place the gearshift lever in Neutral position, then raise car on a hoist.

2. Insert a ¼ in. rod into the alignment holes of the shift levers.

3. If the holes are not in exact alignment, check for bent connecting rods or loose lever locknuts at the rod ends. Make replacements or repairs, then adjust as follows.

4. Loosen the three rod-to-lever retaining locknuts and move the levers until the ¼ in. gauge rod will enter the alignment holes. Be sure that the transmission shift levers are in Neutral, and the Reverse shifter lever is in the Neutral detent.

5. Install shift rods and torque locknuts to 18–23 ft lbs.

6. Remove the ¼ in. gauge rod.

7. Operate the shift levers to assure correct shifting.

8. Lower the car and road-test.

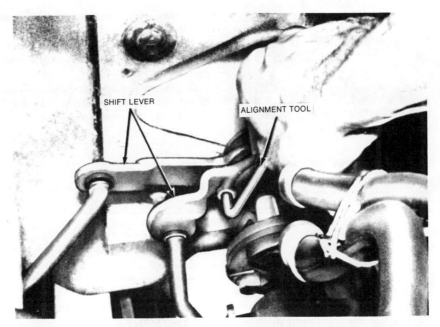

Column-mounted gearshift linkage adjustment

TRANSMISSION AND CLUTCH REMOVAL AND INSTALLATION

1. Raise the vehicle on a hoist.
2. Disconnect the driveshaft from the rear U-joint flange and slide the front yoke from the transmission.
3. Insert a cap or rag in the transmission extension housing to prevent fluid leakage.
4. Disconnect the speedometer cable and shifter linkage from the transmission. On models with a four-speed transmission, remove the shifter mounting bracket from the extension housing.
5. On models with a three-speed transmission, disconnect the transmission mount from the crossmember. If equipped with a four-speed transmission, remove the front parking brake cable from the crossmember and remove the crossmember from the car.
6. Remove the bolts which mount the transmission to the bellhousing. On 429 V8s, the upper left-hand transmission attaching bolt is a seal bolt. Carefully note its location so that it may be returned to its original position.
7. Move the transmission rearward until the input shaft clears the bellhousing and lower it from the car.
8. Disconnect the clutch release lever return spring.
9. If equipped with a one-piece aluminum bellhousing, remove the starter and re-

move the bellhousing from the engine. If equipped with a cast iron bellhousing, remove only the inspection cover from the bottom of the bellhousing.
10. Loosen the six pressure plate attaching bolts evenly to release spring pressure, and remove the clutch assembly from the car.
11. To install, position clutch assembly on flywheel and install each pressure plate attaching bolt finger-tight.

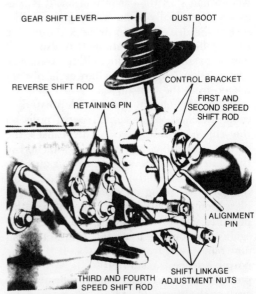

Floor-mounted gearshift linkage adjustment

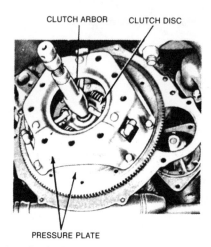

CLUTCH ARBOR   CLUTCH DISC

PRESSURE PLATE

Aligning clutch disc

12. Insert a transmission pilot shaft or other suitable tool to align the clutch disc with the flywheel and alternately tighten the pressure plate attaching bolts until the plate is secured to the flywheel.

13. Reverse above procedure to install transmission and driveshaft.

CLUTCH

The clutch is a system of parts which, when engaged, connects the engine to the transmission. When the clutch is disengaged (clutch pedal pushed in), the turning motion of the engine crankshaft is separated from the transmission. Since the engine does not produce enough torque at idle to turn the rear wheels and start the car in motion, it is necessary to gradually connect the engine to the rest of the drive train to prevent the engine from stalling on acceleration. It is also much easier to shift the gears within a manual transmission when engine power is disconnected from the transmission.

When the clutch pedal is depressed, a cable attached to the clutch pedal pulls on the clutch release lever. This causes the clutch release bearing, which is attached to the clutch release lever, to press against the release fingers of the pressure plate. This removes the spring pressure of the pressure plate from the clutch disc. Since it was this pressure which was holding the clutch disc against the engine flywheel, the clutch can now move away from the flywheel. If engine power is to be transmitted to the rest of the power train, the clutch must be firmly held against the flywheel (which is attached to,

and turns with, the crankshaft). By depressing the clutch pedal you allow the clutch disc to move away from the flywheel, thus isolating engine power from the rest of the drive train.

The following engine displacement/clutch disc diameter chart will prove useful the next time the clutch needs replacement:

Engine	Disc Diameter (in.)
240 Six	9.5
302 V8	10.0
240, 302 Heavy-Duty	11.0
351, 390, 400 V8	11.0
429 V8	11.5

CLUTCH PEDAL FREE TRAVEL ADJUSTMENT

1. Disconnect the clutch return spring from the release lever.

2. Loosen the release lever adjusting nut and locknut, 2 or 3 turns.

3. Move the clutch release lever rearward until the throwout bearing can be felt to lightly contact the pressure plate fingers.

4. Adjust the rod length until the rod seats in the pocket in the release lever.

5. Insert a feeler gauge of specified thickness between the adjusting nut and swivel sleeve. Tighten the nut against the feeler gauge. Correct feeler gauge thicknesses are: 1968–0.206 in., 1969–71–0.194 in.

6. Tighten the locknut against the adjusting nut, being careful not to disturb the adjustment.

7. Connect the clutch return spring.

8. Make a final check with the engine running at 3,000 rpm, and transmission in Neutral. Under this condition, centrifugal weights on release fingers may reduce the clearance. Readjust, if necessary, ot obtain at least ½ in. free-play while maintaining the 3,000 rpm to prevent fingers contacting release bearing. This is important.

AUTOMATIC TRANSMISSION

All automatics used from 1968 to the present are aluminum case, dual-range, three-speed units. The medium-duty C4 au-

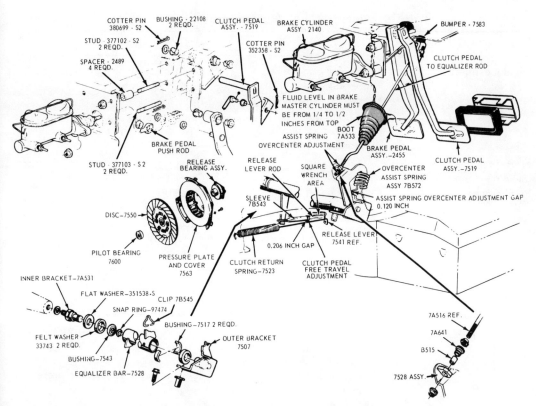

COTTER PIN
380699 - S2

BUSHING - 22108
2 REQD.

CLUTCH PEDAL
ASSY. - 7519

BRAKE CYLINDER
ASSY 2140

BUMPER - 7583

STUD - 377102 - S2
2 REQD.

COTTER PIN
352358 - S2

CLUTCH PEDAL
TO EQUALIZER ROD

SPACER - 2489
4 REQD.

FLUID LEVEL IN BRAKE
MASTER CYLINDER MUST
BE FROM 1/4 TO 1/2
INCHES FROM TOP

BOOT
7A533

BRAKE PEDAL
PUSH ROD

ASSIST SPRING
OVERCENTER ADJUSTMENT

BRAKE PEDAL
ASSY. —2455

CLUTCH PEDAL
ASSY. —7519

STUD - 377103 - S 2
2 REQD.

RELEASE
BEARING ASSY.

RELEASE
LEVER ROD

SQUARE
WRENCH
AREA

OVERCENTER
ASSIST SPRING
ASSY 7B572

DISC—7550

SLEEVE
7B543

ASSIST SPRING OVERCENTER ADJUSTMENT GAP
0.120 INCH

PILOT BEARING
7600

0.206 INCH GAP

RELEASE LEVER
7541 REF.

INNER BRACKET—7A531

PRESSURE PLATE
AND COVER
7563

CLUTCH RETURN
SPRING—7523

CLUTCH PEDAL
FREE TRAVEL
ADJUSTMENT

FLAT WASHER—351538-S

CLIP 7B545

7A516 REF.

SNAP RING—97474

7A641

FELT WASHER
33743 2 REQD.

BUSHING—7517 2 REQD.

OUTER BRACKET
7507

B515

BUSHING—7543

7528 ASSY.

EQUALIZER BAR—7528

Clutch pedal and linkage adjustment—1968

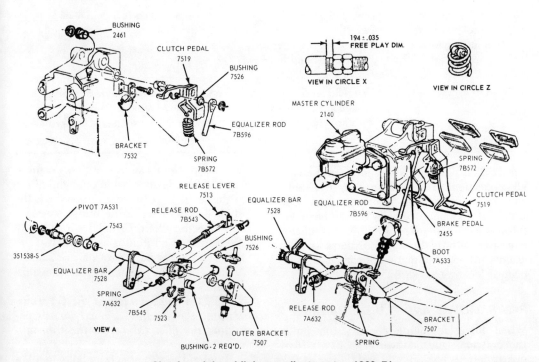

BUSHING
2461

CLUTCH PEDAL
7519

BUSHING
7526

194 ±.035
FREE PLAY DIM.

VIEW IN CIRCLE X

VIEW IN CIRCLE Z

MASTER CYLINDER
2140

EQUALIZER ROD
7B596

BRACKET
7532

SPRING
7B572

SPRING
7B572

CLUTCH PEDAL
7519

RELEASE LEVER
7513

EQUALIZER BAR
7528

EQUALIZER ROD
7B596

PIVOT 7A531

RELEASE ROD
7B543

BRAKE PEDAL
2455

7543

BOOT
7A533

351538-S

BUSHING
7526

EQUALIZER BAR
7528

SPRING
7A632

RELEASE ROD
7A632

BRACKET
7507

7B545

7523

VIEW A

OUTER BRACKET
7507

SPRING

BUSHING - 2 REQ'D.

Clutch pedal and linkage adjustments—1969–71

Troubleshooting the Automatic Transmission

Problem	Is Caused By	What to Do
Fluid leakage	• Defective pan gasket • Loose filler tube • Loose extension housing to transmission case • Converter housing area leakage	• Replace gasket or tighten pan bolts • Tighten tube nut • Tighten bolts • Have transmission checked professionally
Fluid flows out the oil filler tube	• High fluid level • Breather vent clogged • Clogged oil filter or screen • Internal fluid leakage	• Check and correct fluid level • Open breather vent • Replace filter or clean screen (change fluid also) • Have transmission checked professionally
Transmission overheats (this is usually accompanied by a strong burned odor to the fluid)	• Low fluid level • Fluid cooler lines clogged • Heavy pulling or hauling with insufficient cooling • Faulty oil pump, internal slippage	• Check and correct fluid level • Drain and refill transmission. If this doesn't cure the problem, have cooler lines cleared or replaced. • Have transmission checked professionally
Buzzing or whining noise	• Low fluid level • Defective torque converter, scored gears	• Check and correct fluid level • Have transmission checked professionally
No forward or reverse gears or slippage in one or more gears	• Low fluid level • Defective vacuum or linkage controls, internal clutch or band failure	• Check and correct fluid level • Have unit checked professionally
Delayed or erratic shift	• Low fluid level • Broken vacuum lines • Internal malfunction	• Check and correct fluid level • Repair or replace lines • Have transmission checked professionally

tomatic is installed in six-cylinder and small V8 applications. The medium-duty FMX automatic is installed in most midsized V8s (e.g., 351 and some 400 V8s). A similar CW automatic is installed in 1974–75 Ford sedans equipped with the 2.75:1 rear axle ratio. The heavy-duty C6 automatic appears in Ford's biggest V8s (e.g., 390, 428, 429, 460 V8).

PAN REMOVAL AND FLUID DRAINING

When filling a completely dry (no fluid) transmission and converter, install five quarts of transmission fluid and then start the engine. Shift the selector lever through all gear positions briefly and set at Park position. Check the fluid level and add enough fluid to raise the level to between the marks on the dipstick. Do not overfill the transmission.

The procedure for a partial drain and refill of the transmission fluid is as follows:

1. Raise the car on a hoist or jack stands.
2. Place a drain pan under the transmission pan.

NOTE: *On some models of the C4 transmission, the fluid is drained by disconnecting the filler tube from the transmission fluid pan.*

3. Loosen the pan attaching bolts to allow the fluid to drain.

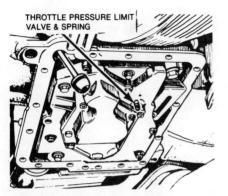

THROTTLE PRESSURE LIMIT VALVE & SPRING

C4 throttle pressure limit valve and spring. They are held in place in the valve body by the filter. The valve is installed with the large end toward the valve body; the spring fits over the valve stem

4. When the fluid has stopped draining to level of the plan flange, remove the pan bolts starting at the rear and along both sides of the pan, allowing the pan to drop and drain gradually.

5. When all the transmission fluid has drained, remove the pan and the fluid filter and clean them.

CAUTION: *When removing the filter on C4 transmissions, be careful not to lose the throttle pressure limit valve and spring when separating the filter from the valve body.*

6. After completing the transmission repairs of adjustments, install the fluid filter screen, a new pan gasket, and the pan on the transmission. Tighten the pan attaching bolts on C4 and C6 transmissions to 12–16 ft lbs. On FMX and CW transmissions, tighten the pan attaching bolts to 10–13 ft lbs.

NOTE: *Be sure to use Type "F" transmission fluid. The use of any other type of fluid such as Type "A" suffix "A," or DEXRON will materially affect the service life of the transmission.*

7. Install three quarts of transmission fluid through the filler tube. If the filler tube was removed to drain the transmission, install the filler tube using a new O-ring.

8. Start and run the engine for a few minutes at low idle speed and then at the fast idle speed (about 1,200 rpm) until the normal operating temperature is reached. Do not race the engine.

9. Move the selector lever through all gear positions and place it at the Park position. Check the fluid level, and add fluid until the level is between the "add" and "full" marks on the dipstick. Do not overfill the transmission.

BAND ADJUSTMENTS

C4 Intermediate Band

1. Clean all the dirt from the adjusting screw and remove and discard the locknut.

2. Install a new locknut on the adjusting screw using a torque wrench, tighten the adjusting screw to 10 ft lbs.

3. Back off the adjusting screw *exactly* 1¾ *turns.*

4. Hold the adjusting screw steady and tighten the locknut to the proper torque.

TOOL—T59P-77370-B

C6 intermediate band adjustment

TOOL—T59P-77370-B

C4 intermediate band adjustment

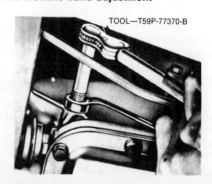

TOOL—T59P-77370-B

C4 low-Reverse band adjustment

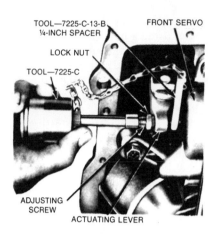

FMX front band adjustment

C4 Low-Reverse Band

1. Clean all dirt from around the band adjusting screw, and remove and discard the locknut.

2. Install a new locknut of the adjusting screw. Using a torque wrench, tighten the adjusting screw to 10 ft lbs.

3. Back off the adjusting screw *exactly three full turns*.

4. Hold the adjusting screw steady and tighten the locknut to the proper torque.

C6 Intermediate Band Adjustment

1. Raise the car on a hoist or place it on jack stands.

2. Clean the threads of the intermediate band adjusting screw.

3. Loosen the adjustment screw locknut.

4. Tighten the adjusting screw to 10 ft lbs and back the screw off *exactly 1½ turns*. Tighten the adjusting screw locknut.

FMX, CW Front Band Adjustment

1. Drain the transmission fluid and remove the oil pan, fluid filter screen, and clip.

2. Clean the pan and filter screen and remove the old gasket.

3. Loosen the front servo adjusting screw locknut.

4. Pull back the actuating rod and insert a ¼ in. spacer bar between the adjusting screw and the servo piston stem. Tighten the adjusting screw to 10 in. lbs torque. Remove the spacer bar and tighten the adjusting screw *an additional ¾ turn*. Hold the adjusting screw fast and tighten the locknut securely (20–25 ft lbs).

5. Install the transmission fluid filter screen and clip. Install pan with a new pan gasket.

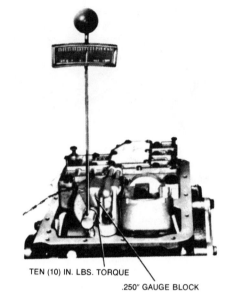

CW front band adjustment

FMX, CW rear band adjustment

6. Refill the transmission to the mark on the dipstick. Start the engine, run for a few minutes, shift the selector lever through all positions, and place it in Park. Recheck the fluid level and add fluid if necessary.

FMX, CW Rear Band Adjustments

On certain cars with a console floor shift, the entire console shift lever and linkage will have to be removed to gain access to the rear band external adjusting screw.

1. Locate the external rear band adjusting screw on the transmission case, clean all dirt from the threads, and coat the threads with light oil.

NOTE: *The adjusting screw is located on the upper right-side of the transmission case. Access is often through a hole in the front floor to the right of center under the carpet.*

2. Loosen the locknut on the rear band external adjusting screw.

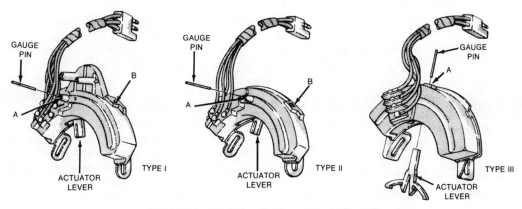

Neutral start switch adjustment—column shift

3. Using a torque wrench tighten the adjusting screw to 10 ft lbs torque. If the adjusting screw is tighter than 10 ft lbs torque, loosen the adjusting screw and retighten to the proper torque.

4. Back off the adjusting screw *exactly 1½ turns*. Hold the adjusting screw steady while tightening the locknut to the proper torque (35–40 ft lbs).

NEUTRAL START SWITCH ADJUSTMENT

1968–71 Column Shift

1. With manual linkage properly adjusted, try to engage starter in each position on quadrant. Starter should engage only in Neutral or Park position.

2. Place shift lever in Neutral detent.

3. Disconnect start switch wires at plug connector. Disconnect vacuum hoses, if any. Remove screws securing neutral start switch to steering column and remove switch. Remove actuator lever along with Type III switches.

4. With switch wires facing up, move actuator lever fully to the left and insert gauge pin (No. 43 drill) into gauge pin hole at point A. See accompanying figure. On Type III switch, be sure gauge pin is inserted a full ½ in.

5. With pin in place, move actuator lever to right until positive stop is engaged.

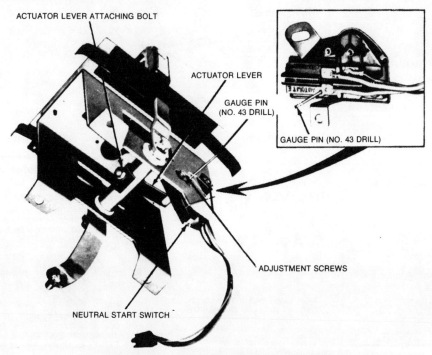

Neutral start switch adjustment—console shift

6. On Type I and Type II switches, remove gauge pin and insert it at point B. On Type III switches, remove gauge pin, align two holes in switch at point A and reinstall gauge pin.

7. Reinstall switch on steering column. Be sure shift lever is engaged in Neutral detent.

8. Connect switch wires and vacuum hoses and remove gauge pin.

9. Check starter engagement as in Step 1.

1972 and Later Column Shift.

1972 and later models which are equipped with a column-mounted shift lever are not equipped with neutral start switch. Instead, an ignition lock cylinder-to-shift lever interlock prevents these models from being started in any gear other than Park or Neutral.

1968–71 Console Shift

1. With manual linkage properly adjusted, try to engage starter at each position on quadrant. Starter should engage only in Neutral and Park positions.

2. Remove shift handle from shift lever, and console from vehicle.

3. Loosen switch attaching screws, and move shift lever back and forward until gauge pin (No. 43 drill) can be inserted fully.

4. Place shift lever firmly against Neutral detent stop and slide switch back and forward until switch lever contacts shift lever.

5. Tighten switch attaching screws, and check starter engagement as in Step 1.

6. Reinstall console and shift linkage.

AUTOMATIC TRANSMISSION LINKAGE ADJUSTMENT

All Column and Console Shift

1. With engine off, loosen clamp at shift lever so shift rod is free to slide.

2. Position selector lever in D1 position (large green dot) on dual range transmissions. On select shift transmission (P R N D 2 1)

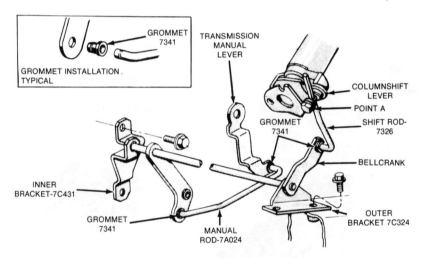

Manual linkage—1968 C6 column shift

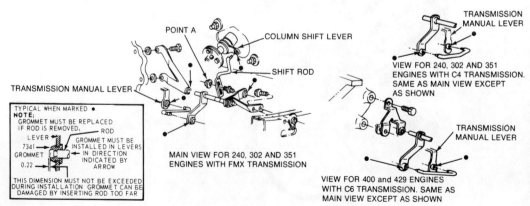

Manual linkage—1969–76 column shift

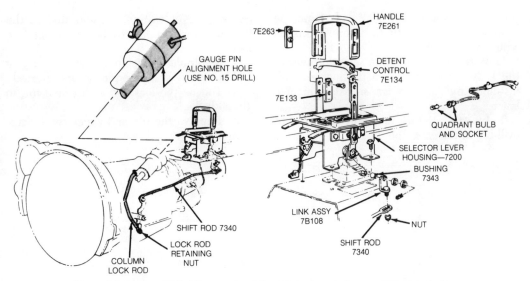

Manual linkage—1970–71 console shift with lock rod shown, 1968–69 similar

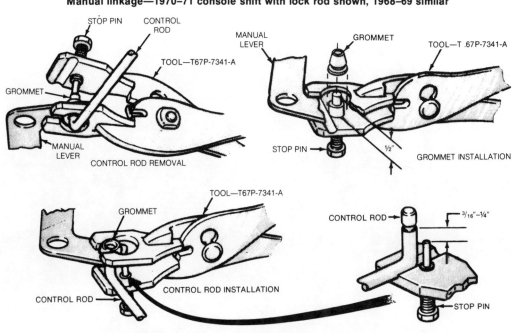

Removing or installing shift linkage grommets

position lever in D position tightly against the D stop.

3. Shift lever at transmission into D1 detent position on dual range transmissions or into D position on select shift transmissions.

NOTE: *D1 position is second from rear on all dual-range transmissions. D position is third from rear on all column shift select shift transmissions and 1968 console shift select shift transmissions. D position is fourth from rear on 1969–72 console shift select shift transmissions.*

4. Tighten clamp and torque nut to 8–13 ft lbs on 1968 column shifts and 10–20 ft lbs on 1969–77 column shifts. Torque 1968 console shift nuts to 20–25 ft lbs and 1969–72 console shift nuts to 10–20 ft lbs.

LOCK ROD ADJUSTMENT

All 1970–71 models equipped with a floor or console-mounted selector lever incorporate a transmission lock rod to prevent the transmission selector from being moved out of the Park position when the ignition lock is in the Off position. The lock rod connects the shift tube in the steering column to the transmission manual lever. The lock rod cannot be properly adjusted until the manual linkage adjustment is correct.

1. With the transmission selector lever in the Drive position, loosen the lock rod adjustment nut on the transmission manual lever.

2. Insert a .180 in. diameter rod (No. 15 drill bit) in the gauge pin hole in the steering column socket casting, it is located at the 6 o'clock position directly below the ignition lock.

3. Manipulate the pin so that the casting will not move when the pin is fully inserted.

4. Torque the lock rod adjustment nut to 10–20 ft lbs.

5. Remove the pin and check the linkage operation.

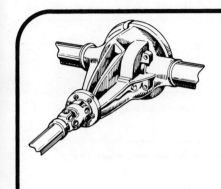

7

Drive Train

DRIVELINE

The driveshaft is the means by which the power from the engine and transmission (in the front of the car) is transferred to the differential and rear axles, and finally to the rear wheels.

The driveshaft assembly incorporates two universal joints—one at each end—and a slip yoke at the front end of the assembly, which fits into the back of the transmission.

All driveshafts are balanced when installed in a car. It is therefore imperative that before applying undercoating to the chassis, the driveshaft and universal joint assembly be completely covered to prevent the accidental application of undercoating to their surfaces, and the subsequent loss of balance.

Driveshaft and U-Joints

DRIVESHAFT REMOVAL

The procedure for removing the driveshaft assembly—complete with universal joint and slip yoke—is as follows:

1. Mark the relationship of the rear drive-

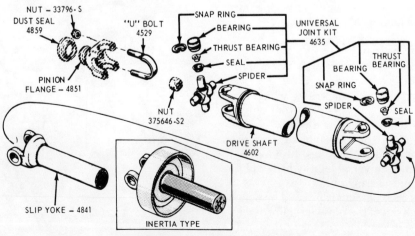

Driveshaft and U-joints disassembled

Troubleshooting the Driveline

The Problem	Is Caused By	What to Do
Shudder as car accelerates from stop or low speed	• Loose U-joint • Defective center bearing	• Tighten U-joint or have it replaced • Have center bearing replaced
Loud clunk in driveshaft when shifting gears	• Worn U-joints	• Have U-joints replaced
Roughness or vibration at any speed	• Out-of-balance, bent or dented driveshaft • Worn U-joints • U-joint clamp bolts loose	• Have driveshaft serviced • Have U-joints serviced • Tighten U-joint clamp bolts
Squeaking noise at low speeds	• Lack of U-joint lubrication	• Lubricate U-joint; if problem persists, have U-joint serviced
Knock or clicking noise	• U-joint or driveshaft hitting frame tunnel	• Correct overloaded condition

shaft yoke and the drive pinion flange of the axle. If the original yellow alignment marks are visible, there is no need for new marks. The purpose of this marking is to facilitate installation of the assembly in its exact original position, thereby maintaining proper balance.

2. Remove the four bolts which hold the rear universal joint or the circular coupling flange on 1979 models to the pinion flange. Wrap tape around the loose bearing caps in order to prevent them from falling off the spider.

3. Pull the driveshaft toward the rear of the vehicle until the slip yoke clears the transmission housing and the seal. Plug the hole at the rear of the transmission housing or place a container under the opening to catch any fluid which might leak.

UNIVERSAL JOINT OVERHAUL

1. Position the driveshaft assembly in a sturdy vise.

2. Remove the snap-rings which retain the bearings in the slip yoke (front only) and in the driveshaft (front and rear).

3. Using a large punch or an arbor press, drive one of the bearings in toward the center of the universal joint, which will force the opposite bearing out.

4. As each bearing is pressed or punched far enough out of the universal joint assembly that it is accessible, grip it with a pair of pliers, and pull it from the driveshaft yoke.

Drive or press the spider in the opposite direction in order to make the opposite bearing accessible, and pull it free with a pair of pliers. Use this procedure to remove all bearings from both universal joints.

5. After removing the bearings, lift the spider from the yoke.

6. Thoroughly clean all dirt and foreign matter from the yokes on both ends of the driveshaft.

NOTE: *When installing new bearings in the yokes, it is advisable to use an arbor press. However, if this tool is not available, the bearings should be driven into position with extreme care, as a heavy jolt on the*

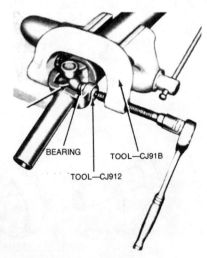

BEARING   TOOL—CJ91B

TOOL—CJ912

Removing universal joint bearing

needle bearings can easily damage or mis-align them, greatly shortening their life and hampering their efficiency.

7. Start a new bearing into the yoke at the rear of the driveshaft.

8. Position a new spider in the rear yoke and press (or drive) the new bearing ¼ in. below the outer surface of the yoke.

9. With the bearing in position, install a new snap-ring.

10. Start a new bearing into the opposite side of the yoke.

11. Press (or drive) the bearing until the opposite bearing—which you have just installed—contacts the inner surface of the snap-ring.

12. Install a new snap-ring on the second bearing. It may be necessary to grind the surface of this second snap-ring.

13. Reposition the driveshaft in the vise, so that the front universal joint is accessible.

14. Install the new bearings, new spider, and new snap-rings in the same manner as you did for the rear universal joint.

15. Position the slip yoke on the spider. Install new bearings, nylon thrust bearings, and snap-rings.

16. Check both reassembled joints for freedom of movement. If misalignment of any part is causing a bind, a sharp rap on the side of the yoke with a brass hammer should seat the bearing needles and provide the desired freedom of movement. Care should be exercised to firmly support the shaft end during this operation, as well as to prevent blows to the bearings themselves. Under no circumstances should a driveshaft be installed in a car if there is any binding in the universal joints.

DRIVESHAFT INSTALLATION

1. Carefully inspect the rubber seal on the output shaft and the seal in end of the transmission extension housing. Replace them if they are damaged.

2. Examine the lugs on the axle pinion flange and replace the flange if the lugs are shaved or distorted.

3. Coat the yoke spline with chassis lube.

4. Remove the plug from the rear of the transmission housing.

5. Insert the yoke into the transmission housing and onto the transmission output shaft. Make sure that the yoke assembly does not bottom on the output shaft with excessive force.

6. Locate the marks which you made on the rear driveshaft yoke and the pinion flange prior to removal of the driveshaft assembly. Install the driveshaft assembly with the marks properly aligned.

7. Install the U-bolts and nuts which attach the universal joint to the pinion flange. Torque the U-bolt nuts to 8–15 ft lbs on models through 1978. 1979 models are attached to the rear differential flange with a circular coupling. New bolts must be used whenever the driveshaft is removed. Torque the bolts to 70–90 ft lbs.

REAR AXLE

Two basic types of rear axles are used; a removable differential carrier type and an integral carrier type which occurs in three variations; a standard type, a light duty (WER) version, and a WGY version used on all 1979 models. All WER and WGY types use C-locks on the inside end of the axle shaft to retain it, while removable carrier axles have no C-locks. To properly identify a C-lock axle, drain the lubricant, remove the rear cover and look for the C-lock on the end of the axle shaft in the differential side gear bore. All Traction-Lok (limited slip) axles are of the removable carrier type. The axle type and ratio are stamped on a plate attached to a rear housing cover bolt. If the second letter of the axle model code is F, it is a Traction-Lok axle. Always refer to the axle tag code and ratio when ordering parts.

AXLE SHAFT REMOVAL AND INSTALLATION AND/OR BEARING REPLACEMENT

Removable Carrier Axle

NOTE: *Bearings must be pressed on and off the shaft with an arbor press. Unless you have access to one, it is inadvisable to attempt any repair work on the axle shaft and bearing assemblies.*

1. Remove the wheel, tire, and brake drum. On cars equipped with rear disc brakes, remove the caliper and disc as outlined in Chapter 9.

2. Remove the nuts holding the retainer plate to the backing plate. Disconnect the brake line.

3. Remove the retainer and install nuts, finger-tight, to prevent the brake backing plate from being dislodged.

4. Pull out the axle shaft and bearing assembly, using a slide hammer.

NOTE: *If end-play is found to be excessive, the bearing should be replaced. Shimming the bearing is not recommended as this ignores end-play of the bearing itself and could result in improper seating of the bearing.*

5. Using a chisel, nick the bearing retainer in 3 or 4 places. The retainer does not have to be cut, but merely collapsed sufficiently to allow the bearing retainer to be slid from the shaft.

6. Press off the bearing and install the new one by pressing it into position.

7. Press on the new retainer.

NOTE: *Do not attempt to press the bearing and the retainer on at the same time.*

8. Assemble the shaft and bearing in the housing, being sure that the bearing is seated properly in the housing.

9. Install the retainer, drum, wheel, and tire. Bleed the brakes. On cars equipped with rear disc brakes, install the disc and caliper as outlined in Chapter 9.

AXLE SHAFT SEAL REPLACEMENT

Removable Carrier Axle

1. Remove the axle shaft from the rear axle assembly, following the procedures previously discussed.

2. Using a two-fingered seal puller (slide hammer), remove the seal from the axle housing.

3. Thoroughly clean the recess in the rear axle housing from which the seal was removed.

4. Position a new seal on the housing and drive it into place with a seal installation tool. If this tool is not available, a wood block may be substituted.

NOTE: *Although the right and left-hand seals are identical, there are many different types of seals which have been used on Ford rear axle assemblies. It is advisable to have one of the old seals with you when you are purchasing new ones.*

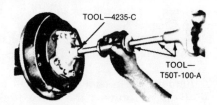

TOOL—4235-C

TOOL—
T50T-100-A

Removing axle shaft

Removing rear wheel bearing retaining ring

5. When the seal is properly installed, install the axle shaft.

AXLE SHAFT, BEARING, AND SEAL REMOVAL AND INSTALLATION

Integral Carrier Type WER and WGY Axle

1. Jack up and support the rear of the car.

2. Remove the wheels and tires from the brake drums. On cars equipped with rear disc brakes, remove the caliper and disc as outlined in Chapter 9.

3. Place a drain pan under the housing and drain the lubricant by loosening the housing cover.

4. Remove the clips securing the brake drums to the axle shaft lug nut studs and remove the drums.

5. Remove the housing cover and gasket.

6. Position jackstands under the rear frame member and lower the axle housing. This is done to give easy access to the inside of the differential.

7. Working through the opening in the differential case, remove the side gear pinion shaft lockbolt and the side gear pinion shaft.

8. Push the axle shafts inward and remove the C-locks from the inner end of the axle shafts.

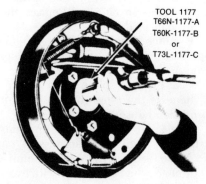

TOOL 1177
T66N-1177-A
T60K-1177-B
or
T73L-1177-C

Installing rear wheel bearing oil seal

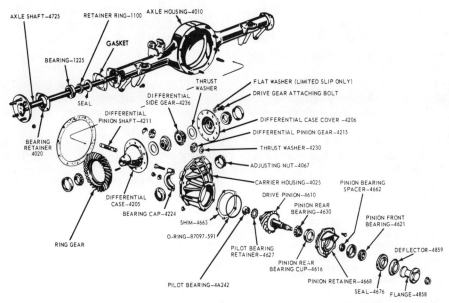

AXLE SHAFT–4725   RETAINER RING–1100   AXLE HOUSING–4010

GASKET

BEARING–1225

THRUST WASHER

DIFFERENTIAL SIDE GEAR–4236

SEAL

DIFFERENTIAL PINION SHAFT–4211

BEARING RETAINER 4020

DIFFERENTIAL CASE–4205

BEARING CAP–4224

RING GEAR

O-RING–87097-591

PILOT BEARING–4A242

FLAT WASHER (LIMITED SLIP ONLY)

DRIVE GEAR ATTACHING BOLT

DIFFERENTIAL CASE COVER –4206

DIFFERENTIAL PINION GEAR–4215

THRUST WASHER–4230

ADJUSTING NUT–4067

CARRIER HOUSING–4025

DRIVE PINION–4610

PINION REAR BEARING–4630

PINION BEARING SPACER–4662

PINION FRONT BEARING–4621

DEFLECTOR–4859

SHIM–4663

PILOT BEARING RETAINER–4627

PINION REAR BEARING CUP–4616

PINION RETAINER–4668

SEAL–4676   FLANGE–4858

Rear axle disassembled—typical removable carrier with conventional differential

9. Remove the axle shafts with a slide hammer. Be sure the seal is not damaged by the splines on the axle shaft.

10. Remove the bearing and oil seal from the housing. Two types of bearings are used on some axles, one requiring a press fit and the other a loose fit. A loose fitting bearing does not necessarily indicate excessive wear.

11. Inspect the axle shaft housing and axle shafts for burrs or other irregularities. Replace any worn or damaged parts. A light yellow color on the bearing journal of the axle shaft is normal, and does not require replacement of the axle shaft. Slight pitting and wear is also normal.

12. Lightly coat the wheel bearing rollers with axle lubricant. Install the bearings in the axle housing until the bearing seats firmly against the shoulder.

13. Wipe all lubricant from the oil seal bore, before installing the seal.

14. Inspect the original seals for wear. If necessary, these may be replaced with new seals, which are prepacked with lubricant and do not require soaking.

15. Install the oil seal.

CAUTION: *Installation of the seal without the proper tool can cause distortion and seal leakage. Oil seals for the right-side are marked with green stripes and the word RIGHT. Seals for the left-side are marked yellow with the word LEFT. Do not interchange seals from side to side.*

LOCK BOLT

DIFFERENTIAL PINION SHAFT

Differential shaft and lockbolt—Integral type axle

AXLE SHAFT

C-LOCK

Removing C-locks—Integral type axle

16. Carefully slide the axle shafts into place. Be careful that you do not damage the seal with the splined end of the axle shaft. Engage the splined end of the shaft with the differential side gears.

17. Install the axle shaft C-locks on the inner end of the axle shafts and seat the C-locks in the counterbore of the differential side gears.

18. Rotate the differential pinion gears until the differential pinion shaft can be installed. Install the differential pinion shaft lockbolt.

19. Install the brake drum on the axle shaft flange. On cars, equipped with rear disc brakes, install the disc and caliper as outlined in Chapter 9.

20. Install the wheel and tire on the brake drum or disc and tighten the attaching nuts.

21. Clean the gasket surface of the rear housing and install a new cover gasket and the housing cover.

22. Raise the rear axle so that it is in the running position. Add the amount of specified lubricant to bring the lubricant level to the bottom of the filler plug hole.

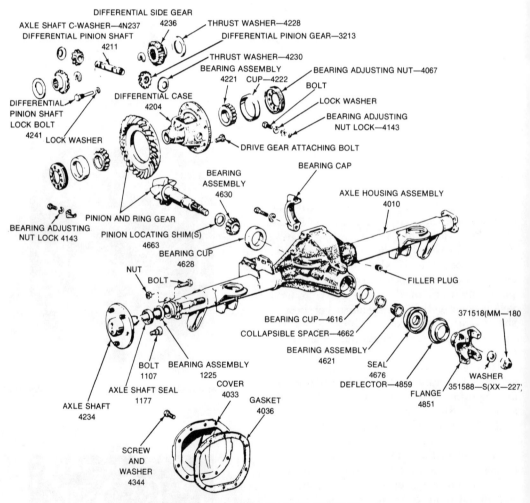

Integral carrier type rear axle assembly

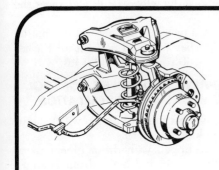

8

Suspension and Steering

FRONT SUSPENSION

Each front wheel rotates on a spindle. The spindle's upper and lower ends attach to the upper and lower ball joints which mount to an upper and lower arm respectively. Through 1978 the upper arm pivots on a bushing and shaft assembly bolted to the frame. The lower arm pivots on the No. 2 cross-member bolt. The coil spring is seated between the lower arm and the top of the spring housing on the underside of the upper arm. A shock absorber is bolted to the lower arm at the bottom and the top of the spring housing. For 1979, the front suspension was redesigned. The arm and strut assembly has been replaced by a new lower "A" arm. The upper ball joint incorporates a new low fric-

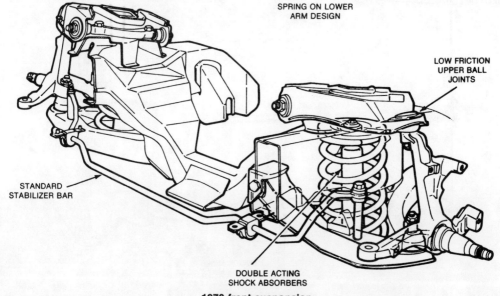

SPRING ON LOWER
ARM DESIGN

LOW FRICTION
UPPER BALL
JOINTS

STANDARD
STABILIZER BAR

DOUBLE ACTING
SHOCK ABSORBERS

1979 front suspension

tion design, and the lower ball joint has a built-in wear indicator. A front stabilizer bar is standard.

Front Shock Absorber Replacement

1. Remove the nut, washer, and bushing from the upper end of the shock absorber.

2. Raise the vehicle on a hoist and install jackstands under the frame rails.

3. Remove the two bolts securing the shock absorber to the lower arm and remove the shock absorber.

4. Inspect the shock absorber for leaks. Extend and compress the unit several times to check the damping action and remove any trapped air. Replace in pairs if necessary.

5. Install a new bushing and washer on the top of the shock absorber and position the unit inside the front spring. Install the two lower attaching bolts and torque them to 8–15 ft lbs.

6. Remove the safety stands and lower the vehicle.

7. Place a new bushing and washer on the shock absorber top stud and install the attaching nut. Torque to 22–30 ft lbs.

COIL SPRING AND LOWER CONTROL ARM REMOVAL AND INSTALLATION

1. Raise car and support with stands placed back of lower arms.

2. If equipped with drum type brakes, remove the wheel and brake drum as an assembly. Remove the brake backing plate attaching bolts and remove the backing plate from the spindle. Wire the assembly back out of the way.

3. If equipped with disc brakes, remove the wheel from the hub. Remove two bolts and washers which hold the caliper and brake hose bracket to the spindle. Remove the cali-

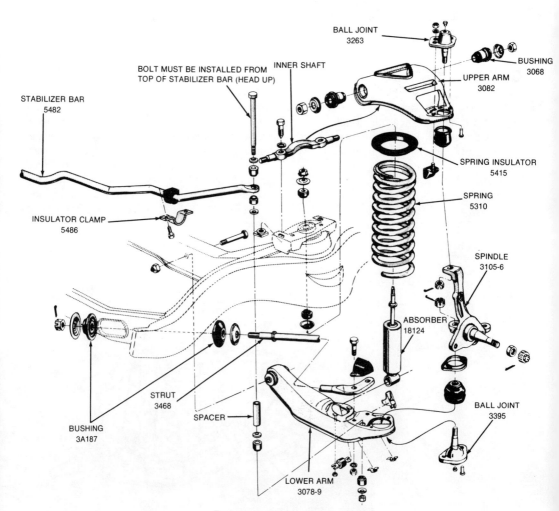

Front suspension disassembled

per from the rotor and wire it back out of the way. Then, remove the hub and rotor from the spindle.

4. Disconnect lower end of the shock absorber and push it up to the retracted position.

5. Disconnect stabilizer bar link from the lower arm.

6. Remove the cotter pins form the upper and lower ball joint stud nuts.

7. Remove two bolts and nuts holding the strut to the lower arm. (through 1978 only)

8. Loosen the lower ball joint stud nut two turns. Do not remove this nut.

9. Install spreader tool between the upper and lower ball joint studs.

10. Expand the tool until the tool exerts considerable pressure on the studs. Tap the spindle near the lower stud with a hammer to loosen the stud in the spindle. Do not loosen the stud with tool pressure only.

11. Position floor jack under the lower arm and remove the lower ball joint stud nut.

12. Lower floor jack and remove the spring and insulator.

13. Remove the A-arm-to-crossmember attaching parts, and remove the arm from the car.

14. Reverse above procedure to install. If lower control arm was replaced because of damage, check front end alignment. Torque lower arm-to-No. 2 crossmember nut to 60–90 ft lbs. Torque the strut-to-lower arm bolts to 80–115 ft lbs. The caliper-to-spindle bolts are torqued to 90–120 ft lbs. Torque the ball joint-to-spindle attaching nut to 60–90 ft lbs.

UPPER CONTROL ARM REMOVAL AND INSTALLATION

1. Perform Steps 1–12 of the previous "Coil Spring and Lower Control Arm Removal and Installation" procedure.

2. Remove the upper arm inner shaft attaching bolts and remove the arm and shaft from the chassis as an assembly.

3. Reverse above procedure to install. Torque the ball joint-to-spindle attaching nut to 60–90 ft lbs.

4. Adjust front end alignment.

LOWER BALL JOINT INSPECTION
Through 1978

1. Raise the vehicle by placing a floor jack under the lower arm or, raise the vehicle on a hoist and place a jackstand under the lower

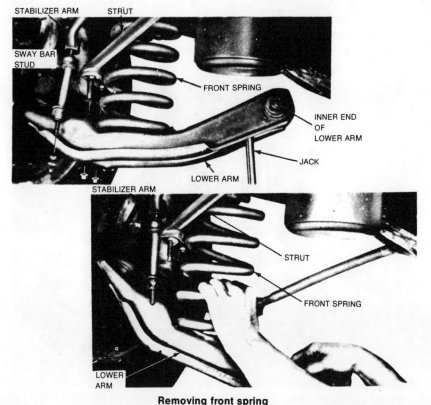

Removing front spring

arm and lower the vehicle onto it to remove the preload from the lower ball joint.

2. Have an assistant grasp the top and bottom of the wheel and apply alternate in and out pressure to the top and bottom of the wheel.

3. Radial play of ¼ in. is acceptable mea-

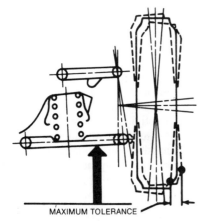

Measuring lower ball joint radial play

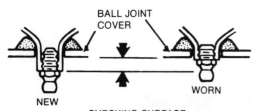

1979 Lower ball joint wear indicator

sured at the inside of the wheel adjacent to the lower arm.

NOTE: *This radial play is multiplied at the outer circumference of the tire and should be measured only at the inside of the wheel.*

1979

1979 lower ball joints have built-in wear indicators. The checking surface is the round boss into which the grease fitting is threaded. If the ball joint is not worn, the checking surface should project outside the cover. If the joint is worn out, the checking surface will be flush with the cover. Do not jack the vehicle up to perform this check.

LOWER BALL JOINT REPLACEMENT

NOTE: *Ford Motor Company recommends replacement of control arm and ball joint as an assembly, rather than replacement of the ball joint only. However, aftermarket replacement parts are available.*

1. Raise the vehicle on a hoist and allow the front wheels to fall to their full down position.

2. Drill a ⅛ in. hole completely through each ball joint attaching rivet.

3. Use a ⅜ in. drill in the pilot hole to drill off the head of the rivet.

4. Drive the rivets from the lower arm.

5. Place a jack under the lower arm and lower the vehicle about 6 in.

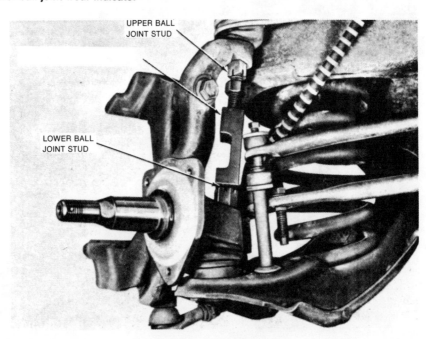

Loosening lower ball joint stud

6. Remove the lower ball joint stud cotter pin and attaching nut.

7. Using a suitable tool, loosen the ball joint from the spindle and remove the ball joint from the lower arm.

8. Clean all metal burrs from the lower arm and install the new ball joint, using the service part nuts and bolts to attach the ball joint to the lower arm. Do not attempt to rivet the ball joint again once it has been removed.

9. Check front end alignment.

UPPER BALL JOINT INSPECTION

1. Raise the vehicle by placing a floor jack under the lower arm. Do not allow the lower arm to hang freely with the vehicle on a hoist or bumper jack.

2. Have an assistant grasp the top and bottom of the tire and move the wheel in and out.

3. As the wheel is being moved, observe the upper control arm where the spindle attaches to it. Any movement between the upper part of the spindle and the upper ball joint indicates a bad ball joint which must be replaced.

NOTE: *During this check, the lower ball joint will be unloaded and may move; this is normal and not an indication of a bad ball joint. Also, do not mistake a loose wheel bearing for a defective ball joint.*

UPPER BALL JOINT REPLACEMENT

NOTE: *Ford Motor Company recommends replacement of control arm and ball joint as an assembly, rather than replacement of the ball joint only. However, aftermarket replacement parts are available.*

1. Raise the vehicle on a hoist and allow the front wheels to fall to their full down position.

2. Drill a ⅛ in. hole completely through each ball joint attaching rivet.

3. Using a large chisel, cut off the head of each rivet and drive them from the upper arm.

4. Place a jack under the lower arm and lower the vehicle about 6 in.

5. Remove the cotter pin and attaching nut from the ball joint stud.

6. Using a suitable tool, loosen the ball joint stud from the spindle and remove the ball joint from the upper arm.

7. Clean all metal burrs from the upper arm and install the new ball joint, using the service part nuts and bolts to attach the ball

joint to the upper arm. Do not attempt to rivet the ball joint again once it has been removed.

8. Check front end alignment.

Wheel Alignment

NOTE: *The procedure for checking and adjusting front wheel alignment requires specialized equipment and professional skills. The following descriptions and adjustment procedures are for general reference only.*

Front wheel alignment is the position of the front wheels relative to each other and to the vehicle. It is determined, and must be maintained to provide safe, accurate steering with minimum tire wear. Many factors are involved in wheel alignment and adjustments are provided to return those that might change due to normal wear to their original value. The factors which determine wheel alignment are dependent on one another; therefore, when one of the factors is adjusted the others must be adjusted to compensate.

Descriptions of these factors and their affects on the car are provided below.

NOTE: *Do not attempt to check and adjust the front wheel alignment without first making a thorough inspection of the front suspension components.*

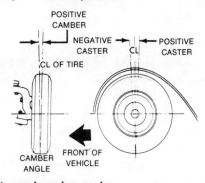

Caster and camber angles

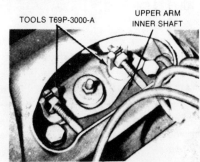

Caster and Camber adjusting tool installed

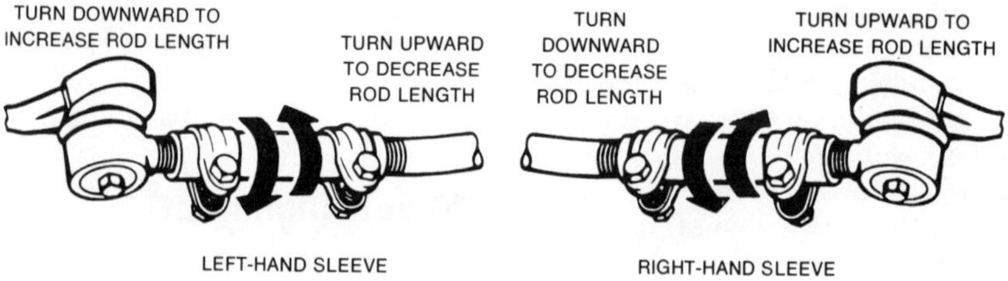
TURN DOWNWARD TO
INCREASE ROD LENGTH
TURN UPWARD
TO DECREASE
ROD LENGTH
TURN
DOWNWARD
TO DECREASE
ROD LENGTH
TURN UPWARD TO
INCREASE ROD LENGTH
LEFT-HAND SLEEVE
RIGHT-HAND SLEEVE

Tie-rod (toe-in) adjustments

CAMBER

Camber angle is the number of degrees that the centerline of the wheel is inclined from the vertical. Camber reduces loading of the outer wheel bearing and improves the tire contact patch while cornering.

CASTER

Caster angle is the number of degrees that a line drawn through the steering knuckle pivots is inclined from the vertical, toward the front or rear of the car. Caster improves directional stability and decreases susceptibility to crosswinds or road surface deviations.

TOE-IN

Toe-in is the difference of the distance between the centers of the front and rear of the front wheels. It is most commonly measured

Wheel Alignment Specifications

		CASTER		CAMBER				WHEEL PIVOT RATIO (deg)	
Year	*Model*	*Range (deg)*	*Pref Setting (deg)*	*Range (deg)*	*Pref Setting (deg)*	*Toe-in (in.)*	*Steering Axis Inclin (deg)*	*Inner Wheel*	*Outer Wheel*
'68–'69	All	0 to 2P	1P	1/4N to 1 1/4P	3/4P	1/8 to 1/4	7 3/4	20	18 1/8
'70–'71	All	0 to 2P	1P	1/4N to 1 1/4P	1/2P	1/16 to 5/16	7 3/4	20	19 4/25
'72	All	1N to 3P	1P	1/2N to 1 1/2P	1/2P	1/16 to 7/16	7 3/4	20	19 4/25
'73	All	0 to 4P	2P	1N to 1P	0	1/16 to 7/16	7 3/4	20	18 3/4
'74	All	0 to 4P	2P	①	②	3/16	9 1/2	20	18 3/4
'75	All	0 to 4P	2P	③	②	3/16	9 1/2	20	18 3/4
'76–'77	All	1 1/4P to 2 3/4P	2P	④	②	3/16	9 1/2	20	18 3/4
'78	All	1 1/4P to 2 3/4P	2P	④	②	1/16 to 5/16	9.44	20	18.69
'79	All	2 1/4P to 3 3/4P	3P	1/4N to 1 1/4P	1/2P	1/16 to 5/16	11.20	20	18

① Left wheel—0 to 1P
Right wheel—1/4N to 3/4P
② Left wheel—1/2P
Right wheel—1/4P
③ Left wheel—1/2N to 1 1/2P
Right wheel—3/4N to 1 1/4P
N Negative P Positive
④ Left wheel—1/4N to 1 1/4P
Right wheel—1/2N to 1P

in inches, but is occasionally referred to as an angle between the wheels. Toe-in is necessary to compensate for the tendency of the wheels to deflect rearward while in motion. Due to this tendency, the wheels of a vehicle, with properly adjusted toe-in, are traveling straight forward when the vehicle itself is traveling straight forward, resulting in directional stability and minimum tire wear.

Steering wheel spoke misalignment is often an indication of incorrect front end alignment. Care should be exercised when aligning the front end to maintain steering wheel spoke position. When adjusting the tie-rod ends, adjust each an equal amount (in the opposite direction) to increase or decrease toe-in. If, following toe-in adjustment, further adjustments are necessary to center the steering wheel spokes, adjust the tie-rod ends an equal amount in the same direction.

ADJUSTMENT PROCEDURES

Install Ford tool T65P-3000D, or its equivalent, on the frame rail, position the hooks around the upper control arm pivot shaft, and tighten the adjusting nuts slightly. Loosen the pivot shaft retaining bolts to permit adjustment.

To adjust caster, loosen or tighten either the front or rear adjusting nut. After adjusting caster, adjust the camber by loosening or tightening both nuts an equal amount. Tighten the shaft retaining bolts to specifications, remove the tool, and recheck the adjustments.

Adjust toe-in by loosening the clamp bolts, and turning the adjuster sleeves at the outer ends of the tie-rod. Turn the sleeves an equal amount in the opposite direction, to maintain steering wheel spoke alignment.

REAR SUSPENSION

The rear suspension through 1978 is a coil-link design. Large, low-rate coil springs are mounted between rear axle pads and frame supports. Parallel lower arms extend forward of the spring seats to rubber frame anchor to accommodate driving and braking forces. A third link is mounted between the axle and the frame to control torque reaction forces from the rear wheels.

Lateral (side sway) motion of the rear axle is controlled by a rubber bushed rear track bar, linked laterally between the axle and frame.

The 1979 rear suspension is a four-link coil spring design. The coil springs are mounted between the top of the axle and the frame pads, providing room for vertical placement of the shock absorbers in front of the axle. Two lower arms mount to the axle forward of the outer ends, while the two shorter upper arms mount near the top center of the axle, with an included angle of 90°.

COIL SPRINGS REMOVAL AND INSTALLATION

1. Place car on hoist and lift under rear axle housing. Place jack stands under frame side rails.

2. Disconnect track bar at the rear axle housing bracket. (through 1978).

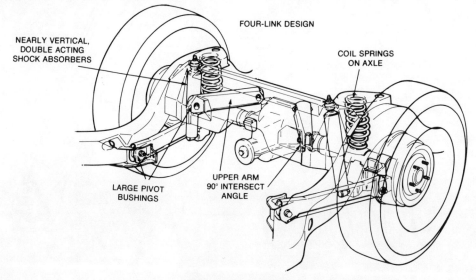

FOUR-LINK DESIGN

NEARLY VERTICAL, DOUBLE ACTING SHOCK ABSORBERS

COIL SPRINGS ON AXLE

LARGE PIVOT BUSHINGS

UPPER ARM 90° INTERSECT ANGLE

1979 rear suspension

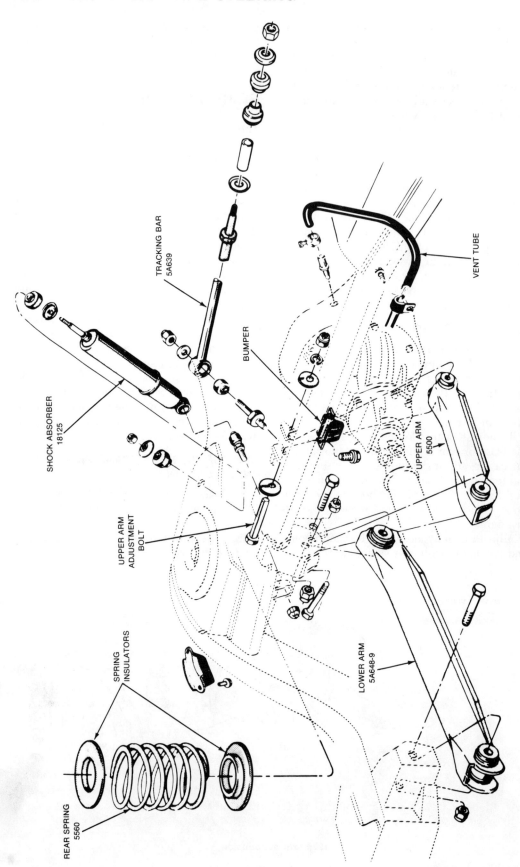

TRACKING BAR
5A639

VENT TUBE

SHOCK ABSORBER
18125

BUMPER

UPPER ARM
5500

UPPER ARM
ADJUSTMENT
BOLT

LOWER ARM
5A648-9

SPRING
INSULATORS

REAR SPRING
5560

Rear suspension disassembled (through 1978)

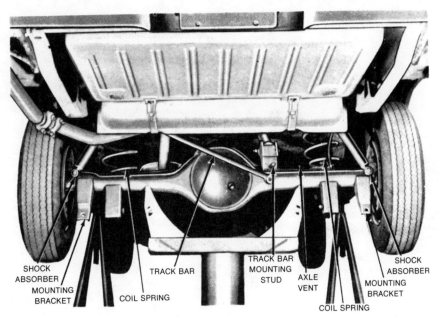

SHOCK
ABSORBER
MOUNTING
BRACKET

TRACK BAR

COIL SPRING

TRACK BAR
MOUNTING
STUD   AXLE
VENT

COIL SPRING

SHOCK
ABSORBER
MOUNTING
BRACKET

Removing rear springs

3. Disconnect rear shock absorbers from the rear axle housing brackets.

4. Disconnect hose from axle housing vent. Disconnect the rear of the front-to-rear brake tube from the rear brake hose at the No. 4 crossmember bracket. Remove the brake hose-to-bracket clip.

5. Lower hoist with axle housing until coil springs are released.

6. Remove spring lower retainer with bolt, nut, washer and insulator.

7. Remove spring with large rubber insulator pads from car.

8. Install in reverse of above. Bleed the brakes as outlined in Chapter 9.

REAR SHOCK ABSORBER REPLACEMENT

1. Raise the rear of the vehicle. Install jack stands beneath the frame.

2. Remove the shock absorber attaching nut, washer, and insulator from the stud at the top side of the spring upper seat. Compress the shock absorber sufficiently to clear the spring seat hole and remove the inner insulator and washer from the upper attaching stud.

3. Remove the locknut and disconnect the shock absorber lower stud at the mounting bracket on the axle housing.

4. Remove the shock absorber from the vehicle and check for leakage. If the shock absorber is in good condition, compress and expand the unit several times to expel any trapped air prior to reinstallation.

5. Position the inner washer and insulator on the upper attaching stud. Place the shock absorber in such a position that the upper attaching stud enters the hole in the spring upper seat. While maintaining the shock absorber in this position, install the outer insulator, washer, and new nut on the stud from the top side of the spring upper seat. Torque the attaching nut to 14–26 ft lbs.

6. Extend the shock absorber. Locate the lower stud in the mounting bracket hole on the axle housing. Install and torque the locknut to 50–85 ft lbs.

7. Remove the jack stands and lower the car. Road-test the car.

STEERING

The steering gear on all models with manual steering is the worm and recirculating ball type. The sector shaft is straddle-mounted in the cover above the gear and a housing mounted roller bearing below the gear.

All full size Fords with power steering use the integral type power steering gear. On this type of steering, hydraulic assist is provided directly to the steering gear, eliminating all hoses and hardware which was previously mounted under the chassis. The most common type of steering gear used with integral power steering is the Ford torsion bar model. The torsion bar type power steering unit includes a worm and one-piece rack

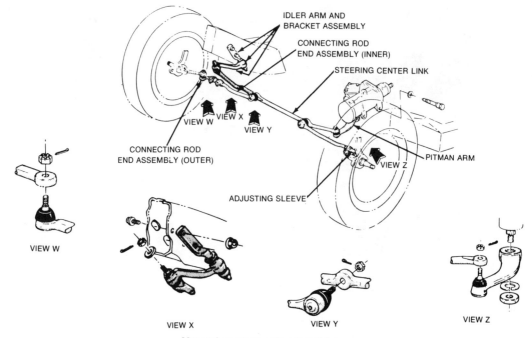

IDLER ARM AND
BRACKET ASSEMBLY

CONNECTING ROD
END ASSEMBLY (INNER)

STEERING CENTER LINK

VIEW W   VIEW X
VIEW Y

CONNECTING ROD
END ASSEMBLY (OUTER)

VIEW Z

PITMAN ARM

ADJUSTING SLEEVE

VIEW W

VIEW X

VIEW Y

VIEW Z

Manual or power steering linkage

TOOL T67L-3000-A

Steering wheel removal

piston, which is meshed with the gear teeth on the steering sector shaft.

The steering linkage consists of a steering (pitman) arm, a pitman arm-to-idler arm rod, and idler arm, and tie-rods.

Steering Wheel Removal and Installation

1. Disconnect the negative battery cable.
2. Remove the horn ring or hub cap by pushing it down and rotating it counterclockwise. Remove the retaining screws (from underside of steering wheel) and the crash pad. On 1969–70 Fords with speed control, the switch bezels must be pried up with a thin knife blade and the center trim plate removed to gain access to the crash pad retaining screws. On later models with speed control, the switches simply snap into plastic retainers inside the crash pad. Disconnect the horn and speed control wires.

3. Remove the steering wheel nut. Install a steering wheel puller on the end of the shaft and remove the wheel.

CAUTION: *The use of a knock-off type steering wheel puller or the use of a hammer on the steering shaft will damage the column bearing and, on collapsible columns, the column itself may be damaged.*

4. Lubricate the steering shaft bushing with white grease. Transfer all serviceable parts to the new steering wheel.

5. With the front wheels pointing in a straight-ahead direction, and with the alignment marks on steering wheel and the steering shaft lined up, install the steering wheel and locknut.

6. Connect the horn and speed control wires and install the horn ring or hub cap. Install the crash pad and retaining screws.

7. Connect the negative battery cable.

Turn Signal Switch Replacement

1. Disconnect the negative battery cable.
2. Remove the steering wheel as pre-

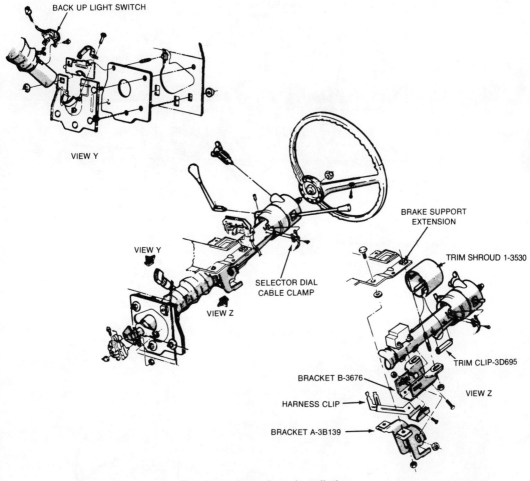

BACK UP LIGHT SWITCH

VIEW Y

VIEW Y

VIEW Z

SELECTOR DIAL
CABLE CLAMP

VIEW Z

BRAKE SUPPORT
EXTENSION

TRIM SHROUD 1-3530

TRIM CLIP-3D695

BRACKET B-3676

HARNESS CLIP

BRACKET A-3B139

Fixed steering column installation

viously outlined in the "Steering Wheel Removal and Installation" section.

3. Unscrew the turn signal lever from the side of the column. Remove the emergency flasher retainer and knob, if so equipped.

4. Locate and remove the finish cover on the steering column and disconnect the wiring connector plugs.

5. On all 1968 models and all models with a tilt steering column it is necessary to separate the wires from the connector plug in order to remove the switch and wires. First note the location and color code of each wire, prior to removal, with the wire terminal removal tool. Remove the plastic cover from the wiring harness. Attach a piece of heavy cord to the switch wires to pull them down through the column during installation.

6. Remove the retaining clips and screws from the turn signal switch and lift the switch

and wire assembly from the top of the column.

7. Tape the ends of the new switch wires together and transfer the pull cord to these wires.

8. Pull the wires down through the column with the cord and attach the new switch to the column hub.

9. If the switch wires were separated from the connector plug, press the wires into their proper location. Connect the wiring connector plugs and install the finish cover on the column.

10. Install the turn signal lever. Install the emergency flasher retainer and knob, if so equipped.

11. Install the steering wheel as outlined in the "Steering Wheel Removal and Installation" section.

12. Connect the negative battery cable

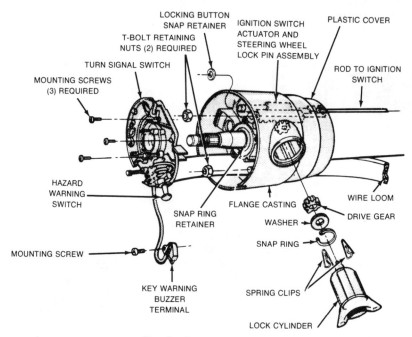

LOCKING BUTTON
SNAP RETAINER

IGNITION SWITCH
ACTUATOR AND
STEERING WHEEL
LOCK PIN ASSEMBLY

PLASTIC COVER

T-BOLT RETAINING
NUTS (2) REQUIRED

TURN SIGNAL SWITCH

ROD TO IGNITION
SWITCH

MOUNTING SCREWS
(3) REQUIRED

HAZARD
WARNING
SWITCH

WIRE LOOM

FLANGE CASTING

DRIVE GEAR

SNAP RING
RETAINER

WASHER

SNAP RING

MOUNTING SCREW

SPRING CLIPS

KEY WARNING
BUZZER
TERMINAL

LOCK CYLINDER

Fixed column components

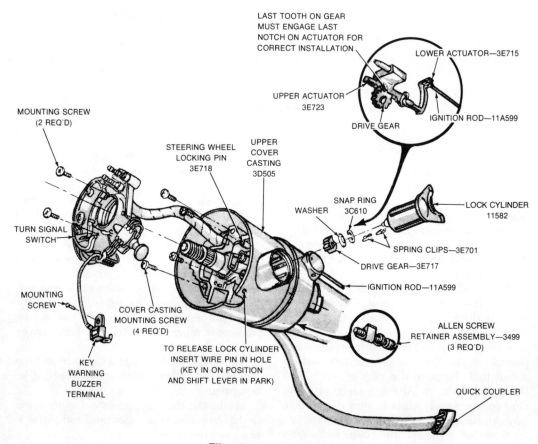

LAST TOOTH ON GEAR
MUST ENGAGE LAST
NOTCH ON ACTUATOR FOR
CORRECT INSTALLATION

LOWER ACTUATOR—3E715

UPPER ACTUATOR
3E723

IGNITION ROD—11A599

DRIVE GEAR

MOUNTING SCREW
(2 REQ'D)

STEERING WHEEL
LOCKING PIN
3E718

UPPER
COVER
CASTING
3D505

SNAP RING
3C610

WASHER

LOCK CYLINDER
11582

TURN SIGNAL
SWITCH

SPRING CLIPS—3E701

DRIVE GEAR—3E717

MOUNTING
SCREW

IGNITION ROD—11A599

COVER CASTING
MOUNTING SCREW
(4 REQ'D)

ALLEN SCREW
RETAINER ASSEMBLY—3499
(3 REQ'D)

KEY
WARNING
BUZZER
TERMINAL

TO RELEASE LOCK CYLINDER
INSERT WIRE PIN IN HOLE
(KEY IN ON POSITION
AND SHIFT LEVER IN PARK)

QUICK COUPLER

Tilt column components

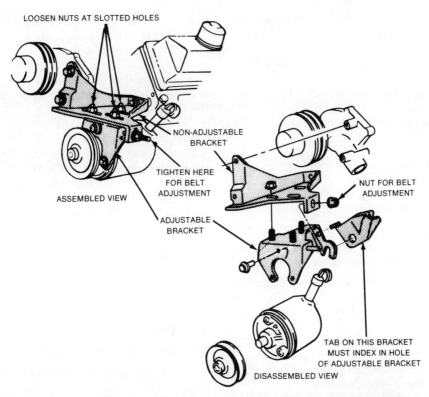

LOOSEN NUTS AT SLOTTED HOLES

NON-ADJUSTABLE
BRACKET

TIGHTEN HERE
FOR BELT
ADJUSTMENT

NUT FOR BELT
ADJUSTMENT

ASSEMBLED VIEW

ADJUSTABLE
BRACKET

TAB ON THIS BRACKET
MUST INDEX IN HOLE
OF ADJUSTABLE BRACKET

DISASSEMBLED VIEW

Power steering pump installation—351W, 351C, 351M, 400, 429, 460 V8 installations

and test the operation of the turn signals, horn, emergency flashers, and speed control, if so equipped.

POWER STEERING PUMP AND REMOVAL AND INSTALLATION

1. Drain the fluid from the pump reservoir by disconnecting the fluid return hose at the pump. Then, disconnect the pressure hose from the pump.

2. Remove the mounting bolts from the front of the pump. On eight cylinder engines, there is a nut on the rear of the pump which must be removed. After removal, move the pump inward to loosen the belt tension and remove the belt from the pulley. Then, remove the pump from the car.

3. To reinstall the pump, position on mounting bracket and loosely install the mounting bolts and nuts. Put the drive belt over the pulley and move the pump outward against the belt until the proper belt tension is obtained. Measure the belt tension with a belt tension gauge for the proper adjustment. Only in cases where a belt tension gauge is not available should the belt deflection method be used. If the belt deflection method is used, be sure to check with a belt

tension gauge as soon as possible, since deflection method is not accurate.

4. Tighten the mounting bolts and nuts.

IGNITION LOCK CYLINDER REPLACEMENT

1968–69

1. Insert key and turn to Acc. position.
2. With stiff wire in hole, depress lock pin and rotate cylinder counterclockwise, then pull out cylinder.

1970 and Later

1. Disconnect the negative battery cable.
2. On cars with a fixed steering column, remove the steering wheel trim pad and the steering wheel. Insert a stiff wire into the hole located in the lock cylinder housing. On cars with a tilt steering wheel, this hole is located on the outside of the steering column near the emergency flasher button and it is not necessary to remove the steering wheel.
3. Place the gearshift lever in Reverse on cars with manual transmission and in Park on cars with automatic transmission, and turn the ignition key to the ON position.
4. Depress wire and remove lock cylinder and wire.

5. Insert new cylinder into housing and turn to the OFF position. This will lock the cylinder into position.

6. Reinstall steering wheel and pad if removed.

7. Connect negative battery cable.

IGNITION SWITCH REPLACEMENT

1968–69

1. Remove cylinder as above.

2. Unscrew the bezel from the ignition switch and remove switch from panel.

3. Remove insulated plug from rear of switch.

4. Install in reverse of above.

1970 and Later

1. Disconnect the negative battery cable.

2. Remove the shrouding from the steering column, and detach and lower the steering column from the brake support bracket.

3. Disconnect the switch wiring at the multiple plug.

4. Remove the two nuts that retain the switch to the steering column.

5. On vehicles with column-mounted gearshift lever, detach the switch plunger from the switch actuator rod and remove the switch. On vehicles with console-mounted gearshift lever, remove the pin connecting the plunger to the actuator and remove the switch.

6. To reinstall the switch, place both the lock mechanism at the top of the column and the switch itself in lock position for correct adjustment. To hold the column in the lock position, place the automatic shift lever in PARK or manual shift lever in Reverse, and turn to LOCK and remove the key. New switches are held in lock by plastic shipping pins. To pin existing switches, pull the switch plunger out as far as it will go and push it back into the first detent. Insert a $3/32$ in. diameter wire in the locking hole in the top of the switch.

7. Connect the switch plunger to the switch actuator rod.

8. Position the switch on the column and install the attaching nuts. Do not tighten them.

9. Move the switch up and down to locate mid-position of rod lash, and then tighten the nuts.

10. Remove the locking pin or wire.

11. Attach the steering column to the brake support bracket and install the shrouding.

Tie-Rod Ends

REMOVAL AND INSTALLATION

1. Firmly apply the parking brake and place blocks behind the rear wheels.

2. Jack up the front of the car and install jackstands beneath the frame members.

3. Remove the cotter pin and castellated nut from the tie-rod end ball joint. Pull the ball joint from the socket in the spindle arm.

4. Loosen the jam nut on the tie-rod. Unscrew the tie-rod end from the tie-rod, taking care to record the number of turns needed to remove the rod end.

5. Reverse the above procedure to install, taking care to turn the tie-rod end the correct amount of turns onto the tie-rod. This is necessary to maintain proper toe-in.

9

Brakes

HYDRAULIC SYSTEM

All post-1966 Fords utilize a dual hydraulic brake circuit in accordance with Federal safety regulations. Each circuit is independent of the other, incorporating a tandem master cylinder, a pressure differential warning valve, and, on disc brake models, a proportioning valve. One circuit services the front brakes (rear of master cylinder) and the other, the rear brakes (front of master cylinder). In case of a leak or other hydraulic failure, ½ braking efficiency will be maintained. A brake system failure will decentralize the pressure differential warning valve, actuating a warning light on the dash. A proportioning valve located between the rear brake system inlet and outlet ports in the pressure differential warning valve serves to regulate the rear brake hydraulic pressure on disc brake models to prevent premature rear wheel lockup during hard braking. On models equipped with disc front/drum rear brakes, a metering valve is used to delay pressure buildup to the front discs upon initial application. The metering valve extends pad life by preventing the front discs from carrying the majority of the braking load at low operating line pressures.

Most full-sized Fords have been equipped with power brakes. On all drum brake equipped cars, as well as those equipped with a disc front/drum rear brake configuration, the power assist has been supplied by a manifold vacuum-operated servo, located between the master cylinder and the firewall. All models equipped with the 4 wheel disc brake system utilize a hydraulically-operated servo, also located between the master cylinder and firewall. This system, known as the hydro-boost system, is connected to the power steering pump via hydraulic hoses, using steering pump fluid pressure to supply and circulate the fluid (type ATF) to the servo.

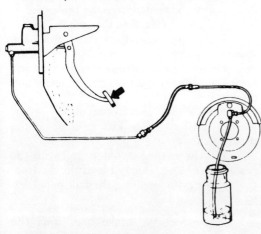

Bleeding brake hydraulic system

The hydro-boost unit contains a spool valve with an open center which controls the strength of pump pressure when braking occurs. A lever assembly controls the valve's position. A boost piston provides the force necessary to operate the conventional master cylinder on the front of the booster.

A reserve of at least two assisted brake applications is supplied by a spring-loaded accumulator, which retains power steering fluid under pressure.

The brakes can be operated without assist, once the reserve is depleted.

Hydraulic System Bleeding

NOTE: *The front and rear hydraulic systems are independent. If it is known that only one system has to be bled. Always bleed the brakes in a sequence that starts with the wheel cylinder farthest from the master cylinder and ends with the wheel cylinder or caliper closest to the master cylinder.*

1. Fill the master cylinder with brake fluid.

2. Install a ⅜ in. box-end wrench to the bleeder screw on the right rear wheel.

3. Push a piece of small-diameter rubber tubing over the bleeder screw until it is flush against the wrench. Submerge the other end of the rubber tubing in a glass jar partially filled with clean brake fluid. Make sure the rubber tube fits on the bleeder screw snugly.

4. Have a friend apply pressure to the brake pedal. Open the bleeder screw and observe the bottle of brake fluid. If bubbles appear in the glass jar, there is air in the system. When your friend has pushed the pedal to the floor, immediately close the bleeder screw before he releases the pedal.

5. Repeat this procedure until no bubbles appear in the jar. Refill the master cylinder.

6. Repeat this procedure on the left rear, right front and left front wheels, in that order. Periodically refill the master cylinder so that it does not run dry.

7. Center the pressure differential warning valve as outlined in the "Pressure Differential Warning Valve" section.

PRESSURE DIFFERENTIAL WARNING VALVE CENTERING

Since the introduction of dual master cylinders to the hydraulic brake system, a pressure differential warning signal has been added. This signal consists of a warning light

on the dashboard activated by a differential pressure switch located below the master cylinder. The signal indicates a hydraulic pressure differential between the front and rear brakes of 80–150 psi, and should warn the driver that a hydraulic failure has occurred.

After repairing and bleeding any part of the hydraulic system the warning light may remain on due to the pressure differential valve remaining in the off-center position. To centralize the valve on 1968–69 models, a pressure difference must be created in the opposite branch of the hydraulic system that was repaired or bled last.

NOTE: *Front wheel balancing of cars equipped with disc brakes may also cause a pressure differential in the front branch of the system.*

To centralize the valve:

1. Turn the ignition to either the ACC or ON position.

2. Check the fluid level in the master cylinder reservoirs. Fill to within ¼ in. of the top if necessary.

3. Depress the brake pedal firmly. The valve will centralize itself causing the brake warning light to go out.

4. Turn the ignition off.

5. Prior to driving the vehicle, check the operation of the brakes and obtain a firm pedal.

MASTER CYLINDER REMOVAL AND INSTALLATION

Non-Power Brakes

1. Working under the dash, disconnect the master cylinder pushrod from the brake pedal. The pushrod cannot be removed from the master cylinder.

2. Disconnect the stoplight switch wires and remove the switch from the brake pedal, using care not to damage the switch.

3. Disconnect the brake lines from the master cylinder.

4. Remove the attaching screws from the firewall and remove the master cylinder from the car.

5. Reinstall in reverse of above order, leaving the brake line fittings loose at the master cylinder.

6. Fill the master cylinder, and with the brake lines loose, slowly bleed the air from the master cylinder using the foot pedal.

Power Brakes

1. Disconnect the brake lines from the master cylinder.

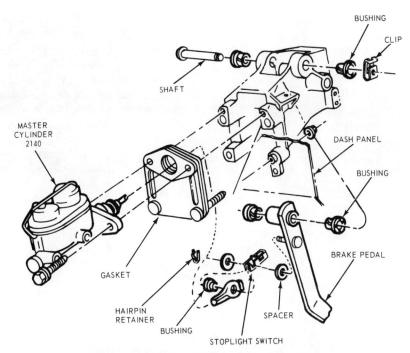

BUSHING

CLIP

SHAFT

MASTER
CYLINDER
2140

DASH PANEL

BUSHING

BRAKE PEDAL

GASKET

HAIRPIN
RETAINER

BUSHING

STOPLIGHT SWITCH

SPACER

Master cylinder installation—non-power brakes

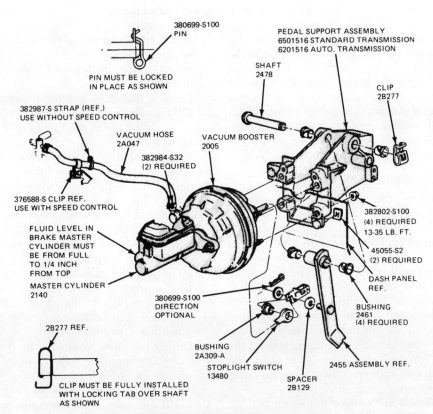

380699-S100
PIN

PEDAL SUPPORT ASSEMBLY
6501516 STANDARD TRANSMISSION
6201516 AUTO. TRANSMISSION

PIN MUST BE LOCKED
IN PLACE AS SHOWN

SHAFT
2478

CLIP
2B277

382987-S STRAP (REF.)
USE WITHOUT SPEED CONTROL

VACUUM HOSE
2A047

VACUUM BOOSTER
2005

382984-S32
(2) REQUIRED

376588-S CLIP REF.
USE WITH SPEED CONTROL

382802-S100
(4) REQUIRED
13-35 LB. FT.

FLUID LEVEL IN
BRAKE MASTER
CYLINDER MUST
BE FROM FULL
TO 1/4 INCH
FROM TOP

45055-S2
(2) REQUIRED

DASH PANEL
REF.

MASTER CYLINDER
2140

380699-S100
DIRECTION
OPTIONAL

BUSHING
2461
(4) REQUIRED

2B277 REF.

BUSHING
2A309-A

STOPLIGHT SWITCH
13480

SPACER
2B129

2455 ASSEMBLY REF.

CLIP MUST BE FULLY INSTALLED
WITH LOCKING TAB OVER SHAFT
AS SHOWN

Master cylinder installation—power brakes

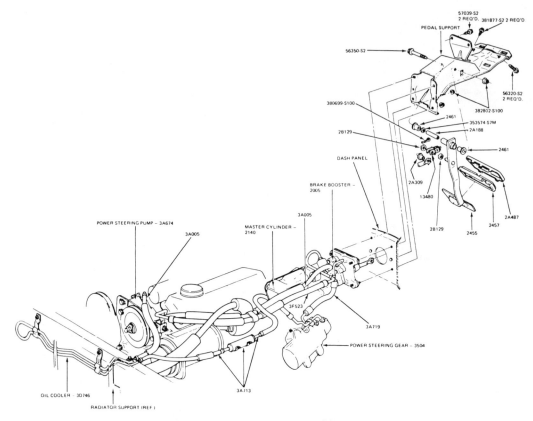

Hydro-Boost assembly and related parts

2. Remove the two nuts and lockwashers which attach the master cylinder to the brake booster.

3. Remove the master cylinder from the booster.

4. Reverse above procedure to reinstall.

5. Fill master cylinder and bleed entire brake system.

6. Refill master cylinder.

MASTER CYLINDER OVERHAUL

Referring to the accompanying exploded view of the dual master cylinder components, disassemble the unit as follows: Clean the exterior of the cylinder and remove the filler cover and diaphragm. Any brake fluid remaining in the cylinder should be poured out and discarded. Remove the secondary piston stop bolt from the bottom of the cylinder and remove the bleed screw, if required. With the primary piston depressed, remove the snap-ring from its retaining groove at the rear of the cylinder bore. Withdraw the pushrod and the primary piston assembly from the bore.

NOTE: *Do not remove the screw that retains the primary return spring retainer,*

return spring, primary cup and protector on the primary piston. The assembly is adjusted at the factory and should not be disassembled.

Remove the secondary piston assembly.

NOTE: *Do not remove the outlet tube seats, outlet check valves and outlet check valve springs from the cylinder body.*

All components should be cleaned in clean isopropyl alcohol or clean brake fluid and inspected for chipping, excessive wear and damage. Check to ensure that all recesses, openings and passageways are clear and free of foreign matter. Dirt and cleaning solvent may be removed by using compressed air. After cleaning, keep all parts on a clean surface. Inspect the cylinder bore for etching, pitting, scoring or rusting. If necessary, the cylinder bore may be honed to repair damage, but never to a diameter greater than the original diameter plus 0.003 in.

During the assembly operation, be sure to use all parts supplied with the master cylinder repair kit. With the exception of the master cylinder body, submerge all parts in extra heavy duty brake fluid. Carefully insert the complete secondary piston and return spring

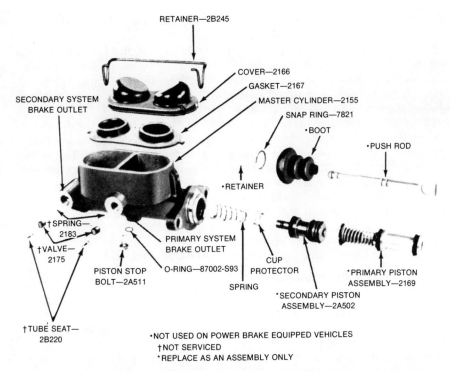

RETAINER—2B245

COVER—2166

GASKET—2167

MASTER CYLINDER—2155

SNAP RING—7821

•BOOT

•PUSH ROD

SECONDARY SYSTEM
BRAKE OUTLET

•RETAINER

†SPRING—
2183

†VALVE—
2175

PRIMARY SYSTEM
BRAKE OUTLET

PISTON STOP
BOLT—2A511

O-RING—87002-S93

CUP
PROTECTOR

SPRING

•PRIMARY PISTON
ASSEMBLY—2169

*SECONDARY PISTON
ASSEMBLY—2A502

†TUBE SEAT—
2B220

•NOT USED ON POWER BRAKE EQUIPPED VEHICLES
†NOT SERVICED
*REPLACE AS AN ASSEMBLY ONLY

Master cylinder disassembled—drum brakes

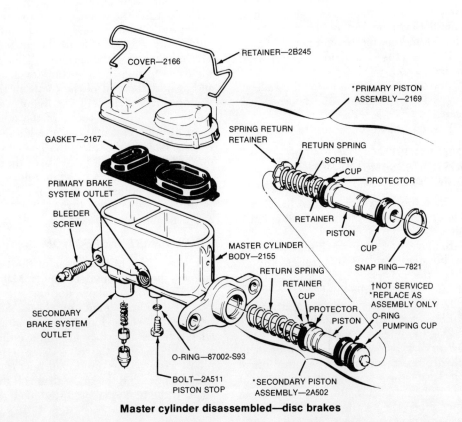

RETAINER—2B245

COVER—2166

*PRIMARY PISTON
ASSEMBLY—2169

SPRING RETURN
RETAINER

RETURN SPRING

SCREW

CUP

PROTECTOR

GASKET—2167

PRIMARY BRAKE
SYSTEM OUTLET

BLEEDER
SCREW

RETAINER

PISTON

CUP

MASTER CYLINDER
BODY—2155

SNAP RING—7821

RETURN SPRING

RETAINER

CUP

PROTECTOR

PISTON

†NOT SERVICED
*REPLACE AS
ASSEMBLY ONLY

SECONDARY
BRAKE SYSTEM
OUTLET

O-RING
PUMPING CUP

O-RING—87002-S93

BOLT—2A511
PISTON STOP

*SECONDARY PISTON
ASSEMBLY—2A502

Master cylinder disassembled—disc brakes

assembly into the cylinder bore and install the primary piston assembly into the bore. With the primary piston depressed, install the snap-ring into its groove in the cylinder bore. Install the pushrod, boot and retainer (if equipped), then install the pushrod assembly into the primary piston. Be sure that the retainer is properly seated and is holding the pushrod securely. Position the inner end of the pushrod boot (if equipped) in the master cylinder body retaining groove. Install the secondary piston stop bolt and O-ring at the bottom of the master cylinder body. Install the bleed screw (if equipped) and position the gasket on the master cylinder filler cover. Be sure that the gasket is securely seated. Install the cover and secure with the retainer.

VACUUM BOOSTER REMOVAL AND INSTALLATION

1. Working from inside the car, beneath the instrument panel, remove the booster pushrod from the brake pedal.

2. Disconnect the stop light switch wires and remove the switch from the brake pedal. Use care not to damage the switch during removal.

3. Raise the hood and remove the master cylinder from the booster without disconnecting the brake lines. Carefully position the master cylinder out of the way, being careful not to kink the brake lines.

4. Remove the manifold vacuum hose from the booster.

5. Remove the booster to firewall attaching bolts and remove the booster from the car.

6. Reverse above procedure to reinstall.

HYDRO-BOOST ACCUMULATOR (BOOSTER ASSEMBLY) REMOVAL AND INSTALLATION

1. Open the hood and remove the 2 nuts attaching the master cylinder to the brake booster.

2. Remove the master cylinder from the hydro-boost accumulator (booster assembly).

3. Set the master cylinder aside without disturbing the hydraulic lines.

4. Disconnect the pressure, steering and return lines from the accumulator.

5. Plug the lines and ports.

6. Working below the dash, disconnect the hydro-boost pushrod from the brake pedal. To do this, disconnect the stoplight switch at the connector. Remove the hairpin retainer. Slide the spotlight switch from the brake pedal pin far enough to clear the switch

outer pin hole. Remove the switch from the pin.

7. Loosen the hydro-boost attaching nuts and remove the pushrod, washers and bushing from the brake pedal pin.

8. Remove the accumulator (booster assembly).

9. Installation is the reverse of removal. Top up the power steering pump reservoir. Run the engine until all air is expelled from the system, which will escape out of the reservoir with the cap off. Then, once steering and brake assist is operational, road-test the car.

DRUM BRAKES

Drum brakes on all Fords employ single-anchor, internal-expanding, and self-adjusting brake assembles. The automatic adjuster continuously maintains correct operating clearance between the linings and the drums by adjusting the brake in small increments in direct proportion to lining wear. When applying the brakes while backing up, the linings tend to follow the rotating drum counterclockwise, thus forcing the upper end of the primary shoe against the anchor pin. Simultaneously, the wheel cylinder pushes the upper end of the secondary shoe and cable guide outward, away from the anchor pin. This movement of the secondary shoe causes the cable to pull the adjusting lever upward and against the end of the tooth on the adjusting screw starwheel. As lining wear increases, the upward travel of the adjusting lever also increases. When the linings have worn sufficiently to allow the lever to move upward far enough, it passes over the end of the tooth and engages it. Upon release of the brakes, the adjusting spring pulls the adjuster lever downward, turning the starwheel and expanding the brakes.

DRUM BRAKE INSPECTION

1. Raise the front or rear of the car and support the car with safety stands. Make sure that the parking brake is not on.

2. If you are going to check the rear brakes, remove the lug nuts which attach the wheels to the axle shaft and remove the tires and wheels from the car. Using a pair of pliers, remove the tinnerman nuts from the wheel studs. Pull the brake drum off the axle shaft. If the brakes are adjusted too tightly to remove the drum, see Step 4. If you can remove the drum, see Step 5.

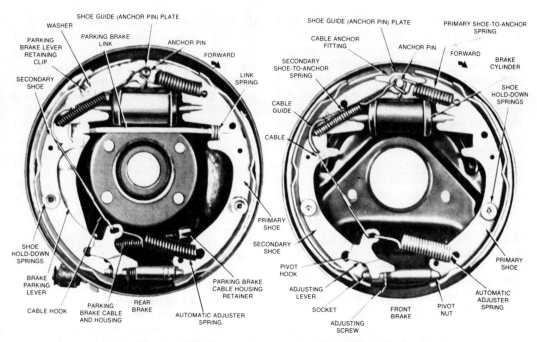

WASHER
SHOE GUIDE (ANCHOR PIN) PLATE
PARKING BRAKE LEVER RETAINING CLIP
PARKING BRAKE LINK
ANCHOR PIN
FORWARD
SECONDARY SHOE
LINK SPRING
SHOE HOLD-DOWN SPRINGS
BRAKE PARKING LEVER
CABLE HOOK
PARKING BRAKE CABLE AND HOUSING
REAR BRAKE
AUTOMATIC ADJUSTER SPRING
PARKING BRAKE CABLE HOUSING RETAINER

SHOE GUIDE (ANCHOR PIN) PLATE
CABLE ANCHOR FITTING
ANCHOR PIN
PRIMARY SHOE-TO-ANCHOR SPRING
FORWARD
BRAKE CYLINDER
SECONDARY SHOE-TO-ANCHOR SPRING
CABLE GUIDE
CABLE
SHOE HOLD-DOWN SPRINGS
PRIMARY SHOE
SECONDARY SHOE
PIVOT HOOK
ADJUSTING LEVER
SOCKET
ADJUSTING SCREW
FRONT BRAKE
PIVOT NUT
PRIMARY SHOE
AUTOMATIC ADJUSTER SPRING

Self-adjusting drum brake assemblies

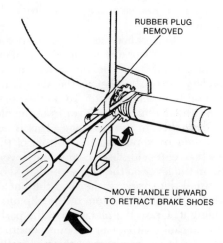

RUBBER PLUG REMOVED

MOVE HANDLE UPWARD TO RETRACT BRAKE SHOES

Backing off brake adjustment

3. If you are going to check the front brakes, then the front tire, wheel and brake drum can be removed as an assembly. Remove the hub cap, then either pry the dust cover off the spindle with a screwdriver or pull it off with a pair of pliers. Remove the cotter pin from the spindle. Slide the nut lock off the adjusting nut, then loosen the adjusting nut until it reaches the end of the spindle. Do not remove the adjusting nut yet. Grab the tire and pull it out toward yourself, then push it back into position. This will free the outer wheel bearing from the drum hub. If the brakes are adjusted up too tightly to allow the drum to be pulled off them, go to Step 4 and loosen up

the brakes, then return here. Remove the adjusting nut, washer and outer bearing from the spindle. Pull the tire, wheel, and brake drum off the spindle.

4. If the brakes are too tight to remove the drum, get under the car (make sure that you have safety stands under the car to support it) and remove the rubber plug from the bottom of the brake backing plate. Shine a flashlight into the slot in the plate. You will see the top of the adjusting screw starwheel and the adjusting lever for the automatic brake adjusting mechanism. To back off on the adjusting screw, you must first insert a small thin screwdriver or a piece of firm wire (coathanger wire) into the adjusting slot and push the adjusting lever away from the adjusting screw. Then, insert a brake adjusting spoon into the slot and engage the top of the starwheel. Lift up on the bottom of the adjusting spoon to force the adjusting screw starwheel downward. Repeat this operation until the brake drum is free of the brake shoes and can be pulled off.

5. Clean the brake shoes and the inside of the brake drum. There must be at least $1/16$ in. of brake lining above the heads of the brake shoe attaching rivets. The lining should not be cracked or contaminated with grease or brake fluid. If there is grease or brake fluid on the lining, it must be replaced and the source of the leak must be found and corrected. Brake fluid on the lining means leaking wheel cylinders. Grease on the brake

lining means a leaking grease retainer (front wheels) or axle seal (rear brakes). If the lining is slightly glazed but otherwise in good condition, it can be cleaned up with medium sandpaper. Lift up the bottom of the wheel cylinder boots and inspect the ends of the wheel cylinders. A small amount of fluid in the end of the cylinders should be considered normal. If fluid runs out of the cylinder when the boots are lifted, however, the wheel cylinder must be rebuilt or replaced. Examine the inside of the brake drum; it should have a smooth, dull finish. If excessive brake shoe wear caused grooves to wear in the drum it must be machined or replaced. If the inside of the drum is slightly glazed, but otherwise good, it can be cleaned up with medium sandpaper.

6. If no repairs are required, install the drum and wheel. If the brake adjustment was changed to remove the drum, adjust the brakes until the drum will just fit over the brakes. After the wheel is installed it will be necessary to complete the adjustment. See "Brake Adjustment" later in this chapter. If a front wheel was removed, tighten the wheel bearing adjustment nut to 17–25 ft lbs while rotating the wheel. This will seat the bearing. Loosen the adjusting nut ½ turn, then retighten it to 10–15 in. lbs.

BRAKE DRUM REMOVAL AND INSTALLATION

See Steps 3 and 4 under "Drum Brakes Inspection."

BRAKE SHOE REMOVAL AND INSTALLATION

NOTE: *If you are not thoroughly familiar with the procedures involved in brake replacement, disassemble and assemble only one side at a time, leaving the other wheel intact as a reference.*

1. Remove the brake drum. See the inspection procedure.

2. Place the hollow end of a brake spring service tool (available at auto parts stores) on the brake shoe anchor pin and twist it to disengage one of the brake retracting springs. Repeat this operation to remove the other spring.

CAUTION: *Be careful the springs do not slip off the tool during removal, as they could cause personal injury.*

3. Reach behind the brake backing plate and place a finger on the end of one of the brake hold-down spring mounting pins. Using a pair of pliers, grasp the washer on the top of the hold-down spring which corresponds to the pin that you are holding. Push down on the pliers and turn them 90° to align the slot in the washer with the head on the spring mounting pin. Remove the spring and washer and repeat this operation on the hold-down spring on the other brake shoe.

4. Place the tip of a screwdriver on the top of the brake adjusting screw and move the screwdriver upward to lift up on the brake adjusting lever. When there is enough slack in the automatic adjuster cable, disconnect the loop on the top of the cable from the anchor. Grasp the top of each brake shoe and move it outward to disengage it from the wheel cylinder (and parking brake link on rear wheels). When the brake shoes are clear, lift them from the backing plate. Twist the shoes slightly and the automatic adjuster assembly will disassemble itself.

5. If you are working on rear brakes, grasp the end of the brake cable spring with a pair of pliers and, using the brake lever as a fulcrum, pull the end of the spring away from the lever. Disengage the cable from the brake lever.

6. The brake shoes are installed as follows: If you are working on the rear brakes, the brake cable must be connected to the secondary brake shoe before the shoe is installed on the backing plate. To do this, first transfer the parking brake lever from the old secondary shoe to the new one. This is accomplished by spreading the bottom of the horseshoe clip and disengaging the lever. Position the lever on the new secondary shoe and install the spring washer and the horseshoe clip. Close the bottom of the clip after installing it. Grasp the metal tip of the parking brake cable with a pair of pliers. Position a pair of side cutter pliers on the end of the cable coil spring and, using the pliers as a fulcrum, pull the coil spring back with the side cutters. Position the cable in the parking brake lever.

7. Apply a *light* coating of high-temperature grease to the brake shoe contact points on the backing plate. Position the primary brake shoe on the front of the backing plate and install the hold-down spring and washer over the mounting pin. Install the secondary shoe on the rear of the backing plate.

8. If working on the rear brakes, install the parking brake link between the notch in the primary brake shoe and the notch in the parking brake lever.

9. Install the automatic adjuster cable loop end on the anchor pin. Make sure that

the crimped side of the loop faces the backing plate.

10. Install the return spring in the primary brake shoe and, using the tapered end of a brake spring service tool, slide the top of the spring onto the anchor pin.

CAUTION: *Be careful to make sure that the spring does not slip off the tool during installation, as it could cause injury.*

11. Install the automatic adjuster cable guide in the secondary brake shoe, making sure that the flared hole in the cable guide is inside the hole in the brake shoe. Fit the cable into the groove in the top of the cable guide.

12. Install the secondary shoe return spring through the hole in the cable guide and the brake shoe. Using the brake spring tool, slide the top of the spring onto the anchor pin.

13. Clean the threads on the adjusting screw and apply a light coating of high-temperature grease to the threads. Screw the adjuster closed, then open it one-half turn.

14. Install the adjusting screw between the brake shoes with the starwheel nearest to the secondary shoe. Make sure that the starwheel is in a position that is accessible from the adjusting slot in the backing plate.

15. Install the short hooked end of the automatic adjuster spring in the proper hole in the primary brake shoe.

16. Connect the hooked end of the automatic adjuster cable and the free end of the automatic adjuster spring in the slot in the top of the automatic adjuster lever.

17. Pull the automatic adjuster lever (the lever will pull the cable and spring with it) downward and to the left and engage the pivot hook of the lever in the hole in the secondary brake shoe.

18. Check the entire brake assembly to make sure that everything is installed properly. Make sure that the shoes engage the wheel cylinder properly and are flush on the anchor pin. Make sure that the automatic adjuster cable is flush on the anchor pin and in the slot on the back of the cable guide. Make sure that the adjusting lever rests on the adjusting screw starwheel. Pull upward on the adjusting cable until the adjusting lever is free of the starwheel, then release the cable. The adjusting lever should snap back into place on the adjusting screw starwheel and turn the wheel one tooth.

19. Expand the brake adjusting screw until the brake drum will just fit over the brake shoes.

20. Install the wheel and drum and adjust the brakes. See "Brake Adjustment."

DRUM BRAKE ADJUSTMENT

NOTE: *Drum brakes installed in Fords are self-adjusting. All that is normally required to adjust the brakes is to apply them moderately hard several times while carefully backing the car in Reverse. However, if this action proves unsatisfactory, or if it proves necessary to readjust the brakes after replacing the linings or removing the drum, the following procedure may be used.*

1. Raise the car and support it with safety stands.

2. Remove the rubber plug from the adjusting slot on the backing plate.

3. Insert a brake adjusting spoon into the slot and engage the lowest possible tooth on the starwheel. Move the end of the brake spoon downward to move the starwheel upward and expand the adjusting screw. Repeat this operation until the brakes lock the wheel.

4. Insert a small screwdriver or piece of firm wire (coat-hanger wire) into the adjusting slot and push the automatic adjuster lever out and free of the starwheel on the adjusting screw.

5. Holding the adjusting lever out of the way, engage the topmost tooth possible on the starwheel with a brake adjusting spoon. Move the end of the adjusting spoon upward to move the adjusting screw starwheel downward and contract the adjusting screw. Back off the adjusting screw starwheel until the wheel spins freely with a minimum of drag. Keep track of the number of turns the starwheel is backed off.

6. Repeat this operation for the other side. When backing off the brakes on the other side, the adjusting lever must be backed off the same number of turns to prevent side-to-side brake pull.

7. Repeat this operation on the other set of brakes (front or rear).

8. When all four brakes are adjusted, make several stops, while backing the car, to equalize all of the wheels.

9. Road-test the car.

WHEEL CYLINDER REMOVAL AND INSTALLATION

1. Remove the brake shoes.

2. On rear brakes, loosen the brake line on the rear of the cylinder but do not pull the line away from the cylinder or it may bend.

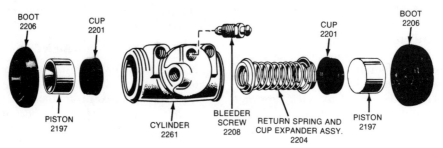

BOOT 2206   CUP 2201   PISTON 2197   CYLINDER 2261   BLEEDER SCREW 2208   RETURN SPRING AND CUP EXPANDER ASSY. 2204   PISTON 2197   CUP 2201   BOOT 2206

Drum brake wheel cylinder disassembled

3. On front brakes, disconnect the metal brake line from the rubber brake hose where they join in the wheel well. Pull off the horseshoe clip that attaches the rubber brake hose to the underbody of the car. Loosen the hose at the cylinder, then turn the whole brake hose to remove it from the wheel cylinder.

4. Remove the bolts and lockwashers which attach the wheel cylinder to the backing plate and remove the cylinder.

5. Position the new wheel cylinder on the backing plate and install the cylinder attaching bolts and lockwashers.

6. Attach the metal brake line or rubber hose by reversing the procedure given in Steps 2 or 3.

7. Install the brakes.

WHEEL CYLINDER OVERHAUL

Since the travel of the pistons in the wheel cylinder changes when new brake shoes are installed, it is possible for previously good wheel cylinders to start leaking after new brakes are installed. Therefore, to save yourself the expense of having to replace new brakes which become saturated with brake fluid and the aggravation of having to take everything apart again, it is strongly recommended that wheel cylinders be rebuilt every time new brake shoes are installed. This is especially true on high-mileage cars.

1. Remove the brakes.

2. Place a bucket or old newspapers under the brake backing plate to catch the brake fluid that will run out of the wheel cylinder.

3. Remove the boots from the ends of the wheel cylinders.

4. Push one piston toward the center of the cylinder to force the opposite piston and cup out the other end of the cylinder. Reach in the open end of the cylinder and push the spring, cup, and piston out of the cylinder.

5. Remove the bleeder screw from the

rear of the cylinder on the back of the backing plate.

6. Inspect the inside of the wheel cylinder. If it is scored in any way, the cylinder must be honed with a wheel cylinder hone or fine emery paper, and finished with crocus cloth if emery paper is used. If the inside of the cylinder is excessively worn, the cylinder will have to be replaced, as only 0.003 in. of material can be removed from the cylinder walls. When honing or cleaning the wheel cylinders, keep a small amount of brake fluid in the cylinder to serve as a lubricant.

7. Clean any foreign matter from the pistons. The sides of the pistons must be smooth for the wheel cylinders to operate properly.

8. Clean the cylinder bore with alcohol and a lint-free rag. Pull the rag through the bore several times to remove all foreign matter and dry the cylinder.

9. Install the bleeder screw and the return spring in the cylinder.

10. Coat new cylinder cups with new brake fluid and install them in the cylinder. Make sure that they are square in the bore or they will leak.

11. Install the pistons in the cylinder after coating them with new brake fluid.

12. Coat the insides of the boots with new brake fluid and install them on the cylinder. Install the brakes.

Front Wheel Bearings
ADJUSTMENT

The front wheels each rotate on a set of opposed, tapered roller bearings as shown in the accompanying illustration. The grease retainer at the inside of the hub prevents lubricant from leaking into the brake drum.

Adjustment of the wheel bearings is accomplished as follows: Lift the car so that the wheel and tire are clear of the ground, then remove the grease cap and remove excess grease from the end of the spindle. Remove

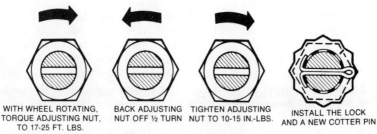

WITH WHEEL ROTATING, TORQUE ADJUSTING NUT, TO 17-25 FT. LBS.   BACK ADJUSTING NUT OFF ½ TURN   TIGHTEN ADJUSTING NUT TO 10-15 IN.-LBS.   INSTALL THE LOCK AND A NEW COTTER PIN

Front wheel bearing adjustment

the cotter pin and nut lock shown in the illustration.

NOTE: *In order to prevent the brake pads from stopping the hub and rotor from seating properly, rock the rotor in and out to push the brake pads back into their bores.* Rotate the wheel, hub, and drum assembly while tightening the adjusting nut to 17–25 ft lbs in order to seat the bearings. Back off the adjusting nut one half turn, then retighten the adjusting nut to 10–15 in. lbs *(inch-pounds)*. Locate the nut lock on the adjusting nut so that the castellations on the lock are lined up with the cotter pin hole in the spindle. Install a new cotter pin, bending the ends of the cotter pin around the castellated flange of the nut lock. Check the front wheel for proper rotation, then install the grease cap. If the wheel still does not rotate properly, inspect and clean or replace the wheel bearings and cups.

REMOVAL, REPACKING, AND INSTALLATION

Drum Brakes

The procedure for cleaning, repacking and adjusting front wheel bearings on vehicles equipped with self-adjusting drum brakes is as follows:

1. Taking proper safety precautions, raise the car until the wheel and tire clear the floor. Install jackstands under the lower control arms.

2. Remove the wheel cover. Remove the grease cap from the hub. Then remove the cotter pin, nut lock, adjusting nut, and flat washer from the spindle. Remove the outer bearing cone and roller assembly.

3. Pull the wheel, hub and drum assembly off the spindle. When encountering a brake drum which will not come off, disengage the adjusting lever from the adjusting screw by inserting a narrow screwdriver through the adjusting hole in the carrier plate. While the lever is disengaged, back off the adjusting screw with a brake adjusting tool. The self-adjusting mechanism will not function properly if the adjusting screw is burred, chipped, or otherwise damaged in the process, so exercise extreme care.

4. Remove the grease retainer and the inner bearing cone and roller assembly from the hub.

5. Clean all grease off from the inner and outer bearing cups with solvent. Inspect the

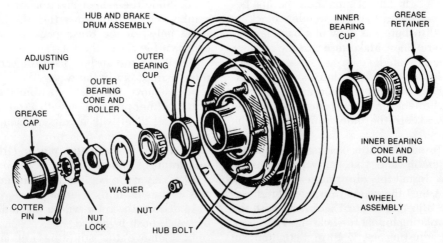

Front hub, wheel bearings and grease retainer

cups for pits, scratches, or excessive wear. If the cups are damaged, remove them with a drift.

6. Clean the inner and outer cone and roller assemblies with solvent and shake them dry. If the cone and roller assemblies show excessive wear or damage, replace them with the bearing cups as a unit.

7. If the new grease retainer is of leather, soak it in light engine oil for 30 minutes, prior to installation. Wipe any excess from the metal portion of the retainer. Clean the spindle and the inside of the hub with solvent to thoroughly remove all old grease.

8. Covering the spindle with a clean cloth, brush all loose dirt and dust from the brake assembly. Remove the cloth carefully so as to not get dirt on the spindle.

9. If the inner and/or outer bearing cups were removed, install the replacement cups on the hub. Be sure that the cups seat properly in the hub.

10. It is imperative that all old grease be removed from the bearings and surrounding surfaces before repacking. The new lithium-base grease is not compatible with the sodium base grease used in the past.

11. Pack the inside of the hub with wheel bearing grease. Add grease to the hub until it is flush with the inside diameter of both bearing cups. Work as much grease as possible between the rollers and cages in the cone and roller assemblies. Lubricate the cone surfaces with grease.

12. Position the inner bearing cone and roller assembly in the inner cup. If a leather grease retainer has soaked for 30 minutes, wipe all excess from the metal portion of the retainer and install. Other grease retainers require a light film of grease on the lips before installation. Using a wooden block to evenly distribute the blow of a hammer, install the retainer. Make sure that the retainer is properly seated.

13. Install the wheel, hub, and drum assembly on the wheel spindle. To prevent damage to the grease retainer and spindle threads, keep the hub centered on the spindle.

14. Install the outer bearing cone and roller assembly and the flat washer on the spindle. Install the adjusting nut.

15. Adjust the wheel bearings by tightening the adjusting nut to 17–25 ft lbs with the wheel rotating to seat the bearing. Then back off the adjusting nut ½ turn. Retighten the adjusting nut to 10–15 in. lbs. Install the locknut so that the castellations are aligned with the cotter pin hole. Install the cotter pin. Bend the ends of the cotter pin around the castellations of the locknut to prevent interference with the radio static collector in the grease cap. Install the grease cap.

16. Remove the adjusting hole cover from the carrier plate and, from the carrier plate side, turn the adjusting screw starwheel upward with a brake adjusting tool. Expand the brake shoes until a slight drag is felt with the drum rotating. Replace the adjusting hole cover.

17. Install the wheel cover.

Disc Brakes

1. Raise the front of the car and support it with safety stands.

2. Remove the front wheels.

NOTE: *In order to remove the rotor, the caliper and anchor plate must be removed from the car.*

3. Loosen, but do not remove, the upper anchor plate attaching bolt with a ¾ in. socket.

4. Using a ⅝ in. socket, remove the lower anchor plate attaching bolt.

NOTE: *When the caliper is removed from the car it must be wired out of the way of the rotor. Also, the brake pads will fall out of the caliper if they are not held in place when the caliper is removed. You will have to insert a small piece of wood or a folded piece of heavy cardboard between the shoes to hold them in place. Have a piece of wire and a piece of wood handy before you start the next step.*

5. Hold the caliper in place and remove the upper anchor plate attaching bolt.

6. Slide the caliper and anchor plate assembly off the rotor, inserting the block of wood between the brake pads as they become visible above the rotor.

7. When the anchor plate is clear of the rotor, wire it out of the way.

8. Remove the dust cap from the rotor hub by either prying it off with a screwdriver or pulling it off with a pair of channel-lock pliers.

9. Remove the cotter pin and the nut lock from the spindle.

10. Loosen the bearing adjusting nut until it is at the end of the spindle.

11. Grasp the rotor with a rag and pull it outward, push it inward.

12. Remove the adjusting nut and the outer bearing.

13. Remove the rotor from the spindle.

14. Place the rotor and tire on a clean, paper-covered surface with the wheel studs facing upward.

15. Working through the hole in the center of the wheel hub, tap the grease seal out of the rear of the hub with a screwdriver or drift.

NOTE: *Be careful not to damage the inner bearing while knocking out the grease seal.*

16. Remove the grease and bearing from under the rotor, and discard the grease seal.

17. Clean the inner and outer bearings and the wheel hub with a suitable solvent. Remove all old grease.

18. Thoroughly dry and wipe clean all components.

19. Clean all old grease from the spindle on the car.

20. Carefully check the bearings for any sign of scoring or other damage. If the roller bearings or bearing cages are damaged, the bearing and the corresponding bearing cup in the rotor hub must be replaced. The bearing cups must be driven out of the rotor hub to the removed. The outer bearing cup is driven out of the front of the rotor from the rear and vice versa for the inner bearing cup.

21. Whether you are reinstalling the old bearings or installing new ones, the bearings must be packed with wheel bearing grease. To do this, place a glob of grease in your left palm, then, holding one of the bearings in your right hand, drag the edge of the bearing heavily through the grease. This must be done to work as much grease as possible through the roller bearings and cage. Turn the bearing and continue to pull it through the grease until the grease is packed between the bearings and the cage all the way around the circumference of the bearing. Repeat this operation until all of the bearings are packed with grease.

22. Pack the inside of the rotor hub with a

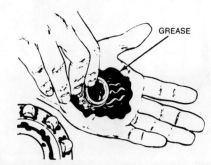

GREASE

Packing bearings

moderate amount of grease, between the bearing cups. Do not overload the hub with grease.

23. Apply a small amount of grease to the spindle.

24. Place the rotor, face down, on a protected surface and install the inner bearing.

25. Coat the lip of a new grease seal with a small amount of grease and position it on the rotor.

26. Place a block of wood on top of the grease seal and tap on the block with a hammer to install the seal. Turn the block of wood to different positions to seat it squarely in the hub.

27. Position the rotor on the spindle.

28. Install the outer bearing and washer on the spindle, inside the rotor hub.

29. Install the bearing adjusting nut and tighten it to 17–25 ft lbs while spinning the rotor. This will seat the bearing.

30. Back off the adjusting nut one half turn.

31. Tighten the adjusting nut to 10–15 in. lbs.

32. Install the nut lock on the adjusting nut so two of the slots align with the holes in the spindle.

33. Install a new cotter pin and bend the ends back so that they will not interfere with the dust cap.

34. Install the dust cap.

35. Install the front tires if they were removed.

DISC BRAKES

Front disc brakes have been available as an option on big Fords since the mid 1960s. From 1968 to 1972 floating caliper front disc brakes were available on all models. Starting in 1973, sliding caliper front discs were made standard equipment with vacuum power assist.

Beginning with 1976 models, a 4-wheel disc brake system utilizing sliding caliper rear disc brakes is standard equipment on all station wagons and police interceptor packages, and optional on all sedans. When equipped with the 4-wheel disc brake system, brake assist is provided by a hydraulically-operated servo system known as Hydro-Boost, in lieu of the traditional vacuum-assist type. In 1979, the four wheel disc brake option was discontinued.

The rear sliding caliper assembly is similar to the one used on the front, except for the parking brake mechanism and a bigger anti-rattle spring. The parking brake lever on the caliper is cable-operated by depressing (or releasing), the parking brake pedal under the dash panel.

When the pedal is depressed, the cable rotates the parking brake lever (on the back of the caliper) and the operating shaft (inside the caliper). Three steel balls, which are located in pockets on the opposing heads of the shaft and thrust screw, roll between ramps formed in the pockets. The motion of the balls forces the thrust screw away from the shaft which, in turn, forces the piston and pad assembly against the disc to create braking action.

An automatic adjuster in the piston compensates for pad wear by moving the thrust screw.

BRAKE PAD REPLACEMENT

Floating Caliper Front Disc Brakes—1968–72

1. Raise the vehicle on a hoist and remove the front wheels.
2. Remove the lockwires from the two mounting bolts and lift the caliper away from the disc.
3. Remove the retaining clips with a screwdriver and slide the outboard pad and retaining pins out of the caliper. Remove the inboard pad.
4. Slide the new inboard pad into the caliper so that the tabs are between the retaining clips and anchor plate and the backing plate lies flush against the piston.
5. Insert the outboard pad retaining pins into the outboard pad and position them in the caliper.

NOTE: *Stabilizer, insulator, pad clips, and pins should alway be replaced when the disc pads are replaced.*

6. Hold the retaining pins in place (one at a time) with a short drift pin or dowel and install the retaining clips.
7. Slide the caliper assembly over the disc and align the mounting bolt holes.
8. Install the lower bolt finger-tight. Install the upper bolt and torque to specification. Torque the lower bolt to specification. Safety-wire both bolts.

CAUTION: *Do not deviate from this procedure. The alignment of the anchor plate depends on the proper sequence of bolt installation.*

9. Check the brake fluid level and pump and brake pedal to seat the lining against the disc. Replace the wheels and rod-test the car.

Sliding Caliper Front Disc Brakes—1973–78

1. Remove approximately ⅔ of the fluid from the rear reservoir of the tandem master cylinder. Raise the vehicle, taking proper safety precautions.
2. Remove the wheel and tire assembly.
3. Remove the key retaining screw from the caliper retaining key.
4. Slide the retaining key and support spring either inward or outward from the anchor plate. To remove the key and spring, a hammer and drift may be used, taking care not to damage the key in the process.
5. Lift the caliper assembly away from the anchor plate by pushing the caliper downward against the anchor plate and rotating the upper end upward out of the anchor plate. Be careful not to stretch or twist the flexible brake hose.
6. Remove the inner shoe and lining assembly from the anchor plate. The inner shoe antirattle clip may become displaced at this time and should be repositioned on the anchor plate. Lightly tap on the outer shoe and lining assembly to free it from the caliper.
7. Clean the caliper, anchor plate, and disc assemblies, and inspect them for brake

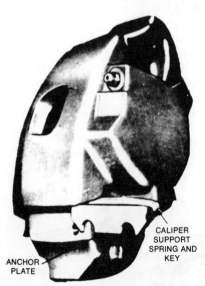

Removing sliding caliper support spring and retaining key

Floating caliper disc brake disassembled

fluid leakage, excessive wear or signs of damage. Replace the pads, if either of them are worn to within $1/32$ in. of the rivet heads.

8. To install new pads, use a 4 in. C-clamp and a block of wood $1\frac{3}{4}$ in. x 1 in. and approximately $\frac{3}{4}$ in. thick to seat the caliper hydraulic piston in its bore. This must be done in order to provide clearance for the caliper to fit over the rotor when the new linings are installed.

9. At this point, the antirattle clip should be in its place on the lower inner brake shoe support of the anchor plate with the pigtail of the clip toward the inside of the anchor plate. Position the inner brake shoe and lining assembly on the anchor plate with the pad toward the disc.

10. Install the outer brake shoe with the lower flange ends against the caliper leg abutments and the brake shoe upper flanges over the shoulders on the caliper legs. The shoe is installed correctly when its flanges fit snugly against the machined surfaces of the shoulder.

11. Remove the C-clamp used to seat the caliper piston in its bore. The piston will remain seated.

12. Position the caliper housing lower V-groove on the anchor plate lower abutment surface.

13. Pivot the caliper housing upward toward the disc until the outer edge of the piston dust boot is about $\frac{1}{4}$ in. from the upper edge of the inboard pad.

14. In order to prevent pinching of the dust boot between the piston and the inboard pad during installation of the caliper, place a clean piece of thin cardboard between the inboard pad and the lower half of the piston dust boot.

15. Rotate the caliper housing toward the disc until a slight resistance is felt. At this point, pull the cardboard downward toward the disc centerline while rotating the caliper over the disc. Then remove the cardboard and complete the rotation of the caliper down over the disc.

16. Slide the caliper up against the upper abutment surfaces of the anchor plate and center the caliper over the lower anchor plate abutment.

17. Position the caliper support spring and key in the key slot and slide them into the opening between the lower end of the caliper and the lower anchor plate abutment until the key semicircular slot is centered over the

retaining screw threaded hole in the anchor plate.

18. Install the key retaining screw and torque to 12–16 ft lbs.

19. Check the fluid level in the master cylinder and fill as necessary. Install the reservoir cover. Depress the brake pedal several times to properly seat the caliper and pads.

Check for leakage around the caliper and flexible brake hose.

20. Install the wheel and tire assembly and torque the nuts to 70–115 ft lbs. Install the wheel cover.

21. Lower the car. Make sure that you obtain a firm brake pedal and then road test the car for proper brake operation.

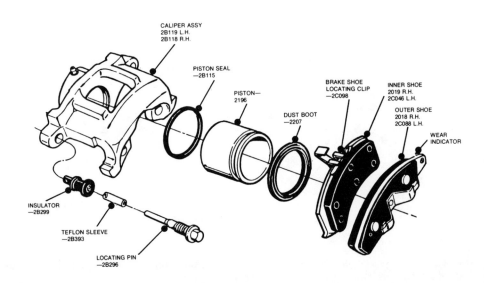

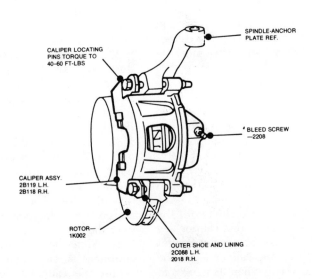

1979 front disc brakes

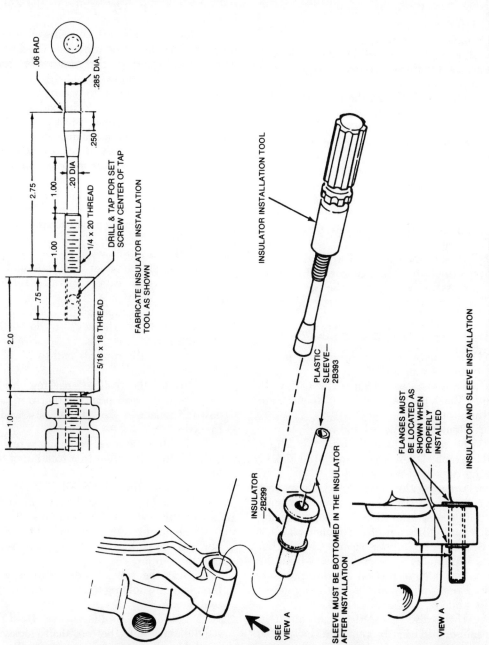

.06 RAD

.285 DIA.

2.75

1.00

1.00

.20 DIA

1/4 x 20 THREAD

DRILL & TAP FOR SET
SCREW CENTER OF TAP

.250

FABRICATE INSULATOR INSTALLATION
TOOL AS SHOWN

.75

2.0

1.0

5/16 x 18 THREAD

INSULATOR INSTALLATION TOOL

PLASTIC
SLEEVE—
2B393

INSULATOR
—2B299

SEE
VIEW A

SLEEVE MUST BE BOTTOMED IN THE INSULATOR
AFTER INSTALLATION

FLANGES MUST
BE LOCATED AS
SHOWN WHEN
PROPERLY
INSTALLED

INSULATOR AND SLEEVE INSTALLATION

VIEW A

1979 insulator and sleeve installation

1979 Models

1. Remove brake fluid from the fluid reservoir until it is half full.

2. Jack up the car and support it with safety stands. Remove the wheel and tire assembly.

3. Remove the caliper locating pins.

4. Lift the caliper assembly from the rotor and remove the brake pads.

5. Remove and discard the plastic sleeves that are located inside the caliper locating pin insulators. These parts *must not* be reused. Also remove and discard the locating insulators. Do not reuse these parts.

6. To install new pads, use a 4 inch C-clamp and a block of wood to seat the caliper piston in its bore.

7. Install new insulators and plastic sleeves in the caliper housing.

8. Install new inner and outer brake pads. The outer pads are marked for right hand or left hand installation. Make sure they are installed correctly.

9. Reinstall the caliper. Torque the locating pins to 40–60 ft lbs. Reinstall the wheel and tire assembly and lower the car.

Sliding Caliper Rear Disc Brakes

NOTE: *This procedure requires the use of a special service tool.*

1. Raise the car and support it with jackstands. Block the front wheels if they remain on the ground.

2. Remove the wheel and tire.

3. Disconnect the cable from the caliper parking brake lever. Be careful not to kink or cut the cable and return spring.

4. Unfasten the setscrew which secures the caliper key. Use a hammer and soft brass drift (if necessary) to slide the support spring and retaining key out of the anchor plate.

5. Push the caliper against the anchor plate and rotate its upper end away from the plate. If a ridge of rust on the disc prevents caliper removal, scrape the rust away with a putty knife or similar blunt tool.

6. If the disc is rusted to the point that the caliper still can't be removed, loosen the caliper end retainer ½-turn, after removing the retaining screw and caliper parking brake lever. Also, be sure to matchmark the caliper housing and end retainer to ensure that the retainer is only given ½-turn.

CAUTION: *Turning the end retainer more than ½-turn could cause internal fluid leaks in the caliper, which would make caliper rebuilding necessary.*

7. Wire the caliper assembly out of the way to avoid stretching or kinking the brake hose.

8. Remove the inner pad assembly from the retaining clip. Tap lightly on the outer pad to free it from the caliper.

9. Mark the pads for proper installation if they are not going to be replaced. Used pads must be returned to the same side from which they were removed.

10. If the pad is worn to within 1/32 in. of any rivet head, replace all of the pads on both rear brakes. Do not replace just one pad or one set of pads; uneven braking will result.

NOTE: *Pad replacement requires the use of a special tool to bottom the piston in its bore.*

11. Inspect the caliper for leaks. Clean any rust off the caliper and anchor plate sliding surfaces or inner brake pad abutment surfaces on the anchor plate.

Installation is as follows:

1. If the end retainer was loosened in order to remove the caliper, perform the following:

   a. Install the caliper on the anchor plate and secure it with the key, but do not install the pads.

   b. Tighten the retainer end to 75–95 ft lbs.

   c. Install the caliper parking brake lever with the arm pointing rearward and down. This allows the cable to pass under the axle.

   d. Tighten the lever retaining screw to 16–22 ft lbs. Check for free rotation of the lever.

   e. Remove the caliper.

2. The following special steps must be performed if new pads are being installed:

   a. Remove the disc and install the caliper less the pads. Use only the key to retain the caliper.

   b. Seat the special tool firmly against the piston by holding the shaft rotating the tool handle.

   c. Loosen the handle ¼-turn. Hold the handle and rotate the tool shaft clockwise until the caliper piston bottoms (it will continue to turn after it bottoms).

   d. Rotate the handle until the piston is firmly seated.

   e. Remove the caliper and install the disc.

3. Confirm that the brake pad antirattle

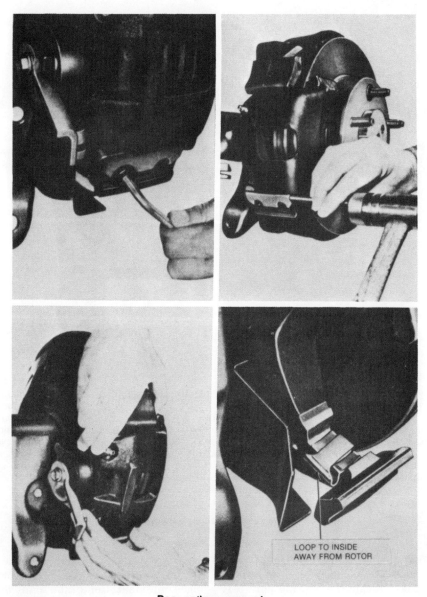

LOOP TO INSIDE
AWAY FROM ROTOR

Rear caliper removal

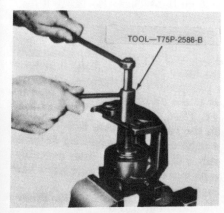

TOOL—T75P-2588-B

Bottoming the caliper piston

clip is correctly positioned in the lower inner brake pad support, the clip loop should face the inside of the anchor plate.

4. Fit the inner pad assembly on the anchor plate, with the lining facing the disc.

5. Install the outer brake pad with its lower flanges against the caliper leg abutments and its upper flanges against the machined shoulder surfaces.

6. Lubricate the caliper and anchor plate sliding surfaces with special brake lubricant. Keep the lubricant off the pad and disc.

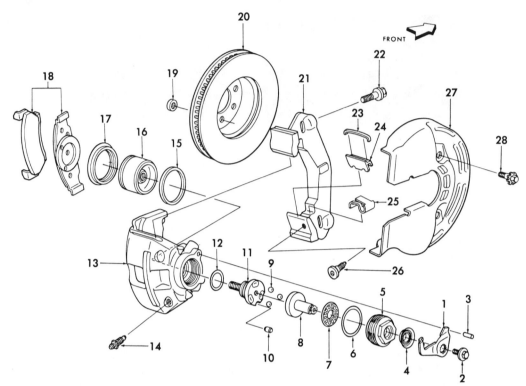

1. Parking brake actuating lever
2. Lever retaining bolt
3. Pin
4. Retainer seal
5. Parking brake end retainer
6. Seal
7. Thrust bearing
8. Parking brake operating shaft
9. Ball bearing
10. Pin
11. Parking brake thrust screw
12. Seal
13. Caliper housing
14. Bleeder screw
15. Piston seal
16. Piston and adjuster assembly
17. Boot
18. Brake pad assemblies
19. Grommet
20. Disc rotor
21. Anchor plate
22. Retaining bolt
23. Caliper support spring
24. Caliper retaining key
25. Anti-rattle clip
26. Retaining screw
27. Anti-splash shield
28. Retaining bolt

Rear sliding caliper assembly

7. Position the caliper housing lower groove against the anchor plate lower abutment surfaces. Rotate the housing until it is completely over the disc. Be careful not to damage the dust boot.

8. Slide the caliper outward until the inner pad is seated firmly against the disc. Measure the outer pad-to-disc clearance. It should be $1/16$ in. or less. If it is more, adjust the piston *outward* with the special tool (See step 2). Each ¼-turn of the piston is about $1/16$ in. of piston movement.

CAUTION: *If piston clearance is more than $1/16$ in., the adjuster may pull out of the piston when the service brakes are applied, causing adjuster failure.*

9. Center the caliper over the lower anchor plate abutment, while holding it over the upper abutment.

10. Install the retaining spring and key in the keyway and slide them into the opening at the lower end of the caliper and anchor plate abutment. Center the semi-circular slot in the key over the anchor plate setscrew hole. Tighten the setscrew to 12–16 ft lbs.

11. Attach the parking brake cable to the lower lever end.

12. If the caliper was completely removed (lines disconnected), bleed the hydraulic system. Run the engine and lightly pump the service brake pedal 40 times; allow one second between brake applications. Check the parking brake for too much travel or too light operating effort. Repeat the pumping and adjust the cable, if necessary.

13. Install the wheel and tire, remove the jacketstand and lower the car.

14. Make sure that the service brake pedal feels firm and then road test the car. Check parking brake operation.

CALIPER REMOVAL, OVERHAUL, AND INSTALLATION

Floating Front Caliper—1968–72

1. Raise the vehicle on a hoist and remove the front wheels.

2. Disconnect and plug the brake line.

3. Remove the lockwires from the two caliper mounting bolts and remove the bolt. Lift the caliper off the disc.

4. Remove and discard the locating pin insulators. Replace all rubber parts at reassembly.

5. Remove the retaining clips with a screwdriver and slide the outboard pad and retaining pins out of the caliper. Remove the inboard pad. Loosen the bleed screw and drain the brake fluid.

6. Remove the two small bolts and caliper stabilizers.

7. Remove the inboard pad retaining clips and bolts.

8. Clean and inspect all parts, and reinstall on the anchor plate. Do not tighten the stabilizer bolts at this time.

9. Remove the piston by applying compressed air to the fluid inlet hole. Use care to prevent the piston from popping out of control.

CAUTION: *Do not attempt to catch the piston with the hand. Use folded towels to cushion it.*

10. Remove the piston boot. Inspect the piston for scoring, pitting, or corrosion. The piston must be replaced if there is any visible damage or wear.

11. Remove the piston seal from the cylinder bore. *Do not use any metal tools for this operation.*

12. Clean the caliper with fresh brake fluid. Inspect the cylinder bore for damage or wear. Light defects can be removed by rotating crocus cloth around the bore. (Do not use any other type of abrasive.)

13. Lubricate all new rubber parts in brake fluid. Install the piston seal in the cylinder groove. Install the boot into its piston groove.

14. Install the piston, open end out, into the bore while working the boot around the outside of the piston. Make sure that the boot lip is seated in the piston groove.

15. Slide the anchor plate assembly onto the caliper housing and reinstall the locating pins. Tighten the pins to specification. Tighten the stabilizer anchor plate bolts.

16. Slide the inboard pad into the caliper so that the tabs are between the retaining clips and anchor plate and the backing plate lies flush against the piston.

17. Insert the outboard pad retaining pins into the outboard pad and position them in the caliper.

18. Hold the retaining pins in place (one at a time) with a short drift pin or dowel and install the retaining clips.

19. Slide the caliper assembly over the disc and align the mounting bolt holes.

20. Install the lower bolt finger-tight. Install the upper bolt and torque to specification. Torque the lower bolt to specification. Safety-wire both bolts.

CAUTION: *Do not deviate from this procedure. The alignment of the anchor plate depends on the proper sequence of bolt installation.*

21. Connect the brake line and bleed the brakes (see "Hydraulic System Bleeding").

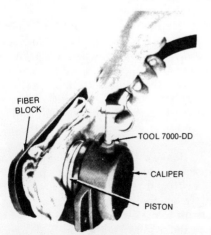

Removing piston from caliper

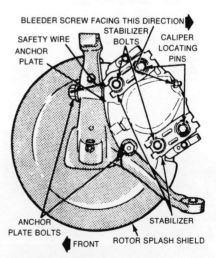

Floating caliper installed—rear view

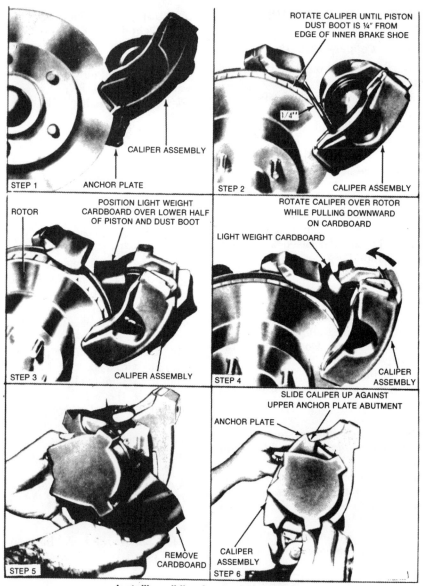

Installing sliding front caliper assembly

Sliding Front Caliper—1973-78

1. Raise the vehicle and place jackstands underneath.

2. Remove the wheel and tire assembly.

3. Disconnect the flexible brake hose from the caliper. To disconnect the hose, loosen the tube fitting which connects the end of the hose to the brake tube at its bracket on the frame. Remove the horseshoe clip from the hose and bracket, disengage the hose, and plug the end. Then unscrew the entire hose assembly from the caliper.

4. Remove the key retaining screw from the caliper retaining key.

5. Slide the retaining key and support spring either inward or outward from the anchor plate. To remove the key and spring, a hammer and drift may be used, taking care not to damage the key in the process.

6. Lift the caliper assembly away from the anchor plate by pushing the caliper downward against the anchor plate and rotating the upper end upward out of the anchor plate.

7. Remove the piston by applying compressed air to the fluid inlet port with a rubber-tipped nozzle. Place a towel or thick cloth over the piston before applying air pressure to prevent damage to the piston. If the piston is seized in the bore and cannot be forced from the caliper, lightly tap around

the outside of the caliper while applying air pressure.

CAUTION: *Do not attempt to catch the piston with your hand.*

8. Remove the dust boot from the caliper assembly.

9. Remove the piston seal from the cylinder and discard it.

10. Clean all metal parts with isopropyl alcohol or a suitable non-petroleum solvent and dry them with compressed air. Be sure that there is no foreign material in the bore or component parts. Inspect the piston and bore for excessive wear or damage. Replace the piston if it is pitted, scored, or if the chrome plating is wearing off.

11. Lubricate all new rubber parts in brake fluid. Install the piston seal in the cylinder groove, being careful not to twist it. Install the dust boot by setting the flange squarely in the outer groove of the bore.

12. Coat the piston with brake fluid and install it in the bore. Work the dust boot around the outside of the piston, making sure that the boot lip is seated in the piston groove.

13. Install the caliper as outlined in Steps 12–18 in the sliding caliper "Shoe and Lining Replacement" procedure.

14. Thread the flexible brake hose and gasket onto the caliper fitting. Torque the fitting to 12–20 ft lbs. Place the upper end of the flexible brake hose in its bracket and install the horseshoe clip. Remove the plug

from the brake tube and connect the tube to the hose. Torque the tube fitting nut to 10–15 ft lbs.

15. Bleed the brake system as outlined in the "Hydraulic System Bleeding" section.

16. Check the fluid level in the master cylinder and fill as necessary. Install the reservoir cover. Depress the brake pedal several times to properly seat the caliper and shoes. Check for leakage around the caliper and the flexible brake hose.

17. Install the wheel and tire assembly and torque the nuts to 70–115 ft lbs. Install the wheel cover.

18. Lower the car. Make sure that you obtain a firm brake pedal and then road test the car for proper brake operation.

1979 Models

1. Raise the car in the air and support it with safety stands.

2. Remove the wheel and tire assembly.

3. Disconnect the flexible brake hose from the caliper.

4. Remove the caliper locating pins. Mark the left and right calipers before removal.

5. Lift the calipers from the anchor plates.

6. Installation is the reverse of removal. Torque the caliper locating pins to 40–60 ft lbs. Torque the brake hose fitting to 20–30 ft lbs.

NOTE: *When the hose is correctly torqued, there should be one or two fitting threads still showing at the caliper. Don't*

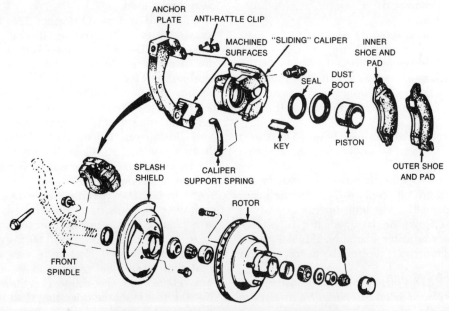

Sliding caliper front disc brake disassembled

attempt to force the hose fitting flush with the caliper.

7. Bleed the brakes.

Sliding Rear Caliper

1. Raise the car and install jackstands beneath the frame. Block the front wheels if they remain on the ground.

2. Remove the wheel and tire.

3. Disconnect and plug the rear brake pipe fitting from the hose end at the frame bracket. Unfasten the horseshoe clip from the hose fitting and separate the hose from the bracket. Unscrew the hose end fitting from the caliper.

4. Follow Steps 3–6 under "Brake Pad Removal" for rear disc brake 1976 cars.

5. Remove the caliper assembly from the car.

6. Remove the retaining screw, parking brake lever, and caliper end retainer.

7. Pull out the operating shaft, thrust bearing, and balls from the caliper.

8. Using either a magnet or tweezers, extract the thrust screw anti-rotation pin.

9. Using a ¼-in. allen key, rotate the thrust screw counterclockwise to remove it.

10. Push the piston/adjuster assembly out of its bore from behind.

NOTE: *A special tool is available to do this. Use care not to scratch the bore or press on the piston adjuster can while removing the piston.*

11. Remove and discard the following:
   a. Piston seal
   b. Boot
   c. Thrust screw O-ring seal
   d. End retainer O-ring
   e. End retainer lip seal

12. Clean all metal parts in isopropyl alcohol. Dry them with compressed air. Be sure that no foreign material remains in the caliper.

13. Inspect the caliper bores. The thrust screw bore must be smooth and show no sign of pitting.

14. If the piston is pitted, scored, or the plating worn off, replace the piston/adjuster as an assembly. The adjuster can should not be loose, high, or damaged, if it is, replace the piston/adjuster assembly. If brake adjustment is incorrect, replace the piston/adjuster assembly.

NOTE: *The piston and the adjuster must be replaced as an assembly. No attempt to repair the adjuster should be made.*

15. If in doubt about adjuster operation, check it as follows:
   a. Install the thrust screw in the piston/adjuster.
   b. Pull the two pieces apart about ¼ in. and release them.
   c. When the pieces are pulled apart, the brass drive ring should remain stationary, causing the nut to turn.
   d. When the pieces are released, the nut should remain stationary and the drive ring rotate.
   e. Replace the piston/adjuster if it fails to operate in this manner.

16. Inspect all bearing, sliding, rotating and rolling surfaces for wear, pitting or brinnelling. Replace any parts necessary. A polished appearance on ball paths or bearing surfaces is OK, as long as there is no sign of wear into the surface.

Assembly is as follows:

1. Coat a new piston seal with clean brake fluid. Seat the seal in the groove of the bore. Be sure it is not twisted.

2. Seat the flange of a new dust boot squarely in the caliper bore outer groove.

3. Coat the piston/adjuster assembly with clean brake fluid. Spread the dust boot over the piston and install the piston. Seat the dust boot in the piston/adjuster groove.

4. Lay the caliper assembly (rear of bore up) in a soft-jawed vise. Do not tighten the vise; housing distortion will result.

5. Fill the piston/adjuster assembly up to the bottom edge of thrust screw bore with clean brake fluid.

6. Install a new O-ring in the thrust screw groove, after coating it with clean brake fluid. Use a ¼ in. allen key to install the thrust screw in the piston adjuster assembly, until its top surface is flush with the bottom of the threaded bore. Align the notches on the thrust screw with those on the caliper housing. Install the anti-rotation pin.

7. Install one ball in each of the three thrust screw pockets. Coat all components of the parking brake mechanism with a liberal amount of silicone grease.

8. Install the parking brake operating shaft over the balls. Coat the thrust bearing with silicone grease and fit it on the shaft.

9. Install a new lip seal and O-ring on the caliper end retainer. Coat both seals with a light film of silicone grease and install the end retainer on the caliper; tighten it to 75–90 ft lbs. Hold the operating shaft so that it is securely seated against the parking brake

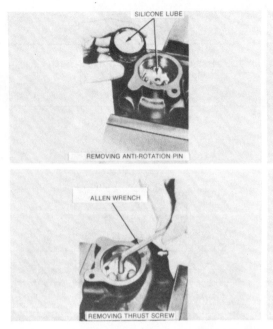
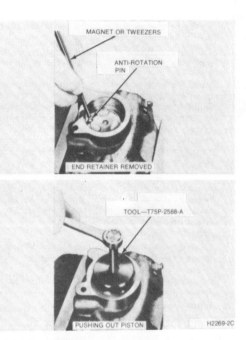

Disassembling rear brake caliper

mechanism during end retainer installation. If the lip seal is dislocated, reseat it.

10. Install the parking brake lever over its keyed spline, so that it points down and rearward. Torque the lever securing screw to 16–22 ft lbs. Check the lever for freedom of movement.

11. Support the caliper and bottom the piston with the special tool as in Steps 2b through d of the "Disc Brake Pad Replacement" procedure.

12. Follow Steps 2–11 under "Brake Pad Installation" for rear disc brake 1976 cars.

13. Place a new gasket on the hose fitting and screw the fitting into the caliper port. Torque to 20–30 ft lbs. Place the upper end of the flexible hose into its bracket and install the horseshoe clip. Do not twist or coil the brake hose. Keep the stripe on the hose straight. Unplug the pipe. Connect the hose to the pipe and tighten the fitting to 10–15 ft lbs.

14. Bleed the hydraulic system. Run the engine and lightly pump the brake pedal 40 times, allowing one second between pedal applications. Check the parking brake for excessive travel or too light an operating effort. Repeat the pumping and adjust the cable, if necessary.

15. Install the wheel and tire. Remove the jackstands and lower the car.

16. Make sure that the brake pedal feels firm, and then road test the car. Recheck parking brake operation.

REAR DISC REMOVAL AND INSTALLATION

1. Remove the caliper assembly and wire it out of the way, unless it is to be serviced. Do not remove the anchor plate.

2. If corrosion makes identification difficult, mark the raised (not the braking) surface of the disc "RIGHT" or "LEFT" prior to removal.

3. Remove the securing nuts and take the disc off the axle shaft.

Installation is as follows:

1. If a new disc is being used, remove its protective coating with carburetor degreaser.

2. Identify the left and right discs before installation. The words "LEFT" and "RIGHT" are cast into the inner surface of the raised section of the disc. This is important, since the cooling vanes cast into the disc must face in the direction of forward rotation.

3. Install the two disc securing nuts.

4. Install the caliper.

PARKING BRAKE

CABLE ADJUSTMENT

All Cars with Rear Drums Brakes

1. Fully release the parking brake.

2. If an axle-type hoist is available, place the transmission in Neutral and raise the vehicle. If the hoist is not available, block the

Brake Specifications

All measurements given are (in.) unless noted

Year	Model	Lug Nut Torque (ft/lb)	Master Cylinder Bore	Brake Disc		Brake Drum			Minimum Lining Thickness	
				Minimum Thickness	Maximum Run-Out	Diameter	Max Machine O/S	Max Wear Limit	Front	Rear
1968–71	all	70–115	1.000	.875	.0007	11.03	11.090	11.090	$\frac{2}{32}$	$\frac{2}{32}$
1972–75	all	70–115	1.000	1.180	.0007	11.03	11.090	11.090	$\frac{2}{32}$	$\frac{2}{32}$
1976–78	all	70–115	1.000	1.120 (front) .895 (rear)	.003 .003	11.03	11.090	11.090	$\frac{1}{8}$	$\frac{3}{32}$
1979	all	70–115	1.000	.972	.003	11.030	11.090	11.090	$\frac{1}{8}$	$\frac{2}{32}$

NOTE: Minimum lining thickness is as recommended by the manufacturer. Because of variations in state inspection regulations, the minimum allowable thickness may be different than recommended by the manufacturer.

front wheels, place a floor jack beneath the axle housing (following the instructions in Chapter 1), place transmission in Neutral, and raise the back of the car. It is important in all cases to raise the car by the rear axle so that the suspension does not become off-loaded thereby stretching the brake cables and giving a faulty adjustment.

NOTE: Install jackstands beneath the frame when using a floor jack.

3. Tighten the equalizer nut against the cable equalizer sufficiently to cause rear wheel brake drag when the wheel is turned by hand. Then, loosen the adjusting nut until the rear brakes just may be turned freely.

There should be no brake drag when the cable is properly adjusted. Tighten the locknut, if so equipped, to 7–10 ft lbs.

4. Remove the jackstands, if used, and lower the car. Check the operation of the parking brake.

Models with Rear Disc Brakes

1. Fully release the parking brake.

2. Place the transmission in Neutral. If it is necessary to raise the car to reach the adjusting nut and observe the parking brake levers, use an axle hoist or a floor jack positioned beneath the differential. This is necessary so that the rear axle remains at the curb

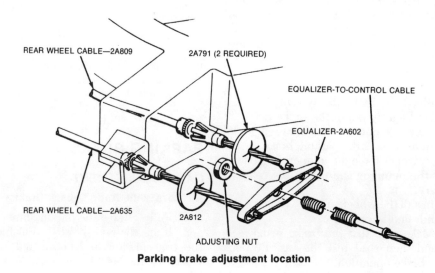

Parking brake adjustment location

attitude, not stretching the parking brake cables.

CAUTION: *If you are raising the rear of the car only, block the front wheels.*

3. Locate the adjusting nut beneath the car on the driver's side. While observing the parking brake actuating levers on the rear calipers, tighten the adjusting nut until the levers just begin to move. Then, loosen the nut sufficiently for the levers to fully return to the stop position.

4. Check the operation of the parking brake. Make sure that the actuating levers return to the stop position by attempting to pull them rearward. If the lever moves rearward, the cable adjustment is too tight, which will cause a dragging rear brake and consequent brake overheating and fade.

10

Body

The list of tools and equipment you may need to fix minor body damage ranges from very basic hand tools to a wide assortment of specialized body tools. Most minor scratches, dings and rust holes can be fixed using an electric drill, wire wheel or grinder attachment, half-round plastic file, sanding block, various grades of sandpaper (#120, which is coarse through #600, which is fine, in both wet and dry types), auto body plastic, primer, touch-up paint, spreaders, newspaper and masking tape. If you intend to try straightening any dents, you'll probably also need a slide hammer (dent puller).

Most auto body repair kits contain all the materials you need to do the job right in the kit. So, if you have a small rust spot or dent you want to fix, check the contents of the kit before you run out and buy any additional tools.

ALIGNING BODY PANELS

Doors

There are several methods of adjusting doors. Your vehicle will probably use one of those illustrated.

Whenever a door is removed and is to be reinstalled, you should matchmark the position of the hinges on the door pillars. The holes of the hinges and/or the hinge attaching points are usually oversize to permit alignment of doors. The striker plate is also moveable, through oversize holes, permitting up-and-down, in-and-out and fore-and-aft movement. Fore-and-aft movement is made by adding or subtracting shims from behind the striker and pillar post. The striker should be adjusted so that the door closes fully and remains closed, yet enters the lock freely.

DOOR HINGES

Don't try to cover up poor door adjustment with a striker plate adjustment. The gap on each side of the door should be equal and uniform and there should be no metal-to-metal contact as the door is opened or closed.

1. Determine which hinge bolts must be loosened to move the door in the desired direction.

2. Loosen the hinge bolt(s) just enough to allow the door to be moved with a padded pry bar.

3. Move the door a small amount and check the fit, after tightening the bolts. Be sure that there is no bind or interference with adjacent panels.

4. Repeat this until the door is properly positioned, and tighten all the bolts securely.

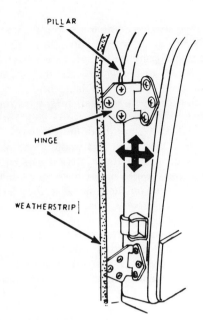

Door hinge adjustment

Hood, Trunk or Tailgate

As with doors, the outline of hinges should be scribed before removal. The hood and trunk can be aligned by loosening the hinge bolts in their slotted mounting holes and moving the hood or trunk lid as necessary. The hood and trunk have adjustable catch locations to regulate lock engagement bumpers at the front and/or rear of the hood provide a vertical adjustment and the hood lockpin can be adjusted for proper engagement.

The tailgate on the station wagon can be adjusted by loosening the hinge bolts in their slotted mounting holes and moving the tailgate on its hinges. The latchplate and

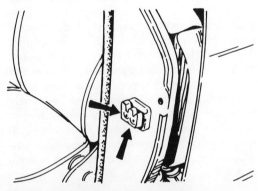

Move the door striker as indicated by arrows

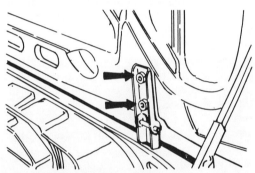

Loosen the hinge boots to permit fore-and-aft and horizontal adjustment

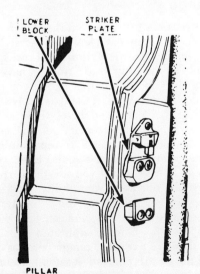

Striker plate and lower block

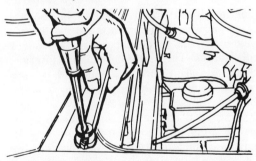

The hood is adjusted vertically by stop-screws at the front and/or rear

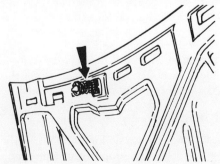

The hood pin can be adjusted for proper lock engagement

latch striker at the bottom of the tailgate opening can be adjusted to stop rattle. An adjustable bumper is located on each side.

RUST, UNDERCOATING, AND RUSTPROOFING

Rust

About the only technical information the average backyard mechanic needs to know about rust is that it is an electro-chemical process that works from **the inside out** on unprotected ferrous metals such as steel and iron. Salt, pollution, humidity—these things and more create and promote the formation of rust. You can't stop rust once it starts. Once rust has started on a fender or a body panel, the only sure way to stop it is to replace the part.

It's a lot easier to prevent rust than to remove it, especially if you have a new car and most late model cars are pretty well rustproofed when they leave the factory. In the early seventies, it seemed like cars were rusting out faster than you could pay them off and Detroit (and the imports) realized that this is not exactly the way you build customer loyalty.

Undercoating

Contrary to what most people think, the primary purpose of undercoating is not to prevent rust, but to deaden noise that might otherwise be transmitted to the car's interior. Since cars are pretty quiet these days anyway, dealers are only too willing to promote undercoating as a rust preventative. Undercoating will of course, prevent some rust, but only if applied when the car is brand-new. In any case, undercoating doesn't provide the protection that a good rustproofing does. If you do decide to undercoat your car and it's not brand-new, you have a big clean-up job ahead of you. It's a good idea to have the underside of the car professionally steam-cleaned and save yourself a lot of work. Spraying undercoat on dirty or rusty parts is only going to make things worse, since the undercoat will trap any rust causing agents.

Rustproofing

The best thing you can do for a new or nearly new car is to have it properly rust-proofed. There are two ways you can go about this. You can do it yourself, or you can have one of the big rustproofing companies do it for you. Naturally, it's going to cost you a lot more to have a big company do it, but it's worth it if your car is new or nearly new. If you own an older car that you plan to hang onto for a while, then doing it yourself might be the best idea. Professional rust-proofing isn't cheap ($100–$250), but it's definitely worth it if your car is new. The rustproofing companies won't guarantee their jobs on cars that are over three months old or have more than about 3000 miles on them because they feel the corrosion process may have already begun.

If you have an older car that hasn't started to rust yet, the best idea might be to purchase one of the do-it-yourself rustproofing kits that are available, and do the job yourself.

Drain Holes

Rusty rocker panels are a common problem on nearly every car, but they can be prevented by simply drilling some holes in your rocker panels to let the water out, or keeping the ones that are already there clean and unclogged. Most cars these days have a series of holes in the rocker panels to prevent moisture collection there, but they frequently become clogged up. Just use a small screwdriver or penknife to keep them clean. If your car doesn't have drain holes, it's a simple matter to drill a couple of holes in each panel.

Repairing Minor Body Damage

Unless your car just rolled off the showroom floor, chances are it has a few minor scratches or dings in it somewhere, or a small rust spot you've been meaning to fix. You just haven't been able to decide whether or not you can really do the job. Well, if the damage is anything like that presented here, there are a number of auto body repair kits that contain everything you need to repair minor scratches, dents, and rust spots. Even rust holes can be repaired if you use the correct kit. If you're unsure of your ability, start out with a small scratch. Once you've mastered small scratches and dings, you can work your way up to the more complicated repairs. When doing rust repairs, remember that unless all the rust is removed, it's going to come back in a year or less. Just sanding the rust down and applying some paint won't work.

Repairing Minor Surface Rust and Scratches

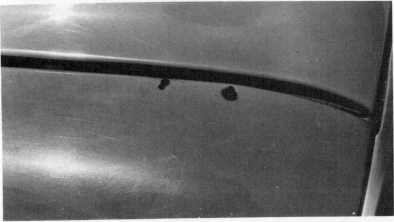

1. Just about everybody has a minor rust spot or scratches on their car. Spots such as these can be easily repaired in an hour or two. You'll need some sandpaper, masking tape, primer, and a can of touch-up paint.

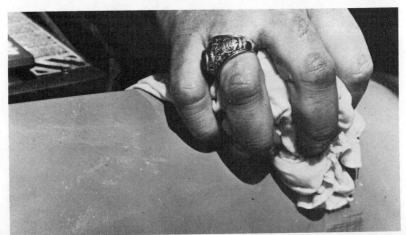

2. The first step is to wash the area down to remove all traces of dirt and road grime. If the car has been frequently waxed, you should wipe it with thinner or some other wax remover so that the paint will stick.

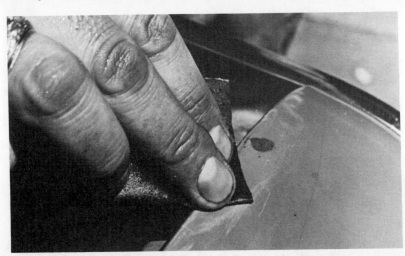

3. Small rust spots and scratches like these will only require light hand sanding. For a job like this, you can start with about grade 320 sandpaper and then use a 400 grit for the final sanding.

4. Once you've sanded the area with 320 paper, wet a piece of 400 paper and sand it lightly. Wet sanding will feather the edges of the surrounding paint into the area to be painted. For large areas, you could use a sanding block, but it's not really necessary for a small job like this.

5. The area should look like this once you're finished sanding. Wipe off any water and run the palm of your hand over the sanded area with your eyes closed. You shouldn't be able to feel any bumps or ridges anywhere. Make sure you have sanded a couple of inches back in each direction so you'll get good paint adhesion.

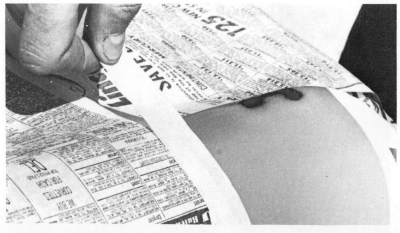

6. Once you have the area sanded to your satisfaction, mask the surrounding area with masking tape and newspaper. Be sure to cover any chrome or trim that might get sprayed. You'll have to mask far enough back from the damaged area to allow for overspray. If you mask right around the sanded spots, you'll end up with a series of lines marking the painted area.

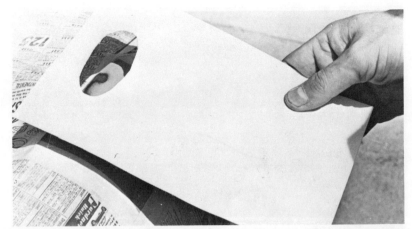

7. You can avoid a lot of excess overspray by cutting a hole in a piece of cardboard that approximately matches the area you are going to paint. Hold the cardboard steady over the area as you spray the primer on. If you haven't painted before, it's a good idea to practice on something before you try painting your car. Don't hold the paint can in one spot. Keep it moving and you'll avoid runs and sags.

8. The primered area should look like this when you have finished. It's better to spray several light coats than one heavy coat. Let the primer dry for several minutes between coats. Make sure you've covered all the bare metal.

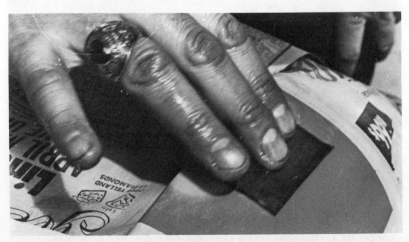

9. After the primer has dried, sand the area with wet 400 paper, wash it off and let it dry. Your final coat goes on next, so make sure the area is clean and dry.

10. Spray the touch-up paint on using the cardboard again. Make the first coat a very light coat (known as a fog coat). Remember to keep the paint can moving smoothly at about 8–12 inches from the surface.

11. Once you've finished painting, let the paint dry for about 15 minutes before you remove the masking tape and newspaper.

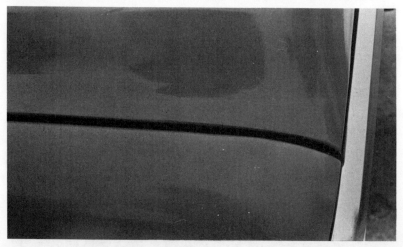

12. Let the paint dry for several days before you rub it out lightly with rubbing compound, and the finished job should be indistinguishable from the rest of the car. Don't rub hard or you'll cut through the paint.

Repairing Rust Holes With Fiberglass

1. The job we've picked here isn't an easy one mainly because of the location. The compound curves make the work trickier than if the surface were flat.

2. You'll need a drill and a wire brush for the first step, which is the removal of all the paint and rust from the rusted-out area.

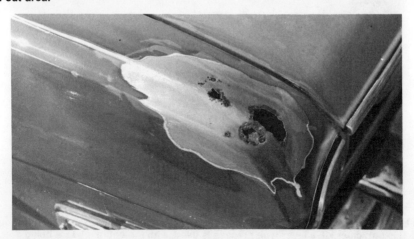

3. When you've finished grinding, the area to be repaired should look like this. Grind the paint back several inches in each direction to ensure that the patch will adhere to the metal. Remove all the **damaged** metal or the rust will return.

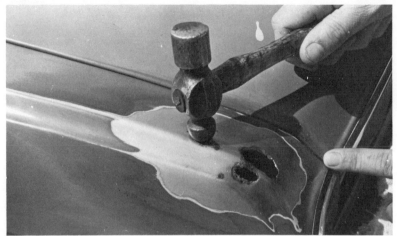

4. Tap the edges of the holes inward with a ballpeen hammer to allow for the thickness of the fiberglass material. Tap lightly so that you don't destroy any contours.

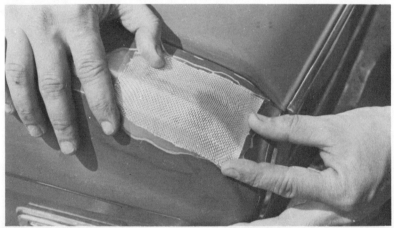

5. Follow the directions of the kit you purchase carefully. With fiberglass repair kits, the first step is generally to cut one or two pieces of fiberglass to cover the hole. Quite often, the procedure is to cut one patch the size of the prepared area and one patch the size of the hole.

6. Mix the fiberglass material and the patching compound together following the directions supplied with the kit. With this particular kit, a layer type process is used, with the entire mixture being prepared on a piece of plastic film known as a release sheet. Keep in mind that not all kits work this way. Be careful when you mix the catalyst with the resin, as too much catalyst will harden the mixture before you can apply it.

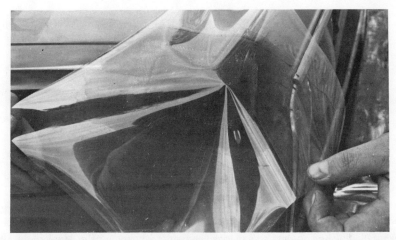

7. Spread the material on the damaged area using the release sheet. This process is essentially meant for smooth flat areas, and as a result, the release sheet would not adhere to the surface properly on our test car. If this happens to you, you'll probably have to remove the release sheet and spread the fiberglass compound out with your fingers or a small spreader.

8. This is what the fiberglass mixture looked like on our car after it had hardened. Because of the contours, we found it nearly impossible to smooth the mixture with a spreader, so we used our fingers. Unfortunately, it makes for a messy job that requires a lot of sanding. If you're working on a flat surface, you won't have this problem.

9. After the patch has hardened, sand it down to a smooth surface. You'll probably have to start with about grade 100 sandpaper and work your way up to 400 wet paper. If you have a particularly rough surface, you could start with a half-round plastic file.

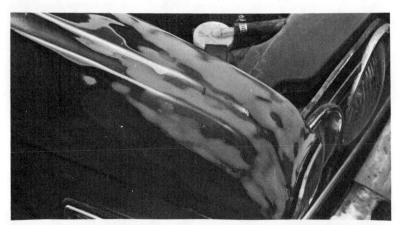

10. This is what the finished product should look like before you apply paint. Many of the kits come with glazing compound to fill in small imperfections left after the initial sanding. You'll probably need some. We did. The entire sanding operation took about an hour. Feather the edges of the repaired area into the surrounding paint carefully. As in any other body job, your hand is the best indicator of what's smooth and what isn't. It doesn't matter if it looks smooth. It's got to feel smooth. Take your time with this step and it will come out right.

11. Once you've smoothed out the repair, mask the entire area carefully, and spray the repair with primer. Keep the spray can moving in steady even strokes, overlap every stroke, and keep the spray can about 8–12 inches from the surface. Apply several coats of primer, letting the primer dry between coats.

12. The finished product (in primer) looks like this. If you were going to just spot paint this area, the next step would be to spray the correct color on the repaired area. This particular car is waiting for a complete paint job.

Appendix

General Conversion Table

Multiply by	To convert	To	
2.54	Inches	Centimeters	.3937
30.48	Feet	Centimeters	.0328
.914	Yards	Meters	1.094
1.609	Miles	Kilometers	.621
.645	Square inches	Square cm.	.155
.836	Square yards	Square meters	1.196
16.39	Cubic inches	Cubic cm.	.061
28.3	Cubic feet	Liters	.0353
.4536	Pounds	Kilograms	2.2045
4.226	Gallons	Liters	.264
.068	Lbs./sq. in. (psi)	Atmospheres	14.7
.138	Foot pounds	Kg. m.	7.23
1.014	H.P. (DIN)	H.P. (SAE)	.9861
—	To obtain	From	Multiply by

Note: 1 cm. equals 10 mm.; 1 mm. equals .0394".

Conversion—Common Fractions to Decimals and Millimeters

Common Fractions	Decimal Fractions	Millimeters (approx.)	Common Fractions	Decimal Fractions	Millimeters (approx.)	Common Fractions	Decimal Fractions	Millimeters (approx.)
1/128	.008	0.20	11/32	.344	8.73	43/64	.672	17.07
1/64	.016	0.40	23/64	.359	9.13	11/16	.688	17.46
1/32	.031	0.79	3/8	.375	9.53	45/64	.703	17.86
3/64	.047	1.19	25/64	.391	9.92	23/32	.719	18.26
1/16	.063	1.59	13/32	.406	10.32	47/64	.734	18.65
5/64	.078	1.98	27/64	.422	10.72	3/4	.750	19.05
3/32	.094	2.38	7/16	.438	11.11	49/64	.766	19.45
7/64	.109	2.78	29/64	.453	11.51	25/32	.781	19.84
1/8	.125	3.18	15/32	.469	11.91	51/64	.797	20.24
9/64	.141	3.57	31/64	.484	12.30	13/16	.813	20.64
5/32	.156	3.97	1/2	.500	12.70	53/64	.828	21.03
11/64	.172	4.37	33/64	.516	13.10	27/32	.844	21.43
3/16	.188	4.76	17/32	.531	13.49	55/64	.859	21.83
13/64	.203	5.16	35/64	.547	13.89	7/8	.875	22.23
7/32	.219	5.56	9/16	.563	14.29	57/64	.891	22.62
15/64	.234	5.95	37/64	.578	14.68	29/32	.906	23.02
1/4	.250	6.35	19/32	.594	15.08	59/64	.922	23.42
17/64	.266	6.75	39/64	.609	15.48	15/16	.938	23.81
9/32	.281	7.14	5/8	.625	15.88	61/64	.953	24.21
19/64	.297	7.54	41/64	.641	16.27	31/32	.969	24.61
5/16	.313	7.94	21/32	.656	16.67	63/64	.984	25.00
21/64	.328	8.33						

Conversion—Millimeters to Decimal Inches

mm	inches	mm	inches	mm	inches	mm	inches	mm	inches
1	.039 370	31	1.220 470	61	2.401 570	91	3.582 670	210	8.267 700
2	.078 740	32	1.259 840	62	2.440 940	92	3.622 040	220	8.661 400
3	.118 110	33	1.299 210	63	2.480 310	93	3.661 410	230	9.055 100
4	.157 480	34	1.338 580	64	2.519 680	94	3.700 780	240	9.448 800
5	.196 850	35	1.377 949	65	2.559 050	95	3.740 150	250	9.842 500
6	.236 220	36	1.417 319	66	2.598 420	96	3.779 520	260	10.236 200
7	.275 590	37	1.456 689	67	2.637 790	97	3.818 890	270	10.629 900
8	.314 960	38	1.496 050	68	2.677 160	98	3.858 260	280	11.032 600
9	.354 330	39	1.535 430	69	2.716 530	99	3.897 630	290	11.417 300
10	.393 700	40	1.574 800	70	2.755 900	100	3.937 000	300	11.811 000
11	.433 070	41	1.614 170	71	2.795 270	105	4.133 848	310	12.204 700
12	.472 440	42	1.653 540	72	2.834 640	110	4.330 700	320	12.598 400
13	.511 810	43	1.692 910	73	2.874 010	115	4.527 550	330	12.992 100
14	.551 180	44	1.732 280	74	2.913 380	120	4.724 400	340	13.385 800
15	.590 550	45	1.771 650	75	2.952 750	125	4.921 250	350	13.779 500
16	.629 920	46	1.811 020	76	2.992 120	130	5.118 100	360	14.173 200
17	.669 290	47	1.850 390	77	3.031 490	135	5.314 950	370	14.566 900
18	.708 660	48	1.889 760	78	3.070 860	140	5.511 800	380	14.960 600
19	.748 030	49	1.929 130	79	3.110 230	145	5.708 650	390	15.354 300
20	.787 400	50	1.968 500	80	3.149 600	150	5.905 500	400	15.748 000
21	.826 770	51	2.007 870	81	3.188 970	155	6.102 350	500	19.685 000
22	.866 140	52	2.047 240	82	3.228 340	160	6.299 200	600	23.622 000
23	.905 510	53	2.086 610	83	3.267 710	165	6.496 050	700	27.559 000
24	.944 880	54	2.125 980	84	3.307 080	170	6.692 900	800	31.496 000
25	.984 250	55	2.165 350	85	3.346 450	175	6.889 750	900	35.433 000
26	1.023 620	56	2.204 720	86	3.385 820	180	7.086 600	1000	39.370 000
27	1.062 990	57	2.244 090	87	3.425 190	185	7.283 450	2000	78.740 000
28	1.102 360	58	2.283 460	88	3.464 560	190	7.480 300	3000	118.110 000
29	1.141 730	59	2.322 830	89	3.503 903	195	7.677 150	4000	157.480 000
30	1.181 100	60	2.362 200	90	3.543 300	200	7.874 000	5000	196.850 000

To change decimal millimeters to decimal inches, position the decimal point where desired on either side of the millimeter measurement shown and reset the inches decimal by the same number of digits in the same direction. For example, to convert 0.001 mm to decimal inches, reset the decimal behind the 1 mm (shown on the chart) to 0.001; change the decimal inch equivalent (0.039″ shown) to 0.000039″.

Tap Drill Sizes

Screw & Tap Size	National Fine or S.A.E. Threads Per Inch	Use Drill Number
No. 5	44	37
No. 6	40	33
No. 8	36	29
No. 10	32	21
No. 12	28	15
1/4	28	3
5/16	24	1
3/8	24	Q
7/16	20	W
1/2	20	29/64
9/16	18	33/64
5/8	18	37/64
3/4	16	11/16
7/8	14	13/16
1 1/8	12	1 3/64
1 1/4	12	1 11/64
1 1/2	12	1 27/64

Tap Drill Sizes

Screw & Tap Size	National Coarse or U.S.S. Threads Per Inch	Use Drill Number
No. 5	40	39
No. 6	32	36
No. 8	32	29
No. 10	24	25
No. 12	24	17
1/4	20	8
5/16	18	F
3/8	16	5/16
7/16	14	U
1/2	13	27/64
9/16	12	31/64
5/8	11	17/32
3/4	10	21/32
7/8	9	49/64
1	8	7/8
1 1/8	7	63/64
1 1/4	7	1 7/64
1 1/2	6	1 11/32

Decimal Equivalent Size of the Number Drills

Drill No.	Decimal Equivalent	Drill No.	Decimal Equivalent	Drill No.	Decimal Equivalent
80	.0135	53	.0595	26	.1470
79	.0145	52	.0635	25	.1495
78	.0160	51	.0670	24	.1520
77	.0180	50	.0700	23	.1540
76	.0200	49	.0730	22	.1570
75	.0210	48	.0760	21	.1590
74	.0225	47	.0785	20	.1610
73	.0240	46	.0810	19	.1660
72	.0250	45	.0820	18	.1695
71	.0260	44	.0860	17	.1730
70	.0280	43	.0890	16	.1770
69	.0292	42	.0935	15	.1800
68	.0310	41	.0960	14	.1820
67	.0320	40	.0980	13	.1850
66	.0330	39	.0995	12	.1890
65	.0350	38	.1015	11	.1910
64	.0360	37	.1040	10	.1935
63	.0370	36	.1065	9	.1960
62	.0380	35	.1100	8	.1990
61	.0390	34	.1110	7	.2010
60	.0400	33	.1130	6	.2040
59	.0410	32	.1160	5	.2055
58	.0420	31	.1200	4	.2090
57	.0430	30	.1285	3	.2130
56	.0465	29	.1360	2	.2210
55	.0520	28	.1405	1	.2280
54	.0550	27	.1440		

Decimal Equivalent Size of the Letter Drills

Letter Drill	Decimal Equivalent	Letter Drill	Decimal Equivalent	Letter Drill	Decimal Equivalent
A	.234	J	.277	S	.348
B	.238	K	.281	T	.358
C	.242	L	.290	U	.368
D	.246	M	.295	V	.377
E	.250	N	.302	W	.386
F	.257	O	.316	X	.397
G	.261	P	.323	Y	.404
H	.266	Q	.332	Z	.413
I	.272	R	.339		

Anti-Freeze Chart

Temperatures Shown in Degrees Fahrenheit +32 is Freezing

Cooling System Capacity Quarts	1	2	3	4	5	6	7	8	9	10	11	12	13	14
	Quarts of ETHYLENE GLYCOL Needed for Protection to Temperatures Shown Below													

Quarts of ETHYLENE GLYCOL Needed for Protection to Temperatures Shown Below

Cooling System Capacity Quarts	1	2	3	4	5	6	7	8	9	10	11	12	13	14
10	+24°	+16°	+ 4°	−12°	−34°	−62°								
11	+25	+18	+ 8	− 6	−23	−47								
12	+26	+19	+10	0	−15	−34	−57°							
13	+27	+21	+13	+ 3	− 9	−25	−45							
14			+15	+ 6	− 5	−18	−34							
15			+16	+ 8	0	−12	−26							
16			+17	+10	+ 2	− 8	−19	−34	−52°					
17			+18	+12	+ 5	− 4	−14	−27	−42					
18			+19	+14	+ 7	0	−10	−21	−34	−50°				
19			+20	+15	+ 9	+ 2	− 7	−16	−28	−42				
20				+16	+10	+ 4	− 3	−12	−22	−34	−48°			
21				+17	+12	+ 6	0	− 9	−17	−28	−41			
22				+18	+13	+ 8	+ 2	− 6	−14	−23	−34	−47°		
23				+19	+14	+ 9	+ 4	− 3	−10	−19	−29	−40		
24				+19	+15	+10	+ 5	0	− 8	−15	−23	−34	−46°	
25				+20	+16	+12	+ 7	+ 1	− 5	−12	−20	−29	−40	−50°
26				+17	+13	+ 8	+ 3	− 3	− 9	−16	−25	−34	−44	
27				+18	+14	+ 9	+ 5	− 1	− 7	−13	−21	−29	−39	
28				+18	+15	+10	+ 6	+ 1	− 5	−11	−18	−25	−34	
29				+19	+16	+12	+ 7	+ 2	− 3	− 8	−15	−22	−29	
30				+20	+17	+13	+ 8	+ 4	− 1	− 6	−12	−18	−25	

For capacities over 30 quarts divide true capacity by 3. Find quarts Anti-Freeze for the ⅓ and multiply by 3 for quarts to add.

For capacities under 10 quarts multiply true capacity by 3. Find quarts Anti-Freeze for the tripled volume and divide by 3 for quarts to add.

To Increase the Freezing Protection of Anti-Freeze Solutions Already Installed

Cooling System Capacity Quarts	From +20° F. to					From +10° F. to					From 0° F. to			
	0°	−10°	−20°	−30°	−40°	0°	−10°	−20°	−30°	−40°	−10°	−20°	−30°	−40°
10	1¾	2¼	3	3½	3¾	¾	1½	2¼	2¾	3¼	¾	1½	2	2½
12	2	2¾	3½	4	4½	1	1¾	2½	3¼	3¾	1	1¾	2½	3¼
14	2¼	3¼	4	4¾	5½	1¼	2	3	3¾	4½	1	2	3	3½
16	2½	3½	4½	5¼	6	1¼	2½	3½	4¼	5¼	1¼	2¼	3¼	4
18	3	4	5	6	7	1½	2¾	4	5	5¾	1½	2½	3¾	4¾
20	3¼	4½	5¾	6¾	7½	1¾	3	4¼	5½	6½	1½	2¾	4¼	5¼
22	3½	5	6¼	7¼	8¼	1¾	3¼	4¾	6	7¼	1¾	3¼	4½	5½
24	4	5½	7	8	9	2	3½	5	6½	7½	1¾	3½	5	6
26	4¼	6	7½	8¾	10	2	4	5½	7	8¼	2	3¾	5½	6¾
28	4½	6¼	8	9½	10½	2¼	4¼	6	7½	9	2	4	5¾	7¼
30	5	6¾	8½	10	11½	2½	4½	6½	8	9½	2¼	4¼	6¼	7¾

Number of Quarts of ETHYLENE GLYCOL Anti-Freeze Required to Increase Protection

Test radiator solution with proper hydrometer. Determine from the table the number of quarts of solution to be drawn off from a full cooling system and replace with undiluted anti-freeze, to give the desired increased protection. For example, to increase protection of a 22-quart cooling system containing Ethylene Glycol (permanent type) anti-freeze, from +20° F. to −20° F. will require the replacement of 6¼ quarts of solution with undiluted anti-freeze.

Index

25 Ways

TO BETTER GAS MILEAGE

The Federal government's goal is to cut gasoline consumption 10% by 1985. In addition to intelligent purchase of a new vehicle and efficient driving habits, there are other ways to increase gas mileage with your present car or truck.

Tests have shown that almost ¾ of all vehicles on the road need maintenance in areas that directly effect fuel economy. Using this book for regular maintenance and tune-ups can increase fuel economy as much as 10%, depending on your vehicle.

1. **Replace spark plugs regularly.** New plugs alone can increase fuel economy by 3%.

2. **Be sure the plugs are the correct type and properly gapped.**

3. **Set the ignition timing to specifications.**

4. If your vehicle does not have electronic ignition, **check the points, rotor and cap as specified.**

5. **Replace the air filter regularly.** A dirty air filter richens the air/fuel mixture and can increase fuel consumption as much as 10%. Tests show ⅓ of all vehicles have air filters in need of replacement.

6. **Replace the fuel filter** at least as often as recommended.

7. **Be sure the idle speed and carburetor fuel mixture are set to specifications.**

8. **Check the automatic choke.** A sticking or malfunctioning choke wastes gas.

9. **Change the oil and filter as recommended.** Dirty oil is thick and causes extra friction between the moving parts, cutting efficiency and increasing wear.

10. **Replace the PCV valve** at regular intervals.

11. **Service the cooling system** at regular recommended intervals.

12. **Be sure the thermostat is operating properly.** A thermostat that is stuck open delays engine warm-up, and a cold engine uses twice as much fuel as a warm engine.

13. **Be sure the tires are properly inflated.** Under-inflated tires can cost as much as 1 mpg. Better mileage can be achieved by over-inflating the tires (never exceed the maximum inflation pressure on the side of the tire), but the tires will wear faster.

14. **Be sure the drive belts (especially the fan belt) are in good condition** and properly adjusted.

15. **Be sure the battery is fully charged for fast starts.**

16. **Use the recommended viscosity motor oil to reduce friction.**

17. **Use the recommended viscosity fluids in the rear axle and transmission.**

18. **Be sure the wheels are properly balanced.**

19. **Be sure the front end is correctly aligned.** A misaligned front end actually has wheels going in different directions, creating additional drag.

20. **Correctly adjust the wheel bearing.** Wheel bearings adjusted too tight increase rolling resistance.

21. **Be sure the brakes are properly adjusted and not dragging.**

22. **If possible, install radial tires.** Radial tires deliver as much as ½ mpg more than bias belted tires.

23. **Install a flex-type fan** if you don't have a clutch fan. Flex fans push more air at low speeds when more cooling is needed. At high speeds the blades flatten out for less resistance.

24. **Check the radiator cap for a cracked or worn gasket.** If the cap doesn't seal properly, the cooling system will not function properly.

25. **Check the spark plug wires for bad cracks, burned or broken insulation.** Cracked wires decrease fuel efficiency by failing to deliver full voltage to the spark plugs.